Behind Kṛṣṇa's Smile

SUNY series in Hindu Studies

Wendy Doniger, editor

Behind Kṛṣṇa's Smile

The Lord's Hint of Laughter in the *Bhagavadgītā* and Beyond

ANTONIO RIGOPOULOS and
GIANNI PELLEGRINI

SUNY
PRESS

Cover: Krsna Pārthasārathi teaching the Bhagavadgītā to Arjuna. Kangra painting, early 19th century. Presently kept at the National Museum in Delhi.

Published by State University of New York Press, Albany

Printed in the United States of America

For information, contact State University of New York Press, Albany, NY
www.sunypress.edu

Library of Congress Cataloging-in-Publication Data

Names: Rigopoulos, Antonio, 1962– author. | Pellegrini, Gianni, author.
Title: Behind Kṛṣṇa's smile : the Lord's Hint of laughter in the Bhagavadgita and beyond / Antonio Rigopoulos and Gianni Pellegrini.
Description: Albany : State University of New York Press, [2024]. | Series: SUNY series in Hindu studies | Includes bibliographical references and index.
Identifiers: LCCN 2024005829 | ISBN 9781438499673 (hardcover : alk. paper) | ISBN 9781438499697 (ebook) | ISBN 9781438499680 (pbk. : alk. paper)
Subjects: LCSH: Krishna (Hindu deity) | Bhagavadgītā—Criticism, interpretation, etc. | Arjuna (Hindu mythological character) | Bhakti. | Śaraṇāgati. | Vaishnavism. | Laughter—Religious aspects—Hinduism. | Laughter in literature. | Vaishnavism.
Classification: LCC BL1220 .R54 2024 | DDC 294.5/2113—dc23/eng/20240705
LC record available at https://lccn.loc.gov/2024005829

To our dear parents
whose loving smile always accompanies us

mahātmānaḥ kila smitapūrvābhibhāṣiṇo bhavantīti ||
"Great souls usually smile before speaking."
(Bhāskara's commentary *ad Bhagavadgītā* 2.10)

"Oh my heart, how could you turn from the smile of your Lord
and wander so far from Him?"
(Excerpt from a poem of the poet-saint Kabīr, fifteenth century)

Contents

Illustrations ix

Preface xi

Acknowledgments xv

Introduction 1

1 On Kṛṣṇa's Hint of Laughter in the *Bhagavadgītā* 13

2 Traditional Commentaries on *Bhagavadgītā* 2.10 57

3 On *prahasann iva* and *hasann iva* in the *Mahābhārata* and *Rāmāyaṇa* 101

4 On Kṛṣṇa's Hint of Laughter in the Arts and in Devotional Literature 135

Notes 181

Bibliography 257

Index 287

Illustrations

Figure 4.1	Kṛṣṇa Pārthasārathi teaching the *Bhagavadgītā* to Arjuna. Chennakesava Temple, Puṣpagiri, Andhra Pradesh, fourteenth century.	144
Figure 4.2	Kṛṣṇa Pārthasārathi teaching the *Bhagavadgītā* to Arjuna. Kangra painting, eighteenth century.	150
Figure 4.3	Kṛṣṇa Pārthasārathi teaching the *Bhagavadgītā* to Arjuna. Kishangarh painting, eighteenth century.	150
Figure 4.4	Illustration taken from Lionel D. Barnett's translation of the *Bhagavadgītā* (London: J. M. Dent, 1928 [1905]).	152
Figure 4.5	Outer View of the Shri Krishna Museum, Kurukṣetra.	153
Figure 4.6	Kṛṣṇa Pārthasārathi blessing Arjuna, contemporary image.	153
Figure 4.7	Kṛṣṇa and Arjuna in a contemporary Kṛṣṇāṭṭam play.	155
Figure 4.8	Ileana Citaristi (right) and Saswat Joshi (left) performing *Parthasarathi*, Odissi dance, July 2017.	156
Figure 4.9	A scene of the film *Bhagvad Gita: Song of the Lord* (1993), directed by G. V. Iyer.	158

Figure 4.10. A scene of the *Bhagavadgītā* episode televised by Doordarshan. 159

Figure 4.11 Kṛṣṇa Pārthasārathi benevolently smiling at Arjuna. 160

Figure 4.12 Child Kṛṣṇa as *navanītacora*. Tanjore painting, late eighteenth century. 164

Figure 4.13 Child Kṛṣṇa as *navanītacora*, contemporary poster. 165

Figure 4.14 Bālakṛṣṇa as *navanītanṛttamūrti*. Chola style, fourteenth century. 166

Figure 4.15 Child Kṛṣṇa granting vision of the universe to his foster-mother Yaśodā, contemporary poster. 167

Figure 4.16 Kṛṣṇa Veṇugopāla with attendant cow. Shirdi Sai Baba temple, Guindy, Chennai. 168

Figure 4.17 Kṛṣṇa in Vṛndāvana riding the swing (*jhūlā*) surrounded by two *gopī*s, contemporary silk painting. 170

Figure 4.18 The *rāslīlā*, Kṛṣṇa dancing with all the *gopī*s. Basohli painting, Punjab Hills, c. 1750. 171

Figure 4.19 Kṛṣṇa lifts the Govardhana mountain, contemporary poster. 172

Figure 4.20 Kṛṣṇa overcoming the serpent-demon Kāliya and dancing upon him. Bronze statue, South India, c. 1300. 173

Figure 4.21 Kṛṣṇa gracefully smiles to Arjuna, blessing him through his *abhāyamudrā*. Contemporary poster. 179

Figure 4.22 Drawing of the Pārthasārathi icon. 242

Preface

ANTONIO RIGOPOULOS

What triggered this study is the shared persuasion that the veritable turning point of the *Bhagavadgītā* poem or the "Song of the Lord," which scholars date somewhere between 200 BCE and 100 CE, is Kṛṣṇa's "hint of laughter" (*prahasann iva*) in *Bhagavadgītā* 2.10. It signals the outpouring of the god's grace (*prasāda*) to Arjuna as a consequence of the latter having taken refuge at his feet. Remarkably, it is from this point that Śaṅkara (c. 700 CE) and other leading theologians begin their commentaries. Arjuna's devout surrender (*prapatti*) to Kṛṣṇa is what attracts the lord's mercy: his hint of laughter conveys his awesome splendor and is the unmistakable sign of his favor, the prelude to the outflow of his liberating teaching (*upadeśa*).

For more than twenty-five years I have been reading the poem with my Sanskrit students at the Ca' Foscari University of Venice and I have been stressing to them the significance of the stock expression *prahasann iva* as the manifestation of Kṛṣṇa's love toward Arjuna, *bhakti* being the essential feature of this celebrated dialogue between master and pupil (*guruśiṣyasaṃvāda*). Although this understanding strikes me as being quite straightforward, in recent years I have found myself wondering when it was that I first read or heard about it since I'm quite sure that it was not originally my idea. The source of this interpretation must inevitably go back to when I was a student of Indian religions in the 1980s. I think I was told of the importance of Kṛṣṇa's hint of laughter/

smile by one of my early teachers in Indology, my cherished professors Mario Piantelli at the University of Turin, or Gerald James Larson at the University of California, Santa Barbara.

What is certain is that the majority of modern English translations and commentaries of the *Bhagavadgītā* written by Indian and Western scholars as well as by Hindu holy men do not offer any particular clue or explanation regarding Kṛṣṇa's *prahasann iva*, which typically goes unnoticed or at best receives a cursory treatment. Even Peter Brook's celebrated staging of the *Mahābhārata* in 1985 failed to capture this fundamental moment, given that the actor that impersonated Kṛṣṇa not only lacked any smile but had a wearied expression on his face, not too different from Arjuna's dejected countenance.

Moreover, while discussing this issue with many Indologists I have come to realize, much to my surprise, that my understanding of Kṛṣṇa's *prahasann iva* is not at all shared knowledge and is far from being a matter of course: for the majority of my interlocutors it usually comes as a revelation and as something to which they had never given any thought before. Even when I venture to explain the significance of *prahasann iva* in public lectures on the *Bhagavadgītā*, the invariable reaction is one of wonder.

When in October 2019 I offered my analysis of Kṛṣṇa's hint of laughter to my dear colleague and friend Gianni Pellegrini at the biannual gathering of the Italian Association of Sanskrit Studies, he was fascinated by it. He also admitted that he had never thought about it in these terms nor had he ever come across any modern commentary that dealt with it. As he later told me, Kṛṣṇa's hint of laughter in *Bhagavadgītā* 2.10 is much like the egg of Columbus: something that is so evident that people don't see it, that is, don't pay attention to. Thus it was that the idea of cowriting a book on this topic first emerged, and I must say that the more Gianni and I probed into it the more our enthusiasm grew since the depth of Kṛṣṇa's *prahasann iva* appears to be inexhaustible, always leading to new insights.

The book is divided into four chapters that are the result of our combined efforts and constant exchange. In particular, I am responsible for chapters 1 and 4 while Gianni Pellegrini is responsible for chapters 2 and 3. After the introduction, which is meant to set the ground for our study, chapter 1 examines Kṛṣṇa's *prahasann iva* in *Bhagavadgītā* 2.10 and its implications in the context of the poem as a whole. As a starting point, we consider its English translations in Western scholarship and offer our own rendering. We investigate its crucial significance and plural meanings, showing how the god's hint of laughter constitutes the text's καιρός, its decisive moment, communicating the outpouring of Kṛṣṇa's grace and words of wisdom to Arjuna. We then consider the impact of *prahasann iva* on the poem's central teachings as they unfold, that is, by taking into account its three traditional subdivisions (*karmayoga, bhaktiyoga,* and *jñānayoga*), evidencing how even Kṛṣṇa's theophany in chapter 11 is somehow in the nature of *prahasann iva*.

Chapter 2 focuses upon the understanding of Kṛṣṇa's hint of laughter in the Sanskrit commentarial tradition. This is pivotal in order to assess how, along the centuries, the most prominent representatives of the schools of Vedānta have understood this stock phrase and have argued about its relevance within the poem. By examining their exegeses, we can detect the main lines of thought in the history of interpretation and appreciate the technicalities of traditional scholarship, the richness and thoroughness that characterize its approach to the text.

Chapter 3 explores the uses of *prahasann iva* and its akin form *hasann iva* within the *Mahābhārata* and *Rāmāyaṇa* epics. The aim is to uncover the various situations in which this expression is utilized along with its principal meanings, depending upon the human and/or divine actors involved. Particular attention is paid to those cases in which Kṛṣṇa himself figures as protagonist. This survey allows to appreciate the broader context in which *prahasann iva* and *hasann iva* are employed and to better situate Kṛṣṇa's hint of laughter in *Bhagavadgītā* 2.10 as part and parcel of the *Mahābhārata*.

Chapter 4 presents the typologies of laughter (*hāsyarasa*) within the *Nāṭyaśāstra* of Bharata (200–300 CE), confronting them with Kṛṣṇa's hint of laughter in the *Bhagavadgītā* and with the representation of the deity in the performing arts. A survey of Kṛṣṇa's figure in epic and purāṇic iconography and literature up to modern times allows the recognition of an aesthetic and literary continuum, evidencing the deep-rootedness of kṛṣṇaite *bhakti* theology and proving the eloquence beyond words of Kṛṣṇa's *prahasann iva*.

To date there are no studies on Kṛṣṇa's hint of laughter in the *Bhagavadgītā* despite the fact that it immediately precedes his conversation with Arjuna, conceptualized as the perennial dialogue between god and man. We are confident that both South Asian scholars and historians of religions will be interested in perusing Kṛṣṇa's *prahasann iva* within the poem and its commentarial tradition and, more broadly, in learning about this stock phrase in the *Mahābhārata* and *Rāmāyaṇa* and the developments of Krsna's hint of laughter in iconography, literature and the performing arts. We also expect that all people who are devout to Kṛṣṇa and to the *Bhagavadgītā*—the Gospel of India, widely revered as the fifth *Veda*—will be eager to read about it and discover new facets of their lord's amazing grace.

All in all, this study explores a set of interrelated issues: (a) an in-depth analysis of Kṛṣṇa's hint of laughter in *Bhagavadgītā* 2.10 and its influence on the poem as a whole, offering new insights into the theological assumptions of the text and its *bhakti* orientation; (b) the interpretation and contextualization of Kṛṣṇa's hint of laughter in Sanskrit commentaries (*bhāṣya*), allowing to detect the shifts of meaning that characterized traditional scholarship over time, highlighting the differences of approach among the main schools of Vedānta; (c) a comprehensive examination of *prahasann iva*/*hasann iva* in both the *Mahābhārata* and *Rāmāyaṇa*, throwing light on its different uses and functions as per the ethos and theology of the epics; (d) an assessment of Kṛṣṇa's hint of laughter in light of the aesthetic experience of the comic in Bharata's *Nāṭyaśāstra* coupled with a survey of the deity's iconography and literature, which allows the recognition of a unified canon that ties together the literary and aesthetical, performative dimensions of Kṛṣṇa's *prahasann iva*. Finally, we hope our Indological investigation may be appreciated as a contribution to the ongoing debate on the fascinating phenomenons of laughter and smile.

Acknowledgments

It is with a smile and filled with gratitude that we wish to thank all those people who in various ways helped us in our research. Special thanks go to the teachers who first kindled our interest in religious studies and in the religions and philosophies of India, in particular to Prof. Franco Michelini Tocci of the University of Venice and Prof. Mario Piantelli of the University of Turin. We also wish to express our debt of gratitude to the late Prof. Gerald James Larson of the University of California, Santa Barbara, for his masterful guidance in the intricacies of Sanskrit grammar and in the reading of the *Bhagavadgītā* between 1987 and 1994.

In India, several people helped us during work on this project. In the first place, we are grateful to the late *brahmalīna* Jagadguru Śaṅkarācārya Svāmī Svarūpānanda Sarasvatī, who through his entire life taught us what *prahasann iva* really means. We are also grateful to his disciple and successor at the *pīṭha* of Jyośimaṭha, the Jagadguru Śaṅkarācārya Svāmī Avimukteśvarānanda Sarasvatī, for his constant encouragement and precious advice.

Without the invaluable guidance of the following Indian scholars we could have never had access to the Sanskrit treatises (*śāstra*) and commentaries (*bhāṣya*) that are at the basis of this study, and thus our thanks to them will always be insufficient: the late Profs. Pārasanātha Dvivedī and Śrī Nārāyaṇa Miśra, Prof. Rāma Kiśora Tripāṭhī, the late *paṇḍita*s Rāma Nivāsa Tivārī and Rāmacandra Tripāṭhī, and *paṇḍita* Vaidyanātha Miśra.

In the course of our work in Italy we profited from the conversations and suggestions of many friends and colleagues: Maurizio Bettini, Cristina Bignami, Giuliano Boccali, Alessandro Cancian,

Pinuccia Caracchi, Marco Castagnetto, Giovanni Ciotti, Alessandra Consolaro, Elisa Freschi, Elisa Ganser, Mrinal Kaul, Frank Koehler, Elena Mucciarelli, Kiyotaka Okita, Stefano Pellò, Massimo Raveri, Francesco Remotti, Francesco Sferra, Federico Squarcini, Raffaele Torella, and Vincenzo Vergiani.

We were lucky to have the opportunity to present talks growing out of our work at the biannual meeting of the Italian Association of Sanskrit Studies held in the island of Procida (Naples) in September–October 2022: we thank all scholars for their stimulating questions and advice. We are also grateful for the constructive comments and suggestions of the anonymous readers at State University of New York Press, who greatly helped us to improve our manuscript.

Preliminary versions of chapters 1 and 2 were originally published in F. Sferra and V. Vergiani, eds., *'Verità e bellezza': Essays in Honour of Raffaele Torella, Series Minor XCVII.2*, Università degli studi di Napoli "L'Orientale"—University of Cambridge (Napoli: UniorPress, 2022), 965–1010 (A. Rigopoulos, "*Prahasann iva*. On Kṛṣṇa's Hint of Laughter in *Bhagavadgītā* 2.10"), 841–99 (G. Pellegrini, "On *prahasann iva*: *Bhagavadgītā* 2.10 in the Light of Traditional Commentaries").

We extend our thanks to all those who encouraged us along the way: Robin Agarwal, Paolo Bà, Tiziana Bertoldin, Michele Botta, Daniela Cancellieri, Alice Cavallo, Claudio Cedolin, Alberico Crafa, Roberto Destro, Tiziana Fantuz, Agnese Garnerone, M. V. Krishnayya, Elisabetta Leonori, Gianna Martelozzo, Monic Mastroianni, Francesco Pellegrini, Bruna Rossi, Enrico Scapin, Paolo Schiavon, Francesca Stefanelli, Mauro Tonon, Peter Zanesco, Purnananda Zenoni, and Andrea Zorzi.

Finally, we wish to acknowledge our debt of gratitude to all the students at the Ca' Foscari University of Venice and at the University of Turin who over many years have patiently read through the *Bhagavadgītā* with us and who have engaged in their own dialogues with Kṛṣṇa.

We feel it appropriate to end our heart-felt thanks with the words of a well-known Sanskrit verse:

gacchataḥ skhalanaṃ kvāpi bhavaty eva pramādataḥ |
hasanti durjanās tatra samādadhati sajjanāḥ ||

> Due to inadvertence, it is certainly possible to stumble while walking:
> whereas mean people laugh at this, gracious people are eager to correct.

And as Śaṅkara states in his commentary *ad Bhagavadgītā* 13.2:

> . . . *na ca mithyājñānaṃ paramārthavastu dūṣayantuṃ samartham* ||

> . . . no erroneous knowledge can ever corrupt Supreme Reality.

Antonio Rigopoulos
Gianni Pellegrini
Venice—Turin, Italy

Introduction

O luce etterna che sola in te sidi,
sola t'intendi, e da te intelletta
e intendente te ami e arridi!

O eternal Light, abiding in yourself alone,
knowing yourself alone, and, known to yourself
and knowing, loving and smiling on yourself!

—Dante Alighieri, *La Divina Commedia,*
Paradiso XXXIII, 124–26

Here it is necessary to know that
the eyes of wisdom are her demonstrations,
by which truth is seen with the greatest certainty,
and her smiles are her persuasions,
in which the inner light of wisdom
is revealed behind a kind of veil;
and in each of them is felt
the highest joy of blessedness,
which is the greatest good of Paradise.

—Dante Alighieri, *Convivio* 3.15.2

In trying to understand the typically human phenomenon of laughter and smile, rivers of ink have been poured from antiquity to the present and various theories have been proposed. Yet even nowadays the subtlety of its nature and of what links laughter to smile is hard to assess and continues to elude us. What is the psychology of smile and laughter? What are their causes and to which stimuli do they respond to? What is their primary function? Are they voluntary or involuntary actions/reactions? Can they be universally classed in fixed typologies?[1] Or is their meaning inevitably linked to the social and cultural contexts in which they manifest themselves, depending on the particular person involved and the ever-changing circumstances? Are they lexically and phrasally produced or without any propositional content?[2]

Among the many theories regarding laughter, one often comes across the "theory of superiority" according to which laughter is resorted to by someone who feels superior to someone else and wants to mark his higher status through mockery. Another theory that has distinguished advocates—including Aristotle (384–322 BCE), Cicero (106–43 BCE) and Quintilian (35–96 CE) up to Thomas Hobbes (1588–1679), Sigmund Freud (1856–1939) and Henri Bergson (1859–1941)—is the "theory of inconsistency," in which laughter is said to be triggered by any incongruous act or utterance, that is, what is known as *anaucitya* (lit. "inappropriateness") in the Indian tradition and that has been thematized by Abhinavagupta (early eleventh century) and referred to by several of the *Bhagavadgītā*'s commentators we will be examining.

From an Indian viewpoint, even the well-known biblical story of the naming of Isaac, a term that literally means "he will laugh," would be rubricated as a case of *anaucitya*. This name was given to him by god himself because of his mother Sarah's incredulous reaction when she ironically laughed at herself at hearing the prediction that she would give birth to a child at her advanced age of ninety years old (*Genesis* 18:10–15). Abraham, who was a hundred years old, was the first to fall on his face and laugh when god announced to him that he would give him a son through her (*Genesis* 17:16–17).[3]

To be sure, both theories of superiority and inconsistency are utilized in the commentarial tradition in order to understand Kṛṣṇa's "hint of laughter" (*prahasann iva*) in *Bhagavadgītā* 2.10, even by viewing them as complementary to one another. Both theories can be applied to god himself, who, as *deus ludens*, laughs at seeing the inadequacy and incongruity of humans and their miseries. Nonetheless, we shall see that in our case Kṛṣṇa's superiority does not manifest itself through a hint of laughter of mere sarcasm toward Arjuna since his *prahasann iva* expresses the pure joy of welcoming him as his dear disciple, signaling the flowing of his grace toward him. Arjuna's *anaucitya* is further underlined by some powerful contrasts: whereas our hero cries and sits despondent in the back of his chariot, the lord stands up exhibiting a cheerful countenance, gracefully dispelling all pain and sorrow by his hint of laughter.

It is noteworthy that Henri Bergson in his famous work on laughter he originally published in 1900—*Le rire: essai sur la signification du comique*—states that although life is essentially inimitable it often happens that we humans cease to be ourselves, that is, deliberately betray ourselves, and start imitating others. Thus he argues that imitation is the very essence of the ludicrous.[4] Along these lines, in the *Bhagavadgītā* the great warrior Arjuna, overcome by anguish, refuses to fight a just (*dharmya*) war stating that he would rather prefer "to eat alms-food" (*BhG* 2.5), that is, to lead the life of a renunciant (*saṃnyāsin*) by imitating his lifestyle. Kṛṣṇa's hint of laughter is but a natural reaction to the hero's betrayal of his princely (*kṣatriya*) class and his wanting to imitate the conduct (*dharma*) of a renunciant that is prescribed only as the final stage (*āśrama*) in a man's life. Again this inversion of roles and imitation of others falls within the sphere of *anaucitya* or inappropriateness. We might also infer that the lord's *prahasann iva* is tinged with surprise, given that Arjuna exhibits this unexpected reaction at the least appropriate time and place, that is, just when the great war is about to begin. Moreover, that our hero's last words to Kṛṣṇa are "I'll not fight" (*BhG* 2.9) despite the fact that he has just surrendered to him as his disciple (*śiṣya*), prove his stubborness and mental confusion: his *anaucitya* is ridiculous, and such ridiculousness is hilarious, which might also explain the lord's hint of laughter.[5]

These introductory observations are far from exhausting the range of possible interpretations of Kṛṣṇa's *prahasann iva*. Laughter as well as smile are such multifaceted and elusive phenomena that it is practically impossible to account for them in any comprehensive way. The reasons and logics that predispose humans—and gods—to laugh/smile depend upon a complex interweaving of factors, in which similarities and contrasts play a major role.

It must be pointed out that laughter is also something that can be viewed as highly dangerous. We are here reminded of Umberto Eco's (1932–2016) famous novel *The Name of the Rose*, first published in Italian in 1980.[6] Its plot is centered upon laughter and its radical condemnation by Christian religious authorities.[7] The motive behind the murders that take place in a Benedictine monastery of northern Italy in the year 1327 is linked to the lost second book of Aristotle's *Poetics*, in which Aristotle is believed to have addressed the issue of comedy and to have revealed what is the essence of the comic.[8] In the novel, the venerable Jorge de Burgos, one of the oldest and most learned monks in the monastery, happens to discover this book in the convent's library and immediately hides it away: the reason behind his homicides is precisely to keep it secret and prevent anyone from reading it. This he does because he is aware that laughter is an antidote to fear. And since religion is understood to be built on fear, he perceives laughter as representing a most dangerous, diabolic force that needs to be shunned at all costs.[9]

Eco thinks that laughter is related to the fact that humans are the only animals that know that they are destined to die and thus he conceives it as a reaction to such awareness that helps us face the tragedies of life. He argues that laughter has the power of projecting a shadow of suspicion on all dogmatic truths and preconceived ideas, and this is the reason why it is opposed not only by theologians but also by philosophers.[10] Already in 1967, as a sort of forerunner to *The Name of the Rose*, he wrote an article for the Italian weekly *L'Espresso* titled *Il nemico dei filosofi* or *The Enemy of Philosophers*, in which he identified laughter as the deceitful enemy of the thinkers of all ages precisely because of its skeptical potential and multiplicity of meaning.[11]

In our context, the elusive nature of laughter is amplified by Kṛṣṇa's own unfathomable personality within the *Mahābhārata*. As Bimal Krishna Matilal observes:

> Kṛṣṇa is an enigma in the *Mahābhārata*. He represents the most confusing kind of moral enigma not only in the epic, but also in the whole of the Hindu ideal of *dharma*. In the icons, he is represented as the Dark Lord, an attractive appearance with a face bearing an enigmatic, mysterious and mischievous smile, the smile, very much unlike the famous smile found in the icons of the Buddha. The Buddha's smile in striking contrast with that of Kṛṣṇa, is straightforward, it radiates with

> compassion, calmness and peace, it strikes confidence in the minds of the viewers. The ethical doctrine of Kṛṣṇa by contrast is different, sometimes it appears to be just the opposite. Kṛṣṇa is a riddle, a paradox.[12]

Though we disagree with Matilal's idea that the Buddha's smile[13] is in "striking contrast" with Kṛṣṇa's smile, given that it is precisely our contention that the latter's *prahasann iva*—at least as far as the *Bhagavadgītā* is concerned—"radiates with compassion, calmness and peace," yet it is certainly true that Kṛṣṇa's character in the epic is ambiguous, paradoxical, and inherently polysemic.[14] If in our study we offer reasons for upholding the idea that the lord's hint of laughter in *Bhagavadgītā* 2.10 is to be understood as the expression of his love and grace toward Arjuna, we also take pains to review the wide range of hermeneutical options that the commentators of the poem have proposed along the centuries.

In the Indian tradition in which grammar (*vyākaraṇa*) is the science of sciences, the two actions of laughing and smiling are expressed by two different verbal roots, that is, √*smi* for smiling and √*has* for laughing. This is important given that although there is an undeniable connection between smiling and laughing, still the fact that Sanskrit accurately distinguishes one from the other is meant to emphasize their difference.[15] Thus with reference to our stock phrase, the noun to which the present active participle *prahasan* refers to is *prahāsa* that the Monier-Williams dictionary translates as "loud laughter," "derision"/"irony,"[16] and the Apte dictionary analogously translates as "violent or loud laughter," "ridicule"/"derision," "irony"/"satire."[17] Herein, the prefix *pra* is understood to mean "loud"/"violent" and points at an intense degree of laughter.

On the other hand, the impact of *pra* + √*has* is mitigated by the indeclinable particle *iva*, which implies a softening of its meaning, that is, that the laughter is only hinted at or somehow suppressed. It is exactly by conflating a strong part and a weak part that our formulaic expression opens itself to a broad range of hermeneutic possibilities and translations. The expression *prahasann iva*—as well as *hasann iva* — embraces both laughter and smile, and this is confirmed by what legions of commentators have written about it. Our own translation of *prahasann iva* as hint of laughter aims at reconciling the two juxtaposed elements of the expression, in which "laughter" renders *prahāsa* and "hint" renders *iva,* the particle having the function of mitigating the former's loudness.

The context in which our *prahasann iva* occurs—immediately after Arjuna has surrendered at Kṛṣṇa's feet as his disciple, placing his burden upon him and recognizing him as his sole refuge—leads us to the conclusion that what the lord's hint of laughter primarily conveys is his boundless grace. Our contention is that Kṛṣṇa's *prahasann iva* is meant to ease the tension, his smiling countenance being an assurance that there is nothing to fear and that everything will be fine, he being in total control of the situation. What Arjuna sees as an unsurmountable tragedy that will result in a disaster for the armies of both Pāṇḍavas and Kauravas is instantaneously resolved by the lord's hint of laughter. Even if we interpret Kṛṣṇa's *prahasann iva* as implying a degree of mockery due to the fact that Arjuna's behavior is contrary to his inherent duty (*svadharma*), such derision is to be viewed as a means (*upāya*) aimed at triggering the hero's discrimination and has an essentially pedagogical function, being motivated by the lord's love toward him.

The *Kāvyaprakāśa* of Mammaṭa (eleventh century CE) states that there are three different styles of beneficial teaching (*hitaśāsana*) prescribed in the authoritative Sanskrit treatises (*śāstra*s): (a) that of the *Veda*s, that teach in a rather severe way through injunctions like a king (*rājasammita*); (b) that of *Itihāsa*s *and Purāṇa*s, that teach in a compassionate way like a friend (*mitrasammita*), and (c) that of *Kāvya* or poetry that teaches in a passionate way like a lover (*kāntāsammita*).[18] Given the epic context and most importantly the bond of friendship (*sakhā*) that exists between Kṛṣṇa and Arjuna, we think that the former's teaching should be interpreted as *mitrasammita,* thus favoring the interpretation of a compassionate hint of laughter. Nonetheless, Kṛṣṇa's teaching could also be interpreted as *rājasammita,* which would imply a rather harsh hint of laughter. To be sure, the three styles of beneficial teaching may be expressed either through sweetness or sourness. If we construe the lord's *prahasann iva* as mockery it would be like a bitter medicine that Kṛṣṇa utilizes in order to cure Arjuna's despondency and trigger his metanoia, as proposed by commentators such as Jñāneśvar (thirteenth century) and Keśava Kaśmīrī Bhaṭṭācārya (c. 1510).

Along these lines, several Indian proverbs celebrate the insults of holy men and renouncers as tokens of their grace. Thus a popular

Hindī saying goes: *sādhu kī gālī kṛpā kī nadī*, that is, "The insult of a *sādhu* is a river of mercy." The antinomian behavior of extreme ascetics such as *paramahaṃsa*s and *avadhūta*s is exemplary in this regard. In ancient times, one is reminded of the lost sect of the *śaiva* Pāśupatas[19]—who indulged in transgressive laughter—and in recent times of a beloved saint such as the Sai Baba of Shirdi (d. 1918) who would often "welcome" the people who came to visit him with a torrent of abuses that were thought to represent a shower of mercy, the idea being that his insults were not directed at the person but at the evil forces that he saw were harming his devotee and that he vanquished through his powerful invectives.[20]

Coming back to our *prahasann iva* and reaffirming our conviction that it should be understood as a sign of Kṛṣṇa's grace toward Arjuna, it must be realized that there is no mutual exclusion between the sweetness of a hint of laughter of pure delight and the sourness of a hint of laughter of pure scorn. Rather, it seems reasonable to envisage a *samuccaya* of the two, that is, a combination of mockery and mirth in the sense of hypothesizing a passage, an almost imperceptible transition from one to the other.

Kṛṣṇa's hint of laughter also points at the god's *līlā*, his disarming ease and playful attitude vis-à-vis the anguish and preoccupations of mortals. In Vedānta, the notion of *līlā* is dealt with in section 2.1.32–33 of the *Brahmasūtra* and its commentarial tradition. What is at stake is the reason (*prayojana*) that prompts the Absolute *Brahman* to manifest the universe, given that *Brahman* is in itself perfect, full (*pūrṇa*), and free of desires (*akāma*). In fact, it is said that there is no reason at all given that only one that has something to accomplish, to avoid or to acquire, involves himself/herself into action (*pravṛtti*).[21] Moreover, one would incur in various logical fallacies if he/she were to affirm that *Brahman*, which is wholly satisfied (*paritṛpta*), is drawn to manifest the universe out of some unmotivated urge (*niṣprayojana*): it would be like the action of a mad person! If this was so, the omniscience of *Brahman*[22] would be contradicted (*bādhita*) and the authoritativeness of the "revealed" texts, that is, the *śruti* said to originate from *Brahman*, would be undermined. In order to refute these misconceptions, *Brahmasūtra* 2.1.33 states: "But [*Brahman*] appears as the world only for its own amusement" (*lokavat tu līlākaivalyam*).

In his *Brahmasūtrabhāṣya*, Śaṅkara (eighth century) argues that in the case of *Brahman* or Īśvara (i.e., god), one cannot postulate any actual reason for the manifestation (*sṛṣṭi*) of the universe and thus it must be understood as an act of pure *līlā*, a gratuitous play or *divertissement* that is inherent to god's nature.[23] He gives the example of a high-ranking person who, though having satisfied all his desires, spends his time in gambling houses and other places of leisure. He also suggests the analogy of breathing, an activity that takes place only due to one's intrinsic nature and that has no extrinsic motivation. Śaṅkara emphasizes the total ease with which Īśvara carries out the seemingly arduous task of manifesting the universe.[24]

Through his *prahasann iva* Kṛṣṇa manifests his wondrous *līlā*. The *kurukṣetra* battlefield of the *Bhagavadgītā* is the *dharmakṣetra*, the "field of *dharma*" in which the forces of good (i.e., Arjuna and the other Pāṇḍavas) face the forces of evil (i.e., Duryodhana and all the Kauravas). It also symbolizes the stage of the world in which each and every person must fight his/her own battle in order to attain the supreme aim of *mokṣa*, freedom from rebirth. In the poem, the lord's *līlā* resonates with the *naiṣkarmya* doctrine that he teaches to Arjuna, that is, the *upadeśa* of disinterested action, with no attachment to its results (*phala*). Humans are called to imitate the divine *līlā* by abandoning all karmic ties and living a selfless life. In other words, they are invited to participate in god's play, to be part of his sublime cosmic drama by cultivating maximum attention and passion for action, performing it at the best of their capacities, but with total equanimity (*samatva*), without any attachment whatsoever (*BhG* 2.47–48). The idea is that one must remain unaffected and not identify himself/herself with the role he/she is playing. Arjuna and all men must absorb themselves in their *svadharma* without seeking any personal advantage, only having in mind the world's welfare (*lokasaṃgraha*; *BhG* 3.20, 3.25). The grace that manifests itself through Kṛṣṇa's *prahasann iva* is devoid of any necessity, it being free and unconditional (*ahetukī*) and beyond human expectations: like his love, it knows no reason and no season. Ultimately, all pain (*duḥkha*) and dichotomies are dissolved in the blissful tranquillity of the lord's hint of laughter.

There are some subtle correspondences that characterize the master-disciple relationship between Kṛṣṇa and Arjuna throughout the poem. It is our contention that Kṛṣṇa's *prahasann iva* in *BhG* 2.10 resonates with Arjuna's *vismaya* or amazement in *BhG* 11.14, after having witnessed his lord's glorious theophany, and a correspondence can also be detected between the hero's surrender to his *guru*-god as a *prapanna* in *BhG* 2.7 and the latter's grace/favor, that is, his *prasāda* toward him and all creatures, as he states near the end of the poem in *BhG* 18.56 and 18.58:

> Even tho all actions ever
> He performs, relying on Me,
> By My grace (*matprasādād*) he reaches
> The eternal, undying station.
> . . . .
> If thy mind is on Me, all difficulties
> Shalt thou cross over by My grace (*matprasādāt*);
> But if thru egotism thou
> Wilt not heed, thou shalt perish.[25]

Among the range of meanings of the term *prasāda* — derived from *pra* + verbal root √*sad*, "to be clear/bright/tranquil," "to be satisfied/pleased/glad"—we also find smile. Kṛṣṇa as the *prasanna*, the adjective derived from *pra* + √*sad*, indicates he who is gracious and serene by nature. The hint of laughter with which he looks at his dear *śiṣya* implies a "bright countenance" (*prasannamukha*) that envelops Arjuna in his blissful radiance.

It should be noted that even Śaṅkara is defined as *prasanna* by his pupils: just before their master's death they fix their eyes on his smiling face and his radious countenance is said to be so powerful as to dispel all their doubts.[26] Padmapāda (c. eighth century CE) at the beginning of his *Pañcapādikā* and Vācaspati Miśra (tenth century CE) in his *Bhāmatī* address him as the one who is both *prasanna* and *gambhīra*, "serene and profound."[27] Both *prasāda* and *prasanna* imply an opening, a blossoming that is characterized by brightness and peace (*śānti*). It is the sign of an inner beatific condition that distinguishes *guru*s and *avatāra*s, being the external manifestation of their blissful nature (*ānandasvarūpa*).

In comparative perspective, Kṛṣṇa's hint of laughter can be compared to the "priestly blessing" (*birkat kohanim*) that is found in the book of *Numbers* (6:24–26), though to be sure the inbuilt sense of ambiguity that we have in *prahasann iva* is absent.[28] Herein, Yahweh addresses Moses and tells him to speak to Aaron and his sons and let them know that from now onward the children of Israel will be blessed through these words:

> The Lord bless you and keep you;
> The Lord make his face shine upon you, and be gracious to you;
> The Lord lift up his countenance upon you, and give you peace.[29]

To this day, this prayer also known as the "lifting of the hands" (*nesiat kapayim*) continues to be devoutly recited by Jews as well as Christians, these words of benediction echoing in synagogues and churches throughout the world especially at the end of service.[30] Significantly, the expression "the Lord make his face shine upon you," refers to Yahweh's luminous smile, which is synonymous of his grace.

And yet we know that in the Jewish tradition seeing Yahweh's face—which symbolizes the whole person as well as the person's interiority—is prohibited and, indeed, it is said to be impossible for man, the idea being that man cannot survive to such an experience. Thus even though Moses conversed with Yahweh on mount Sinai and as a consequence the skin of his face shone, such radiance being derived from the divine encounter that he experienced (*Exodus* 34:29–30.35),[31] nonetheless when he wished to contemplate Yahweh's face the lord explicitly told him that he could not see it for no man can see god's face and live: protected by the lord's sheltering hand, Moses is only allowed to see Yahweh's back,[32] and it is this protective encounter that illuminates him (*Exodus* 33:20–23).[33]

Despite all differences, a parallelism with the situational context of *prahasann iva* may be detected in the background of this "shining face," that is, in the ambivalence and paradox that characterizes the moment at Sinai when Moses found himself *panim al-panim*, "face to face" with the lord, and yet is proscribed from seeing his face. Even in the *Bhagavadgītā* when the hint of laughter blossoms on Kṛṣṇa's face, Arjuna cannot behold it directly given that the poem tells us that he had just taken refuge in him (*tvāṃ prapannam*). This entails that he lay prostrate at his feet, with his eyes either closed or fixed on his lord's feet, having surrendered his mind and heart to his divine *guru* (*BhG* 2.7). Though Arjuna and Moses do not fix their eyes on their lords' face, Kṛṣṇa's and Yahweh's brightness and smiling countenance powerfully radiate toward them, enveloping them in the light of divine love. In both cases, the gods' dazzling brilliance and benevolent gaze are inseparable from one another and are a revelation of their transcendent splendor and beauty.[34]

Thus in *Bhagavadgītā* 7.8 Kṛṣṇa proclaims that he is the radiance (*prabhā*) in the moon and the sun and Arjuna, after witnessing his lord's theophany in chapter 11 and extolling his extraordinary brightness (*bhā*) "like that of a thousand suns in the sky" (*divi sūryasahasrasya*; *BhG* 11.12), praises the "matchless glory" (*apratimaprabhāva*) of his "most venerable *guru*" (*tvam asya pūjyaś ca gurur garīyān*; *BhG* 11.43). All in all, Kṛṣṇa's hint of laughter in *Bhagavadgītā* 2.10 must be appreciated as the first disclosure of the god's effulgence, loving grace, and beauty which instantly illumines and sanctifies Arjuna making him a fit receptacle for undertaking the listening (*śravaṇa*), pondering (*manana*) and meditative realization (*nididhyāsana*) of his liberating teaching.[35]

Chapter 1

On Kṛṣṇa's Hint of Laughter in the *Bhagavadgītā*

When shall I see your lotus face
With its always smiling dawn-red lips,
Joyously swelling the charming flute song
Which is sweetly accompanied by half
closed eyes that widen and dance?

—*Kṛṣṇakarṇāmṛta* 1.44[1]

To every single Arjuna, with heavy heart and empty hand,
Afraid to fight the battle of life on to victory,
You feel He has come for you, to you.
You see Him, silently looking around!
The searchlight eye full circle swings!
How lucky, you are there!
He smiles; He wins you by that smile!
You scarce can take your eyes from off that face,
So alluring, so divine!

—Excerpt from a poem of Narayan Kasturi, 1958

The expression *prahasann iva* is frequently used in the *Mahābhārata* (*MBh*) given that it occurs eighty-four times in its eighteen books, especially in the *Droṇaparvan*, the seventh book (twenty-eight times). In the sixth book of the *Bhīṣmaparvan*, besides the *Bhagavadgītā* (*BhG*) occurrence (*MBh* 6.24.10 = *BhG* 2.10),[2] it figures another eight times.[3] The cognate expression *hasann iva* is also common—thirty-nine occurrences—again mostly in the *Droṇaparvan* (twelve times) while in the *Bhīṣmaparvan* it occurs four times.[4] All in all, there are a total of 123 occurrences of *prahasann iva* + *hasann iva* in the *MBh* (forty occurrences in the *Droṇaparvan,* followed by thirteen in the *Bhīṣmaparvan* and *Karṇaparvan,* nine in the *Śalyaparvan,* etc.). In Vālmīki's *Rāmāyaṇa* (*Rām*), *prahasann iva* occurs thirteen times whereas the cognate *hasann iva* occurs only once.[5]

English Translations of the Expression *prahasann iva* in the *Bhagavadgītā*

The English renderings[6] of *prahasann iva* in *BhG* 2.10 have been varied, ranging from a preference for smile or a semblance of a smile (especially in the early period and up to the 1970s) to a preference for laughter or a hint of laughter (starting with J. A. B. van Buitenen's seminal translation in the early 1980s). Thus Charles Wilkins (1785) in his pioneering rendering translates "smiling,"[7] Sir Edwin Arnold (1900) "with tender smile,"[8] Franklin Edgerton (1944) "with a semblance of a smile,"[9] Sarvepalli Radhakrishnan (1948) "smiling as it were,"[10] Robert Charles Zaehner (1966) "faintly smiling,"[11] and Eliot Deutsch (1968) "smiling as it were."[12] Whereas Johannes Adrianus Bernardus van Buitenen (1981) translates "with a hint of laughter,"[13] Winthrop Sargeant (1984) "beginning to laugh, so to speak,"[14] Barbara Stoler Miller (1986) "mocking him gently,"[15] Angelika Malinar (2007) "almost bursting out in laughter,"[16] Alex Cherniak (2008) "almost laughing,"[17] and Georg Feuerstein and Brenda Feuerstein (2011) "laughingly, as it were."[18]

In the *MBh* the present active participle *prahasan*[19] (masculine nominative singular of *prahasant*), fulfils a quasi-adverbial function.[20] As already noted, it is derived from verbal root √*has*—meaning "to laugh" as well as "to deride" / "to mock"—with the addition of prefix (*upasarga*) *pra* whose primary meaning is "forward," "onward," "forth," "fore," often used pleonastically.[21] The Monier-Williams dictionary translates *pra* + √*has* as "to burst into laughter," "to laugh with," "to laugh at, mock, deride, ridicule,"[22] and Apte's dictionary translates it as "to laugh, smile," "to deride, ridicule, mock," and "to brighten up, look splendid, cheer up."[23]

In dramaturgy, *prahasana* identifies one of ten types of play (*nāṭya*) in which the comic sentiment predominates and in which the object of laughter is furnished by the improper conduct of someone who is criticized and put to shame.[24] Along these lines, the Monier-Williams dictionary translates the noun *prahāsa* as "loud laughter," *pra* being understood to mean "loud."[25] It should be noted that the prefix *pra*—corresponding to Greek προ—has a variety of possible nuances, not always predictable, among which notably are the meanings of "eminence"/"excellence" or "superiority," as for instance in the words *pradyumna* ("the preeminently mighty one"), *pravīra* ("hero"), *pramā* ("true knowledge") and *pramāṇa* ("a means to acquire true knowledge").[26] As a prefix to adjectives, *pra* means "excessively," "very," "much," whereas in nouns of relationship it means "great."[27]

As it happens in almost half of the *pāda*s in the *MBh*, the participle *prahasan* is followed by the indeclinable particle *iva* — "like," "as it were"/"as if," "in a certain manner"/"a little," "nearly"/"almost"—which always follows the word to which it refers and which in such participial usages is not easy to render.[28] With reference to *iva* in Vedic prose, Joel Brereton noted long ago that ". . . with verbs and verbal expressions, *iva* affirms that the action is true but that its realization or its extent is uncertain."[29]

In view of the above, we think that the most appropriate renderings of *prahasann iva* are the ones which translate *prahasan* as "laughing" rather than "smiling," though to be sure the action of laughing is mitigated by the presence of the *iva* particle and *prahasann iva* might be understood as meaning "to smile before laughing."[30] Our favored translation of this formulaic diction is van Buitenen's "with a hint of laughter," followed by Malinar's "almost bursting out in laughter." We agree with Walter Harding Maurer when he writes: "[. . .] *prahasann iva* "almost bursting into laughter," the idea being *not* that Kṛṣṇa is ridiculing or in any way mocking Arjuna's dilemma, but rather mitigating it, with a lighthearted shrug, so to speak, so as to allay Arjuna's distress. The particle *iva* is frequently used to tone down an expression or soften its effect."[31]

The full verse of *BhG* 2.10 may be rendered as follows:

Saṃjaya[32] said: (*saṃjaya uvāca*)
To him [= Arjuna] spoke Hṛṣīkeśa[33] (*tam uvāca hṛṣīkeśaḥ*)
With a hint of laughter, son of Bharata,[34] (*prahasann iva bhārata*)

In between the two armies (*senayor ubhayor madhye*)
As he was despondent, this speech: (*viṣīdantam idaṃ vacaḥ*)

The Expression *prahasann iva* in Context

BhG 2.10 is a crucial moment in the poem given that it is at this juncture that lord (*bhagavat*) Kṛṣṇa starts uttering his salvific teaching (*upadeśa*) to the hero Arjuna who, in his dejection, has finally surrendered himself to him. Significantly Śaṅkara (c. 700 CE), the most prominent representative of nondual (*advaita*) Vedānta, starts his seminal commentary (*bhāṣya*) to the *BhG* from this point, considering the first chapter (*adhyāya*) and the first nine verses of the second as preparatory, setting the scene to the *incipit* and unfolding of Kṛṣṇa's *upadeśa*. In Śaṅkara's own words:

> Now the portion from 1.2 to 2.9 should be interpreted as showing whence arose those evils of grief (*śoka*), delusion (*moha*), etc., which in sentient creatures cause the misery of *saṃsāra*. . . . Grief and delusion are thus the cause of *saṃsāra*. And seeing that their cessation could not be brought about except by Self-knowledge preceded by renunciation of all works, Lord Vāsudeva[35] wished to teach that knowledge for the benefit of the whole world by using Arjuna as the occasion and began His teaching with 2.11.[36]

Form both a poetic and religious point of view, Kṛṣṇa's hint of laughter at 2.10 is to be regarded as the pivotal *trait d'union*, being what immediately precedes his revelatory speech. In order to fully appreciate its import and function we need to contextualize it within the *BhG* and the epic's framework.[37] As Alf Hiltebeitel has noted, "One always has to watch these smiles."[38] In commenting upon the *Mahābhārata* play of the English theater and film director Peter Brook (1925–2022), first staged in July 1985 at the Thirty-Ninth *Festival d'Avignon*, Hiltebeitel poignantly observed:

> Also, Kṛṣṇa, you know, schemes with a smile. But this was missing in the Brook version. Kṛṣṇa is supposed to

> set the stage for some kind of catastrophe with the most subtle grin. That's one of the things that you can't miss if you know what the iconography looks like. That's a statement about seeing what Kṛṣṇa's up to in a *bhakti* kind of mode. But Peter Brook doesn't develop this subtlety, his player doesn't have this Kṛṣṇa smile. Rather, he looks like he's a figure who's going through one long weary scene of dire disaster, and the *Mahābhārata* is not really like that. I thought that this was a failure.[39]

It is noteworthy that besides the *BhG* episode there are various other places in the *MBh* where Kṛṣṇa either smiles or laughs, as when he responds with an enigmatic smile to Gāndhārī's curse in the *Strīparvan*. Throughout the epic Kṛṣṇa's smile/laughter is always to be watched carefully since, as David Dean Shulman points out, in particular his open laugh is "a sure sign that some horror is in the offing."[40]

While Saṃjaya relates to Dhṛtarāṣṭra that on the Kuru field the war between the two armies of Pāṇḍavas and Kauravas is about to begin, with the tumultuous din that made heaven and earth resound (1.19), the course of events is given an unexpected turn when Arjuna,[41] the hero of the Pāṇḍavas, having seen (*dṛṣṭvā*; 1.20) Dhṛtarāṣṭra's sons arrayed in battle order with their bows risen, asks his charioteer (*sārathi*) Kṛṣṇa—whom he calls *acyuta*, "imperishable"—to halt the chariot[42] in between the two armies so that he may give a closer look at those who have marched up eager to fight (1.21–23). Arjuna feels the urge to intently look at the Kauravas and it is precisely this act of seeing that brings about a change in his attitude.

According to political treatises, "standing in between" (*madhyastha*) of two armies exemplifies a neutrality of weakness, and such a position effectively illustrates Arjuna's psychological predicament. By contrast, Kṛṣṇa is wholly detached and uninvolved (*udāsīna*; *BhG* 9.9), and his neutrality is a neutrality of strength.[43] Theologically, Kṛṣṇa represents the intellect (*buddhi*); he is the charioteer of the "chariot" (*ratha*) of the individual soul (*jīva*).[44] By the same token, Arjuna's equidistant placement between the two fighting parties symbolizes the sole point from where it will be possible for him to achieve a condition of equanimity (*samatva*).[45] Such middle position is a space of freedom in which time is symbolically suspended, and from this privileged vantage point Arjuna will be able to exercise discriminative inquiry and detachment (*vairāgya*).[46] Indeed, it is the place where his transformation will be effectively brought about thanks to Kṛṣṇa's teachings.

Having complied with Arjuna's request of positioning the chariot in between the two armies, Hṛṣīkeśa asks him to behold the assembled Kurus (1.25)—Bhīṣma, Droṇa, and all the kings—and the following verses focus upon what the hero sees and its consequences. As in other places in the *MBh*, here the act of seeing is most powerful and is equated with knowing.[47] Arjuna, on the other side, does not see enemies but, in his words, *bandhus* (i.e., relatives): fathers, grandfathers, teachers, uncles, brothers, sons, grandsons, companions, fathers-in-law, and friends (1.26–27). In particular, Arjuna is anguished at the idea of having to fight against his revered teachers Bhīṣma and Droṇa.[48]

As a consequence, Saṃjaya tells us that Arjuna is immediately filled with utmost pity (1.28; *kṛpayā parayāviṣṭo*).[49] Seeing his kinsfolk (*dṛṣṭvaimān svajanān*) arranged in battle-order against him, eager to fight, he is emotionally and physically overwhelmed and breaks down: his limbs sink down, his mouth dries up, he trembles and has goosebumps, his *gāṇḍīva* bow[50] falls from his hand, he feels his skin burning, he gets dizzy, and his mind wanders (1.29–30). Moreover, Arjuna sees inauspicious signs (*nimittāni ca paśyāmi viparītāni*)[51] that are both a warning and an opportunity to prevent what he perceives as an impending catastrophe, since he sees nothing good in killing his kith and kin (1.31).[52]

Refusing to fulfill his own duty (*svadharma*) as a warrior, that is, his *kṣatriyadharma*, Arjuna declares that he desires neither victory (*vijaya*) nor the kingdom (*rājya*).[53] In his speech (1.28–46) he puts forward reasons for peace that are familiar to the reader of the *MBh*,[54] having been voiced in the preceding *Udyogaparvan*, which is dominated by the conflict between *kuladharma* and *kṣatriyadharma* (i.e., the duty pertaining to the family / clan and the one pertaining to the warrior class). Arjuna's argument is as follows (1.32cd–33):

> Of what use to us were kingdom, Govinda,[55]
> Of what use enjoyments or life?
> For whose sake we desire

Kingdom, enjoyments, and happiness,
They are drawn up here in battle,
Giving up life and wealth.[56]

Contrary to his cousin Duryodhana,[57] the chief of the Kauravas, Arjuna rejects *kṣatriyadharma* and regards his clan's prosperity as the paramount value. For him, the purpose of war can only be the welfare of the family. Wishing to be loyal to it, the very idea of fighting against his *bandhus* is something he instinctively repudiates (1.35):

Them I do not wish to slay,
Even though they slay (me), O slayer of Madhu,[58]
Even for three-world-rulership's
Sake; how much less for the sake of the earth![59]

Arjuna ponders over the evil (*pāpa*)[60] of killing one's people, and states that the destruction of the family is a crime (*doṣa*) that must be prevented, even if the others do not see it, their intelligence being overpowered by greed (*lobha*; 1.36–39). His words may be regarded as an anticipation of the mourning for the dead and serve as a last, desperate attempt to avoid the conflict. In his passionate defense of *kuladharma* over *kṣatriyadharma*, Arjuna proceeds to describe the vicious circle that the destruction of family members entails, considering the inevitable disruption of the larger network of social relations defined by the endogamous rules of marriage, which in turn determines lawlessness (*adharma*) and the collapse of the entire society through pernicious caste-admixture (*varṇasaṃkara*).[61] With the destruction of caste (*jātidharma*), the inexorable destiny of each and all is said to be none other than hell (*naraka*, 1.40–44):

Upon the destruction of the family, perish
The immemorial holy laws of the family;
When the laws have perished, the whole family
Lawlessness overwhelms also.
Because of the prevalence of lawlessness, Kṛṣṇa,
The women of the family are corrupted;
When the women are corrupted, O Vṛṣṇi-clansman,[62]
Mixture of caste ensues.

Mixture (of caste) leads to naught but hell
For the destroyers of the family and for the family;
For their ancestors fall (to hell),
Because the rites of (giving) food and water are interrupted.
By these sins of family-destroyers,
(Sins) which produce caste-mixture,
The caste laws are destroyed,
And the eternal family laws.
When the family laws are destroyed,
Janārdana,[63] then for men
Dwelling in hell certainly
Ensues: so we have heard (from the Holy Word).[64]

Arjuna wants to have nothing to do with the impending war—which he regards as a major sin (*mahat pāpam*) motivated by the greed for the joys of kingship (*rājyasukhalobha*)—and is rather willing to be slain in battle by Dhṛtarāṣṭra's men, without opposing any resistance (*apratīkāra*) and unarmed (*aśastra*). Indeed, he views suicidal surrender as more beneficial (*kṣematara*) than being involved in the family slaughter (1.45–46). At the end of chapter 1, Saṃjaya depicts Arjuna as sinking down in the box of his chariot, letting his bow and arrows fall, "his heart smitten with grief" (1.47; *śokasaṃvignamānasa*).

At the beginning of chapter 2, Saṃjaya repeats what he had already said at 1.28, that is, that Arjuna is overwhelmed by pity (2.1; *kṛpayā 'viṣṭam*), his eyes being blurred with tears.[65] At this point, Kṛṣṇa offers a first, brief reply (2.2–3) in which he upholds *kṣatriyadharma* and underlines how Arjuna's faintheartedness is offensive to the noble, excludes him from the heavenly world that awaits all heroes, and causes disgrace.[66] Kṛṣṇa tries to convince him to stop being a eunuch (*klība*), which does not befit him: he must shake off his miserable weakness of heart and get up/arise (*uttiṣṭha*). His reproach to Arjuna of being a eunuch, a symbol of impotence and cowardice,[67] is common in the epic, being addressed to weak heroes who are unable or reluctant to fulfill their *kṣatriya* duties.[68] It must be remembered that Arjuna had spent the thirteenth and last year of his exile disguised as a eunuch at the court of Virāṭa, the king of the Matsyas,[69] and thus Kṛṣṇa's reproach may be interpreted as insinuating that he had learned to play his role so well that he was still behaving as a eunuch, subtly accusing him to have turned into one.[70] Kṛṣṇa wants to hurt Arjuna's pride so as to trigger a manly reaction in him, given that in a warrior society the first commandment in order to maintain social status is to avoid shame by behaving bravely.

In 2.4–8, Arjuna repeats his main argument by saying that he cannot fight against the great heroes Bhīṣma and Droṇa whom he reveres as teachers (*gurus*) worthy of worship (*pūjārhāu*). The importance of his words is signaled by the fact that in verses 5–8 the meter changes from *śloka* to *triṣṭubh*.[71] Arjuna argues that rather than eating food besmeared with blood (i.e., gaining victory by slaying his masters and relatives), he prefers to eat alms food in this world. Again he puts forward an argument for peace, his reference to living from alms (*bhaikṣya*) pointing to the fact that he prefers ascetic renunciation (*saṃnyāsa*) to killing his own dear ones. By embracing a life of renunciation, he thinks he may be able to escape the conflict between contradictory *dharma*s. He is thus ready to relinquish all territorial claims and social status, and to live in the realm of another king.[72] He reiterates that neither a kingdom nor the earth is worth fighting for at the cost of killing his *bandhus*, and once again refuses to follow *kṣatriyadharma*.

Finally, recognizing that his own being (*svabhāva*) is afflicted with the weakness of pity (*kārpaṇyadoṣa*) and that his mind is confused as to what is right (*dharma*), Arjuna turns to Kṛṣṇa as his ultimate resort, desperately seeking his help.[73] Arjuna asks Kṛṣṇa to tell him decidedly (*niścitam*) what is better (*śreyas*),[74] what he ought to do at this critical juncture. Decisive is the close of verse 2.7, in which he falls at Kṛṣṇa's feet seeking refuge in him as his *guru*.[75] He declares that he is his disciple, and asks him to offer his invaluable teaching to him: "I am your pupil, teach me: I surrender to you" (*śiṣyas te 'haṃ śādhi māṃ tvāṃ prapannam*).

Arjuna does not see what else could possibly dispel his grief (*śoka*), which dries up his senses, even if he was to attain unrivaled, prosperous kingship and sovereignty over the gods. For him, *kuladharma* stands above and beyond *kṣatriyadharma* given that he sees his duty as a warrior as harboring demerit, not merit. His conflict over *dharma* is reinforced by the anticipation of the sorrow that the death of his *bandhus* will cause to him, and he definitely wants to avoid it. The hero's tragedy, which makes him utterly despondent and incapable of action, is that he is both intellectually and emotionally dumbfounded by the whole situation.

At 2.9, Saṃjaya reports Arjuna's last words to Govinda: "I will not fight" (*na yotsya iti*), after which he became silent (*tūṣṇīṃ babhūva*). The fact that Arjuna, who is the son of the war-god Indra and the main warrior-hero among the Pāṇḍavas, categorically states that he will not fight, is in itself emblematic of an ironic—and tragic—reversal of roles.[76]

From 2.11, Kṛṣṇa patiently begins to impart his *upadeśa* to Arjuna by pointing out that he is grieving for those he shouldn't grieve for (*aśocyān anvaśocas tvaṃ*), since the wise (*paṇḍitāḥ*) grieve for neither the dead nor the living. And yet, Kṛṣṇa seems to acknowledge that Arjuna has spoken "words of wisdom" (*prajñāvādān*). One needs to understand this statement—which has always been an interpretative crux—as being tinged with sarcasm. Kṛṣṇa's subtle irony at this juncture is in perfect keeping with his hint of laughter at 2.10. The idea is that with his words Arjuna only mimics a true sage since he is just the parody of one who is endowed with real wisdom (*prajñā*). Therefore, we think that the expression *prajñāvādān ca bhāṣase* of 2.11 should be understood to mean "you pretend to speak words of wisdom."[77]

In his first teaching to his *śiṣya*, Kṛṣṇa develops four major themes. First of all, he addresses the hero's sorrow and emotional crisis by imparting a speech of consolation (2.11–30) that teaches the immortality of the "owner of the body" (*dehin, śarīrin*), that is, the Self, vis-à-vis the mortality of the body.[78] At 2.20, he says that only the body can be killed, not the embodied Self which is beyond birth and death.[79] Therefore Arjuna has nothing to worry about—as repeatedly underlined by the formula *na śocitum arhasi* (see 2.25–27, 30)—and must learn to cultivate an equal attitude with respect to happiness and suffering.[80] Death is only an occasion for "changing old clothes" (*vāsāṃsi jīrṇāni*, 2.22), that is, for transmigrating into a new body.[81]

Kṛṣṇa then addresses the hero's conflict over tradition, emphatically endorsing *kṣatriyadharma* given that Arjuna's *svadharma*, his own duty as a warrior, overrules *kuladharma*. Thus he tells him that he must fight since refusing to do so is a sin.[82] The *kṣatriya* must engage in battle at all costs, without caring about winning or losing, that is, indifferent to its consequences since the consequences of war are no criteria for establishing its validity. Moreover, Kṛṣṇa points out that he should consider himself lucky since there is nothing better (*śreyas*) for a warrior than a legitimate, righteous (*dharmya*, 2.33) war.[83] Ultimately Kṛṣṇa's *kṣatriya* ethos is the same as the one upheld by the Kaurava leader Duryodhana, for whom "the warrior has been created for fighting" (*yuddhāya kṣatriyaḥ sṛṣṭaḥ*; see *MBh* 5.158.11–12). The code of honor does not allow for any regrets, afterthoughts, or doubts since a *kṣatriya* must engage himself in fight and never submit to anybody.[84] The idea is that a fighting warrior will always win: both victory and defeat will lead him to Indra's heaven (2.31–37).

Furthermore, Kṛṣṇa criticizes the old ritualistic worldview of *karman* of the followers of the *Veda*s and argues that solely discriminative knowledge purged of all personal interests is the precondition for right action. He thus redefines *karman* as per the famous doctrine of disinterested action (*niṣkāmakarman*, 2.47):

> On action alone be thy interest,[85]
> Never on its fruits;
> Let not the fruits of action be thy motive,
> Nor be thy attachment to inaction.[86]

Action must be carried out at the best of one's abilities, and yet it must not be judged by its results. Most importantly, one must relinquish all desires attached to it: only in this way can one free himself/herself from the bondage of *karman* (i.e., interrupt the ongoing production of karmic retribution). One must always consider the intentions that trigger action and exercise self-control. In order to do this the intellect, the highest faculty that allows to control the lower ones such as ego-consciousness (*ahaṃkāra*) and possessiveness, must be purified through the practice of *yoga* (*buddhiyoga*), poignantly defined as equanimity (*samatva*), so as to leave the realm of "acquisition and conservation" (*yogakṣema*) behind oneself and abandon all attachment (2.38–53).

Kṛṣṇa brings chapter 2 to a close by answering Arjuna's question regarding the characteristics of a man whose insight is firm (*sthitaprajña*, 2.54–72). Herein, he offers a lesson on yogic meditation that shows how perfect detachment from sense-objects results in clarity of mind (*prasāda*) and peace (*śānti*), in a contemplative withdrawal from the world that culminates in liberation, that is, *brahmanirvāṇa*, "the vanishing away that is *Brahman*."[87] Noteworthy is that Kṛṣṇa for the first time in the poem proposes himself as the privileged object of concentration, the "highest goal" (*matpara*) to whom the man of discernment must surrender himself (2.61, our translation):

> Them [= the senses] all restraining,
> Let him sit disciplined, intent upon Me as the highest goal;
> Only when his senses are under control,
> Is his wisdom secure.

To be sure, this is the fundamental teaching of the *BhG*, the most thorough presentation of which is found in chapter 18.54–58. Although some scholars consider this reference to Kṛṣṇa's divinity to be out of context, a later interpolation inserted when the theistic layers of the poem were added,[88] we think this need not be the case. In fact, 2.61 is consonant with 2.7d, which is the critical moment that occasions Kṛṣṇa's *upadeśa*, that is, the time when Arjuna surrenders himself to him, falling at his feet and taking "refuge" (*śaraṇāgati*) in him as his *guru*, which implies that he has accepted him as his beloved lord. The hero's surrender (*prapatti*),[89] his leap of faith (*śraddhā*),[90] is a silent, heartfelt prayer for help that he addresses to his charioteer as his last resort: it expresses the human need for god, which manifests itself in all its imperativeness at the time of existential crises and impending death.[91]

The paradigmatic *guru-śiṣya* relationship between Kṛṣṇa and Arjuna is the foundational presupposition of the *BhG*'s dialogue, its "secret" (*rahasya*) being *bhakti*, that love that has the characteristic of being exclusive.[92] As the *Śvetāśvatara Upaniṣad* proclaims in its closing verse (6.23): "Only in a man who has the deepest love for God, and who shows the same love towards his teacher as towards God, do these points declared by the Noble One shine forth."[93] If Arjuna's act of surrender to the divine master had not preliminarily taken place, Kṛṣṇa's teaching could have never been uttered. The hero's ripeness to receive Kṛṣṇa's *upadeśa* is demonstrated by his *prapatti*. According to Rāmānuja (trad. 1017–1137), the great master of Śrīvaiṣṇavism and the leading theologian of Viśiṣṭādvaita or "non-dualism of the qualified [whole]," the *prapanna* who has surrendered himself to the deity is the one worthy of divine favor (*prasāda*). In its culminating sixth stage known as *kārpaṇya* ("poorness of spirit") or *akiṃcanya* ("nullity"), *prapatti* is characterized by a condition of total vulnerability: one then "belongs" to the deity, his/her ego being shattered. The idea is that when one reaches such κένωσις or complete self-emptying, god intervenes filling him/her with his grace, his *prasāda*. It is especially noteworthy that the term *prasāda*—derived from *pra* + √*sad*, "to become clear/tranquil," "to become satisfied/pleased/glad"—besides its double meaning of clarity/tranquility of mind and divine grace also means good humor and smile.[94]

Having said this, it must be remembered that within the framework of a theology of grace the very possibility of Arjuna's seeking refuge at Kṛṣṇa's feet originates from god's overwhelming love.[95] His initiative is thought to precede and predetermine all human endeavor, suspending/vanquishing the law of *karman* itself. The sublime paradox of *bhakti* lies precisely in this: love is activated/instilled within man by god and man, in turn, is called to reciprocate it, that is, donate it to his/her lord. But how is it possible to donate something that does not actually belong to us since man received it as a gift of grace in the first place? The answer lies in the recognition that there is only love and such love is no "thing" but the very essence of god. Love is therefore to be understood as the foundation of all creatures and of all that exists, it being the alpha and the omega, the way and the goal. There is but one circularity of love, with no beginning nor end, an eternal dynamism of love, and this is what the dialogue (*saṃvāda*) between Kṛṣṇa and Arjuna is all about: its presupposition and its τέλος. As it is taught in the *Nāradabhaktisūtras* (30–33), the superiority of *bhakti* over all other paths (*mārga*) lies precisely in its being both the means and the end.

Even before the *BhG* episode, there are other instances in the *MBh* that reveal Arjuna's devotional pose toward Kṛṣṇa. Thus when Arjuna approaches the latter in order to ask him to be his ally in the war against the Kauravas he stands bowing at the foot of Kṛṣṇa's bed—as Govinda was sleeping—with folded hands (*kṛtāñjali*; 5.7.7), an attitude that contrasts with that of Duryodhana who, having come there for the same purpose of asking Kṛṣṇa to ally himself with him against the Pāṇḍavas, comfortably seats himself on a choice seat toward Kṛṣṇa's head. When Kṛṣṇa leaves them the option of selecting either the army of the Yādavas[96] or himself as a weaponless noncombatant advisor, Arjuna immediately chooses him (i.e., quality), whereas Duryodhana is delighted to have his army (i.e., quantity). And by choosing Kṛṣṇa, who will then act as his charioteer, Arjuna is definitely chosen by him.[97] As Mario Piantelli writes, Arjuna's choice is "the measure of the exceptional preciousness of Vāsudeva's word, of the unlimited power of the divine and of the risk that anyone who approaches such power with uncompromising dedication must face."[98]

The *BhG* aims to establish the legitimate rule of the ideal king who is none other than the god-obeying king, that is Arjuna, given that god (i.e., Kṛṣṇa) is the sole, eternal sovereign of the cosmos. It rejects the claims of those evil rulers who, like Duryodhana, make themselves absolute monarchs and affirm a godlike status for themselves. Within the *BhG*, the religious dimension of *bhakti* is inextricably intertwined with the political dimension of kingship. In the end, Arjuna must fight as a devoted *bhakta* for the cause of the one and only god, Kṛṣṇa, and for the welfare of the world (*lokasaṃgraha*; *BhG* 3.20, 3.25, 12.4). Although keeping to his yogic detachment, Kṛṣṇa shows interest in the world and his devoted king must act as his collaborator in the ongoing endeavor of maintaining its well-being. As Angelika Malinar states: "Kṛṣṇa's position is unique in that he is in command of the creative powers like a *yogin*, protects the created cosmos like a king, and surpasses all cosmic levels and established realms of liberation in that the 'knowing devotee' reaches not just identity with the elements of creation and liberation of the self, but the eternity in which Kṛṣṇa exists. This state of being can be reached only by those who are devoted to him."[99]

The Interpretations of *prahasann iva*

Given such context, we now revert to Hṛṣīkeśa's hint of laughter. From the outset, it must be noted that at this decisive juncture the poet who wrote our text plays on some fundamental oppositions that at the same time complement each other, making up an indissoluble whole since the relation between Kṛṣṇa and Arjuna is one of intimate reciprocity and mutual dependence.[100] Kṛṣṇa the godhead is the necessary companion for Arjuna, who is the ideal king and man since in the theology of the *BhG* god and king/devotee, religion and politics, liberation (*mokṣa*) and kingship are never conceived as separate. Arjuna and Kṛṣṇa, symptomatically "the white/silvery one" and "the black/dark one," are none other than the incarnations of the twin, inseparable sages Nara and Nārāyaṇa, revered as one being in two persons.[101] Arjuna's cry and sad situation is skillfully contrasted with Kṛṣṇa's hint of laughter and otherworldly serenity.[102] The hero represents man who in his despondency can only take refuge at his lord's feet as his *śiṣya*, vis-à-vis the laughing/smiling god who stands in front of him as his *guru*.[103] As god and man, Kṛṣṇa and Arjuna are regarded as unbeatable—as *BhG* 18.78, the last verse of the poem, solemnly states—and represent the perfect relationship, being supportive and respectful of one another.

Whereas Arjuna is lost in despair, Kṛṣṇa opens his mouth (*mukha*) in a hint of laughter, which is the prelude to his nectarine words of grace (*kṛpā, anugraha*), his liberating teaching. His *prahasann iva* is the bridging point between silence and the word: it triggers Arjuna's transformation by interrupting his dejection, that is, who he thinks he is, and leading him to a new understanding of himself—who he truly is.[104] Thanks to Kṛṣṇa's *upadeśa*, the hero will overcome his paralysis and will be prepared to act, having acquired resoluteness. As artfully staged in the *BhG* through these series of oppositions, Arjuna will emerge as the ideal king precisely because as a *bhakta* he is made to represent the ideal human being who, having surrendered to the sovereign of all creatures, will be granted the vision of the lord's universal form in chapter 11 of the poem.

Apparently Kṛṣṇa—who is as much a *kṣatriya* prince as he is the ultimate godhead, descended to earth as an *avatāra* (lit. "descent") for the protection of the good and the reestablishment of *dharma* (*BhG* 4.8)[105]—exhibits the typical reaction of a warrior when someone fails to fulfill his martial duty. In other words, Kṛṣṇa's hint of laughter can straightforwardly be interpreted as a laugh of ridicule and scorn, implicitly accusing Arjuna of being a coward: indeed, his derision is concomitant to what he tells Arjuna at 2.3, when he derogatorily calls him a eunuch. This is confirmed by the frequency of the stock expressions *prahasann iva/hasann iva* in the epic, though as we shall see in chapter 3 by no means all such occurrences are intended to be derisory. Just to mention one example, when at 5.7.9 Duryodhana approaches Kṛṣṇa for asking him to be his ally in the war against the Pāṇḍavas, he introduces his speech by a hint of laughter that he does not intend as sarcastic or offensive.

In Indian literature, the sentiment of laughter (*hāsyarasa*) is said to be induced when a character acts contrary to his own nature and inherent duty. Here Arjuna's behavior is laughable precisely because of its incongruence or inappropriateness (*anaucitya*), given that his sudden despondency and refusal to engage in combat are incompatible with his reputation as a fearless warrior. In the world of the epic, such a misdemeanor is invariably regarded as shameful and therefore laughable[106] and conducive to disgrace (*akīrti*) and loss of social esteem, as Kṛṣṇa further points out to Arjuna at 2.34–36:

> Disgrace, too, will creatures
> Speak of thee, without end;
> And for one that has been esteemed, disgrace
> Is worse than death.
> That thou hast abstained from battle thru fear
> The (warriors) of great chariots will think of thee;
> And of whom thou wast highly regarded,
> Thou shalt come to be held lightly.
> And many sayings that should not be said
> Thy ill-wishers will say of thee,
> Speaking ill of thy capacity:
> What, pray, is more grievous than that?[107]

Undoubtedly, what a warrior fears most is to be laughed at due to his supposed weakness.[108] Strength and manliness (*balapauruṣa*) are the sole values that count within a *kṣatriya* milieu, and Arjuna's crisis and last-minute appeals for peace cannot be deemed acceptable.

Thus, at a prima facie level, the hint of laughter of Arjuna's charioteer appears to be mocking and derisory, a warrior's typical reaction toward another warrior's lack of courage. Along these lines, it can be argued that Kṛṣṇa's derisive laugh/smile has a pedagogical function, being intended to put Arjuna to shame so as to elicit a reaction from him capable of triggering discriminative knowledge. Swami Swarupananda writes: "*Smiling*—to drown Arjuna in the ocean of shame. Krishna's smile at Arjuna's sorrow is like the lightning that plays over the black monsoon cloud. The rain bursts forth, and the thirsty earth is saturated. It is the smile of the coming illumination."[109] On a more subtle level, Kṛṣṇa's hint of laughter is the expression of his pure mirth and of something superhuman, being the sign of his divinity. His laughter/smile conveys a sense of joyful levity and relief, of unburdening and liberation. It indicates his benign sovereignty and transcendent detachment, above and beyond saṃsāric circumstances though being constantly engaged in the protection of the good and the welfare of the world.[110]

Laughing as well as smiling are constitutively ambivalent and ambiguous actions, being as it were suspended at the fringe of reality: they "stand in between" and are akin to a dream experience. The *iva* particle of our text, in its nuance of indefiniteness, reinforces the liminal character of Kṛṣṇa's hint of laughter, which is at the same time human and divine. The Austrian ethologist Konrad Lorenz (1903–1989) noted long ago that laughter is a case of redirected activity, that is, the transformation of an originally threatening movement—as for most animals is the opening of the mouth and the showing of the teeth, signaling the intention to bite—in a reassuring, peaceful gesture.[111]

Our contention is that *prahasann iva* is constitutively polysemic and that both understandings should be acknowledged (i.e., the hint of laughter as mockery and the hint of laughter as mirth). After all, Kṛṣṇa is both a prince (i.e., a warrior) and the supreme godhead, and his hint of laughter must be acknowledged as a skillful means (*upāya*) through which he achieves the transformation of his pupil by resorting to both mockery and mirth. The poet of the *BhG* articulates this adaptive framework by deliberately playing with such polysemy, which also reflects Kṛṣṇa's ambiguous personality within the *Mahābhārata*. In his divine freedom he is a law unto himself and as James L. Fitzgerald writes, there is in his portrayal

> a tension between a placid, typically smiling, surface demeanor, and a boundlessness that might suddenly open up in connection with him, an unexpected flash

> of infinity. . . . [Kṛṣṇa] Vāsudeva [being] characterized by limitless ambition . . . ruthless wiliness . . . sudden, explosive violence . . . his sudden demonstration to Arjuna that he was "time grown old for the destruction of the world," and the ontological point of origin and end of all being, the Puruṣottama . . . and Parameśvara . . . and, ultimately, Nārāyana and Viṣṇu . . . ; and, finally, by his utter transcendence of all the categories distinguishing between the *dvandvas*, "pairs," "oppositions," such as warm-cold, . . . *dharma-adharma*. . . . The divine transcendence of Kṛṣṇa-Vāsudeva that is revealed in the *Bhagavadgītā* . . . and other episodes of the text is easily harmonized with the steady stream of ruthless *nīti* (policy advice) he offers the Pāṇḍavas throughout the narrative, guiding them without reference to *dharma* in politics and war.[112]

Although the understanding of *prahasann iva* as both mockery and mirth may appear to be contradictory, that is, mutually exclusive if taken in isolation, an almost imperceptible and yet decisive movement from one to the other can be inferred: the hint of laughter as mockery of Kṛṣṇa the prince gives way to the sweetest expression of blissful grace of Kṛṣṇa the godhead, that which is to be understood as the beautiful "smile of smiles," resort of all *bhaktas*.[113]

Moreover, we are persuaded that given Arjuna's surrender to Govinda as his *guru* and lord at the close of 2.7, *prahasann iva* rather than as an "ordinary" mocking laugh/smile must be understood primarily as a laugh/smile of pure grace and satisfaction on the latter's part. Kṛṣṇa rejoices at Arjuna having finally sought refuge at his feet and promptly responds to his utter despondency through his benevolent gaze. Most commentators point out that Arjuna's crisis and his seeking refuge at the lord's feet are used by Kṛṣṇa as the long-awaited occasion, the pretext (*vyāja*) for imparting his liberating teaching. The two prefixes *pra* of *pra-pannam* (2.7) and *pra-hasann* (2.10) subtly respond to one another, the former inevitably attracting the latter. The past passive participle *prapanna* (*pra* + *√pad*) literally means "to throw one's self down [at a person's feet]," "to go forward," "to resort to,"[114] and it is precisely Arjuna's act of surrendering at Kṛṣṇa's feet, of moving forward and resorting to him, that attracts the lord's positive response, that is, his hint of laughter/smile toward him.[115]

Arjuna's crisis and utter despair (*viṣāda*) is what constitutes his entitlement (*adhikāra*) to seek discipleship, prompting his surrender. Though our hero's pity (*kārpaṇyadoṣa*; 2.7) is misplaced, it has its own appeal to the lord, who is resolved to transmute it into the renunciation of the attachment to the deed, and the fruits of it. The darkness (*tamas*) of Arjuna's ignorance is infallibly removed thanks to his *śaraṇāgati* to Kṛṣṇa, which ignites the spark of light (*jyotis*) in him. There is an immediate match—a reciprocal attraction and reflection—between Arjuna's surrender and Kṛṣṇa's smile/laugh which manifests the god's effulgence (*prabhā*), that is, his pure love (*preman*) for his pupil. As we read in the *Jñāneśvarī* (18.1461), the Marāṭhī commentary to the poem written by the thirteenth-century poet-saint Jñāneśvar (1275–1296): "Isn't the *Gītā* like a sun which, in the sky of Kṛṣṇa's mouth, illuminates for the world the jewels of all the scriptures?" By opening his mouth the deity communicates his blissful radiance (*tejas*),[116] his incomparable glory and beauty (*saundarya*).[117] The idea that Kṛṣṇa's mouth is the receptacle of an otherworldly effulgence through which he reveals his divinity will become a leitmotif in subsequent devotional literature.[118]

Though Arjuna's last words that he shall not fight (*na yotsya iti*; *BhG* 2.9) evidence the hero's deluded stubbornness and inevitably attract Kṛṣṇa's irony, because of the patent contradiction between his discipleship on the one hand and his claimed independence on the other,[119]such hint of sarcasm is nonetheless secondary with respect to the lord's all-forgiving hint of laughter, given the new, transformative context of the sacred *guru-śiṣya* relation that has just been inaugurated.

Kṛṣṇa's standing in front of Arjuna with a radiant countenance expresses the fullness of god's *prasāda* toward his *bhakta*. It is not a cynical laughter filled with contempt, since Govinda does not laugh at or against Arjuna. His is not a condescending or nasty grimace but rather a cheerful laughter of sympathy and encouragement that welcomes the Pāṇḍava hero as his dear pupil and devotee: Govinda laughs/smiles *for* Arjuna, embracing him in the warmth of his love.[120] Along these lines, Douglas Brooks observes: "Krishna's reply begins with the "hint of a smile," . . . the signal of grace descending (*shakti-pata*), and promises a radical transformation and awakening. This descent of grace comes from the highest, self-luminating reality and is refined in the awareness of the seeker who opens to its presence in her or his own thoughts (*vikalpa*)."[121] Swami Chidbhavananda's commentary is also worth quoting:

> Significant is the smile beaming on the lips of Hrishikesa. As the dawn is the harbinger of day-break, the Lord's smile forecasts the *yoga* and the spiritual enlightenment that are to come on Arjuna. It was *Preyas* [= the gratifying] that he had been receiving till now. What he is going to receive forthwith is *Sreyas* [= the good], the sovereign remedy for all the evils of the mundane existence. It is the inviolable means for the attainment of Beatitude. There is nothing greater than *Sreyas* for man to seek. Existence finds fulfillment in It. Arjuna is going to be initiated into It. Hence this divine smile on the lips of the Lord.[122]

Kṛṣṇa's hint of laughter is the connecting point between the hero's mute anguish and the lord's word of grace, the pivotal moment that immediately precedes the deliverance of the divine teaching. The smile of the *guru* toward his disciple/s marking the effusion of his *upadeśa*—be it through the medium of speech or even through silence—has a long-standing tradition in Indian religions: one is reminded of the Buddha and of Bodhisattvas such as Avalokiteśvara and, within the Hindu milieu, of the figure of Śiva Dakṣiṇāmūrti, who is said to convey the truth of Vedānta through his eloquent silence.[123] Just to offer one example, we quote two elegant verses taken from the *Dakṣiṇāmūrtistotra* attributed to Śaṅkara:

> I have contemplated Him, the One who is rich of inexhaustible compassion,
> The Primeval Teacher seated at the root of the Banyan tree,
> Who through His silence adorned of His gentle smile
> Vanquishes the darkness of ignorance for the multitude of the great seers.
> . . . .
> I bow to the Teacher of Teachers who, by inclining His gaze,

From the corner of His eye discharges
The waves of nectar of His boundless compassion
On the ascetics who are worn-out by the sultriness of the desert of rebirths.[124]

Here Śiva Dakṣiṇāmūrti's grace (i.e., the waves of nectar that he discharges from the corner of his eye), is effectively conveyed through his gentle smile and compassionate look. In the hymn the motif of amazement (*vismaya*) is also present given that Śiva Dakṣiṇāmūrti is depicted as a youthful teacher surrounded by aged disciples: the unexpected contrast of the young god, stainless and serene beyond measure, who bestows the direct knowledge of *Brahman* through silence to his old pupils—mighty sages who nonetheless suffer from the malady of birth and death—is in itself a matter of astonishment.[125]

Kṛṣṇa's hint of laughter anticipates the dissolution of the hero's mortal anguish: it is the definite cure for Arjuna's "disease" caused by *śoka* and *moha*. More to the point, it signals the theological truth that Govinda has already dissolved his negative condition, even before the pouring forth of the nectar of his words. His hint of laughter is the expression of the gushing out of his superabundant grace that eradicates the disciple's doubts[126] and vanquishes the numbness of his mind and body.

As noted, the prefix *pra* can be interpreted as meaning "supreme"/"excellent," pointing at the spiritual dimension of Kṛṣṇa's hint of laughter. A reason that supports such interpretation is the implied body language of the two protagonists: whereas Arjuna's posture as a *prapanna* entails that he has thrown himself at his lord's feet, Kṛṣṇa the *guru* stands up as the *prasanna*—an adjective that is derived from *pra* + √*sad*, just like the noun *prasāda*—that is, the clear/tranquil/gracious one, facing his disciple and illumining him with a hint of laughter that "comes from above" and is indicative of his otherworldly eminence.[127] Arjuna awaits everything from Kṛṣṇa, with his eyes fixed upon him as his last resort—wholly concentrating his attention on Kṛṣṇa's feet, these being the receptacle of divine power and grace[128]—and the lord bountifully turns his beaming countenance and laughing eyes toward him and gives him peace (*śānti*), filling the hero's emptiness with his luminous gaze that annihilates all sins. It is the sacred moment of *darśana*, the transformative experience of seeing the divine person and, most importantly, of being seen by him.[129]

Arjuna's surrender to the lord entails his "falling like a stick, with the eight limbs of his body touching the ground" (*sāṣṭāṅga daṇḍavat*; forehead, chest, palms, knees, and feet): love of god and fear of god are perfectly integrated in the all-important act of prostration, the *praṇipāta* or *namas*.[130] On his part Kṛṣṇa, standing upright, through the first, imperceptible opening of his mouth in laughter/smile asserts his *saṃkalpa* (i.e., his "intention" of love toward his *bhakta*). And through the expansion of his facial muscles, the lord radiates and pours down on Arjuna his invigorating *preman*. Arjuna's devout attitude as a *pra-panna* inevitably attracts Kṛṣṇa's graceful hint of laughter, his *pra-hasann iva*, the call of love being irresistible.

The *prahasann iva* signals the bond of intimacy between the two that characterizes their relation throughout the *BhG*. Even at the beginning of chapter 4, Kṛṣṇa tells Arjuna that he will teach him his ancient (*purātana*) *yoga* precisely because he is his loyal devotee and comrade (*bhakto 'si me sakhā ca*; 4.3). This bond of love between *guru* and *śiṣya* will find its culmination in chapter 11 when the lord will grace his *bhakta* with the vision of his universal form.[131] Indeed, after having had this astonishing revelation Arjuna praises Kṛṣṇa as the father of the world (*pitā 'si lokasya*) and the most venerable *guru* (*tvam asya pūjyaś ca gurur garīyān*), whose greatness is matchless.[132] He then asks Kṛṣṇa to please forgive him if in the past he treated him lightly, as if he was just his friend (11.42–43). In particular, at 11.42 Arjuna says:

> And if I treated Thee disrespectfully, to make sport of Thee (*avahāsārtham*),
> In the course of amusement, resting, sitting or eating,
> Either alone, O unshaken one (*acyuta*), or in the presence of those others,
> For that I beg forgiveness of Thee, the immeasurable one.[133]

Herein the noun *avahāsa*, "jest"/"joke," "derision," originates from *ava* + √*has* meaning "to laugh at"/"deride."[134] Remarkably, it is the only other occurrence in the whole poem besides *prahasan* at 2.10 of a term derived from verbal root √*has*. The compound *avahāsārtham*, which Franklin Edgerton translates "to make sport," can be more appropriately rendered "with jesting / deriding purpose," "by way of a joke."[135] As a prefix to verbs, *ava*—literally "down," "off"—can be used to express disrespect and depreciation.[136] Arjuna prays Kṛṣṇa to forgive him if in the past he "put him down" and treated him disrespectfully (*asatkṛta*). The prefix *ava* of *avahāsārtham*—entailing inferiority / horizontality (i.e., humanity)—stands in complementary contrast to the prefix *pra* of *prahasann iva*, which can be used to express superiority, thus entailing verticality (i.e., divinity).[137] Our suggestion is that Kṛṣṇa's *pra* + √*has* at 2.10 and Arjuna's *ava* + √*has* at 11.42 are an interrelated pair, mirroring two opposite and yet corresponding modes of expression of laugh / jest, the first being sublimely divine, and the second being all too human. Such contrastive wordplay is not casual but consciously aimed at by the poet of the *BhG*.

With regard to the hero's supplicant words to his *guru*-god, Alf Hiltebeitel remarks:

> Friendship (*sakhyam*) is thus a suitable relationship for understanding Krishna's dharmic role, but, as Arjuna says, it is not adequate to carry the devotional appreciation of Krishna in his universal form. Thus, after the theophany, Arjuna apologizes for his earlier familiarity with Krishna, that is, as he puts it, for:
>
> "Whatever I said rashly, thinking Thee my boon companion (*sakhe 'ti matvā*), calling Thee 'Kṛṣṇa, Yādava, Companion (*sakhe*)!' " (11.41)
>
> Arjuna is, of course, forgiven his familiarities, and he stands as the exemplar of both of these relationships to Krishna: those of *sakhi* and *bhakta*, the former implying a variety of social and dharmic relations, the latter a means to salvation.[138]

Hiltebeitel's authority notwithstanding, we think that his final statement needs to be corrected. As Angelika Malinar notes: "Well-established social relationships of kinship (father-son), friendship / comradeship (*sakha*) and love (*priya*) are now placed within the religious framework of *bhakti*."[139] In such framework, friendship (*sakhya*) with the lord is regarded as one of the highest forms of devotion. Significantly, in the much later *Bhāgavata Purāṇa* (ninth–tenth century) *sakhya* figures as the penultimate, eighth limb of the "nine limbs" (*navāṅgāni*) of *bhakti* which culminate in self-surrender, that is, *ātmanivedana*, which is a synonym of *prapatti*.[140] That Arjuna's comradeship with Kṛṣṇa—extolled as the paradigm of *sakhya*[141]—resulted in his falling at the latter's feet must be appreciated as the hero's crowning achievement along the *bhakti* path. Thus, at 11.44 Arjuna states:

> Therefore, bowing and prostrating my body (*praṇamya praṇidhāya kāyaṃ*),
> I beg grace (*prasādaye*) of Thee, The Lord to be revered:
> As a father to his son, as a friend to his friend,
> As a lover to his beloved, be pleased to show mercy, o God![142]

Here Arjuna's prostration to his lord—also expressed at 11.35 ("making a reverent gesture," *kṛtāñjalir*, "having made obeisance," *namaskṛtvā*, "bowing down," *praṇamya*)—corresponds to his having sought refuge in him at 2.7. There is a subtle link between these moments, his first act of surrender being the most crucial and decisive one. Indeed, the hero's *prapatti* to his god and *guru* is the reason why Kṛṣṇa looks at him with tenderness since by submitting himself to his lord he has done the one right thing, which solely counts.

The epithet *acyuta* ("imperishable"/"unshaken"/"changeless") with which Arjuna acknowledges Kṛṣṇa's divinity at 11.42 had already been used by our hero at the very beginning of the poem, that is, at *BhG* 1.21, when he had asked Hṛṣīkeśa to halt the chariot between the two armies. This appellation suggests that Arjuna was all along aware of Kṛṣṇa's divine nature, though his comradeship with him had brought him to forget such truth being misled by the *avatāra*'s humanity (i.e., the veil of Kṛṣṇa's *māyā*).[143] Besides 1.21 and 11.42, *acyuta* is used a third time at the end of the poem, at 18.73, when Arjuna pronounces his last, solemn words:

> Destroyed the confusion; attention (to the truth) is won,
> By Thy grace, on my part, O Changeless One (*acyuta*);
> I stand firm, with doubts dispersed;
> I shall do Thy word.[144]

The curling of the god's lips (*oṣṭha, dantacchada, adhara*), the corners of his mouth turned up, and the glimpse of his glimmering teeth (*danta / daśana*) are for Arjuna as well as for all *bhakta*s the sure sign of the lord's benign favor. Such exquisite, benevolent *darśana* of Kṛṣṇa coexists with the wrathful vision of the god's mouth and terrible tusks (*daṃṣṭrākarāla*) in the theophany of chapter 11 (in particular 11.23, 11.25, and 11.27). Within kṛṣṇaite traditions, the *darśana* of the god's laughter / smile is thought to be so captivating—his teeth being compared to the buds of jasmine flowers,[145] reflecting the splendor of his rosy lips—that his devotees are advised to constantly contemplate such sheer radiant beauty within their hearts, given that the lord "abides in the heart of each and every one" (*sarvasya cā 'haṃ hṛdi saṃniviṣṭo; BhG* 15.15) as their inner controller (*antaryāmin*). Once again the act of seeing plays a key function, being the way through which the god's grace is effectively conveyed.

Through his hint of laughter Kṛṣṇa challenges Arjuna's entanglement to the world by calling attention to what solely is: the *ātman*. The lord's *prahasann iva* exhibits his pure joy (*ānanda*) and blissful equanimity,[146] his *līlā* or playful attitude toward existence that subverts mundane preoccupations and well-established patterns of thought.[147] As Swami Mukundananda notes: "In sharp contrast to Arjuna's words of lamentation, Shree Krishna smiled, displaying that the situation was not making him despair; rather he was perfectly happy with it. Such is the equanimous attitude exhibited by someone with knowledge in all situations."[148]

Kṛṣṇa laughs also because he knows beforehand that his *bhakta* will reach him: then Arjuna's hair will no longer stand on end due to the despondency / grief born out of ignorance (1.29c) but as the unmistakable sign that he has realized Kṛṣṇa's true identity. This is evidenced by the hero's reaction at *BhG* 11.14, after having witnessed his lord's cosmic form, in which he is depicted in the typical position of a devoted disciple worshipping his chosen deity:

> Then filled with amazement (*vismayāviṣṭo*),
> His hair standing upright (*hṛṣṭaromā*), Dhanaṃjaya[149]
> Bowed with his head (*praṇamya śirasā*) to the God,
> And said with a gesture of reverence (*kṛtāñjalir*):[150] . . .

While the hero's crisis was determined by his sentiment of pity, due to which he also got goosebumps (*romaharṣa*), its solution is now represented by another overwhelming emotion: amazement/awe (*vismaya*) at the sight of Kṛṣṇa's theophany. This produces utter astonishment (*vismita*) in all heavenly beings: Rudras, Ādityas, Vasus, Sādhyas, Viśvedevas, Aśvins, Maruts, Ūṣmapas, Gandharvas, Yakṣas, Asuras, and Siddhas (*BhG* 11.22).[151] It is noteworthy that both the noun *vismaya* and the past passive participle *vismita* are derived from *vi* + verbal root √*smi* which means "to smile."[152] This experience of the numinous leads Arjuna to bow to his god and *guru* by performing the *añjalimudrā,* the gesture of reverent honoring.[153]

Our hero and all *bhakta*s are implicitly called to cultivate *vismaya*—which entails humility, that is, literally being "free from pride and arrogance" (*vi-smaya*)[154]—by extending it to everyday life, recognizing god's invisible and wondrous presence at all times.[155] Theologically, Arjuna's and all creatures' *vismaya* is the necessary qualification to proceed along the path that leads to communion with the divine. Arjuna's *vismaya,* his staring at his lord with awe, must be appreciated as the most appropriate response to Kṛṣṇa's *prahasann iva*: this state (*bhāva*) that manifests itself so powerfully at the sight of the lord's cosmic form in chapter 11 was effectively prepared and anticipated by Arjuna's surrender to Kṛṣṇa at 2.7 since the two are linked to one another, *vismaya* being the consequence of pure devotion.[156] The lord makes it clear that Arjuna's vision of his glory is entirely due to his grace, which he calls *prasanna*:

> By Me showing grace (*mayā prasannena*) towards thee, Arjuna, this
> Supreme form has been manifested by My own mysterious power;
> (This form) made up of splendor, universal, infinite, primal,
> Of Mine, which has never been seen before by any other
> Than thee.[157]

In the end, nothing but *bhakti* can lead man to see/know god in his cosmic form and achieve oneness with him. As Kṛṣṇa states at 11.54:

> But by unswerving devotion (*bhaktyā tv ananyayā*) can
> I in such a guise, Arjuna,

Be known (*jñātuṃ*) and seen (*draṣṭuṃ*) in very truth,
And entered into (*praveṣṭuṃ*), scorcher of the foe.[158]

Devotion is therefore indispensable. Arjuna was granted the privilege of seeing the lord's cosmic form precisely because he chose the path of *bhakti*, *bhaktiyoga* being the most excellent kind of spiritual discipline an adept can resort to (*BhG* 14.26).[159]

Eventually, by realizing Kṛṣṇa as the highest godhead one goes beyond all *dharmas*. Along these lines, in *BhG* 18.66 the lord declares:

Abandoning (*parityajya*) all other duties (*sarvadharmān*),
Go to Me as thy sole refuge (*śaraṇaṃ*);
From all evils I thee
Shall rescue (*mokṣayiṣyāmi*): be not grieved![160]

Arjuna's original conflict between *kuladharma* and *kṣatriyadharma*, which led to his tragic breakdown and impasse, has been definitely superseded by his loyalty to "the lord who abides in the region of the heart of all creatures" (*īśvaraḥ sarvabhūtānāṃ hṛddeśe . . . tiṣṭhati*; *BhG* 18.61). The complete surrender of body (*tanu*), mind (*manas*), and all possessions (*dhana*) to the *guru*-god is the acme of *bhakti*,[161] after which nothing else is needed: all duties drop away just as a flower drops off as soon as its fruit appears.[162]

The Impact of Kṛṣṇa's *prahasann iva* on the *Bhagavadgītā*'s Central Teachings: An Overview

Traditionally, the first six chapters of the poem are known as the section on *karmayoga*, "the discipline of action," which is undoubtedly its most original, possibly even oldest, portion (in particular, chapters 2–4).[163] Herein, Kṛṣṇa reveals to Arjuna the doctrine of disinterested action (*naiṣkarmya*), a path to liberation that requires an inner attitude of detachment from the results (*phala*) of one's deeds, both ritual and social.[164] Having already presented the contents of the first two chapters, we offer a brief summary of the main teachings that unfold in chapters 3 through 6.

In chapter 3, Kṛṣṇa tells Arjuna that action is inescapable since there is no life without it. He therefore instructs him to act without any longing and loathing, regarding each and every action as a veritable sacrifice (*yajña*) that he must undertake for the welfare of the world, relinquishing all selfish interests: in this way all deeds and their results, which pertain to the material sphere and not to the self, will not bind him to the wheel of rebirth. The agent must renounce his/her agency and by doing so he/she will be free from the karmic repercussions of his/her inescapable activity. Everyone must be keen to adhere to his/her own *dharma* by continuing to live in the world and performing his/her duties in the best possible way, consecrating all actions as an offering to the lord, that is, casting all karmic burdens upon him. Kṛṣṇa points out that actions are done by the constituents (*guṇa*) of nature (*prakṛti*) alone; it is only the deluded one who thinks "I am the doer" (*kartṛ*; 3.27).

In chapter 4, Kṛṣṇa reveals to Arjuna that he has been teaching this *yoga* from time immemorial, as he manifests himself from age to age in order to reestablish *dharma* and protect the good and punish all evildoers. The devotees that consecrate themselves completely to him become a part of him, and as *karman* does not stain the lord who is not bound by actions in the same way whoever acts without desire for the fruits of his/her deeds will be free from their consequences.

In chapter 5, Kṛṣṇa tells Arjuna that the action that is free from craving is preferable even to renunciation (*saṃnyāsa*). Whoever practices *yoga* with this inner attitude is never polluted by *karman*: he/she sees no difference among creatures, abides in *Brahman*, and attains peace. Finally, in chapter 6 Kṛṣṇa reiterates to Arjuna that true renunciation lies in disinterested action because it is thanks to such action that a *yogin* attains that peace that culminates in *nirvāṇa*. By seeing himself in all creatures and the whole universe in the Bhagavat, the *yogin* achieves the ultimate goal: perfect communion with the lord. Thus the best among *yogin*s is the devotee that consecrates himself to the lord with total faith, the path (*mārga*) of *karmayoga* being ultimately subsumed in *bhakti*.

Coming to an evaluation of the fundamental teaching of *naiṣkarmya* from the perspective of *prahasann iva*, we think that Kṛṣṇa's hint of laughter—that purposely stands in contrast to Arjuna's despondency—is revelatory of the lord's *līlā*, pointing to the proper attitude that our hero and all humans should cultivate toward action. Indeed, god is constantly engaged in the manifestation, maintenance, and dissolution of the cosmos and yet "action does not stain him" (*na māṃ karmāṇi limpanti*; *BhG* 4.14) since his activity is nothing but a gratuitous pastime free from the yearning for the fruits of actions. Kṛṣṇa's hint of laughter is indicative of his perfect serenity in the midst of the sounds of war and sets the example for the ideal *karmayogin*:[165] Arjuna is called to engage in action for the welfare of the world (*lokasaṃgraha*), abandoning all egotistic attachments and being "always satisfied/content" (*nityatṛpto*; *BhG* 4.20).

Even though the term *līlā* as such does not occur in the poem and its theology will be developed in a full-fledged way only in later times,[166] Kṛṣṇa's hint of laughter signals that he as an *avatāra* accomplishes the protection of the good, the destruction of evildoers and the establishment of *dharma* (*BhG* 4.8) with perfect ease. Along these lines, the lord instructs Arjuna to free himself from the burden of selfishness and to perform his duty as a *kṣatriya* without any thought of reward, in a spirit of gratuitous service.[167] Kṛṣṇa gives the example that all should follow in order to participate in his divine play (*BhG* 3.22–23):

> For me, son of Pṛthā,[168] there is nothing to be done
> In the three worlds whatsoever,
> Nothing unattained to be attained;
> And yet I still continue in action.
> For if I did not continue
> At all in action, unwearied,
> My path (would) follow
> Men altogether, son of Pṛthā.[169]

The levity of the lord's *prahasann iva*, his leisurely attitude, hints at the fact that the world is akin to a stage and all creatures are but actors in his play. Though each and every one are instructed to enact their role to the best of their capacities in accordance with their *svadharma*, it is made clear that this whole cosmic drama, this entire material universe made up of the three *guṇa*s, is but an illusion (*māyā*) that only *bhakti* can overcome. By surrendering one's mind and heart to the Bhagavat, the veil of *māyā* can effectively be pierced (*BhG* 4.6, 7.14):

> Tho unborn, tho My self is eternal,
> Tho Lord of Beings,
> Resorting to My own material nature
> I come into being by My own mysterious power (*ātmamāyayā*).
> . . . .
> For this is My divine strand-composed
> Trick-of-illusion (*māyā*), hard to get past;
> Those who resort to Me alone
> Penetrate beyond this trick-of-illusion.[170]

The lord's manifestation (*vyakti; BhG* 10.14) is commonly interpreted as an expression of his *līlāmayasvarūpa*, given that his "own form consists of play."[171] It is by the power of his *māyā* that he causes all beings to revolve "as if fixed on a mechanical device/toy" (*yantrārūḍhāni; BhG* 18.61), "like wooded dolls mounted on a machine" as Śaṅkara perceptively suggests in his commentary.[172] That everything is but god's unfathomable *līlā* is strikingly revealed to Arjuna when Kṛṣṇa grants him the vision of his universal form and he sees the sons of Dhṛtarāṣṭra as well as his own chief warriors enter his mouths "frightful with tusks, and terrifying" (*BhG* 11.27). As the Bhagavat solemnly states (*BhG* 11.32–33):

> I am Time (Death),[173] cause of destruction of the worlds, matured
> And set out to gather in the worlds here.
> Even without thee (thy action), all shall cease to exist,
> The warriors that are drawn up in the opposing ranks.
> Therefore arise thou, win glory,
> Conquer thine enemies and enjoy prospered kingship;
> By Me Myself they have already been slain long ago;
> Be thou the mere instrument, left-handed archer![174]

Kṛṣṇa, the lord of the gods (*deveśa; BhG* 11.25, 11.37, 11.45) who is infinite (*ananta; BhG* 11.37) and has infinite forms (*anantarūpa; BhG* 11.38), swallows all beings with his flaming mouths "like moths entering a burning flame" (*BhG* 11.29): he is the director of the cosmic play and knows beforehand how it will unfold and how it is destined to end. As the supreme lord of *yoga* (*mahāyogeśvara, BhG*

11.9; *yogeśvara, BhG* 11.4, 18.75, 18.78), Kṛṣṇa's *vibhūtis*, that is, the manifestations of his power (*BhG* 10.19–42), are the expression of his sovereignty (*aiśvarya*), which he exercises with absolute ease.[175] Man's duty is but to act with an equanimous attitude, devoutly offering all results (*phala*) (i.e., the fruits of *karman*) to Kṛṣṇa, and leaving the scene at god's appointed time.

Chapters 7 to 12 of the *Bhagavadgītā* are popularly regarded as the *bhaktiyoga* section of the poem, extolling the "discipline of devotion" as a path to liberation that is socially and gender inclusive,[176] thought to supersede and incorporate all other paths through its call to a complete surrender to the lord. In chapter 7, Kṛṣṇa tells Arjuna that true wisdom is the knowledge of he himself, the supreme Bhagavat, who has two natures: one lower, to be identified with the gross elements—the mind and the intellect—and one higher, which pertains to the soul. Nothing exists apart from Kṛṣṇa, the whole universe being strung on him like heaps of pearls on a string. The possessor of knowledge (*jñānin*) is the best among the virtuous ones precisely because he is totally devoted to him, whom he regards as the highest goal. Ultimately, all divine forms are none other than Kṛṣṇa.

Herein, the blissful effulgence of Kṛṣṇa's *prahasann iva* can be appreciated in the god's revelation that he is light. Thus in *BhG* 7.8–10, he tells Arjuna that he is the light in the moon and sun (*prabhā 'smi śaśisūryayoḥ*), the brilliance in fire (*tejas cā 'smi vibhāvasau*), the majesty of the majestic (*tejas tejasvinām aham*). Even in chapter 10 he describes himself as radiant sun (10.21), fire (10.23), thunderbolt (10.28), the splendor (*tejas*) of the splendid (10.36) with a fragment of which he upholds the universe (10.44). Through such splendor the lord communicates the truth that he is the embodiment of beauty and knowledge (*jñāna*), exercising an irresistible power of attraction toward all creatures since all souls, even if unconsciously, long to reunite themselves to him. Already at 4.37, the lord points out that as the kindled fire reduces firewood to ashes, so the fire of knowledge (*jñānāgni*) reduces all actions to ashes. Moreover, at 6.19, he states that the *yogin* who controls his mind and concentrates upon the self (*ātman*) is like a lamp (*dīpa*) in a windless place that does not flicker,[177] a speck of light that is destined to enlightenment, achieving perfect communion with the source of all splendor.[178] As Kṛṣṇa declares at 10.11, it is out of compassion that he dispels the darkness of men, which is born out of ignorance (*ajñānajaṃ tamaḥ*) with the shining lamp of his knowledge (*jñānadīpena bhāsvatā*), again explicitly equating light and knowledge.

In chapter 8, Kṛṣṇa proclaims to Arjuna the supreme reality of *Brahman* and the significance of the ritual act, highlighting that *Brahman* is omnipresent. He points out that at the time of death whoever meditates on the Bhagavat—who is of the color of the sun—will achieve communion with him and will never be reborn again. Beyond this world that is periodically manifested and dissolved is the realm of unmanifest (*avyakta*) materiality, and beyond it is the indestructible (*akṣara*) spirit, the highest goal, Kṛṣṇa's supreme dwelling place. After death there are two paths for the soul: one characterized by darkness, which entails rebirth, and another one characterized by light, which entails nonreturn (i.e., liberation from rebirth).[179]

In chapter 9, Kṛṣṇa teaches Arjuna that all existence originates from him, and yet the Bhagavat is untouched by the ongoing process of manifestation and dissolution, he being its impartial overseer (*adhyakṣa*). Unlike the ignorant fools who despise him, the wise worship the Bhagavat in his manifold forms as the father of the universe, the one to be known, the goal, the witness (*sākṣin*), the refuge, and the imperishable seed (*bījam avyayam*) of all that is. Those who practice Vedic rituals and seek celestial pleasures are destined for rebirth. But those who offer their oblation to Kṛṣṇa with love—be it a leaf, a flower, a fruit, or water—and seek refuge in him who is the same (*sama*) in all beings, unfailingly reach him, as no devotee whose mind is fixed on him ever gets lost.

In chapter 10, Kṛṣṇa states that nobody knows the origin (*prabhava*) of the Bhagavat. Intellect, knowledge, and all virtues arise from him alone. Everything proceeds from him, he being the source of all. To those who love him, he offers the *yoga* of discrimination (*buddhiyoga*), the light of knowledge that allows to reach him. Having recognized Kṛṣṇa as none other than *Brahman*, Arjuna asks him to tell him about his divine *yoga* and the various manifestations of his power (*vibhūti*). Kṛṣṇa tells him that his manifestations are infinite and that it is always he that excels in all categories of beings. Thus, he is the self (*ātman*) that abides in the heart of all creatures and the knowledge of the knowing (*jñānaṃ jñānavatām*). With just a fragment of his splendor (*tejas*) he upholds the entire universe.

In chapters 8 through 10, the presence of Kṛṣṇa's *prahasann iva* reveals itself in the god's *prasāda* or tranquility, in the otherworldly serenity and clarity of mind that are the distinctive features of the Bhagavat and of the *jñānayogin* who is instructed to plunge himself in concentration and contemplation. This fundamental attitude is already anticipated at 2.64–66:

> But with desire-and-loathing-severed
> Senses acting on the object of sense,
> With (senses) self-controlled, he, governing his self,
> Goes unto tranquility (*prasādam adhigacchati*).
> In tranquility (*prasāde*), of all griefs
> Riddance is engendered for him;
> For of the tranquil-minded (*prasannacetaso*) quickly
> The mentality (*buddhi*) becomes stable.
> The undisciplined has no (right) mentality,
> And the undisciplined has no efficient-force (*bhāvanā*);
> Who has no efficient-force has no peace;
> For him that has no peace how can there be bliss?[180]

At 6.8, Kṛṣṇa teaches that the true *yogin* is the one who is satisfied with knowledge and discrimination, who is unchanging and with conquered senses: for the disciplined one (*yukta*) a clod, a stone, and gold are all the same (*sama*). This essential characteristic of perfect serenity is later underlined at 17.16:

> Serenity of mind (*manaḥprasādaḥ*), kindliness,
> Silence, self-control,
> And purification of being, this
> Is called austerity of mind.[181]

Even at 18.37, Kṛṣṇa praises the pure joy that originates from the serenity of the soul and intellect (*ātmabuddhiprasādajam*), and at 18.54 he describes to Arjuna the characteristics of the one who has achieved the highest culmination of knowledge:

Having become *Brahman*, serene-souled (*prasannātmā*),
He neither grieves nor longs;
Alike (*samaḥ*) to all beings,
He attains supreme devotion to Me.[182]

Furthermore, we are reminded of the lord's *prahasann iva* by the importance that he assigns to silence (*mauna*), given that smile and silence are subtly linked to one another. It is our contention that the moment of the Bhagavat's silent smile—this magical, suspended juncture that immediately precedes his speech—is in and of itself eloquent and "full" (*pūrṇa*), containing *in nuce* the entire *upadeśa* that he will discursively offer to his disciple. Significantly, at 10.25 Kṛṣṇa tells Arjuna that "of sacrifices (*yajña*) he is silent prayer (*japa*)," that is, the muttered repetition of a *mantra* or of the name of god, and most importantly at 10.38 he states that "of secrets (*guhya*) he is silence." The lord's eloquent silence at 2.10—the mark of wisdom, *jñāna*—stands in opposition to Arjuna's desperate "becoming silent" (*tūṣṇīṃ babhūva*) at 2.9—the mark of man's ignorance, *ajñāna*. The Bhagavat's silent *prahasann iva* must be appreciated as god's compassionate answer to Arjuna's and all humans' anguished cry for help.

As noted, at 17.16 Kṛṣṇa presents silence as a fundamental characteristic of the austerity of the mind (*tapo mānasam*). It is noteworthy that he praises the *muni*, the "silent one," as being the best among sages: thus at 10.26 he identifies himself with the *muni* Kapila, the founder of Sāṃkhya and the best among the perfect ones (*siddha*), and at 10.37 he identifies himself with Vyāsa, extolled as the best among *muni*s.[183] Moreover, at 12.19 he points out that the one who practices silence (*maunin*) is dear to him. *Muni*s and liberating knowledge (*jñāna*) are de facto inseparable: as the Bhagavat states at the beginning of chapter 14, it is by knowing the best of all knowledge (*jñānam uttamam*) that *muni*s reach supreme perfection. Already at 2.56, Kṛṣṇa had offered a memorable definition of the *muni*:

When his mind is not perturbed in sorrows,
And he has lost desire for joys,
His longing, fear, and wrath departed,
He is called a stable-minded holy man (*muni*).[184]

At 2.69, the silent one who is fixed in *jñāna* is contrasted with the condition of deluded ordinary beings. It is said that the time in which all creatures are awake is night for the *muni* who sees (*yasyāṃ jāgrati bhūtāni sā niśā paśyato muneḥ*). Along these lines, at 5.6 the lord declares that the *muni* who is disciplined in *yoga* quickly attains *Brahman*, and at 5.28 he reiterates:

> Controlling the senses, thought-organ, and intelligence,
> The sage (*muni*) bent on final release,
> Whose desire, fear, and wrath are departed—
> Who is ever thus, is always released.[185]

Moreover, at 6.3 Kṛṣṇa proclaims:

> For the sage (*muni*) that desires to mount to discipline (*yoga*)
> Action (*karman*) is called the means;
> For the same man when he has mounted to discipline
> Quiescence (*śama*) is called the means.[186]

We have already highlighted some subtle correspondences of *adhyāya* 11 with 2.10. Thanks to a divine eye (*divyacakṣu*) that the lord gifts to Arjuna, the latter is granted the exclusive privilege of beholding Kṛṣṇa's cosmic form that comprises the whole universe within his glorious body and that fills our hero with astonishment and terror. The revelation of the Bhagavat as a mass of unimaginable splendor is consistent with the inherent luminosity of Kṛṣṇa's face and hint of laughter. Arjuna extols the lord's overwhelming brightness by utilizing this beautiful and justly famous metaphor (11.12):

> Of a thousand suns in the sky
> If suddenly should burst forth
> The light, it would be like
> Unto the light of that exalted one.[187]

The god appears to him as a mass of radiance (11.17), whose face/mouth is flaming fire (11.19). The revelation of Kṛṣṇa as light is a constant refrain throughout the poem: thus at 13.17 the lord presents the supreme *Brahman*—which is none other than he himself—as "the light of lights" (*jyotiṣām api taj jyotis*) and at 13.33 he states:

> As alone illumines
> This whole world the sun,
> So the Field-owner (= Kṛṣṇa as the *ātman*) the whole Field
> (= the body of humans)
> Illumines, son of Bharata.[188]

Besides the already discussed motif of Arjuna's *vismaya* — which also characterizes the narrator Saṃjaya in the poem's penultimate verse (18.77): "And as I recall again and again that / Most wondrous (*atyadbhutam*) form of Hari, / Great is my amazement (*vismayo*), O king, / And I thrill (*hṛṣyāmi*) with joy again and again"[189]—what is revelatory of Kṛṣṇa's hint of laughter/smile is the grace (*prasāda*) with which he is ready to fill his devotee who earnestly implores it (*prasīda*) from him (see 11.25, 11.31, 11.44–45, 11.47). Ultimately it is only through love, *bhakti*, that it is possible to know/contemplate the Bhagavat as he truly is, that is, as "the imperishable, the existent and the non-existent, and that which is beyond both" (*akṣaraṃ sad asat tatparaṃ yat*; 11.37).

In chapter 12, Kṛṣṇa explains to Arjuna that the best ones among the adepts of *yoga* are those who have *bhakti* toward him and as a consequence give up the fruits of their actions. As he points out in 12.6–7:

> But those who, all actions
> Casting on Me, intent on Me,
> With utterly unswerving discipline
> Meditating on Me, revere Me,
> For them I the Savior
> From the sea of the round of deaths
> Become right soon, son of Pṛthā,
> When they have made their thoughts enter into Me.[190]

The idea is that genuine *jñāna*, knowledge, naturally leads to *bhakti*. In fact, *jñāna* itself can emerge only thanks to one's surrender to the *guru*-god, as is evidenced at the beginning of the poem when Arjuna surrenders at the feet of his lord at 2.7. But finally the possibility of such an act of surrender is itself the consequence of the lord's grace. In verse 12.12, Kṛṣṇa states that knowledge is better than practice (*abhyāsa*) and that contemplation (*dhyāna*) is better than knowledge. Moreover, the abandonment of the fruits of action (*karmaphalatyāga*) is better than contemplation and from such abandonment immediately ensues peace (*śānti*). From 12.13 to 12.20, the lord offers a list of the virtues of those who are dear to him in which compassion and equanimity play a key role.[191] In this chapter centering on *bhakti*, the presence of the Bhagavat's *prahasaṁn iva* shows itself in the meaning of *prasāda* as both clarity of mind—the precondition for achieving equanimity and contemplating the unmanifest (*akṣara*; 12.4–5)—and pure grace, thanks to which one can resort to the lord and, endowed with faith, be constantly intent upon him (12.11, 12.20).

Chapters 13 to 18 of the *Bhagavadgītā* are traditionally known as the *jñānayoga* section of the poem, extolling the "discipline of knowledge." In chapter 13, Kṛṣṇa defines the human body as the field (*kṣetra*) and he himself as the knower of the field (*kṣetrajña*). He explains what true knowledge is and what needs to be known, that is, *Brahman*, and illustrates the characteristics of nature (*prakṛti*) and of the spiritual principle (*puruṣa*). He asserts the omnipresence of the Bhagavat who is the supreme *puruṣa*, and reiterates how it is only *prakṛti* that is involved in action, whereas *puruṣa* neither acts nor can it ever be polluted (see 3.27, 4.14). Herein, besides the identification of Kṛṣṇa with the light of lights and the light of the self that have already been pointed out (13.17, 13.33), the presence of the lord's *prahasann iva* can be appreciated in his serenity and equanimity: thus at 13.8–9 he extols detachment (*vairāgya*), the absence of attachment (*asakti*) and the constant equanimity of mind (*samacittatva*), at 13.22 he magnifies the supreme *puruṣa* as the uninvolved witness/spectator (*upadraṣṭṛ*), and at 13.27–28 he calls Arjuna and all creatures to discern the presence of the same (*sama*), supreme lord in all beings.

In chapter 14, Kṛṣṇa teaches Arjuna that the great *Brahman* is the womb (*yoni*) in which the lord deposits the germ (*garbha*) from which all beings originate. In each and every body the imperishable embodied (*dehin*, i.e., the *ātman*) is bound by the three qualities (*guṇa*) sprung from *prakṛti* (i.e., *sattva*, *rajas* and *tamas*). The different characteristics of all beings depend upon the prevalence of one or the other of the three *guṇas*. The luminous *sattva* causes attachment to happiness and knowledge, *rajas* to action and desire, and the dark *tamas* to negligence and ignorance. All beings are subject to the dominance of the *guṇas* and are thus destined to rebirth, a higher rebirth if *sattva* is prevalent and a lower one if *tamas* is prevalent. But the one who is capable of altogether transcending the *guṇas* attains immortality and achieves oneness with *Brahman*.

Here again the pivotal *darśana* of Kṛṣṇa's serene hint of laughter discloses itself in the equanimity that substantiates his teaching. At 14.22–25, he explains to Arjuna the distinguishing features of one who has gone beyond the *guṇas*: such a person sits apart unperturbed (*udāsīnavat*) and looks at the ongoing operations of the three qualities as a witness to whom pain and pleasure are alike and clods, stones, and gold are all the same (*sama*). To such a one, blame and praise, honor and disgrace are equal (*tulya*). The loving gaze that is inherent in the lord's *prahasann iva* is made manifest in the words with which he brings this chapter to a close, in which he reveals himself as the foundation of *Brahman* to whom a devotee must completely surrender himself/herself:

> And whoso Me with unswerving
> Discipline of devotion (*bhaktiyoga*) serves,
> He, transcending these Strands,
> Is fit for becoming *Brahman*.
> For I am the foundation (*pratiṣṭhā*) of *Brahman*,
> The immortal and imperishable,
> And of the eternal right (*dharma*),
> And of absolute bliss (*sukha*).[192]

In chapter 15, Kṛṣṇa narrates to Arjuna the parable of the mythic *aśvattha* tree, with roots above and branches below,[193] that represents life in the world and that man must cut with the stout axe of nonattachment (*asaṅga*). He tells him of his mysterious presence in the whole of reality and particularly in the heart of all beings. He further illustrates the characteristics of the two spirits (*puruṣa*), the perishable that are all creatures and the imperishable that is called the immovable (*kūṭastha*), and reveals to him the reality of a third, supreme *puruṣa* or *paramātman*, the undying lord that is he himself, the Puruṣottama who supports the three worlds. In this *adhyāya*, we are reminded of Kṛṣṇa's *prahasann iva* in his repeated identification with light (15.12):

> The splendor (*tejas*) that belongs to the sun,
> Which illumines the whole world,
> And that which is in the moon and in fire,
> Know that to be My splendor.[194]

In fact, his transcendent splendor is beyond the natural light that humans can conceive of, it being beyond comprehension (15.6):

> The sun does not illumine that,
> Nor the moon, nor fire;
> Having gone to which they return not:
> That is My highest station (*dhāma paramam*).[195]

We are also reminded of the lord's hint of laughter/smile in his instruction that one must take refuge in him in order to achieve liberation, just as Arjuna did at 2.7. Thus, at 15.4 we read:

> Then that place (*padam*) must be sought
> To which having gone men no more return,
> (Thinking:) 'I take refuge (*prapadye*) in that same primal spirit (*ādyaṃ puruṣam*),
> Whence issued forth of old the (whole cosmic) activity.'[196]

As he tells to Arjuna at the closing of this chapter (15.19), the man who is undeluded (*asammūḍhas*) and knows him as the Puruṣottama is truly all-knowing (*sarvavid*) and worships (*bhajati*) him with his whole being (*sarvabhāvena*), which again points to the fact that the real *jñānin* is the one who ultimately resorts to *bhakti*.

In chapter 16, Kṛṣṇa illustrates to Arjuna the virtues of those men who are endowed with a divine nature and then dwells on the vices that characterize those who have a demonic nature, describing their hellish destiny. At 16.21, he points out that what one should abandon (*tyajet*) are desire (*kāma*), anger (*krodha*), and greed (*lobha*), since these three are the ruin of the soul, and at 16.24 he concludes his speech by telling Arjuna that relative to what is and what is not to be done (*kāryākārya*), the authority (*pramāṇa*) are the scriptures (*śāstra*): thus he should perform action in this world by following the prescribed scriptural injunctions (*śāstravidhāna*).

Herein, the presence of Kṛṣṇa's *prahasann iva*, that is, of his *prasāda* both as tranquility of mind and compassionate grace, emerges in many of the qualities that distinguish those who are born to a divine destiny (16.1–3): purity of heart (*sattvasaṃśuddhi*), steadfastness in *jñānayoga* (*jñānayogavyavasthiti*), generosity (*dāna*), self-control (*dama*), austerity (*tapas*), abandonment (*tyāga*), peace (*śānti*), compassion toward all beings (*dayā bhūteṣu*), gentleness (*mārdava*), modesty (*hrī*), steadiness (*acāpala*), splendor/majesty (*tejas*), patience (*kṣamā*), fortitude (*dhṛti*), purity (*śauca*), and benevolence (*adroha*).

In chapter 17, Kṛṣṇa explains to Arjuna that on the basis of the three *guṇas* it is possible to distinguish three types of faith, food, sacrifice, austerities, and gifts. And three are also the monosyllables that designate *Brahman*, i.e., *oṃ*, *tat* and *sat*. He points out that no practice of piety has any value if it is done without faith (*śraddhā*). Here we must appreciate the fact that through his surrender to Kṛṣṇa at 2.7 Arjuna proves himself to be the ideal representative of those men whose faith is pure, *sāttvic*, and thus worship the gods (17.4; see also 17.14). Kṛṣṇa again underlines that the best of all sacrifices (*yajña*)—and of all actions—is that offered without desiring its fruit, since this is what makes it *sāttvic* (17.11). As noticed, the presence of the lord's hint of laughter, his *prasāda*, can be detected at 17.16 where Kṛṣṇa states that mental austerity (*tapo mānasam*) is defined by serenity of mind (*manaḥprasāda*), gentleness (*saumyatva*), silence (*mauna*), self-restraint (*ātmavinigraha*), and the purification of being (*bhāvasaṃśuddhi*). Its presence can be extended to his definition of the austerity of the body (*śārīraṃ tapas*) and the austerity of speech (*vāṅmayaṃ tapas*), which he gives in the two preceding verses (17.14–15):

> To gods, brahmans, reverend elders, and wise men
> Respectful homage (*pūjanam*); purity (*śaucam*), uprightness (*ārjavam*),
> Chastity (*brahmacaryam*), and harmlessness (*ahiṃsā*);
> This is called austerity of the body.
> Words that cause no disturbance (*anudvegakaraṃ vākyam*),

That are true (*satyam*), and pleasingly beneficial (*priyahitam*);
Also practice of recitation in study (of sacred texts) (*svādhyāyābhyasanam*);
This is called austerity of speech.[197]

In chapter 18, the poem's last *adhyāya*, Kṛṣṇa expounds to Arjuna the difference between renunciation (*saṃnyāsa*) and abandonment (*tyāga*) and teaches that the acts of sacrifice, giving, and austerity should always be performed with no attachment to their fruits.[198] He illustrates the three types of abandonment on the basis of the three *guṇa*s and explains the five factors for the accomplishment of action, the three impulses to action, and the three bases of action. He also presents the three types of knowledge, action, agent, intellect, will, and happiness, all dependent upon the three *guṇa*s. He further explains the actions proper to each of the four social categories (*varṇa*s) and that depend on the *guṇa*s that predominate in them, pointing out that each and every one must adhere to his/her own duty (*svadharma*) since this is the way to perfection. Indeed, this is the path that leads to oneness with *Brahman* and to the bond of love with Kṛṣṇa: such bond of love is the supreme goal of all creatures. Therefore, Arjuna must rely on his lord who abides in the heart of all beings, surrendering himself totally to him. By his grace (*prasāda*) he will be freed from all evils and will reach the highest objective (i.e., peace). Finally, Kṛṣṇa gives assurance of the *phalaśruti*, the reward that all those who will study and transmit this divine teaching will reap. The poem ends with the words of the narrator Saṃjaya, who, addressing Dhṛtarāṣṭra, praises the marvelous and holy dialogue of the *Bhagavadgītā* and in the last verse (18.78) declares that where Kṛṣṇa and Arjuna are, there splendor (*śrī*), victory (*vijaya*), wealth (*bhūti*), and statecraft (*nīti*) are firmly fixed.

The qualities of calmness/clarity of mind, equanimity and sheer *līlā* that the lord's *prahasann iva* reveals are implied in several *śloka*s of this chapter in which Kṛṣṇa recapitulates his *upadeśa*. We already noted how at 18.54 he points out that one who is absorbed in *Brahman* (*brahmabhūtaḥ*), whose self is serene (*prasannātmā*), neither mourns nor desires. Such a person achieves supreme devotion to him (*madbhaktiṃ parām*) once he is impartial (*samaḥ*) among all beings. Along these lines, in verses 42, 49 and 51–53 we read:

Calm (*śama*), (self-)control (*dama*), austerities (*tapas*), purity (*śauca*),
Patience (*kṣānti*), and uprightness (*ārjava*),
Theoretical and practical knowledge, and religious faith (*āstikya*),
Are the natural-born actions of brahmans.
. . . .
His mentality unattached (*asaktabuddhi*) to any object,
Self-conquered (*jitātman*), free from longings (*vigataspṛha*),
To the supreme perfection of actionlessness (*naiṣkarmya*)
He comes thru renunciation.
. . . .
With purified mentality disciplined,
And restraining himself with firmness,
Abandoning (*tyaktvā*) the objects of sense, sounds and the rest,
And putting away desire and loathing (*rāgadveṣa*),
Cultivating solitude, eating lightly,
Restraining speech, body, and mind,
Devoted to the discipline of meditation (*dhyānayoga*) constantly,
Taking refuge in dispassion (*vairāgya*),
From egotism (*ahaṃkāra*), force (*bala*), pride (*darpa*),
Desire (*kāma*), wrath (*krodha*), and possession (*parigraha*)
Freed (*vimucya*), unselfish (*nirmama*), calmed (*śānta*),
He is fit for becoming *Brahman*.[199]

The lord's smile of grace is insisted upon in this final chapter that celebrates love as the ultimate goal of life and as Kṛṣṇa's paramount teaching. We noticed how at 18.73 Arjuna declares that his delusion (*moha*) has been destroyed and that he has gained wisdom (*smṛti*) thanks to the lord's grace (*tvatprasādān*): it is thanks to his *prasāda* that his doubts (*saṃdeha*) are dissipated, and he is ready to act as he commands.[200] In verses 56, 58, and 62 we find an emphasis on Kṛṣṇa's grace. The idea is that in the end everyone is dependent upon god's wondrous mercy: that is, his smiling, benevolent look. What the lord expects from Arjuna and all creatures is that they seek refuge in him, reciprocating his love:

Even tho all actions ever
He performs, relying on Me (*madvyapāśrayaḥ*),
By My grace (*matprasādād*) he reaches
The eternal, undying station.
. . .
If thy mind is on Me, all difficulties
Shalt thou cross over by My grace (*matprasādāt*);
But if thru egotism thou
Wilt not heed, thou shalt perish.
. . . .
To Him alone go for refuge (*tam eva śaraṇaṃ gaccha*)
With thy whole being, son of Bharata;
By His grace (*tatprasādāt*), supreme peace
And the eternal station shalt thou attain.[201]

All in all, by his *prahasann iva* Kṛṣṇa manifests his divine mercy through which he inspires Arjuna and all beings to tread the triune paths of *karmayoga, bhaktiyoga,* and *jñānayoga* so as to achieve—via the renunciation of the fruits of action, one's love for god and the inner awareness of the reality of the self (*ātman*)—the sublime communion with the Bhagavat, which is the consummation and culminating secret (*rahasya*) of the poem's integrative teaching.

Chapter 2

Traditional Commentaries on *Bhagavadgītā* 2.10

We now focus attention on the Sanskrit commentarial readings of the *BhG*'s *prahasann iva*. *BhG* 2.10 represents the *trait d'union* between the first part of the text—from 1.1. to 2.9—and the teaching itself, which begins at 2.11 and ends at 18.66 (Uskokov 2021, 72–75). The lord's hint of laughter of *BhG* 2.10 is the bridge that leads Arjuna, that is, each and every human being, to the nectar of Kṛṣṇa's divine utterances that dispel the darkness of delusion and anguish. In fact, it is our contention that the lord's *prahasann iva* is not only the means for crossing the ocean of *saṃsāra*, but represents in and of itself the veritable end, the supreme goal. Arjuna's surrender to Kṛṣṇa as his disciple is the pivotal point, since from 2.7 onward the poem embodies the unhindered flow of the *guru*'s grace, which is as much conveyed by his hint of laughter as it is conveyed by his liberating instruction.

The verses that precede 2.10 contextualize Kṛṣṇa's *upadeśa*, which is placed within an unusual setting: a battlefield where two armies confront one another at the eve of war.[1] While the first chapter concentrates on the causes of Arjuna's grief, in the first verses of the second, Arjuna's anguish and delusion reach their peak. Indeed, though in 2.7 Arjuna pleads Kṛṣṇa to instruct him, already in 2.8 he says that nothing can remove his grief, neither on earth nor in the heavens. Moreover, in *BhG* 2.9 Arjuna states decidedly that he will not fight and remains mute. Verse 2.10 highlights Arjuna's tragic predicament: positioned in between the two armies, he is completely overwhelmed by despondency. And it is at this moment that Kṛṣṇa, immediately after exhibiting his hint of laughter, begins his teaching. Convinced as we are that *prahasann iva* hides more than what appears on the surface, we investigate the commentarial tradition so as to obtain further clues on its inner meaning (*gūḍhārtha*) and function.

If Karl Potter in his *Bibliography* of the *Encyclopedia of Indian Philosophies* (1995, 1464–66; see also Sarkar 1975, 190–203) reviews a huge number of commentaries on the *BhG*, here we limit ourselves to twenty-four of them (twenty-three in Sanskrit, one in Marāṭhī). Our choice has been driven by two objectives: 1) to present those commentaries that are most relevant to our topic, detailing the chief interpretations of *prahasann iva* that were developed over time; 2) to offer a comprehensive survey of the *BhG*'s commentarial tradition by taking into consideration the main schools of thought and their representative authors, from Śaṅkara's eighth-century seminal commentary up to the works of Vaṃśīdhara Miśra and Śrībellaṅkoṇḍa Rāmarāya Kavi in the nineteenth and twentieth centuries. We focus attention on the commentaries' introductions and their understanding of chapter 2, especially verses 2.6 to 2.11. Our aim is to map the various readings of *prahasann iva* and discern some fundamental hermeneutic patterns. In order to be faithful to the commentators' thought, we have tried to be as literal as possible in our translations.[2]

What follows is the list of authors and works we will be looking at. In chronological order: Śaṅkara's (eighth century) *Gītābhāṣya* or *Advaitabhāṣya*; Bhāskara's (eighth century) *Bhagavadāśayānusaraṇa*; Abhinavagupta's (tenth to eleventh century) *Gītārthasaṃgraha*; Rāmānuja's (eleventh century; traditional dates 1017–1137) *Gītābhāṣya* or *Viśiṣṭādvaitabhāṣya*; Jñāneśvar's (thirteenth century) *Jñāneśvarī* or *Bhāvārthadīpikā*; Śaṅkarānanda Sarasvatī's (1290) *Tātparyabodhinī*; Śrīdhara Svāmin's (thirteenth to fourteenth century) *Subodhinī*; Veṅkaṭanātha/Vedānta Deśika's (1268–1369) *Tātparyacandrikā* on Rāmānuja's *Gītābhāṣya*; Ānanda Giri's (fourteenth century) *Gītābhāṣyavivecana*; Jaya Tīrtha's (possibly 1340–1388) *Prameyadīpikā*; Daivajña Paṇḍita Sūrya's (ca. 1440) *Paramārthaprapā*; Sadānanda Yogīndra's (1500) *Bhāvaprakāśa*; Keśava Kaśmīrī Bhaṭṭācārya's (1510) *Tattvaprakāśikā*; Madhusūdana Sarasvatī's (sixteenth century) *Gūḍhārthadīpikā*; Śrīveṅkaṭanātha's (sixteenth to seventeenth century) *Brahmānandagiri*; Vallabha's (seventeenth century) *Tattvadīpikā*; Rāghavendra's (c. 1640) *Arthasaṃgraha*; Ānandavardhana's (seventeenth century) *Jñānakarmasamuccayavyākhyā*; Viśvanātha Cakravartī Ṭhākura's (seventeenth century) *Sārārthavarṣiṇīṭīkā*; Nīlakāṇṭha Caturdhara's (second half of seventeenth century) *Bhāvadīpa*; Dhanapati Sūri's (eighteenth century) *Bhāṣyotkarṣadīpikā*; Baladeva Vidyābhūṣaṇa's (eighteenth century, 1700–1793?) *Gītābhūṣaṇa*; Vaṃśīdhara Miśra's (nineteenth to twentieth century) *Vaṃśī*; Śrībellaṅkoṇḍa Rāmarāya Kavi's (nineteenth to twentieth century) *Bhāṣyārkaprakāśa*.

Though following a strictly chronological order might be helpful in detecting how the interpretation of *prahasann iva* evolved over time, yet in order to better appreciate these works within their own axiological viewpoints we think it preferable to group them according to their philosophical affiliations (Saha 2017, 259): Advaita (nondualism), Kashmirian Śaiva Bhedābheda (difference-and-non-difference), Jñāneśvar's Advaita-oriented Marāṭhī gloss, Viśiṣṭādvaita (non-dualism of the qualified [whole]), Dvaita (dualism), Dvaitādvaita (dualism and nondualism), Śuddhādvaita (pure nondualism) and Acintyabhedābheda (unconceivable difference and nondifference). In this way, one can get a sense of the developing perspective of Kṛṣṇa's hint of laughter within the various schools of thought.

The commentarial tradition confirms the multiplicity of possible interpretations of *prahasann iva*. Our stock phrase is placed in a crucial position being in between the epic frame and the philosophical frame, which is the introductory part and the beginning of Kṛṣṇa's teaching (Ježić 1979). Each and every author interprets *prahasann iva* according to his own axiological position: either as implying mirth and benevolence or mockery and derision, some of them positing that it should be interpreted as a combination of the two. Moreover, we will see that some commentators interchange the root √*has* with other verbs and play with different prefixes such as *pari*, *apa*, and *upa*. The indeclinable particle *iva*, which is greatly important in the analysis of several authors, marks the polyvalence of our stock phrase since it mitigates the force of the present participle *prahasan*.

It seems to us that none of the glosses analyzed can claim to exhaust the richness of the *BhG*'s *prahasann iva*, though taken together they offer us a comprehensive picture of its purport.

Almost all commentators link Kṛṣṇa's hint of laughter to verse 2.11, as Veṅkaṭanātha/Vedānta Deśika states more clearly than others: "The verse that begins with *aśocyān* is the content of *prahasann iva*." Recalling what Bhāskara says, "Great souls usually smile before speaking," Kṛṣṇa can be seen as the model of the *paṇḍitas* mentioned in 2.11, a term uniformly interpreted as wise men, i.e., knowers of the Self, who mourn neither over the destruction of the body, for it is unavoidable, nor over the destruction of the Self, for it is impossible as it is imperishable. As noted in chapter 1, Kṛṣṇa's statement that Arjuna has spoken "words of wisdom" (*prajñāvādān*) is tinged with sarcasm. The lord's irony at this juncture is definitely in keeping with his *prahasann iva,* since Arjuna is only a caricature of one who is endowed with real wisdom (*prajñā*).

Nonetheless, we will see that the interpretation of *prahasann iva* as nothing more than mockery is not favored by our authors. Rather, several of them interpret the lord's hint of laughter as a sign of his benevolence, spontaneously arising on the occasion of the childish babbling of meaningless words on the part of his disciple. This is a subject that we also find in the *Upaniṣads*: for instance in the dialogue between Sanatkumāra and Nārada in *Chāndogya Upaniṣad* 7 and, from another perspective, in the dialogue between Yama-Mṛtyu and Naciketas in the *Kaṭha Upaniṣad*. The idea is that Arjuna is sick, and his disease causes him to cry; Kṛṣṇa, as the supreme doctor, offers him the remedy of his hint of laughter that anticipates his *upadeśa*. In other words, the lord's *prahasann iva* is a medicine that, though it can be bitter and hurt Arjuna's pride, in the end reveals itself to be sweet as pure nectar offering the secret of immortality (*amṛta*): the inappropriate inaction of Arjuna prompts the gracious, appropriate action of Kṛṣṇa, that is, his hint of laughter followed by his instruction.

Kṛṣṇa's *prahasann iva* takes place after Arjuna has surrendered himself to his lord (*īśvarapratipatti*) at 2.7, when he declares himself to be his *śiṣya,* and the majority of commentators agree that a disciple cannot be laughed at by his *guru*. This is the reason why in the end Kṛṣṇa's hint of laughter appears to sublimate all dichotomies pointing at a superior level: that is, the lord's loving grace. In this regard, especially telling are the readings of Madhusūdana Sarasvatī and Keśava Kaśmīrī Bhaṭṭācārya. But let us now turn to an analytical review of the commentators' interpretations.

Advaita

The *BhG* commentators are numerous: some are independent interpreters while others are subcommentators of Śaṅkara's *bhāṣya*.[3] Be that as it may, all Advaita Vedānta glosses are indebted to Śaṅkara's work. In the following section, we examine twelve commentaries starting with Śaṅkara's foundational *bhāṣya*.

Śaṅkara

It is well known that Śaṅkara fixed the standard text of the *BhG* in its seven hundred verses, the so-called vulgate version. In his *Bhagavadgītābhāṣya* or "Commentary on the *Bhagavadgītā*" (hereafter *BhGBh*), apart from a short introduction that focuses on the purport of the poem Śaṅkara does not comment on the first chapter nor on the first nine verses of the second. Rather, he contextualizes Arjuna's need to be instructed and argues that *BhG* 1.2 to 2.9 is meant to identify the root of the defects that are intrinsic to worldly life (*saṃsāra*): anguish (*śoka*) and delusion (*moha*). Arjuna is overwhelmed by both because, out of affection for his kinsfolk, he is tormented by the erroneous idea of "I am their own! They are mine!" (*aham eteṣāṃ mamaite iti*).[4] These feelings are so perturbing as to subjugate Arjuna's discriminating faculty (*abhibhūtavivekavijñāna*), and this is why he thinks of abandoning his duty as a warrior and turn to a life of alms, as renunciates do.

Ordinary people who follow their duties constantly long to gain and enjoy the fruits thereof. Due to the increasing and decreasing of merit (*dharma*) and demerit (*adharma*), the unceasing becoming (*saṃsāra*) characterized by auspicious and inauspicious births flows unobstructed (*anuparata*). This is the reason why anguish and delusion are depicted as the seeds of *saṃsāra*. In order to uproot them, there is nothing but the knowledge of the Self (*ātmajñāna*), which must be preceded by the total renunciation of actions (*sarvakarmasaṃnyāsa*), ritual as well as secular. Śaṅkara points out that this *upadeśa* begins at 2.11 and that it is geared to benefit all human beings (*sarvalokānugrahārtha*). Precisely in order to accomplish such a task, Arjuna functions as the appropriate instrument (*nimitta*). Here are the opening lines of his elaborate commentary *ad* 2.11:[5]

> Though he (= Arjuna)—whose discriminating intellect was subdued by anguish and delusion—was ready for war, which is a warrior's duty, [he] withdrew from the battle and [developped the wish of] following another's duty, i.e., the [wandering] life of a beggar. Hence, the abandonment of one's own duty and the undertaking of something prohibited naturally occurs to all those living beings whose soul is pervaded by anguish and delusion. Even for those who are committed in word, mind and body to their own duty, an active engagement occurs presupposing an aspiration for the fruits [of that action], and with a sense of egotism as well. Under these circumstances, due to the accretion of merits and demerits, the becoming (*saṃsāra*)—characterized by the gaining of pleasure and pain, [respectively] in desirable and non-desirable births—is not interrupted. Thus, anguish and delusion are the seeds of becoming, and their withdrawal does not take place without the knowledge of the Self preceded by the renunciation of all actions. Thus, eager to teach this, having used Arjuna as a means for the benefit of all worlds, the glorious Vāsudeva said "Those who are not to be mourned . . ." (2.11, *aśocyān*)

Śaṅkara then offers a lengthy explanation against the view that ritual activities and knowledge are equally involved in the attainment of liberation (*karmajñānasamuccaya*; BhG1 2000, 74; BhG3 1936, 41; BhG4 2015, 33–40). At the end of his commentary on this verse (BhG1 2000, 79), he calls Arjuna *mūḍha*, which means "deluded," someone who, being the victim of delusion (*moha*), is lost in ignorance. According to Śaṅkara, "those who are not to be mourned" (*aśocya*) are Bhīṣma, Droṇa, and the other heroes arrayed on the opposite side. They are *aśocya* for two reasons: from the point of view of *dharma*, their conduct is faultless; from the absolute point of view, they are ultimately nothing but *ātman*, the immortal Self. Therefore, there is no point in mourning for them.[6] Arjuna does so because he is utterly confused, though he thinks he is saying wise words, words that are usually pronounced by sages.[7] Śaṅkara paraphrases Kṛṣṇa's words to Arjuna as follows:

> Like a madman, you show in yourself both foolishness and wisdom, which are [mutually] opposed (*tad etat mauḍhyaṃ pāṇḍityaṃ ca viruddham ātmani darśayasy unmatta iva ity abhiprāyaḥ* |). True sages (*paṇḍita*), knowers of the Self, neither grieve for the departed nor for the living. Moreover, this wisdom (*paṇḍā*) is a kind of thought (*buddhi*)—namely a cognitive tendency, an understanding—whose specific content is the Self (*ātmaviṣayā*), as stated by the *śruti*: "Thus, having surpassed wisdom . . ." (*Bṛhadāraṇyaka Upaniṣad* 3.5.1)[8]

Though Śaṅkara does not gloss 2.10, it is clear that for him Kṛṣṇa's hint of laughter is part and parcel of his essential teaching at 2.11. It is its prelude but also, we surmise, its embodied content. Indeed, Kṛṣṇa's *prahasann iva* foreshadows the uprooting of *śoka* and *moha*: it expresses the lord's sublime ease, which announces the doctrine of *naiṣkarmya* and the renunciation of all actions that ultimately leads to *ātmajñāna*. As Kṛṣṇa's hint of laughter informs his teaching throughout the poem, it can similarly be argued that it incapsulates Śaṅkara's own commentarial position.

Ānanda Giri

Ānanda Giri appears to be somewhat later than Anubhūtisvarūpācārya and is surely indebted to him.[9] He wrote the *Gītābhāṣyavivecana* or "Examination of the Commentary on the *BhG*," a detailed gloss on the *BhGBh*. In his reading of Śaṅkara's introduction, he glosses the opening verses and clears up various points. At the beginning of his commentary to *BhGBh* 2.1, he says that the first chapter and the first verses of the second are self-evident and that the subject of the *BhG* is the double "firm point of view" (*niṣṭhā*) which represents the goal (*sādhya*) as well as the method (*sādhana*) of final realization.

In his commentary to *BhG* 2.10,[10] he elucidates *prahasann iva* as follows: *upāhasaṃ kurvann iva tadāśvāsārtham*, "'with a hint of laughter,' [that is] ridiculing [him] (*upāhasa*) in order to make him believe [in himself]." Here mockery is a means through which Kṛṣṇa stimulates Arjuna's reaction, so that he may regain confidence. Since Śaṅkara's commentary to 2.11 is quite detailed, Ānanda Giri's gloss is even longer. Useful in highlighting the purport of 2.10 is the *incipit* of Ānanda Giri's work, where he states that *BhG* 1.1 is an independent verse, the function of which is to connect (*sambandha*) the *BhG* with the rest of the *Mahābhārata*. Then, from 1.2 to 2.9, we have a section (*vākya*) that is meant to show that anguish (*śoka*) and delusion (*moha*)—the seeds of *saṃsāra*—are brought about by ignorance of the Self, and therefore must be removed (*ātmājñānotthanirvartanīyaśokamohākhya saṃsārabījapradarśanaparatvam*). At this point Ānanda Giri says that *BhG* 2.10 represents a transition in the text, which is especially helpful in opening up to the rest of the poem, which begins at 2.11 and is dedicated to teaching correct knowledge so as to dispel becoming and transmigration, along with its cause (*sahetukasaṃsāranirvartakasamyagjñānopadeśe tātparyam*).[11] In his interpretation of 2.11, Ānanda Giri closely follows Śaṅkara's commentary. What is remarkable is the independent status he attributes to 2.10, which he views as a bridge between the causes of saṃsāric disease—anguish (*śoka*), delusion (*moha*) and ultimately ignorance (*ajñāna*)—and their antidote, namely the knowledge of the Self.

Daivajña Paṇḍita Sūrya

This author wrote the *Paramārthaprapā* or "The Fountain (= Bestower) of the Supreme Aim," a subcommentary to Śaṅkara's *BhGBh*. While it is not easy to determine its date, there is a close relation between this text and Sadānanda Yogīndra's *Bhāvaprakāśa*. This might suggest an indebtedness of the latter to the former. In addition, the same topics are also dealt with by Śaṅkarānanda (BhG2 2001, 55).

In the introduction to the *Paramārthaprapā* (BhG2 2001, 12–13), Paṇḍita Sūrya—like Sadānanda—points out a correspondence between the initial verses of the *BhG* and the four preliminary requirements (*sādhanacatuṣṭaya*) of Advaita Vedānta: "discrimination between permanent and impermanent entities" (*nityānityavastuviveka*; 1.38c, 1.26c); "detachment form the enjoyments of the here-world and the after-world" (*ihāmutraphalabhogavirāga*; 1.35c); "trust in the words of the *guru* and the deity" (*gurudaivatavākyaviśvāsa*; 2.7c); "the longing for release" (*mumukṣājuṣa*).[12] He notes that detachment has already arisen (*utpannavairāgya*) in Arjuna, hence he is eligible for the knowledge (*jñānādhikārin*) that Kṛṣṇa is about to offer.[13] *Ad BhG* 2.10, Paṇḍita Sūrya says:

> Hereafter the glorious lord spoke to Arjuna—*tam uvāca*—who, having decided—due to anguish—"I will not fight!" (2.9), remained silent. The lord of the sense faculties, who knows the inner purports [of all living beings], with a hint of laughter, spoke these words to Arjuna, as if they were filled with mockery. [Doubt:] Although on that occasion of grief no laugh happened, then how come does he say "with a hint of laughter"? [Reply:] On this [issue] it must be pointed out that [in Arjuna's case] the arousal of anguish is not justified, because it is seen that anguish arises only when afflicted people or orphans are killed. In the case under examination Bhīṣma, Droṇa, Karṇa, Duryodhana and all the other [Kauravas] who do not reckon even Śakra (= Indra) as a hero, engage themselves [in fighting] following their own martial duty, and [clearly] not out of stupidity! Then, how can they be considered as reservoirs of pity? [. . .] Therefore, the said cause of anguish is a mere deception which has no place along the liberating path of non-action (*naiṣkarmya*). This is why [Kṛṣṇa] spoke with a slightly smiling face: this is the meaning.[14]

In this passage, Paṇḍita Sūrya links the lord's *prahasann iva* to Arjuna's inappropriate reaction when faced with his martial duty. The emphasis is placed on the impropriety (*anaucitya*) of Arjuna's anguish, in particular his misplaced pity toward his enemies, which inevitably triggers Kṛṣṇa's reaction: his hint of laughter at the hero's *anaucitya*.

Śrīveṅkaṭanātha

Another important gloss on the *BhGBh* is the *Brahmānandagiri* or "The Mountain of the Bliss of *Brahman*" (BhG1 2000). Unlike the Viśiṣṭādvaita author, this Śrīveṅkaṭanātha was a younger contemporary of Madhusūdana Sarasvatī. As a matter of fact, the *Brahmānandagiri* quotes and criticizes Madhusūdana's *Gūḍhārthadīpikā* (hereafter *GAD*) in several places.[15] Śrīveṅkaṭanātha was probably a disciple of Nṛsiṃhāśrama (sixteenth century) and the teacher of Dharmarāja Adhvarin (seventeenth to eighteenth century), the author of the well-known primer *Vedāntaparibhāṣā* (Pellegrini 2018, 589–99).

In his gloss *ad BhG* 2.7 (BhG1 2000, 69), Śrīveṅkaṭanātha writes that in the world, namely in ordinary conversation, whoever asks for instruction without a sincere desire is ignored by the interlocutor, since he/she is not really eager to listen attentively to his/her words (*loke hy aśiṣyabhāvena pṛcchan vaktrā svoktārthānavadhāraṇe saty upekṣyate*). On the contrary, Arjuna is definitely anguished and so he asks with the proper feeling and a sincere desire to know: he is a true disciple, and this is the reason why he is not ignored. Hence, the duty (*dharma*) of Kṛṣṇa is to teach, and, through the use of various tools, to make his disciple understand things properly. Śrīveṅkaṭanātha further points out that in saying *gurūn hatvā* at *BhG* 2.5, Arjuna perceives himself as a disciple of Bhīṣma and Droṇa too. Then, why is it that Kṛṣṇa accepts him as his own *śiṣya*? Śrīveṅkaṭanātha observes that this is due to the fact that at *BhG* 2.7 Arjuna has completely surrendered himself to him (*tvāṃ prapannam*): Arjuna has taken refuge in Kṛṣṇa (*śaraṇāgatam*) and this act of total surrender occurs only when there is no other way out.[16]

Śrīveṅkaṭanātha's commentary on *BhG* 2.10 (BhG1 2000, 73) is quite elaborate. The anguish tormenting Arjuna is not like the uneasiness commonly experienced in everyday life, which sooner or later fades away. Arjuna's is a different kind of anguish, deeper and stronger. In order to show this, the text uses the present active participle *viṣīdantam*. Had such a despondency occurred during the battle, it could have been solved at the opportune moment; on the contrary, it occurs when the two armies are facing each other, and the heroes—weapons in hand—are about to fight. This is why Arjuna's anguish is a big problem.[17] Nonetheless, despite the difficulty of the situation the text introduces a note of lightheartedness with the expression *prahasann iva*,[18] meaning "uttering a sentence of mockery" (*parihāsavākyaṃ vadann ity arthaḥ*):[19]

> [Moreover,] since Arjuna is not rendering a true service to his forefathers, at every step there are some enunciations of mockery (*parihāsa*) by the glorious lord to Arjuna. Thus,

> even during [such] crisis, the glorious lord—desirous of dispelling it—in a mocking mood pronounced these words—beginning with *aśocyān* (2.11)—the meaning of which is very profound, being the very essence of the whole Vedānta (= the *Upaniṣads*). Moreover, if in the world it is well known that mockery results in amusing pleasure, herein for Arjuna this [very circumstance] results in generating the knowledge of reality. Hence, in the expression *prahasann iva* the indeclinable *iva* [is used] to highlight its difference from ordinary mockery. Through the word Hṛṣīkeśa (= "controller of the sense faculties") what is conveyed is that for the one who stimulates every cognition[20] it is easy to generate knowledge even with a simple laugh (*hāsa*).[21]

The idea is that through his *parihāsa* the lord conveys a reprimand which is meant to shake Arjuna's conscience. To be sure, Kṛṣṇa's intention is not one of mere derision for it aims at awakening his disciple. Thus the lord's hint of laughter ultimately displays his grace toward his *śiṣya*.

Śrīveṅkaṭanātha's interpretation of *BhG* 2.11 (BhG1 2000, 81–82) begins with a further explanation of *prahasann iva*:[22] "Henceforth Kṛṣṇa, not seeing any other means for the emancipation of Arjuna—who was deeply immersed in the sea of illusion—than the knowledge of the reality of the Self, extended the mockery (*apahāsa*) directed toward him, expressed through the *prahasann iva* of the preceding verse, and revealed such knowledge of the reality of the Self." All in all, Śrīveṅkaṭanātha interprets *prahasann iva* as an expression of cheerful derision. While in a worldly context a mocking attitude is intended to ridicule someone, here its aim is nothing but supreme knowledge. The indeclinable *iva* is used precisely to mark this difference. Kṛṣṇa is the almighty inner controller and his *prahasann iva* highlights the ease with which he is able to bring about liberating gnosis. As we shall see in the next chapter, one of the possible semantic nuances of the stock phrase *prahasann iva* has to do with one's effortlessness in accomplishing even the toughest task. Such ease reminds us of a well-known passage from the *Bṛhadāraṇyaka Upaniṣad* (2.4.10)[23] that is often quoted by Vedānta authors in order to show that the supreme being manifests everything without any effort. In turn, this is reminiscent of the notion of *līlā* or "divine sport," the lighthearted attitude through which god carries out every action—starting with the manifestation of the universe—for pure amusement (see *Brahmasūtra* 2.1.33: *lokavat tu līlākaivalyam*).

Śrīveṅkaṭanātha asks himself: how is it possible that Kṛṣṇa bestows his *upadeśa* in this atmosphere of war and convulsion? And how can Arjuna benefit from his teaching, given the circumstances? He answers these questions by saying that for the blessed lord (*bhagavat*) spatial and temporal conditions are ultimately insignificant.[24] He then proceeds to analyze *BhG* 2.11 viewing it as a summary of the poem's entire teaching (BhG1 2000, 81). He calls it the "seed-verse" (*bījaśloka*) and says that whatever was spoken by Arjuna in the first chapter is summarized in the first word of this verse (i.e., *aśocyān*). The second word—*anvaśocaḥ*—sums up what had been said from the beginning of the second chapter to verse 2.4. The second part of 2.11 is said to encapsulate the knowledge of the reality of the nondual Self that the lord will expound throughout the subsequent chapters.[25] Ultimately, the aim of the text is to dispel all anguish and delusion in conformity with several passages of the *śruti*:[26] "Therefore, just as the entire shape of a tree is [hidden] in a seed, since the meaning of the entire *Bhagavadgītā* is included here [in 2.11], this is the "seed-verse": this is the secret behind the *Bhagavadgītā*."[27] Śrīveṅkaṭanātha points out that although Arjuna seems to speak wise words, he is not wise at all. As evidenced in *BhG* 2.7b (*pṛcchāmi tvāṃ dharmasammūḍhacetāḥ*) and 2.7d (*śiṣyas te 'haṃ śādhi māṃ tvāṃ prapannam*), he is not behaving like a wise man. He is not even respecting the proper boundaries of a disciple (*śiṣyamaryādā*) since he decides to leave the battle (*na yotsye*, *BhG* 2.9c) without resorting to his teacher. Arjuna's feelings and behavior—a mixture of foolishness (*mauḍhya*) and wisdom (*prājñatva*), discipleship (*śiṣyatva*) and independence (*svātantrya*)—are contradictory: this is what prompts Kṛṣṇa's laugh.[28]

Dhanapati Sūri

A well-trained scholar who lived between the second half of the eighteenth and the first half of the nineteenth century, Dhanapati wrote a lengthy gloss on Śaṅkara's *BhGBh*,[29] the *Bhāṣyotkarṣadīpikā* or "The Lantern on the Excellence of [Śaṅkara's] Commentary," where he quotes Madhūsudana Sarasvatī's *GAD* several times and criticizes him whenever he deviates from Śaṅkara's readings (Saha 2014, 291–95).[30] In his gloss on *BhG* 2.10, Dhanapati says:[31]

> After that what did the glorious lord do? Then [the text] says: *tam*. To him, to Arjuna who was dismayed in between the two armies, while he was [passively] accepting anguish and delusion, Hṛṣīkeśa, the glorious lord Vāsudeva, with a hint of laughter [that means] "I am happy for you, who are under the control of my authority!," uttered these words [to him], i.e., the speech which is about to be expressed. Some say: "Like plunging him into the sea of shame by exhibiting [his] inappropriate conduct."[32] Others [say]: "With a hint of laughter, since 'Although he is a fool, he speaks as if he were not one.' "[33] [. . .]

Dhanapati's interpretation of *prahasann iva*—"I am happy for you, who are under the control of my authority!"—is aimed at showing that the lord's hint of laughter is the revelation of the divine master's happiness, that is, of his grace. Kṛṣṇa's *kṛpā* descends upon Arjuna who, having surrendered (*prapanna*) to his lord, is now eligible (*adhikārin*) for receiving the instruction. Indeed, Arjuna has come to realize that he cannot get rid of his anguish by himself.[34]

Śrībellaṅkoṇḍa Rāmarāya Kavi

Born on December 27, 1875, this author subcomments the *BhGBh* with the *Bhāṣyārkaprakāśa* or "The Light of the Sun that is [Śaṅkara's] Commentary." His aim is to establish once and for all the supremacy of Śaṅkara's interpretation, in opposition to Rāmānuja's *Gītābhāṣya* and Veṅkaṭanātha's *Tātparyacandrikā*.

In his gloss *ad BhG* 1.1, Rāmarāya Kavi notes that the *BhG*'s first *śloka* is 2.11 (BhG4 2015, 4). Along these lines, he states that the benedictory invocation (*maṅgala*) of the text is "The glorious lord said" (*bhagavān uvāca*), just before *BhG* 2.11 (BhG4 2015, 15). Consequently, he argues that 2.10 concludes the introductory portion (*upodghāta*; BhG4 2015, 31). Kṛṣṇa is said to laugh because Arjuna is talking nonsense. And this same irony characterizes the lord's words in *BhG* 2.11, that is, *prajñāvādāṃś ca bhāṣase*:[35] "O descendant of Bharata, o Dhṛtarāṣṭra! To that Arjuna, who was lamenting in between the two armies, Hṛṣīkeśa, with a hint of laughter—his hint of laughter follows the hearing of Arjuna's words, similar to the prattling of a fool: this is the meaning—uttered these words in the form of the instruction of the *Bhagavadgītā*, beginning with *aśocyān* (2.11) and ending with *mā śucaḥ* (18.66)."[36] Significantly, in his gloss on 2.11 (BhG4 2015, 43–44) he quotes from Rāmānuja and Veṅkaṭanātha and refutes the latter according to whom the anguished words of Arjuna are the object of Kṛṣṇa's mockery. Rāmarāya Kavi highlights that Arjuna is immersed in the sea of sorrow and as a consequence has surrendered at the feet of Kṛṣṇa as his *śiṣya*. Therefore, it is unlikely that the lord would simply make fun of him (*mahati śokasāgare nimagne svacaraṇaṃ śaraṇaṃ prapanne pārthe bhagavataḥ kṛṣṇasya parihāsodbhāvodayāsaṅgatyāt*). Rāmarāya Kavi appears to favor the interpretation of *prahasann iva* as the expression of Kṛṣṇa's grace who makes Arjuna the worthy recipient of his teaching. On the other hand, Rāmarāya Kavi agrees with Veṅkaṭanātha that verses 2.10 and 2.11 must be taken together since the latter gives the meaning of *prahasann iva* (BhG4 2015, 44).

Śrīdhara Svāmin

Śrīdhara Svāmin (thirteenth to fourteenth century) is an *advaitin* whose effort is to harmonize knowledge (*jñāna*) and devotion (*bhakti*), as can be seen in his commentary to the *Bhāgavata Purāṇa*. He wrote a gloss on the *BhG* titled *Subodhinī* or "Easy Explanation."

While glossing *BhG* 2.10, Śrīdhara writes *prahasann iveti prasannamukhaḥ sann ity arthaḥ* (BhG2 2001, 74), that is, "the meaning of *prahasann iva* is having a happy face," without adding anything else. The mention of Kṛṣṇa's happy face conveys what in the performing arts is known as *hasita* or "slight laughter," which is the sure sign of Kṛṣṇa's grace toward Arjuna (see chapter 4). The compound *prasannamukha*, where the adjective *prasanna* means "delighted, bright, glad, cheerful, showing favor," evidences Kṛṣṇa's loving disposition toward his interlocutor (Vireswarananda 1991, 32–33).

In his introduction to the gloss *ad* 2.11 (BhG2 2001, 74), Śrīdhara adds that "Arjuna's anguish comes from the lack of discrimination between the body and the Self, therefore the glorious lord first shows how to discriminate between these two domains" (*dehātmanor avivekād asyaivaṃ śoko bhavatīti tadvivekapradarśanārthaṃ śrībhagavān uvāca*) and then begins his teaching.

Śrīdhara also offers a short outline of the *BhG*. He notices that starting from verse 1.28 the poem highlights that the object of Arjuna's anguish are his kinsfolk. Though admonished by Kṛṣṇa in verse 2.2, Arjuna keeps on speaking like a discriminating sage, albeit not being one.[37]

Śaṅkarānanda Sarasvatī

This author lived between the thirteenth and fourteenth centuries and wrote a clear gloss on the *BhG*, the *Tātparyabodhinī* or "The Explainer of the Purport," which closely follows Śaṅkara's commentary.[38] The *incipit* of Śaṅkarānanda's gloss to the *BhG*'s second chapter (BhG2 2001, 55–56) suggests a connection between verses 2.1–10 and the Upaniṣadic requirements for approaching a master for instruction.

He argues that thanks to the discrimination (*viveka*) between the real and the unreal, the sharp detachment arisen out of such discrimination and the will to achieve release, a Brahmin who has abandoned every action and longs only for liberation (*mokṣa*) acquires the eligibility to investigate into *Brahman*, as stated by the first aphorism of the *Brahmasūtras* (1.1.1): "Now, then, the desire to know *Brahman*" (*athāto brahmajijñāsā*). Preceded by a reverent approach to a teacher established in *Brahman* and well-versed in the Vedic texts (*Muṇḍaka Upaniṣad* 1.2.12), this investigation proceeds in three steps, as stated by the *śruti* (*Bṛhadāraṇyaka Upaniṣad* 2.4.5, 4.5.6): "The Self, indeed, o beloved, is to be realized; it is to be heard about,. . . ." Hence, the *BhG*'s second chapter begins by showing that Arjuna—who discriminates between the real and the unreal and longs for the supreme goal—has surrendered to the lord (starting from 2.7). Moreover, the chapter is meant to convey the instruction concerning the knowledge of the Self and the non-Self.[39] Following the *śruti* passage "Here I am, o lord, a suffering man! Please, make me overcome the limits of grief!" (*Chāndogya Upaniṣad* 7.1.3), once he who longs for release has taken refuge in his *guru* the latter should proceed to instruct him. Accordingly, Kṛṣṇa offers his teaching to Arjuna.[40] What is given prominence here is the subject of grace that the lord is willing to bestow upon whoever surrenders to him. Though Śaṅkarānanda glosses 2.10 in a cursory way, the Advaita character of his interpretation deserves notice:[41]

> O descendant of Bharata, thus at the mercy of grief in between the two armies [Arjuna,] in this way anguished, [thought:] "These [people] of mine will be killed" [and] "Because of the sin of killing them I will go to hell." Having Arjuna superimposed—due to beginningless ignorance—non-Self and its characteristics on the inactive Self—which is unchanging, free from properties like agency, etc., and [ideas such as] "I am the agent, I am the enjoyer"—and having Kṛṣṇa seen him lamenting, the greatly merciful lord thought in this way with an opposite feeling: "Without the knowledge of the identity of the Self and *Brahman*—expressed by well-known *śruti* passages such as 'What bewilderment, what sorrow can there be, regarding the Self of he who sees this oneness?' (*Īśa Upaniṣad* 7)—[. . .] he will never overcome the ocean of grief the root of which lies in illusion." Therefore, [the lord] uttered such a speech desirous of teaching the knowledge of that [identity] preceded by an analytical clarification on the meaning of the words ["Thou" (*tvam*) and "That" (*tat*)],[42] [. . .] as if he were laughing at his behavior [through ironic expressions such as] "You are a sage!" or "I think that you possess wisdom."

The actual *upadeśa* begins at *BhG* 2.11 (BhG2 2001, 73). Paraphrasing Śaṅkara, Śaṅkarānanda proceeds to explain Arjuna's inappropriate anxiety, anguish, and delusion. While Kṛṣṇa points out that true wisdom is seeing *Brahman* always and everywhere (*sadā sarvatra brahmadarśanaṃ pāṇḍityam*), "Arjuna is without such a characteristic and thus he is a fool and not a wise man" (*ata uktalakṣaṇābhāvāt tvaṃ mūḍha eva na tu paṇḍita iti*; BhG2 2001, 73).[43]

Sadānanda Yogīndra

Sadānanda Yogīndra (fifteenth century), author of the popular Advaita primer *Vedāntasāra*, also wrote the *Bhāvaprakāśa* or "Light on the Inner Meaning," which is a versified gloss on the *BhG* in the *anuṣṭubh* meter.[44] As he himself recognizes at the beginning of the *Bhāvaprakāśa*, he follows for the most part Śaṅkara's *BhGBh* (vss. 9–10, 33–39; BhG2 2001, 7–8).

In this work, Sadānanda divides the *BhG* into three sections (*kāṇḍa*) on the basis of the Upaniṣadic saying (*mahāvākya*) "Thou art That" (*tat tvam asi; Chāndogya Upaniṣad* 6.8.7–16): chapters 1–6 are said to explain the word *tvam*; chapters 7–12 are said to explain the word *tat*; and chapters 13–18 are said to elucidate the identity of the two (vss. 42–43).

In his commentary on *BhG* 2.7 (BhG2 2001, 66), Sadānanda underlines that *saṃsāra* is an ocean of defects (*doṣavāridhi*) and he lists the preliminary Vedāntic requirements beginning with the discrimination between the real and the unreal (*vivekādisādhanāni*). The *BhG* verses 1.31–32, 1.35, 1.38, 1.46 and 2.5 are said to offer details on the qualifications needed in order to have access to the teaching (*nityānityavastuviveka, ihāmutraphalavirāga, śama, dama, nirlobha, titikṣā*) coupled with the reverent approach one must have toward the *guru* (*gurūpasadana*, vss. 3–7). In verses 6–7 of the gloss *ad BhG* 2.8 (BhG2 2001, 68), Sadānanda points out that Arjuna is endowed with "detachment from the enjoyments of the here-world and the after-world" (*ihāmutraphalavirāga*). This means that he is eligible to receive the lord's *upadeśa* (vs. 12). The brief gloss *ad* 2.10 is worth quoting:[45]

> Thus, even though Arjuna disregarded the war, the lord certainly did not overlook it. In this way Saṃjaya replied to the blind [king]. And, having arrived in between the two armies for the war-enterprise, showing with a laugh at Arjuna—who was the victim of anguish and delusion, which prevented him from [entering into] battle—the inappropriateness of his behavior, the lord, the inner controller, as if he were soaking him in a sea of shame, uttered these very deep and essential words, which are about to be revealed.

What is remarkable according to Sadānanda is the peculiar mixture of discipleship and disobedience that characterizes Arjuna: he is on the one hand the exemplary *śiṣya*, the ideal reservoir of the lord's grace, and on the other he disobeys Kṛṣṇa's words. Overall, it is the hero's inappropriateness (*anaucitya*) that causes the lord's hint of laughter, which is aimed at triggering his discrimination.

Commenting on 2.11, Sadānanda informs us that Arjuna is the victim of two types of delusion (BhG2 2001, 74). Before explaining how to uproot them, he describes them in detail. The first kind of delusion depends upon the superimposition of the threefold body[46] on the pure and unchanging Self. This raises wrong ideas concerning the phenomenal world and the illusory notion of the Self being the body. The second kind of delusion is that Arjuna perceives the performance of his *svadharma* as a warrior as leading to injustice. Following Śaṅkara, Sadānanda states that when wisdom (*pāṇḍitya*) and foolishness (*mauḍhya*) occur in the same person it is an extraordinary and unusual (*adbhūta*) event. Furthermore, Sadānanda puts this question in Arjuna's mouth: "Why do even sages feel anguish on separating from their friends?" To this, Kṛṣṇa replies:[47] "O [Arjuna], it is not like that! That is not intelligence, [rather] it is definitely [something] fit for derision. [On the contrary] the wise ones, having heard from their teacher the word whose content is Vedānta and reflecting with [solid] reasoning on the oneness of *Brahman*, and meditating upon it for a long time, these sages—once the filth of ignorance has been annihilated—realize the reality of the Self." Following 2.11, the final verses maintain that the wise do not mourn neither for the dead nor for the living, be they friends or relatives (vvs. 17–18). Sadānanda gives an example:[48] "Just as in a dream a companion—dead or alive—becomes an object of sorrow but the delusion generated from this does not follow when one wakes up, in the same way dead or alive companions—[thus] conceived by an illusion arisen from ignorance—do not provoke anguish and delusion in the sages that have awoken to reality." Kṛṣṇa exhorts Arjuna to behave as a true sage (*paṇḍita*)—namely, as a knower of the Self, capable of discriminating between impermanent bodies and the permanent Self—abandoning the anguish caused by his epistemic blindness and establishing himself in the firmness of the Self's reality. On the whole, Sadānanda interprets *prahasann iva* as mockery, without considering the value of the particle *iva*. Kṛṣṇa's laugh, however, is not purely for the sake of derision since by putting Arjuna to shame he teaches him that he needs to react and overcome his weakness.

Madhusūdana Sarasvatī

One of the most important pre-modern authors of Advaita Vedānta is surely Madhusūdana Sarasvatī (sixteenth century; Pellegrini 2015). He wrote a detailed gloss on the *BhG*, the *Gūḍhārthadīpikā* or "The Lantern on the Hidden meaning" (*GAD*), which mainly follows Śaṅkara though he sometimes disagrees with him. An important issue to be kept in mind is the kṛṣṇaite background of Madhusūdana. The verses are widely commented in a lucid style and plain language, far from the complex technicalities of Madhusūdana's other works. Moreover, unlike Śaṅkara, Madhusūdana comments upon the entire first chapter and the opening ten verses of the second.

At the beginning of *GAD* (GAD 2005, 7; BhG2 2001, 5; BhG3 1936, 8), after a long series of introductory verses, Madhusūdana states that the main purpose (*prayojana*) of the *BhG* is to be found in 2.11, a verse concerned with dispelling impurities—such as anguish and delusion—through the performance of one's own duty, which leads to the accomplishment of life's goal. Like the dialogue between Janaka and Yājñavalkya in the *Upaniṣad*s, the dialogue between Kṛṣṇa and Arjuna in the *BhG* is dedicated to extolling knowledge. But what is happening to Arjuna, who is notoriously a valorous man? How does it happen that his intellect is subdued by anguish and delusion due to his affection for masters and companions? Indeed, he wants to abandon the battlefield—the duty of a warrior—in order to follow another's duty—that is, a wandering life of alms: this is why he plunges deeply into confusion. But having secured Kṛṣṇa's supreme wisdom, all his anguish and doubts will be ultimately dispelled. Arjuna will thus revert to his own duty and become fulfilled. The idea is that Arjuna, as the lord's pupil, is the model of every eligible person.

As done by Daivajña Paṇḍita Sūrya and Sadānanda Yogīndra, while commenting on *BhG* 2.6 Madhusūdana highlights the Vedāntic requirements as they are expressed in the *BhG*. He shows that some qualifications of the person who is eligible for receiving the teaching (*adhikāriviśeṣaṇāni*) are present in the previous part of the text (*prāktanena granthena*). Thus when he comments on *BhG* 1.31cd[49] Madhusūdana recollects the passage on acquisitions (*yoga*) and their conservation (*kṣema*) of *BhG* 9.22[50] and equates the destiny of a warrior slain in battle with that of a wandering ascetic who aims at attaining the *summum bonum* as established by several *śruti* passages such as "The good is one thing, the gratifying is quite another" (*Kaṭha Upaniṣad* 1.2.1). Whatever differs from this supreme goal is not the *summum bonum*: here Madhusūdana detects the discrimination between what is permanent and what is impermanent (*nityānityavastuviveka*). *BhG* 1.32ab[51] conveys the detachment from both here-world results and those of the other-world (*aihikaphalavirāga*) and *BhG* 1.35[52] underlines this point. *BhG* 1.44[53] teaches that the Self is beyond the gross body. *BhG* 1.32c[54] refers to mental control (*śama*) and *BhG* 1.32d[55] to sensory control (*dama*). *BhG* 1.38[56] conveys the absence of greed (*nirlobhatā*) and *BhG* 1.46[57] the virtue of forbearance (*titikṣā*). The idea is that the *BhG*'s first chapter is dedicated to the means of renunciation, and—on the basis of 2.5[58]—the second one treats the life of wandering renunciates.

In the gloss to *BhG* 2.7 (GAD 2005, 50–52; BhG2 2001, 65–66; BhG3 1936, 36), Madhusūdana continues to link several verses of the poem to the steps that lead a pupil to approach an authoritative teacher (*gurūpasadana*) and attain the Vedāntic teaching. Eligible for such an instruction is he who is aware of the defects of phenomenal experience and totally rejects it. Then, as Arjuna does with Kṛṣṇa, such a man reverently approaches a teacher according to the rules.

In *BhG* 2.7, Arjuna's desire to approach Kṛṣṇa as a teacher arises due to the anguish that grips him at the sight of Bhīṣma and the other heroes. So, having highlighted Arjuna's aspiration for a life of alms, as described by the *śruti* passage ". . . they rise above, and conduct a wandering life" (*Bṛhadāraṇyaka Upaniṣad* 3.5.1), resorting to the stratagem of his despondency, with the word *kārpaṇya*, that is, "pity," the text discloses his reverent approach to the master.[59]

Possibly borrowing his observations from Keśava Kaśmīrī Bhaṭṭācārya, Madhusūdana focuses on the meaning of the word *kārpaṇya*. In the world of everyday life, "miser" (*kṛpaṇa*) is someone who does not tolerate even the slightest loss of money or goods. On the other hand, in the *śruti* it is written that "the one who indeed, o Gārgī, departs without having known the immutable, he is a miser" (*Bṛhadāraṇyaka Upaniṣad* 3.8.10):[60] a miser (*kṛpaṇa*) is whoever does not know the Self and has not attained the supreme goal. The abstract form of the word *kṛpaṇa* is *kārpaṇya*, which is nothing but the superimposition (*adhyāsa*) of the non-Self on the Self. Due to this superimposition, a defect such as the stubborn attachment characterized by the sense of mine has obscured the *kṣatriya* nature of Arjuna.[61]

Ad 2.8, Madhusūdana states that Kṛṣṇa alone is capable of removing the anguish and delusion of Arjuna, just like Nārada did with sage Sanatkumāra in *Chāndogya Upaniṣad* 7.1.3 (GAD 2005, 54–55; BhG2 2001, 68; BhG3 1936, 37–38).[62] Here he emphasizes a fundamental point, namely the act of total surrender (*prapatti*) of the devotee Arjuna to his lord (see Lester 1966, 266–82; Raman 2007).[63]

After this, Madhusūdana focuses on the nature of the two kingdoms, that of this world and that of the otherworld, and—as it is said in *Chāndogya Upaniṣad* 8.1.6—[64] he points out that both are impermanent. Hence, what follows is an inferential formula based on a positive invariable concomitance (*anvayavyāpti*):[65] "Whatever is produced is impermanent" (*yat kṛtakaṃ tad anityam*). Madhusūdana adds that besides inference direct perception (*pratyakṣa*) also proves that objects of this world are subject to destruction. More than this, all the enjoyments of this world, as well as of the other world, are ultimately unable to remove anguish.

In the gloss *ad BhG* 2.9 (GAD 2005, 55–56; BhG2 2001, 69; BhG3 1936, 38), Madhusūdana simply contextualizes the verse and provides a para-etymological derivation of the name Govinda who is none other than Hṛṣīkeśa, the one who triggers all sense faculties (*sarvendriyapravartakatvena*), the inner controller (*āntaryāmiṇam*). Addressing Kṛṣṇa with these epithets, the *BhG* suggests that he is the almighty. Thus it is very easy for him to remove Arjuna's delusion (*govindahṛṣīkeśapadābhyāṃ sarvajñatvasarvaśaktitvasūcakābhyāṃ bhagavatas tanmohāpanodanam anāyāsasādhyam iti sūcitam*), and it is precisely this effortlessness that justifies his hint of laughter.

Madhusūdana's reading of *BhG* 2.10 is worth quoting:[66]

> [. . .] To him, who—having reached the position in between the two armies for war-engagement—experiences anguish and a delusion which is opposed to that

> [war], Hṛṣīkeśa—the glorious lord and inner controller—with a hint of laughter, as though plunging him into the sea of shame by exhibiting [his] inappropriate conduct,[67] uttered to [that] Arjuna those words starting with *aśocyān* (*BhG* 2.11) which are about to be expressed, whose meaning is utterly profound, and which throw light on [his] inappropriate conduct (*anucita*). By displaying an inappropriate conduct, derision (*prahāsa*) generates shame and such shame is substantiated by sorrow. And the content of its primary [meaning] is repulsion. Nonetheless, since Arjuna is the reservoir of the grace of the glorious lord and since throwing light on his inappropriate behavior is done with the aim of triggering discrimination in him, such derision is only metaphoric [. . .]. In order to express this, there is the indeclinable particle *iva*. [. . .] Indeed, if [Arjuna] had disregarded the war by staying at home he would have not done something inappropriate. But having reached the battlefield with great enthusiasm, his avoidance of the war is definitely inappropriate.

The goal of the *bhagavat*'s hint of laughter is highlighted by the particle *iva*, that suggests that his derision is aimed at triggering Arjuna's discrimination (*viveka*). The lord's *prahasann iva* is understood as an act of grace, so as to stimulate Arjuna's pride as a warrior. Madhusūdana interprets Kṛṣṇa's hint of laughter as a skillful means (*upāya*), willingly resorted to in order to transform his pupil's mind and heart. Indeed, the aim of the *guru* is the transformation of his disciple by removing all his doubts and sorrows. In Kṛṣṇa's *prahasann iva* there is no opposition or tension between mirth and mockery since they both concur to the same objective. This shows the inconsistency of an either/or interpretation: mirth and mockery can coexist since the lord conveys his *prasāda* through both of them. Madhusūdana ends his gloss on 2.10 by saying that his last statements will become clear in *GAD ad* 2.11. Herein, he writes:[68] "Although it has arisen by nature, Arjuna's inclination towards his own duty—called war—is obstructed by two kinds of delusion, and by the anguish caused by them."[69] Such a twofold delusion of Arjuna must be removed (*dvividho mohas tasya nirākaraṇīyaḥ*). The first delusion is the superimposing of false identities on the Self. This superimposition is common to all living beings and takes place because of lack of discrimination due to a threefold limiting condition constituted by the two bodies (gross and subtle) and their respective cause, i.e., the causal body. The realization of the Self is what removes this kind of delusion.[70] The second delusion has to do with the defect of pity which afflicts Arjuna, who sees in the violence of war a form of injustice. This delusion is erased by understanding that—even though full of violence—war is a warrior's own duty (*svadharma*) and therefore it cannot be unjust (*adharma*).[71] Madhusūdana closes his reasoning by saying that once the causes of anguish have withdrawn, anguish itself comes to an end:[72] there is no need of any further means.[73]

Nīlakāṇṭha Caturdhara

Nīlakāṇṭha Caturdhara (second half of the seventeenth century) was an *advaitin* who wrote the *Bhāratabhāvadīpa* or "The Light on the Meaning of the *Mahābhārata*" (also known as *Bhāvadīpa*, "The Light on the Meaning"), a commentary on the entire *Mahābhārata*. The *Bhāratabhāvadīpa* obviously covers the *BhG* as well.[74] What characterizes this work is a kind of formalized expression that is typical of the period, dominated by the *navya* style and a meta-idiom.

While commenting *ad BhG* 2.1–3 (BhG1 2000, 64), Nīlakāṇṭha says that the words of Arjuna in *BhG* 1.37 (*svajanaṃ hi kathaṃ hatvā sukhinaḥ syāma mādhava*) are not due to a compassion characterized by the desire to eradicate others' sorrows (*na tu dayayā paraduḥkhaprahāṇecchārūpayā*) but are rather caused by his affection (*snehena*) for masters, relatives and friends. This is a form of delusion (*moha*), which reaches its peak in *BhG* 2.6 (*yān eva hatvā na jijīviṣāmas*).

Nīlakāṇṭha's gloss to *BhG* 2.10 (BhG1 2000, 73) is very brief: "This is about to be expressed [by verse 2.11], that 'Even though he is a fool, he is speaking as if he were not one;' [this is the reason for] *prahasann iva*" (*mūḍho 'py ayam amūḍhavad vadatīti prahasann iva | idaṃ vakṣyamāṇam*).

Like Madhusūdana, in his gloss *ad* 2.11 (BhG1 2000, 82–83) Nīlakāṇṭha states that Arjuna is the victim of two types of delusion: 1. the idea that the Self dies with the death of the body; and 2.

the idea that his own duty—war—constitutes *adharma* (*arjunasya dehanāśe ātmanāśadhīḥ svadharme yuddhe cādharmadhīr iti mohadvayam*).[75] The lord uproots the first type of delusion through twenty *ślokas*—beginning with 2.11—that are similar to the aphorisms on the knowledge of *Brahman* (*brahmavidyāsūtrabhūta*).[76] The axiom is that only the body is subject to death, so that when Arjuna is pained for Bhīṣma, etc. he is completely wrong. This is why even though he utters wise words—as in 1.42 (*patanti pitaro hy eṣām*) and 1.44 (*narake niyataṃ vāso*)—he acts like a fool. The *probans* (i.e., the logical reason [*hetu*] for this) is given in 2.11cd: *gatāsūn agatāsūṃś ca nānuśocanti paṇḍitāḥ*, that is, "the wise do not mourn for the dead or for the living." From this we deduce that what is truly desired is the vital breath (*prāṇa*), not the body (*deha*).[77] Inferentially speaking: "the Self is different from the body because it is sentient unlike a pot; [and] the body is not sentient because it can be experienced to be like a pot" (*tasmād ātmā dehād anyaḥ, cetanatvāt, vyatirekeṇa ghaṭavat | deho na cetanaḥ, dṛśyatvāt, ghaṭavat*).[78]

Vaṃśīdhara Miśra

There is very scanty information on Vaṃśīdhara Miśra. He wrote a gloss of Advaita inspiration to the *BhG*, the so-called *Vaṃśī* or "[The Gloss] of Vaṃśīdhara." *Ad BhG* 2.10, he explains *prahasann iva* thus:[79]

> This is the meaning of *prahasann iva*: [Hṛṣīkeśa], by laughing, produced a strong laugh like a common man, he became happy-faced, [that is], displayed a happy face. The glorious lord—who wished to illustrate the supreme principle whose fruit is the rescue of all his devotees—is the compeller of the sense faculties, the inner controller of all and the beloved of his devotees. Having recourse to the anguish and delusion of Arjuna as a pretext (*nimitta*), in the lord's consciousness arose [the thought]: "the right occasion has arrived," and it manifested itself in his moon-face. This is the purport.

Kṛṣṇa's joyful laugh is due to the fact that Arjuna's anguish is the pretext for the lord's intervention, which will lead his devotee to the supreme goal. The god's laughter makes his face resemble the moon, which hints at his extraordinary charm and beauty. The central theme of Kṛṣṇa's grace is once again emphasized. The originality of Vaṃśīdhara's interpretation lies in the fact that for him *prahasann iva* is not just a hint of laughter or a slight laughter (*hasita*) but a hearty laugh. The use of the term *nimitta* is also important since it underlines that Arjuna's despondency is the occasion for the outpouring of the lord's grace (see *BhG* 11.33 and *BhGBh ad* 2.11).

In his commentary to 2.11 (BhG7 1990, 34–35), Vaṃśīdhara divides the *BhG* in two main sections: from 1.1 to 2.10 we have the introductory part (*prastāvakakathānirūpaṇam*), which is useful for showing that the cause of all evil—anguish, delusion, etc.—is ignorance (*avidyā*). Then from 2.11 to 18.66 we have the actual text (*aṅgī granthaḥ*), where Arjuna is instructed in the ultimate spiritual teaching (*adhyātmaśāstra*).

Kashmirian Śaiva Bhedābheda

In this section we shall briefly deal with some of the commentators of the Kashmirian traditions[80] starting with Bhāskara. The reason for including Bhāskara in this group is because he chiefly[81] glossed the Kashmirian recension of the *BhG* (hereafter *BhGk*). What is remarkable in the *BhGk* (Piano 2017, 98–99; Kato 2016, 1109) is the reading of 2.12b (vulgate 2.11b) as *prajñāvan nābhibhāṣase*, "you do not speak as a wise man," instead of the vulgate's problematic *prajñāvādāṃś ca bhāṣase*. Kato (2016) has offered a precious survey of traditional interpretations of 2.11b and the scholars' understanding of it, arriving at the conclusion that the *BhGk*'s reading is more plausible, even though *abhibhāṣase* is comparatively rarer than *bhāṣase*.

Bhāskara

In addition to a commentary on the *Brahmasūtra*, Bhāskara (eighth century) also wrote the *Bhagavadāśayānusaraṇa* on the *BhG* (Saha 2017, 272–73). This seems to be the oldest commentary after Śaṅkara's *BhGBh*. The *Bhagavadāśayānusaraṇa* or "Following the

Intention of the Glorious Lord," was edited by Subhadropādhyaya (1965) and studied by van Buitenen (1965) and Kato (2014, 1144–45).

Bhāskara's commentary on *BhG* 2.10 is terse and ignores the indeclinable *iva* as well as the prefix *pra-*:[82] "To that Arjuna, seated in the said way in between the two armies, who had abandoned enthusiasm toward war, Hṛṣīkeśa, laughing, uttered this sentence which is about to be expressed." Despite the scanty gloss, Bhāskara adds an illuminating statement: "Great souls usually smile before speaking" (*mahātmānaḥ kila smitapūrvābhibhāṣiṇo bhavantīti*). This remark emphasizes once more the pivotal role of grace. It hints at a topic that we shall deal with in our next chapter, namely that gods, sages, and *guru*s herald their teachings by resorting to a benign hint of laughter. The idea that Kṛṣṇa, like all *mahātma*s, smiles before speaking indicates a shared characteristic, herein expressed by an *upapada* compound ending with an agentive adjective where the first member is the nominalized form *smita* (from verbal root √*smi*) meaning "smile." Moreover, the next verse of the *BhGk* seems to hint at a double entendre given that in place of 2.11 of the vulgate edition it reads:[83] "You—whose soul is troubled by pity due to overwhelming anguish and delusion—are without discernment. You have been seized by tenderness having seen [your] companions approaching the jaws of death."[84] This verse together with *BhGk* 2.12 (= vulgate 2.11; *prajñāvādāṃś ca bhāṣase*) sketches a clear picture of what Kṛṣṇa is saying to Arjuna (i.e., that he is obnubilated and lacks *viveka*), he being concerned with what he should not be concerned. Yet the lord's hint of laughter is not meant to be disparaging. It rather shows Kṛṣṇa's surprise, given that at such a crucial time the great warrior Arjuna is unrecognizable. The lord's *prahasann iva* is brought about by the disciple's *anaucitya* and is tinged with astonishment (*vismaya*) given the latter's unusual behavior. Arjuna being the prototype of the valiant hero, Kṛṣṇa doesn't believe his eyes when he sees him in such a despondent condition. It should be noted that in the *BhG* and in the entire *MBh* it is typically Arjuna who is filled with wonder toward Kṛṣṇa,[85] not the other way around. Right now, however, Arjuna's discriminating faculty (*saṃjñānaṃ saṃjñā viśiṣṭā buddhiḥ*) is obstructed having somehow collapsed (*vigatā vyavahitā vā saṃjñā*): this is the reason for the lord's chiding laugh (*itaś copahāsakāraṇam*).[86]

Abhinavagupta

The commentary on the *BhGk* of the well-known Kashmirian thinker Abhinavagupta (tenth to eleventh century) is the *Gītārthasaṃgraha* or "The Compendium of the Meaning of the *BhG*." Abhinavagupta briefly introduces his work by pointing out that the *BhG*'s first chapter is just an introduction to the rest of the poem (BhG3 1936, 8). According to him, the enmity between the Pāṇḍavas and the Kauravas should be symbolically interpreted as a perpetual conflict between knowledge (*vidyā*) and ignorance (*avidyā*): each tries to subdue the other (*abhibhāvya-abhibhāvaka*). Abhinavagupta observes that there are two types of people who are ineligible to receive the teaching (*upadeśabhajana*): 1. the ignorant ones, who don't have even a speck of knowledge (*anutpannavidyāleśāvakaśa*); and 2. the wise ones, who have totally eradicated ignorance (*nirmūlitasamastāvidyāprapañca*). Any instruction given to these two categories is fruitless. Best candidates for the *upadeśa* that leads to liberation (*mokṣamārgopadeśana*) are the doubtful ones. This division reminds us of the opening of the second *vallī* of the *Kaṭha Upaniṣad* (1.2.4), which focusses on the eligibility of Naciketas. Herein, Yama-Mṛtyu points out the difference between *vidyā* and *avidyā*: "Far apart and widely different are these two: ignorance and what is known as knowledge. I take Naciketas as one yearning for knowledge; the many desires do not confound you."[87]

While glossing *BhG* 2.5–6 (BhG3 1936, 35–36, 39), Abhinavagupta anticipates that the sentence in 2.10 "in between the two armies" (*senayor ubhayor madhye*) suggests that Arjuna is overcome by doubt but has not yet decided to withdraw from the war. This is why Arjuna wishes to be instructed: his doubt is precisely what makes him eligible for the teaching. Finding himself in between the two armies, he is exactly in between knowledge and ignorance. Abhinavagupta does not say anything else on 2.10.[88] What he concentrates on is Arjuna's full eligibility (*adhikāra*) to receive Kṛṣṇa's *upadeśa*.

Ānandavardhana

For his commentary on the *BhG* titled *Jñānakarmasamuccayavyākhyā* or "Combination of Knowledge and Action," also known as *Ānanda-*

vardhinī or "Increasing the Bliss," the Kashmirian Ānandavardhana follows the *BhGk*. Though Saha (2017, 274) states that the author is the same as the Kashmirian rhetorician Ānandavardhana (ninth century, author of the *Dhvanyāloka*), Belvalkar (1941, 5) disagrees: he convincingly argues that the Ānandavardhana of the *Jñānakarmasamuccayavyākhyā* is a commentator of the seventeenth century since he quotes from Abhinavagupta, who is certainly later than the author of the *Dhvanyāloka*. On *BhG* 2.10, Ānandavardhana writes:[89]

> To the son of Pṛthā who in the said way sat in between the two armies overwhelmed by anguish, with the enthusiasm for war lost, the lord who is the compeller of the sense-organs and of all faculties, the glorious of the nature of the supreme Self with its four states, with a hint of laughter, [that is] nearly mocking him by observing his modified gestures, desirous of leading him again to his own [fighting] occupation by showing him how the body and its owner are associated and separated from one another, following the teaching "The removal of the false notion that arises from the idea of 'I' [superimposed] on the body is possible," thus spoke to him. This is the meaning.

Ānandavardhana's interpretation of *prahasann iva* as "nearly mocking" is based on an implicit recognition of Arjuna's *anaucitya*. He does not add anything else on our topic.

Jñāneśvar

Besides the Sanskrit commentarial tradition, there are countless vernacular glosses on the *BhG*. Though our analysis is based on Sanskrit sources, we deal here with a single outstanding exception, that is, the Marāṭhī *Jñāneśvarī* or *Bhāvārtha Dīpikā*, "The Lantern of the Inner Meaning," composed around 1290 by Jñāneśvar (or Jñāndev, traditional dates 1275–1296). This text is rightly regarded as the most significant vernacular commentary on the *BhG* (Davis 2014, 65–71). As Ian M. P. Raeside noted: "In *Jñāneśvarī* we have a marvelous text, a tremendous sustained sermon on life with a sweep and gusto, a piling on of imagery, and a development of simile that is almost numbing in its power" (Kripananda 1989, ix). Jñāneśvar was the founder of the Vārkarī Panth and advocated a synthesis of Advaita Vedānta tenets, Kṛṣṇa *bhakti* and the *śaiva* Nātha tradition.

Commenting on Arjuna's refusal to fight (*BhG* 2.9), verse 2.83 of the *Jñāneśvarī* ends with these words: "Lord Krishna was astonished to see him in such a condition" (Kripananda 1989, 17). Kṛṣṇa's astonishment (*vismaya*) is thus explicitly recognized, being the primary emotion that prompts his hint of laughter. Jñāneśvar dedicates seven verses (2.84–90) to the interpretation of *BhG* 2.10:

> He said to Himself, what is he thinking of? Arjuna is quite ignorant. What can be done? (84) How can he be brought back to his senses? How can he be made to take heart? Just as an exorcist considers how to cast out an evil spirit, (85) or just as a physician who finds someone suffering from a dangerous illness, as the crisis approaches, instantly prescribes a magic remedy like nectar, (86) similarly, between the two armies, Krishna reflected on how Arjuna could cast off his infatuation. (87) Having decided what to do, He began to speak in an angry tone, just as a mother's love is often concealed in her anger. (88) The potency of nectar is hidden in the bitter taste of medicine. Even though it is not outwardly visible, it is revealed by the effectiveness of the medicine. (89) In the same way, Krishna spoke to Arjuna with words which, though seemingly bitter, were actually very sweet. (90) (Kripananda 1989, 17–18)

Kṛṣṇa's apparently harsh behavior, his angry tone and bitter words, are thought of as a medicine, that is, the medium of his nectarine grace (*prasāda*). As *BhG* 18.37ab will later state: "That [joy] which is at the beginning like poison, but then transforms [itself] into nectar [. . .]" (*yat tad agre viṣam iva pariṇāme 'mṛtopamam*). If *prahasann iva* is mockery, then it must be understood as the remedy that restores Arjuna's mental clarity and discriminative power.

Viśiṣṭādvaita

Other important commentators of the *BhG* are found among the followers of the school known as "non-dualism of the qualified [whole]" (*viśiṣṭādvaita*). This school was started by Nāthamuni (ninth century) and it flourished through such figures as Yāmuna Muni (917–1037; Uskokov 2021, 68),[90] Rāmānuja (eleventh century) and Veṅkaṭanātha (1269–1370; Uskokov 2021, 69). Along with Bhāskara, the *vaiṣṇava viśiṣṭādvaitin*s were the earliest adversaries of Śaṅkara's interpretation of the *BhG*.

Rāmānuja

Rāmānuja (traditional date 1017–1137) is acknowledged as the great commentator or *bhāṣyakāra* of Viśiṣṭādvaita. He commented on the *Brahmasūtra*s with the *Śrībhāṣya* and two other works—the *Vedāntasāra* and the *Vedārthadīpa*—and on the *BhG* with the *Gītābhāṣya,* also known as *Viśiṣṭādvaitabhāṣya.* Although not directly initiated by him, he is traditionally believed to be a disciple of Yāmuna Muni. Due to his pivotal position, Rāmānuja's commentary on the *BhG* is highly esteemed. There exist two main hermeneutic tools for investigating his commentary on the *BhG*, one earlier and one later: Yāmuna Muni's *Gītārthasaṃgraha* and the lucid subcommentary *Tātparyacandrikā* by Veṅkaṭanātha / Vedānta Deśika (Raghavachar 1990, xi).

Like Śaṅkara, Rāmānuja observes that in the *BhG* Kṛṣṇa is not simply addressing Arjuna but all living beings who long for release. The central theme is devotion to the supreme Kṛṣṇa Nārāyaṇa since in Viśiṣṭādvaita *bhakti* is considered the utmost way for realizing the divine, its acme being one's surrender (*prapatti*) by taking refuge (*śaraṇāgati*) in the lord (Raman 2007, 26–34; Uskokov 2021, 73–75). Devotion is said to develop through knowledge (*jñāna*) and action (*karman*). These main themes are synthetically anticipated in Rāmānuja's introduction to the poem and find an analytical focus in specific *loci* of his commentary (Raghavachar 1990: xii–xiii).

Like Yāmuna, Rāmānuja divides the *BhG* into three hexads (*ṣaṭka*). The first hexad is said to be dedicated to the method one must follow in order to vanquish bondage. For comprehending the nature of the Self, one must first resort to *karmayoga* and then to *jñānayoga*. The second hexad focuses on *bhaktiyoga* and its object, namely the supreme lord, his nature, attributes and glories. Following Yāmuna, Rāmānuja maintains that the third *ṣaṭka* develops the contents of the other two with a theoretical clarification of the paths of *karman, jñāna* and *bhakti*. It also investigates the status of *prakṛti, puruṣa* and *puruṣottama*, highlighting the supremacy of the latter (Raghavachar 1990, xiv).

In his introduction to the *BhG*, Rāmānuja says that the nature of the *bhagavat* and the supreme aim of human life (*puruṣārtha*) are achievable through *bhaktiyoga*, accompanied by a combination (*samuccaya*) of *karman* and *jñana* (BhG1 2000, 6). He briefly comments on the first chapter in order to summarize the scene of the battlefield (from *BhG* 1.25 to 1.47) and observes that this introduction extends to the opening verses of the second chapter. *Ad BhG* 2.8, he points out that Arjuna has surrendered as a disciple to the *bhagavat*, thus recalling his *prapatti* to the lord. Rāmānuja's detailed commentary begins *ad BhG* 2.10. On *prahasann iva* he writes:[91]

> Having thus seen him, the descendant of Pṛthā, between the two armies ready for battle all of a sudden discouraged, pervaded by anguish due to the ignorance of the real nature of the body and the Self, while he (= Kṛṣṇa) was about to put forward the truth of the knowledge of the Self as distinct from the body, they being mutually opposed to one another, [to him]—with a hint of laughter—the supreme person said this. [Almost laughing at Pārtha, that is] as though pronouncing a mocking sentence, he revealed to him—beginning with "Never indeed was I not . . ." (2.12) and ending with "I will free you from all sins, do not worry!" (18.66)—what are the contents of the path of action and the path of devotion in order to obtain that [goal] which concerns the real nature of the [individual] Self and the supreme Self. This is the meaning.

Rāmānuja reads *prahasan* as a mocking laugh that is mitigated by the particle *iva*. *Ad BhG* 2.11 (BhG1 2000, 79) he clarifies a few points mentioned in 2.10 but doesn't add anything substantial on Kṛṣṇa's hint of laughter. He focuses on the source of Arjuna's anguish: quoting *BhG* 1.42cd,[92] he says that all the hero's problems are due to his identification of the Self with the body, which is also what triggers his seemingly wise words (*dehātmasvabhāvaprajñānimittavādān*). Rāmānuja points out that those who are free from this error, that is, who know that the body is distinct from the Self (*tatsvabhāvayāthātmyavid*), do not suffer any anguish whatsoever on similar occasions (*dehātmasvabhāvajñānavatāṃ nātra kiñcic chokanimittam asti*).

Veṅkaṭanātha

In addition to the *Gītārthasaṃgraharakṣā* on Yāmuna Muni's *Gītārthasaṃgraha*,[93] Veṅkaṭanātha (traditional dates 1268–1369)—also known as Vedānta Deśika—composed a subcommentary on Rāmānuja's commentary on the *BhG*: the *Tātparyacandrikā* or "The Moonlight on the Purport." This text glosses the *Gītābhāṣya*'s introduction at length, mentioning Śaṅkara several times in order to refute him. While glossing the *Gītābhāṣya*'s first chapter, Veṅkaṭanātha closely follows Rāmānuja without adding anything new. The *Tātparyacandrikā* touches upon some interesting points *ad BhG* 2.1 (BhG1 2000, 62), where it says that whereas the center of the first chapter is Arjuna's anguish and delusion (*prathame 'dhyāye arjunasya śokamohau varṇitau*) the focus of the second is the teaching capable of uprooting them, namely the instruction on *Brahman* and *ātman* (*dvitīye tu tannivartakabrahmātmatattvajñānopadeśo 'nuvarṇyate*). In his gloss *ad BhG* 2.2 (BhG1 2000, 62), Veṅkaṭanātha concentrates on Arjuna's out-of-place (*asthāne*) delusion (*moha*), which leads to his refusal to fight (*na yotsya iti*; *BhG* 2.9). It is precisely this delusion that needs to be taken into consideration, not the people for whom Arjuna is distressed (*tathā ca etādṛśas tava moha evānuśocyaḥ, na tu tvadanuśocito jana iti*).

In commenting on *BhG* 2.6–8 (BhG1 2000, 68), Veṅkaṭanātha points out that a war is usually fought with the aim of defending one's beloved. But in the *Mahābhārata* conflict the enemy is one's kith and kin: this inevitably generates confusion, diminishing the ability to reach decisions due to the feelings of affection for one's relatives and friends.[94] Only Kṛṣṇa can solve the problem and dispel all doubts by revealing what Arjuna's best option is (*śreyas*; see *Kaṭha Upaniṣad* 1.2.1). Moreover, in his gloss *ad*

BhG 2.9 (BhG1 2000, 72) Veṅkaṭanātha asks himself: if the first chapter is centered upon Arjuna's despondency brought about by an out-of-place affection (*asthānasneha*), then why is the lord's teaching focused on the methods (*yoga*) of action, knowledge and devotion (*apṛṣṭakarmayogajñānayogabhaktiyogādiviṣayaṃ śāstram*)?[95] It does not seem appropriate to offer such an instruction, given that what the *bhagavat* will reveal is a content that requires ascending degrees of secrecy (*cāyaṃ guhyaguhyataraguhyatamaprakāro 'rthaḥ sahasopadeṣṭum ayuktaḥ*). This becomes evident in subsequent passages of the poem, i.e., at 2.18d[96] and 2.37d,[97] where the lord emphasizes that Arjuna must engage in battle. To this objection Veṅkaṭanātha replies by reverting to *BhG* 2.7 (BhG1 2000, 72). He argues that though the expression "what is best" (*yac chreyaḥ*) is indeterminate, yet Arjuna is by now a *bhakta* consecrated to his *guru*-god, and thus it must be inferred that he has the desire to know *Brahman* (*paramaniśśreyasaparyantajijñāsopapatteḥ*). This is why the lord offers him his sublime teaching. Even the imperative form "fight" (*yudhyasva*; *BhG* 2.18d) must be understood as a means to achieve the supreme goal. For this reason, it is correct (*yukta*) to undertake the teaching. Veṅkaṭanātha then proceeds to comment upon Rāmānuja's *bhāṣya ad* 2.10:[98]

> To [highlight] the suitability for mockery [the pronoun] *tam* is recalled, and [Rāmānuja consequently] says *evam*, etc. [. . .]. In such case there is no good reason—such as injustice or defeat—to withdraw from the war. On the other hand, becoming an object of mockery [is something that] happens when an undertaken enterprise is abandoned without reason. This is the idea [. . .]. Conversely, since he (= Kṛṣṇa) is the lord of the sense faculties, having agitated the valiant Arjuna, with a hint of laughter he revealed to him his teaching so as to benefit the whole universe. . . . since mockery (*prahāsa*) is legitimate when amusement (*parihāsa*) is its purpose [. . .].

It is noteworthy that Veṅkaṭanātha links mockery to amusement, thus skillfully relating it to the notion of divine play (*līlā*). His analysis leads to an appreciation of Kṛṣṇa's ease and grace toward Arjuna:[99] "[. . .] Therefore, the freshness and ease of the [expression] *prahasann iva,* is [the prelude to] an effortless speech whose majestic meaning is hidden in the cave of the conclusion of all revealed texts (= the *Upaniṣads*). The object of the word *idam* are the sentences of the glorious lord that are about to be uttered. Moreover, by means of what is indicated he (= Rāmānuja) alludes to what is meant by [the expression] 'mocking [sentence].'" The above passage reiterates the theme of Kṛṣṇa's otherworldly naturalness/effortlessness. His *prahasann iva* reveals the god's graceful *līlā,* his privileged way of communicating himself to his confused disciple and bringing about his spiritual renewal:[100]

> Indeed, since the verse *aśocyān* (2.11) also bears a shadow of mockery, its aim is to draw attention to the meaning of the teaching. Simply introducing the text from "Never, indeed, I was not . . ." (*na tv evāham,* 2.12) does not display the nature of a direct, [benefic] instruction. This is what has been said [by Rāmānuja]. In other words, here the verse *aśocyān* is the content of *prahasann iva,* and *na tv evāham* is the meaning of the word *idam* [. . .].

Dvaita

The Dvaita school of Vedānta emerged between the thirteenth and fourteenth centuries thanks to the works of Madhva, also known as Ānandatīrtha (1198–1277 or 1238–1317; Sharma 1981, 77–79).[101] Besides presenting a dualist axiology and a method of realization based on devotion, the textual production of Dvaita authors addresses the refutation of Śaṅkara's nondualism. Madhva wrote the *Gītābhāṣya,* which like Śaṅkara's *BhGBh,* begins *ad* 2.10. He doesn't gloss on Kṛṣṇa's *prahasann iva,* however, possibly because he took its meaning to be self-evident. After Madhva comes an early stage of development of dualist writings that culminates in the "standardization of Dvaita thought" (Sharma 1981, 235) under the multifarious genius of Jaya Tīrtha.

Jaya Tīrtha

Jaya Tīrtha (possibly 1340–1388; Sharma 1981, 245) was a wide-ranging author who won the title of *ṭīkācārya* for his *Nyāyasudhā,* a highly sophisticated subcommentary on Madhva's *magnum opus*

Anuvyākhyāna. Jaya Tīrtha also wrote the *Prameyadīpikā*, "The Lantern on the Knowable [Principle]," a subcommentary on Madhva's *Gītābhāṣya*[102] which also begins *ad* 2.10. Commenting on 2.11 (BhG1 2000, 80), he says that Madhva condensed the *BhG* verses from 1.1 to 2.11 in the *incipit* of his work since their content is crystal-clear. Still, an objector (*pūrvapakṣin*) raises a question: as neither *dharma* nor any principle (*tattva*) is dealt with in this part of the text (*BhG* 1.1–2.11) why is it included in the body of the *BhG*? To this the *Prameyadīpikā* answers by saying that the *BhG* is keen to present the context in which Kṛṣṇa offered his salvific teaching to Arjuna: therefore, there is no inconsistency in including it.

Arjuna's delusion and attachment—his affection (*sneha*) toward masters, companions, and relatives (*bāndhavādiviṣayo moho*)—takes the form of this false conception (*mithyāpratyaya*): "They are mine! I am their own! They will die because of me! How could I live without them? I will be afflicted by sin; in addition, victory is doubtful!" (*mamaite, aham eteṣām, ete ca mannimittaṃ naṅkṣyanti, katham etair vinā 'haṃ bhaveyam? pāpaṃ ca me bhaviṣyati, jayaś ca sandigdhaḥ*). Being caught in the net of these feelings, Arjuna is a victim of despondency, which can be interpreted as a weakness of the mind resulting from the anguish generated by bewilderment (*viṣādo nāma mohanimittāc chokād yanmanodaurbalyam, yasmin sati sarvavyāpāroparamo bhavati*).

Jaya Tīrtha then raises another question that pertains to *BhG* 2.10: Why is it that the hero's despondency occurs just when the battle is about to begin? Indeed, Arjuna was all along aware that in the Kauravas army could be found many of his masters, friends, and relatives. And he knew that the war would cause enormous losses.[103] To this, Jaya Tīrtha replies by saying that though it is well known that when one recollects a great offence suffered from a relative or friend the original rage reemerges, in the case of a sensitive person like Arjuna such rage tends to soften giving way to one's affection for kith and kin, out of which arises delusion. Nonetheless, as Arjuna is ultimately a sage his imprisonment in the net of *moha* is said to be minimal.[104]

Rāghavendra

The *dvaitin* Rāghavendra (c. 1640) wrote a *BhG* gloss called *Arthasaṃgraha* or "The Compendium of the Meaning." *Ad* 2.10, he offers a brief comment on *prahasann iva* (BhG2 2001, 71): "The word *iva* (like, nearly, almost) in *prahasann iva* suggests a laugh, revealing the expressions in [Arjuna's] sentences that are objects of mockery" (*prahasann iveti parihāsakaravākyoktiddyotakahāsasya sūcanāyevaśabdaḥ*).

In his gloss *ad* 2.11 (BhG2 2001, 75), the interpretation of the conjunction *ca* in *gatāsūn agatāsūṃś ca* is also worth mentioning since Rāghavendra argues that it should be read as *iva*: "The [conjunction] *ca* implies comparison [as expressed by the indeclinable] *iva*. Therefore, dead persons are just like those who are not dead" (*gatāsūn āsannavināśān agatāsūn ivety upamārthaś cakāraḥ*).

Dvaitādvaita

The school of Dvaitādvaita ("duality and non-duality" or "duality in non-duality"), also known as Bhedābheda ("difference and non-difference"), had the *vaiṣṇava* Nimbārka (twelfth to thirteenth century) as its chief exponent. His *magnum opus* is the *Vedāntapārijātasaurabha*, a short commentary on the *Brahmasūtras*. Although he did not write any commentary on the *BhG*, the Dvaitādvaita interpretation of the poem was later developed by Keśava Kaśmīrī Bhaṭṭācārya (Uskokov 2018, 2–4).

Keśava Kaśmīrī Bhaṭṭācārya

The Kashmirian Keśava Kaśmīrī Bhaṭṭācārya (or Bhaṭṭa, c. 1510) is the author of the *Tattvaprakāśikā* or "[The Gloss] Illuminating Reality." It is noteworthy that he did not follow the vulgate version of the *BhG* but a text of 745 verses that differs even from the *BhGk* (Saha 2017, 270). This sophisticated gloss of Keśava Kaśmīrī is one more proof of how the exegesis of the *BhG* was widely diffused among the various intellectual traditions and all the Vedānta schools (Clémentin-Ojha 2011, 429). Some of Keśava Kaśmīrī's interpretations were later adopted by other commentators, such as Nīlakāṇṭha Caturdhara and Madhusūdana Sarasvatī.

Keśava Kaśmīrī says that the *BhG*'s first chapter is essential in order to learn the causes of Arjuna's despondency since the teaching of the *bhagavat* that unfolds from 2.11 is meant to dispel the hero's anguish and delusion (BhG2 2001, 3).[105] In commenting on *BhG* 2.7

(BhG2 2001, 65), the *Tattvaprakāśikā* focuses on the meaning of the word *kārpaṇya* quoting a passage from the *Bṛhadāraṇyaka Upaniṣad* (1.4.15, 3.8.10)[106] that is most likely the source of Madhusūdana's similar observations. The *kṛpaṇa* is someone who does not know his/her own nature nor the qualities of the "imperishable" (*akṣara*) supreme being[107] and who is unable to tolerate even the smallest loss of wealth and goods. Due to this kind of weakness (*kārpaṇya*), Arjuna's discrimination is obscured, and he is incapable of finding any reason for fighting against his own people. With his intellect darkened by delusion and utterly confused with regard to his duty, Arjuna resorts to the omniscient lord who is completely free from defects.[108]

In the opening line of the *Tattvaprakāśikā ad BhG* 2.10 (BhG2 2001, 70), we find an original insertion. The following thought is attributed to Dhṛtarāṣṭra: "If Arjuna will abandon the battlefield, my sons will live happily." Saṃjaya points out to Dhṛtarāṣṭra that it is totally improper for a king born in the heroic lineage of Bharata to think in this way.[109] In the first part of the *scholium*, Keśava Kaśmīrī quotes the expression *prahasann iva*. The gloss presents the construction (*anvaya*) of the passage, that is, that Arjuna was despondent in between the two armies and that the glorious lord, with a hint of laughter, spoke to him. Then Keśava Kaśmīrī observes:[110]

> But this does not fit with the son of Pāṇḍu (= Arjuna), who is celebrated as a [great] warrior. The expression *prahasann iva* has been said in order to generate rage [in him], caused by shame. It is not proper to use Arjuna as a means for mockery, because the glorious lord—who is ready to destroy all the [enemies'] armies—being a *guru* and having accepted [him as his disciple], is a beneficial instructor ready to make him turn again toward his own duty. Nonetheless, such speech is intended to produce eligibility for the knowledge of reality by eliminating all pride, thanks to the strength of such an understanding. This is the purport of the word *iva*.

Once again, the idea is that Kṛṣṇa's hint of laughter has a therapeutic function and is an expression of his grace meant to trigger Arjuna's discrimination (*viveka*). The lord's *prahasann iva* is like a bitter medicine, a means resorted to in order to hurt the hero's pride, in a way similar to *BhG* 2.3 when Kṛṣṇa tells him to stop behaving like a eunuch. The context recalls the episode narrated in the *MBh*'s fourth book: if at the court of King Virāṭa Arjuna was under the guise of Bṛhannaḍā / Bṛhannalā, a eunuch dance teacher, here Kṛṣṇa is telling him that it is time to dismiss such role and behave like a warrior. According to Keśava Kaśmīrī, the lord's hint of laughter is not meant to mock Arjuna since this would be incongruous. Having just accepted him as disciple, it would be inappropriate for the *guru* to laugh at the despondency of his *śiṣya*.

The gloss *ad BhG* 2.11 opens with a series of quotations from the *śruti* and the *smṛti* in order to throw light on a science (*vidyā*) whose subjects are the nature and qualities of the supreme *Brahman*, denoted by the words Nārāyaṇa, Hari, Vāsudeva, the unchanging Being whose nature is both different and nondifferent from everything, the all-pervasive Self of all (BhG2 2001, 72). Such a science removes all bewilderment, anguish, and delusion.

Finally, Keśava Kaśmīrī observes that Arjuna's sorrow is summarized in verse 1.31,[111] where our hero states that without Bhīṣma, Droṇa and his other teachers, friends, and relatives there is no point in living or gaining the kingdom. The *Tattvaprakāśikā* defines Arjuna's despondency as dullness or foolishness (*mūrkhatva*), even though the words he utters in verses 1.36,[112] 1.44[113] and 2.5[114] disclose a wisdom of sorts, as indicated by the phrase *prajñāvādāṃś ca bhāṣase*. However, Arjuna's arguments as well as his superficial wisdom are ultimately useless.

The *nimbārkī* perspective—which is specifically kṛṣṇaite—emphasizes devotion as the means to achieve liberation. The complete surrender (*prapatti*) of oneself to lord Kṛṣṇa, who is perceived as inseparable from his consort Rādhā, is the foremost among the five forms of *sādhanā*[115] recognized by this school. Catherine Clémentin-Ojha rightly notes the importance of *prapatti* in the Nimbārka *sampradāya* (2011, 442): "There are broadly two types of *sādhanā* or spiritual disciplines in the sect. The first is the complete surrender directly to Kṛṣṇa (*prapatti* or *śaraṇāgati*) or through dedication to the *guru* (*gurūpasatti*), which can be adopted by all, irrespective of birth and social status." In the *BhG*, *prapatti* and *gurūpasatti* are one and the same since in Kṛṣṇa the figures of the supreme lord and of the *guru* coincide: just as Arjuna's surrender is understood to be the ultimate form of devotion (*parābhakti*), Kṛṣṇa's hint of laughter is the anticipation of the outpouring of his boundless grace, of his sweetest nectar (*mādhuryarasa*).

Śuddhādvaita

Another *vaiṣṇava* interpretation of Vedānta was developed by the Śuddhādvaita ("pure non-dualism") school whose main author was Vallabha (fifteenth to sixteenth century). He doesn't seem to have written a commentary on the *BhG* though he focused on our poem in an independent work (i.e., the *Tattvārthadīpikā,* also known as *Tattvadīpanibandha*) together with his own gloss *Prakāśa* (Bhatt 1949, 131). Successors of Vallabha such as Viṭṭhalanātha (1518–1588) glossed the *BhG* or some verses of it in works like the *Gītārthavivaraṇa* together with the *Gītātātparya,* the *Nyāsādeśa* on *BhG* 18.66 and the *Gītāhetunirṇaya* (Saha 2017, 271; see also Bhatt 1949, 131–34).

Vallabha

The fifth grandson in Vallabha's lineage was another Vallabha (seventeenth century). He wrote an independent commentary on the *BhG*: the *Tattvadīpikā* or "The Lantern on Reality" (Saha 2017, 272). The gloss *ad BhG* 2.10 is as brief as it is notable. Having refused to fight, Arjuna sits silent on the floor of his chariot. The *Tattvadīpikā* asks:[116] "After that what happened? [The lord] 'said to him.' With this idea in mind: 'Alas, how great is such cowardice due to the ignorance of the reality of the Self.' Here the [lord's] hint of laughter is adequate since he (= Arjuna) is greatly virtuous. This is the meaning." Arjuna is said to be *dharmiṣṭha,* "greatly virtuous," even though his behavior is not virtuous. It should be noted that in the final part of the first chapter and at the beginning of the second, Kṛṣṇa addresses Arjuna with his usual heroic epithets. Thus in *BhG* 2.3 we witness the contrast of Arjuna behaving like a eunuch and Kṛṣṇa nonetheless calling him *paraṃtapa,* "scorcher of the enemies." This is understood to be a teaching strategy.[117]

Acintyabhedābheda

The last section of our survey on the *BhG*'s commentarial literature concerns another branch of Vedānta, the Acintyabhedābheda ("inconceivable difference and non-difference"), intimately linked to *gauḍīya* Vaiṣṇavism and philosophically indebted to both Madhva and Rāmānuja. Apparently, the initiator of this school was the Beṅgālī saint Caitanya (1486–1534).

Viśvanātha Cakravartī Ṭhākura

The first *gauḍīya* commentary on the *BhG* is the *Sārārthavarṣiṇīṭīkā* or "The Gloss Pouring the Meaning in [its] Essence," of Viśvanātha Cakravartī Ṭhākura (1626–1708?), a Beṅgālī author active in Vṛndāvana (Burton 2000, 9–29). At the end of his gloss *ad BhG* 2.7, Kṛṣṇa is said to scold Arjuna (BhG8 1966, 30):[118] "'If you, considering yourself a sage, keep on refuting my words, then why should I continue to speak?' At this point [Arjuna] says: 'I am your disciple! From now on, I shall no more reject [your words].' This is the idea." Then, without commenting on *BhG* 2.9, the *Sārārthavarṣiṇīṭīkā* glosses *BhG* 2.10 (BhG8 1966, 33):[119] "[Kṛṣṇa] then mocked him in a friendly mood [and said to Arjuna]: 'Alas, such lack of discrimination has indeed taken hold of you!' Thus the lord soaked him in the sea of shame by manifesting the inappropriateness [of his behavior]. [Anyhow], on this occasion his laughing at [Arjuna] who had reached the condition of disciple, is inappropriate. Therefore, the meaning [of *prahasann iva*] is 'curling the lower lip and hiding the laughter.'" Again we find the idea of a gentle mockery caused by Arjuna's inappropriate (*anaucitya*) behavior. Even for Viśvanātha the lord's hint of laughter is a means to trigger Arjuna's discrimination and thus an instrument of Kṛṣṇa's grace. He denies that Kṛṣṇa laughs at Arjuna out of scorn since he has accepted him as his disciple and a *guru* can never laugh at his disciple. This is why Kṛṣṇa's laughter is hidden by a contraction of his lower lip. And such hidden laughter is a manifestation of Kṛṣṇa's love for Arjuna, as the following passage confirms (BhG8 1966, 33):[120] "Even though by [resorting to the epithet] "Hṛṣīkeśa" love had indeed inspired Arjuna's words, it is now [Kṛṣṇa] who, out of love, controls Arjuna's mind being his benefactor: this is the idea. Indeed, "in between the two armies" the glorious lord has equally witnessed—together with the two armies—the anguish and the awakening of Arjuna. This is the meaning." In his gloss *ad BhG* 2.11, Viśvanātha does not add anything relevant to our subject.

Baladeva Vidyābhūṣaṇa

Another important *gauḍīya* author is Baladeva Vidyābhūṣaṇa (1700–1793?), a later follower of Caitanya who, along with a commentary on the *Brahmasūtras* known as *Govindabhāṣya,* wrote a commentary on the *Gītā,* the *Gītābhūṣaṇa* or "The Ornament of the *Gītā.*" *Ad* 2.7, while elaborating on Viśvanātha's commentary, he quotes some passages from the *śruti*[121] and emphasizes the need to become the disciple of a master. Baladeva interprets the word *kārpaṇya* as meaning "not knowing *Brahman*" (*abrahmavittva*): this is the problem that afflicts Arjuna and prevents him from accomplishing his duty. His interpretation of *BhG* 2.10 follows that of Viśvanātha (BhG8 1966, 33):[122]

> [. . .] To Arjuna who had spoken in an inappropriate way being immersed in the sea of doubt and who was in anguish, [the lord,] smiling in a friendly mood, [said]: "Alas, is this your discrimination . . . ?" This is the meaning. [The word] *iva* [means that,] since at that moment he (= Arjuna) had reached discipleship, then a [mocking] laugh was improper. This is why the meaning is "with his lower lip trembling a bit." In order to point out that Arjuna's anguish and the [consequent] teaching of the glorious lord can be experienced by all, [the verse states] this: "Between the two armies."

Through the words "who had spoken in an inappropriate way being immersed in the sea of doubt" (*anaucityabhāṣitvena trapāsindhau nimajjayan ity arthaḥ*), the inappropriateness (*anaucitya*) that occasions Kṛṣṇa's *prahasann iva* is once again emphasized. Baladeva's understanding of *prahasann iva* as "with his lower lip trembling a bit" is meant to point out that it should be interpreted as a sympathetic smile aimed at dispelling Arjuna's anguish (*śoka*) and delusion (*moha*).

Concluding Remarks

Throughout these pages we have provided an analysis of the main commentarial readings of the *BhG*'s *prahasann iva,* placing it in its larger context. Though some commentators lack a specific interpretation of the formula, nonetheless all of them help us to reconstruct the prewar setting and lay the ground for a more in-depth understanding. Despite the difficulty in systematizing the topic, we think that a useful overview of the possible explanations of *prahasann iva* is offered by Veṅkaṭanātha in his *Tātparyacandrikā,* where he sketches four interpretative keys:

1. Mockery: whoever abandons without reason an action that he/she has undertaken becomes an object of derision;

2. A seeming mockery in view of a superior end: Arjuna is mortally anguished and Kṛṣṇa, through his hint of laughter, reveals the *BhG* for his benefit and the benefit of the whole world;

3. Derision and mockery are impossible since Arjuna has surrendered himself to Kṛṣṇa: *prahasann iva* introduces an effortless and sublime speech, replete with the meanings that are hidden in the *Upaniṣads*;

4. *BhG* 2.10 must be understood in the light of 2.11, which also implies a shade of mirth along with a shade of derision: both are needed in order to shake Arjuna out of his *moha* and prepare him to assimilate the teaching and achieve discrimination.

We agree with Ānanda Giri that the function of 2.10 is that of being a connective link (*sambandha*) between Arjuna's self-surrendering to Kṛṣṇa and the latter's flow of love through his *upadeśa.* The end of 2.9 (*tuṣṇīm babhūva ha*) is the climax of Arjuna's passivity, mirroring his utter despondency. This extreme condition symbolized by his having no more words to say is broken by the opening of Kṛṣṇa's mouth and the beginning of his instruction in 2.11: *prahasann iva* stands right in the middle and operates the passage from the hero's deluded muteness to the lord's enlightened word. The dramatic tension at the center of the battlefield is eased by the reassuring sign of Kṛṣṇa's hint of laughter.

If in verses 2.2–3 Kṛṣṇa had openly mocked Arjuna for behaving like a eunuch, in verse 2.10 mockery—if at all present—is utilized by Kṛṣṇa as a means to bring about Arjuna's transformation, it being motivated by his love for his *śiṣya*. The lord's hint of laughter comes after Arjuna has surrendered at his feet as his pupil (2.7d; *śiṣyas te 'haṃ śādhi māṃ tvāṃ prapannam*), a decisive move that had not yet taken place in 2.2–3. From 2.7, what is pivotal in the relationship between Kṛṣṇa and Arjuna is the bond of *bhakti* that unites them. The mercy of the *guru*-god is contained in his *prahasann iva*, his *upadeśa* being its natural consequence. The very moment in which Kṛṣṇa opens his mouth and manifests his hint of laughter is the veritable καιρός that signals the rescue of his *śiṣya* from the dreadful quagmire of delusion and sorrow.

Of the authors we have scrutinized, most of the Advaita Vedāntins and Kashmirian commentators interpret *prahasann iva* as the expression of Kṛṣṇa's benevolent attitude toward his disciple, despite the latter's *anaucitya* or inappropriate behavior. A second group of exegetes that is linked to the so-called *vaiṣṇava* school of Vedānta is more diversified in its interpretation: it oscillates between an apparently harsher mockery—meant to shake Arjuna by soaking him in the sea of shame so as to trigger his metanoia—and a more positive attitude that comes close to the understanding of the majority of the *advatins*. The gloss of Madhusūdana Sarasvatī, a nondualist thinker devoted to Kṛṣṇa, can be appreciated as operating a kind of synthesis. This is important since the various interpretative options we have reviewed, some of which are striking in their psychological depth, are not to be regarded as being mutually exclusive.

Having acknowledged the plurality of possible meanings of Kṛṣṇa's *prahasann iva*, for the majority of commentators what is crucial is the recognition that his hint of laughter reveals his grace: even when it is interpreted as derision it still expresses the lord's *prasāda* since the intention (*saṃkalpa*) that guides the *guru* is the ultimate good of his *śiṣya*. In the end, Kṛṣṇa's *prahasann iva* must be appreciated as the divine sign that instantly relieves Arjuna from the ignorance in which he is trapped.

Chapter 3

On *prahasann iva* and *hasann iva* in the *Mahābhārata* and *Rāmāyaṇa*

We now come to an evaluation of the occurrences of *prahasann iva* and *hasann iva* within the *Mahābhārata* (*MBh*) and Vālmīki's *Rāmāyaṇa* (*Rām*).[1] This textual survey aims at appreciating the meaning of these expressions in their specific settings, so as to effectively compare them with the *prahasann iva* of the *BhG* and arrive at a comprehensive understanding of the latter within the epic milieu.

Situated in the *Bhīṣmaparvan* which is the narrative pivot of the *MBh*, the *BhG* is recognized as the veritable heart of the epic. Its structure in eighteen *adhyāyas* reflects the structure of the *MBh* in eighteen *parvans* (eighteen are also the *akṣauhiṇīs*,[2] that is, the armies that confront each other on the Kurukṣetra field—eleven on the Kaurava side, seven on the Pāṇḍava side—and eighteen are the days of war).[3] Though the *BhG* circulated as an independent work from an early date, and as we have seen in chapters 1 and 2 it is often treated as a stand-alone text, yet its epic background is essential. The *BhG* is by all standards an integral part of the *MBh* and one must explore the latter with care since it matters to the internal development of the *BhG* itself, the complexity of the textual layers of the epic notwithstanding (Ježić 1979). Indeed, the *BhG* needs to be interpreted within the context of the *MBh* not only because it constitutes its highest reflection on ultimate realities and the aims of human life[4] but also because the key to its full comprehension is to be found in the epic as a whole (van Buitenen 1981, 1–6). The *BhG* being the theological peak of the

MBh, its *prahasann iva* is to be regarded as the most significant occurrence of this formulaic diction in the entire epic corpus.

The *BhG* bears important connections with the theoretical (Sāṃkhya-Yoga) and devotional, *bhakti*-oriented sections of the *MBh*, presupposing the epic setting in which it is embedded. We find evidence of this in the *Sanatsujātīya* of the *Udyogaparvan* (5.42–45) and in the *Mokṣadharma* of the *Śāntiparvan* (12.174–365; containing the *Yogakathana* section, 12.289–306, and the *Nārāyaṇīya* section, 12.321–339), as well as in the other *Gītā*s of the epic, first and foremost in the *Anugītā* or *Uttaragītā* (14.16–51).[5] It is noteworthy that the central teaching of the *BhG*, that is, action performed without any expectation of its fruits (*niṣkāmakarman*), is already outlined in a dialogue between Yudhiṣṭhira, Bhīma, and Draupadī, which occupies nine chapters of the *Vanaparvan* (3.27–35). Even the glorious theophany described in the eleventh chapter of the *BhG* finds several correlates in the *MBh*, where various sages and heroes have the privilege of experiencing divine visions. Thus Arjuna witnesses the theophany of Śiva who had taken the form of a wild hunter (*kirāta*; *MBh* 3.40), Bhīma has the vision of the ancient form of Hanumān (*MBh* 3.146–150) and Aśvatthāman, who is about to carry out the night massacre, experiences the terrifying appearances of Kṛṣṇa and Śiva (*MBh* 10.6–7). Moreover, Kṛṣṇa reveals his eternal form to Bhīṣma (*MBh* 12.51.3–10) and in a dialogue between Kṛṣṇa and Uttaṅka (*MBh* 14.52–53) the former manifests his glory to the latter (*MBh* 14.54.1–3). In the *Udyogaparvan* (5.129.1–16), Kṛṣṇa reveals his cosmic form to the terrified Kauravas and this is a prelude to Arjuna's vision in the eleventh *adhyāya* of the *BhG* (Piano 1994, 28–34).

There are several reasons behind the reading of the *BhG* as an independent work. In the first place, it is a short and manageable text, and its language is simple and easily accessible. Its narrative fabric is grounded in a literary *topos* that is shared by all philosophical and religious traditions: the *BhG* is a dialogue (*saṃvāda*) between a *guru* and a *śiṣya*, a divine teacher and his disciple (i.e., between god and man). As Śaṅkara himself explains in the introduction to his *BhG* commentary using Arjuna as model (*nimittīkṛtya*), the message of the text is universal since it is addressed to the human being as such who is faced with a terrible crisis. In addition, according to the vast majority of the Hindu traditions the *BhG* offers plural solutions to the human predicament. This is why the poem is taken as a paradigm of salvific instruction, being capable of speaking directly to each and every soul. It would be impossible to achieve the same effectiveness by approaching the epic of the *MBh* in its entirety.[6] As a counterfactual example, it must be noted that in the Indian exegetical tradition there exists only one commentary on the whole *MBh* (i.e., Nīlakāṇṭha Caturdhara's *Bhāratabhāvadīpa*).

As seen in chapter 2, all *BhG* commentators belong to schools that search for a definitive solution to the problem of suffering. Being viewed as the essence of the *MBh*, the *BhG* was selected as one of the fundamental texts to be scrutinized by all schools of Vedānta, together with the *Upaniṣad*s and the *Brahmasūtra*s: these three are regarded as the *prasthānatraya* or the "triad of the points of departure." In the colophons to the eighteen *adhyāya*s of the *BhG* one finds the formula *śrīmadbhagavadgītāsūpaniṣatsu*, i.e., "[. . .] in that *Upaniṣad* [= secret teaching] that is the *Bhagavadgītā* [. . .]." Given its immense prestige, the *BhG* is explicitly equated to an *Upaniṣad*, thus elevating it to the rank of *śruti*.[7]

Before focusing attention on the two classical epics (*itihāsa*), it is useful to go through a quick overview of the *Upaniṣad*s themselves, which represent a fundamental source for both the *MBh* and *Rām*. Herein, the occurrences of root √*has*[8] are scarce. In *Chāndogya Upaniṣad* 3.17.3 we find the present indicative *hasati* in a list of verbs associated with the recitations performed by a Brahmin during the Soma sacrifice, which are preceded by a sacrificial consecration (3.17.1) and preparatory rites (3.17.2). *Chāndogya Upaniṣad* 3.17.6 states that these instructions were taught by Ghora Āṅgirasa to Kṛṣṇa, the son of Devakī (*tad haitad ghora āṅgirasaḥ kṛṣṇāya devakīputrāyoktvovāca*; Olivelle 1998, 212; see also Brodbeck 2018, 202–3 and Ježić 2009, 221). In addition, in *Jaiminīya Upaniṣad Brāhmaṇa* 3.25.8 there is a similar sacrificial context where we find the occurrence of the words *hasaḥ* "laughter," *krīḷā* [= *krīḍā*] "play," and *mithunam* "sexual congress" (*haso me krīḷā me mithunaṃ me*; Oertel 1896, 185).

A passage that deserves mention is that of *Bṛhadāraṇyaka Upaniṣad* 4.3.13, where Yājñavalkya instructs King Janaka on the nature of dream: "Travelling in sleep to places high and low, the god creates many a visible form—now dallying with women, now laughing, now seeing frightful things" (*svapnānta uccāvacam īyamāno rūpāṇi devaḥ kurute bahūni | uteva stribhiḥ saha modamāno jakṣad utevāpi bhayāni paśyan ||* Olivelle 1998, 112–13). Here the present participle *jakṣad*, "laughing," which is followed by *iva* (*utevāpi* = *uta iva api*, where *uta* is merely a conjunction), comes from √*jakṣ* "to laugh," which is the reduplicated form of √*has*. The subject of the sentence is *devaḥ*, "the god," that Śaṅkara in his commentary to the *Bṛhadāraṇyaka Upaniṣad* interprets as the *ātman*. Significantly, Śaṅkara glosses *jakṣad . . . iva* as *hasann iva* and says that it is the self-luminous *ātman* (*svayaṃ jyotir ātmā*) that exhibits this hint of laughter (Śāstrī 1986, 321).[9]

In the late *Mahā Upaniṣad* 3.35, *hasanti* refers to some family members who laugh at a man who behaves like a mad person (*hasanty unmattakam iva naram*; Śāstrī 1970, 433). Finally, *hasati* in *Yogaśikhā Upaniṣad* 6.67 is inserted in a list of verbs used to describe the physical and emotional behavior of an enlightened person, all connected with laugh, mirth, playfulness, and delight (*hasaty ullasati prītyā krīḍate modate tadā*; Śāstrī 1970, 472). What emerges is the scanty use of the root √*has* if compared to its frequency in the epics.[10] Furthermore, there is no occurrence of root √*has* with prefix *pra-*. All in all, the theme of smile/laughter did not receive special attention in the Vedic period, its emergence being linked to the development of epic theology and the *bhakti* movements centered upon divine grace (*kṛpā, prasāda*).

The Occurrences of *prahasann iva* and *hasann iva* in the *Mahābhārata* and *Rāmāyaṇa*

When one surveys the *MBh* with a view to find all the occurrences of *prahasann iva* and *hasann iva*, what appears is that it is a frequent formulaic expression, there being a total of eighty-four occurrences of *prahasann iva* and thirty-nine occurrences of *hasann iva*.[11] The *Bhīṣmaparvan*, which comprises the *BhG* (6.23–40), besides *BhG* 2.10 (6.24.10) displays eight other occurrences of *prahasann iva*, whereas *hasann iva* is found four times. The *Droṇaparvan* stands out as the book with the highest numbers: twenty-eight occurrences of *prahasann iva* and twelve of *hasann iva*. From the tenth *parvan*, the *Sauptikaparvan*, up to the end of the *MBh*, the use of *prahasann iva* diminishes considerably—fourteen occurrences—and *hasann iva* is found only three times.

On the whole, there are one hundred and twenty-three occurrences of *prahasann iva* + *hasann iva* in the *MBh*. In particular, there are forty in the *Droṇaparvan*, thirteen in the *Bhīṣmaparvan* and the *Karṇaparvan*, ten in the *Ādiparvan* and the *Āraṇyakaparvan*, and nine in the *Śalyaparvan*. Table 3.1 shows their distribution within the *MBh* eighteen *parvans*.

Table 3.1. Occurrences of *prahasann iva* and *hasann iva* in the *Mahābhārata*

Parvan	*prahasann iva*	*hasann iva*
1. *Ādiparvan*	9	1
2. *Sabhāparvan*	1	1
3. *Āraṇyakaparvan*	8	2
4. *Virāṭaparvan*	4	/
5. *Udyogaparvan*	4	1
6. *Bhīṣmaparvan*	9	4
7. *Droṇaparvan*	28	12
8. *Karṇaparvan*	5	8
9. *Śalyaparvan*	2	7
10. *Sauptikaparvan*	/	2
11. *Strīparvan*	/	/
12. *Śāntiparvan*	6	/
13. *Anuśāsanaparvan*	1	/
14. *Āśvamedhikaparvan*	5	1
15. *Āśramavāsikaparvan*	/	/
16. *Mausalaparvan*	1	/
17. *Mahāprasthānikaparvan*	/	/
18. *Svargārohaṇaparvan*	1	/
Total	84	39

According to Sellmer (2015, 198), in the *MBh* present participles[12] appear most frequently at the beginning of even *pāda*s—as in *BhG* 2.10b—and among these participles *prahasan* is one of the commonest. As a matter of fact, of the 123 occurrences of *prahasann iva* and *hasann iva* the majority of them are found at the end of *pāda*s and especially at the end of the second or at the end of the fourth one.

To complete the picture, in Vālmīki's *Rām* we find thirteen instances of *prahasann iva* and only one of *hasann iva*. Table 3.2 shows how they are distributed within the *Rām*'s seven *kāṇḍa*s.

One might ask: If the expressions *prahasann iva* and *hasann iva* are so frequent in the *MBh*, doesn't this diminish their relevance?[13] The answer to this is that their frequency is counterbalanced by the fact that there are different applications of *prahasann iva*/*hasann iva*, that is, at least three different employments. Besides, one must keep in mind the remarkable multivalence of *prahasann iva*. The hint of laughter of *BhG* 2.10 recapitulates the main usages that we will be looking at, constituting the quintessential *prahasann iva* just as the *Bhagavadgītā* is the quintessence of the *Mahābhārata*: it simultaneously incorporates pure grace—undoubtedly its primary meaning—irony/mockery, and easiness, which links it to the notion of *līlā*.

Table 3.2. Occurrences of *prahasann iva* and *hasann iva* in the *Rāmāyaṇa*

Kāṇḍa	*prahasann iva*	*hasann iva*
1. *Bālakāṇḍa*	2	/
2. *Ayodhyākāṇḍa*	2	1
3. *Araṇyakāṇḍa*	1	/
4. *Kiṣkindhākāṇḍa*	2	/
5. *Sundarakāṇḍa*	1	/
6. *Yuddhakāṇḍa*	1	/
7. *Uttarakāṇḍa*	4	/
Total	13	1

On the Different Uses of *prahasann iva* and *hasann iva* in the *Mahābhārata* and *Rāmāyaṇa*

When the subject is a hero, be he positive or negative, human or divine—such as Duryodhana, Bhīṣma, Droṇa, Yudhiṣṭhira, Bhīma, Karṇa, Śiva, Indra and of course Kṛṣṇa and Arjuna—he exhibits a hint of laughter that indicates the extraordinary ease with which he accomplishes his martial deeds, as if they were a child's play.[14] A second salient use is when the hint of laughter blossoms on the face of deities, sages, and *guru*s since it indicates their grace and words of wisdom. A third typology is when the two participles are used to express mockery, with varying degrees of intensity, or even delight and surprise. Finally, *prahasann iva* and *hasann iva* are used in ambiguous or seemingly incongruous situations, where the reason that prompts them is less recognizable. We will illustrate significant examples of each of these applications, focusing attention on the *prahasann iva*/*hasann iva* of deities—and among them of Kṛṣṇa—as it is typologically closer to *BhG* 2.10. Following each survey of the *MBh*, we will consider one analogous passage from the *Rām*.

Prahasann iva and *hasann iva* as Markers of Heroic Ease

The first semantic nuance of *prahasann iva* and *hasann iva* concerns a hero's ease—that is, the capacity of various *kṣatriya*s to accomplish difficult tasks with no effort whatsoever. In the *MBh*, this is the widest use of our formulaic diction. What differentiates these types of occurrences from those treated in the following sections is that here *prahasann iva* and *hasann iva* do not precede any locutionary act. In this section we also include instances of a hero's disregard of danger and fear[15] and his involvement in leisure activities such as hunting. With regard to the effortlessness of these *kṣatriya*s in accomplishing their heroic feats, Peter Sloterdijk's (2013, 196) transcultural observations on asceticism and acrobatics are worth quoting: "Acrobatics is involved whenever the aim is to make the impossible seem simple. It is not enough, therefore, to walk the tightrope and perform the *salto mortale* at a great height; the acrobat's decisive message lies in the smile with which he bows after the performance. It speaks even more clearly in the nonchalant hand gesture before his exit, the gesture one could take for a greeting to the upper tiers." We have seen that the theme of ease is especially underlined by some of the commentators of *BhG* 2.10, and this same subject will surface in our assessment of Kṛṣṇa's iconography and devotional literature in the next chapter. Among the seventy-one instances of *prahasann iva* and *hasann iva* as markers of heroic effortlessness and fearlessness that are found in the *MBh* we survey nine of them.[16]

MBh

1) 1.151.7b[17] = while Bhīma is eating the food of a demon (*rākṣasa*), he listens to his threatening words with a hint of laughter (*prahasann iva*); disregarding him, he keeps eating with his back turned on the enemy. The hero's hint of laughter proves his fearlessness and self-confidence.

2) 1.151.14d[18] = a few verses later, Bhīma postpones the attack against the *rākṣasa* and keeps eating his food. Finally, he stands up ready for battle with a hint of laughter (*prahasann iva*) on his face, and with his left hand throws back a tree which the demon had thrown at him in wrath. The effortlessness of Bhīma's deed is emphasized by the reference to his left hand, which is believed to be weaker and impure.

3) 6.49.15d[19] = during the battle, the hero Droṇa exhibits a hint of laughter (*hasann iva*) and with a mighty spear thwarts Dhṛṣṭadyumna's attack three times. The hint of laughter signals Droṇa's strength and ease in contrasting the valiant Dhṛṣṭadyumna, commander-in-chief of the Pāṇḍavas's army.

4) 6.79.48e[20] = Due to a trick, the Madrarāja (i.e., Śalya, Madrī's brother) is forced to fight against the Pāṇḍavas and, with a hint of laughter (*prahasann iva*), wipes out a shower of arrows shot at him by Sahadeva.[21] His hint of laughter sketches the ease with which a great warrior accomplishes a wondrous act, which would be impossible for any ordinary person.

5) 6.107.2d[22] = extremely enraged, with a hint of laughter (*prahasann iva*), Mādhava (i.e., Kṛṣṇa) pierces a demon (*rākṣasa*) with nine arrows. This is a significant occurrence since the hero Kṛṣṇa shows his strength in battle. Again, the emphasis is on the

effortlessness with which a valiant warrior accomplishes a difficult task as if it were a child's play.

6) 7.37.13b[23] = after a brave deed performed by Saubhadra (i.e., Abhimanyu), all members of his army praise him, whereas his enemies say: "You will not escape alive" (7.37.12).[24] While they are saying so, Saubhadra looks at them with a hint of laughter (*prahasann iva*). The hero's attitude indicates his fearlessness and utter disregard of danger.

7) 7.173.48b = this episode takes place following the death of Droṇa, when—as in *BhG* 1.1—Dhṛtarāṣṭra asks Saṃjaya what his sons and the sons of Pāṇḍu have done. At this time, when the Kauravas had nearly been defeated, Arjuna asks Vyāsa to explain to him the vision he had had of a man bright as fire who stood in front of him without touching the ground and who, without using his spear, annihilated all enemies through the radiance of his weapons, while all other warriors thought that such a massacre was being carried out by Arjuna (7.173.1–9). Vyāsa explains that the man who preceded him in battle was none other than the three-eyed Śaṅkara (i.e., Śiva), the ultimate refuge of the universe. He points out that Śiva, when angry, can terrify even divine beings and praises him as Vīrabhadra, in whose form the great god destroyed Dakṣa's sacrifice:[25]

> Then that fearless one, being enraged, struck the [embodied] sacrifice by shooting an arrow with his bow, which screamed loudly. (42) The gods could find no shelter and no peace, so while the great lord was furious the [embodied] sacrifice all of a sudden ran away. (43) Due to the crack of the bowstring all worlds trembled, o Arjuna, and gods and antigods fell down and became his slaves. (44) All waters became rough, the earth shook, the mountains disappeared, and the quarters of the sky and the clouds became dark. (45) The worlds—blind and covered in darkness—were not visible, he destroyed the radiance of all stars together with the sun. (46) Vedic poets—who desire their own good as well as the good of all beings—screamed in terror and searched for peace. (47) [Then] Śaṅkara, with a hint of laughter (*prahasann iva*), attacked Pūṣan and made his teeth fall out while

> he was eating the sacrificial cakes (*puroḍāśa*). (48) Thus the trembling gods came out and bowed down to him, but he again shot a sharp, flaming arrow against them: (49) they then established Rudra's special part of the sacrifice. O king, out of fear the thirty [gods] fell down on earth for shelter. (50)[26]

The fact that the great god Śiva, just before attacking Pūṣan, almost laughs, underlines the extreme ease with which he accomplishes his mighty task.

8) 8.24.94c = throughout this chapter, Duryodhana narrates the myth of the three sky-cities of the antigods (*asura*) that were destroyed by Śiva as Tripurāntaka (Hiltebeitel 1984, 15–21). When the three worlds were tormented by the three *asura*s, Tarakākṣa, Kamalākṣa, and Vidyunmālin, the gods along with Brahmā came to Śiva to win his favor. After honoring him with a hymn and several prayers, Śiva agreed to help them to remove the cause of their distress (8.24.1–56). Śiva, however, told them that he would be unable to kill the three enemies on his own and thus sought the assistance of all the gods who agreed to give him half of their strength: thus Śiva became known as Mahādeva, the great god. Armed with bow and arrows, he assured them he would kill the *asura*s, piercing them with just one dart, and asked the gods to provide him with a chariot. Accordingly, they asked Viśvakarman to build Mahādeva's chariot (8.24.57–77). On that chariot, Śiva placed all the weapons given to him by the gods. His bow was forged out of the year and the six seasons, and its string was made by the frightening and destructive black night (*kālarātrī*) of human beings (8.24.78–93). Then we read: "The shining benefactor armed with a sword, arrow and bow, with a hint of laughter (*hasann iva*), asked the deities: 'Who will be the charioteer?'[27] (94). To him, the host of deities replied: 'Whoever you shall appoint, o lord of gods, shall be your charioteer, there is no doubt!' (95) The lord, best among all, furious, told them: 'Choose for me a charioteer; carefully ponder your decision, but don't take too long.' "[28] (96) Apart from the curiosity as to whom shall be Śiva's charioteer,[29] this passage displays a deity who sets out to accomplish a heroic deed with absolute self-confidence. Mahādeva's *hasann iva* announces his ease in defeating the *asura*s as well as his eagerness to fight.[30]

9) 12.125.18d[31] = Sumitra, king of the Haihayas, goes hunting and releases an arrow against a group of deer (*mṛga*). The leader of the herd moves off the arrow's trajectory with ease and stands looking at him with a hint of laughter (*prahasann iva*). Here the hint of laughter displays the transfer of a human feeling to an animal: disregarding the danger, the deer fearlessly challenges Sumitra.[32]

Rām

3.27.28f[33] = lord Rāma, with a hint of laughter (*prahasann iva*), breaks the bow and arrows of the demon Khara with his thunderlike arrow and then pierces Khara to death. Similar to Indra, he displays his heroism with nonchalance.[34]

Prahasann iva and *hasann iva* as Expressions of Divine Grace

The second major use of our stock phrase is especially linked to *BhG* 2.10 since it concerns the hint of laughter of deities, sages, and *gurus*. In many cases, the *prahasann iva*/*hasann iva* on their faces precedes locutionary acts in the form of teachings or advice that manifest their grace (*prasāda*). Besides expressing itself through the granting of boons, their favor is also revealed through injunctions. Exceptionally, the hint of laughter may precede a punishment that is meant to teach a lesson. Herein, we review fifteen of the twenty instances[35] of this kind present in the *MBh*.

MBh

1) 1.211.16b = Kṛṣṇa looks at Arjuna and addresses him with a hint of laughter (*prahasann iva*). The context is as follows:

> While they were moving about, they saw in the midst of [her] companions the beautiful daughter of Vasudeva, well-adorned and prosperous. (14) The very moment he saw her, love struck Arjuna. So Kṛṣṇa stared at Pārtha, whose mind was one-pointed. (15) Then, o descendent of Bharata, the lotus-eyed [Kṛṣṇa], with a hint of laughter, said: "Does love for this forest-dweller agitate your mind? (16) O Pārtha, she is my sister, the uterine sister

> of Sāraṇa (= one of Kṛṣṇa's brothers). If you have this idea, I myself will talk to [her] father." (17)[36]

Though the situation is entirely different from the one described in the *BhG*, there are nonetheless some analogies. Here the heart/mind (*manas*) of Arjuna is captured by Kṛṣṇa's beautiful sister Subhadrā. Having recognized his confused state of mind, Kṛṣṇa addresses a few words to Arjuna. Seeing that he has been struck by the arrow of love, Kṛṣṇa, with a hint of laughter, discloses his advice and intentions in order to satisfy Arjuna's passion. Thus the lord's *prahasann iva* signals his grace, announcing the satisfaction of his companion's desire.

2–3) 3.38.36b, 3.38.39b = here we have another relevant context where two occurrences of *prahasann iva* appear one after the other. Yudhiṣṭhira tells Arjuna that Vyāsa has revealed something to him. Following Vyāsa's instruction, Arjuna is to move toward the north in search of the divine weapons kept by Indra, who will donate them to him (3.38.1–13). Arjuna prepares himself for the journey, receives the blessings of various sages and Brahmins, and quickly arrives at his destination on the sacred mountain Indrakīla, where he hears a celestial voice that tells him to stop. Here Arjuna sees a radiant ascetic with matted locks of hair at the foot of a tree. The latter tells him that in this abode of peaceful ascetics devoted to penance there is no reason to move around armed with bow and weapons: Arjuna is advised to get rid of them. As our hero does not follow the ascetic's advice and keeps his weapons to himself, the ascetic again repeats the same words to him (3.38.14–35). Then we read:

> The delighted twice-born, with a hint of laughter, spoke to him thus: "Choose a boon that is dear to you, o destroyer of enemies, I am Śakra (= Indra)!" (36) Once he spoke in this way, the heroic Dhanaṃjaya, the best of the Kurus, bowing down with folded hands replied to the thousand-eyed Indra: (37) "Indeed this is the desire I wish to have satisfied, please bestow this boon upon me: today, o Glorious one, I wish to obtain all weapons from you!" (38) Pleased, the Great Indra, with a hint of laughter, replied to him: "O Dhanaṃjaya, what do you

> wish to do with weapons, now that you have come here? Choose rather satisfaction of desires and heavenly worlds: you have attained the utmost abode." (39)[37]

Arjuna's steadiness is emphasized in the following verses, when Indra reveals to him that once he has Śiva's vision he will obtain all weapons. The sequel of the story notwithstanding, what is of interest is that Indra's speech is twice opened by a hint of laughter that communicates his benevolent grace toward Arjuna.

4) 3.186.116b = the ageless sage Mārkaṇḍeya tells Yudhiṣṭhira how Viṣṇu appeared to him in disguise as a divine boy:[38] "Then, o hero, with a hint of laughter (*prahasann iva*) that resplendent boy, wearing the *śrīvatsa* mark,[39] clothed in yellow and of great effulgence, addressed me."[40] The hint of laughter that blossoms on the radiant boy's face and immediately precedes his speech represents the flowing of his grace, which instantly sanctifies the old sage.

5) 5.73.1b = having heard a speech that was unusual for Bhīma, Kṛṣṇa, with a hint of laughter, incites him with his powerful words. In order to clarify the context, it is worthwhile quoting a few additional verses (5.73.1–11). Kṛṣṇa's *prahasann iva* responds to Bhīma's despondency, just like in *BhG* 2.10 it responds to Arjuna's despondency:

> The strong-armed Keśava, having heard such sensitive words by Bhīma and having considered them unusual, like the lightness of a mountain or like coldness in fire, Bālarāma's younger brother (= Kṛṣṇa), the son of Vasudeva bearer of the corneous bow (*śārṅga*), with a hint of laughter, spurring the wolf-bellied one (= Bhīma) with words like wind for fire, spoke to Bhīma who sat overwhelmed by pity: (1–3) "O Bhīma, on other occasions you praised the war, longing for the death of Dhṛtarāṣṭra's cruel sons who rejoice in killing. (4) O destroyer of enemies, you do not sleep, you stay awake, you lie down with your face downward; you always pronounce terrible, violent and offensive words. (5) Sighing like fire, scorched by your own rage, o Bhīma, you have an agitated mind like fire with smoke. (6) While sighing, you lie all alone like a weak man troubled by

> a burden. Some people who come to know this, even think that you are mad. (7) O Bhīma, you run about the earth groaning like an elephant that having torn down uprooted trees, shatters and demolishes them with its feet. (8) O son of Pāṇḍu, you do not rejoice with these people and move alone—night and day—never pleased with anyone. (9) Moreover, you sit all alone smiling without reason as though you were crying, for a long time keeping your head between your knees with eyes closed. (10) Furthermore, you have been seen repeatedly furrowing your brow and biting your lips. O Bhīma, all this is due to your rage." (11)[41]

What is remarkable here is that Bhīma, just like Arjuna in the *BhG*, sits overwhelmed by pity (*kṛpā*) and utters words that are inappropriate for a warrior, to the point that he is unrecognizable. To his state of utter shock, Kṛṣṇa responds with a benign hint of laughter that accompanies his speech, which is full of grace toward Bhīma.

6) 5.89.23d = this is an episode in the *Udyogaparvan*, where Kṛṣṇa visits the Kauravas before the beginning of the war. Seeing him approaching, they stand up in obeisance and invite him to sit on a precious canopy, offering him a cow and some milk. Duryodhana, the son of Dhṛtarāṣṭra, goes to the extent of offering him a kingdom and beautiful palaces and begs him to accept some food, but Kṛṣṇa does not accept any of these things from him (5.89.1–13). Thus, beckoning to Karṇa, Duryodhana kindly asks Kṛṣṇa (5.89.13–15):

> O Janārdana, why don't you accept the food, the beverages, the clothes and canopies that have been prepared for you? (13) You who are a beloved relative of Dhṛtarāṣṭra, o Mādhava, you gave assistance to both [parties], being intent upon the welfare of both. (14) O Govinda, you definitely know both *artha* and *dharma*, the pursuing of worldly success and the sacred norm, hence I wish to hear from you the reason for such behavior, o holder of the disc and the mace. (15)[42]

Having been addressed in this way, Govinda, with a thundering yet calm and clear voice (5.89.16–17) says:[43]

> "The messengers who accomplish their mission accept honors and eat [what is offered to them], and you with your counsellors will honor me [only] when I will fulfill my aim." (18) Having said so, the son of Dhṛtarāṣṭra replied to Janārdana: "You happened to come amongst us at the right moment, (19) whether you succeed or not, o slayer of Madhu. We try to honor you, o Govinda, but we cannot, (20) and we do not know the reason why—o slayer of Madhu—you do not accept our worship full of affection, o best among men. (21) There is neither hostility nor division between you and us, o Govinda: therefore, taking this into consideration, you should not speak thus." (22) Then Janārdana, with a hint of laughter (*prahasann iva*), looking at the son of Dhṛtarāṣṭra and all his ministers said to him: (23) "I never disregard the norm (*dharma*) because of desire, neither out of arrogance or hatred, nor for the sake of controversy or covetousness. (24) O king, neither delectable foods nor those that are eaten during calamities satisfy me, not even if you fall into disgrace. (25) O king, from birth you hate the Pāṇḍavas who are your brothers and who pursue love and possess all virtues. (26) Furthermore, such useless hatred toward the sons of Pṛthā has no suitable reason: the sons of Pāṇḍu abide in *dharma*, and indeed who can accuse them of anything? (27) Who hates them hates me, who is close to them is close to me: be aware of my total intimacy with the Pāṇḍavas, who follow *dharma*. (28) Indeed, [the ones who know] define whoever follows desire and anger because of delusion and opposes and hates a virtuous person as the vilest among men. (29) Whoever wishes to hate relatives who are full of noble qualities due to delusion and covetousness, such a man—unable to subjugate anger and to control himself—will not prosper for long. (30) On the other hand, whoever welcomes the virtuous ones with

> affection—even if they are not dear to his heart—rests for long in glory. (31) Hence, I cannot eat all this food associated with the wicked; I can only eat the [food] of the charioteer: this is what I think." (32)[44]

This passage is especially relevant since Kṛṣṇa instructs Duryodhana and his attendants regarding the proper attitude one should have toward the virtuous and, specifically, one's relatives. Duryodhana himself is said to be a victim of illusion. Kṛṣṇa's hint of laughter reminds us of the *BhG,* though Duryodhana and Arjuna are confused by opposite feelings: while Arjuna is overwhelmed by pity, Duryodhana is blinded by envy, desire, anger, and greed. Nonetheless, in both cases the remedy is the lord's *prahasann iva,* which signals the outpouring of his bounteous *upadeśa.*

7) 6.41.16d = the battle is about to begin, and the two armies of the Pāṇḍavas and Kauravas face one another on the battlefield sounding their conches, drums, and horns. Then king Yudhiṣṭhira, the elder among the Pāṇḍava brothers,

> [. . .] unfastened his armor and put down his fine weapon. He quickly dismounted from his chariot and proceeded on foot with folded hands. Yudhiṣṭhira the King Dharma espied Grandfather and strode in silence eastward to the enemy army. Kuntī's son Dhanaṃjaya also dismounted at once, when he saw the other stride forward, and followed him with his brothers. The blessed Lord Vāsudeva followed behind, and after him came eagerly the other kings according to their rank. Arjuna said: "King, what do you have in mind, leaving us behind and going on foot eastward to the enemy army?" Bhīma said: "Where are you going, Indra of kings, doffing armor and weapons while the enemy troops are armed to the teeth, leaving your brothers behind?" Nakula said: "Terror is striking my heart, when I see you, my eldest brother, in this state, Bhārata! Tell me, where are you going?" Sahadeva said: "While there are a score of terrible battles to be fought, where are you going, facing the enemies?" (van Buitenen 1981, 145–47)

Despite these legitimate worries and the utter astonishment of his brothers, Yudhiṣṭhira keeps walking straight toward the Kauravas' army without answering their queries.[45] It is at this point that Kṛṣṇa intervenes (6.41.16–19):

> The extremely sagacious, great-souled Vāsudeva, with a hint of laughter (*prahasann iva*), said to them: "I have understood his purport! (16) Our king will fight against the enemies only after obtaining the assent of Bhīṣma and Droṇa, Gautama and Śalya and all [his *gurus*]. (17) Indeed, in former eras whoever fought without previously obtaining the assent of his *gurus* was looked upon with contempt by the virtuous ones. (18) On the contrary, whoever fights against his own *gurus* having asked [their] prior permission, as required by the sacred texts, surely gains victory in battle: this is my firm opinion!"[46] (19)

Seeing that Yudhiṣṭhira is approaching them unarmed, even the Kauravas are caught by surprise being unable to comprehend the reason behind his strange behavior (6.41.20–24). What is remarkable is Kṛṣṇa's interpretation of Yudhiṣṭhira's intentions. While both Pāṇḍavas and Kauravas are confused by Yudhiṣṭhira's seeming loss of control, Kṛṣṇa rightly deduces that the behavior of the king is in accordance with the *śāstras* and thus begins his enlightening explanation with a hint of laughter that dispels the fear and bewilderment of the Pāṇḍavas.

8) 7.57.46b = Arjuna is anguished at the eve of his fight against Jayadratha. In order to relieve his despondency, Kṛṣṇa reminds him of the formula for activating the powerful *pāśupata* weapon,[47] which, once known, confers victory over all enemies: if Arjuna will learn the *mantra* he will certainly vanquish Jayadratha (7.57.1–15). As an alternative, he should meditate upon Śiva in order to obtain the boon of the weapon from him (7.57.16–18). Arjuna then concentrates upon Śiva and, together with Kṛṣṇa, travels to Śiva's abode by ascending to the celestial worlds (7.57.19–32). Here Arjuna sees Śiva radiant like a thousand suns, deeply immersed in austerities, with all his attributes, with matted locks and a thousand eyes, together with Pārvatī in the midst of chanting sages and the

dances of divine beings (7.57.33–38). When Kṛṣṇa and Arjuna see Śiva, they bow down to him, revere him as the supreme *Brahman* and seek refuge in him (7.57.39–45). Then we read: "Then Śarva [= Śiva], with a hint of laughter (*prahasann iva*), addressed those who had arrived thus: 'Welcome to you best among men! Get up and forego exhaustion! O heroes, please tell me immediately what you wish to obtain! (46) I will grant it to you! Choose whatever boon and I will give it to you!' (47) Having heard these words, Vāsudeva and Arjuna, those two great intellects, extolled Śarva standing up with folded hands" (48).[48] In this passage, Śiva does not instruct his interlocutors but wishes to offer a boon to Kṛṣṇa and Arjuna. His hint of laughter is the expression of his *kṛpā*: his *prahasann iva* announces his favor, displaying his blissful attitude eager to satisfy the wishes of his devotees.

9) 8.40.85b = following the death of Droṇa, Karṇa has become the commander-in-chief of the Kauravas' army.[49] With his mighty spear[50] he slaughters many enemies while, on the other side of the battlefield, Arjuna succeeds in killing many other foes. Since no other warrior can defeat Karṇa, who is scaring away the Pāṇḍavas' allies, Arjuna asks for Kṛṣṇa's help (8.40.79–84): "Once he heard this, o great king, Govinda, with a hint of laughter (*prahasann iva*), said to Arjuna: 'O son of Pāṇḍu, quickly kill the Kauravas!' " (85)[51] Immediately after Kṛṣṇa's peremptory instruction, Arjuna's chariot is led to where Karṇa is in order to fight against him. Here, Kṛṣṇa's command to Arjuna is of a military nature. The hint of laughter that precedes it is aimed at encouraging Arjuna and signals the lord's grace, being an assurance of victory. Kṛṣṇa's *prahasann iva* indicates that there is no other choice but to fight against Karṇa and that the latter's destiny is sealed.

10) 8.50.2b = this occurrence can be properly understood only by looking back at the previous chapters. From the beginning, we are confronted with something unusual, namely Arjuna's rage against Yudhiṣṭhira: Arjuna is ready to kill his elder brother and king. Previously, Yudhiṣṭhira had harshly reproached Arjuna telling him to give his *gāṇḍīva* bow to Karṇa and become his charioteer since Arjuna appeared to be afraid of Karṇa (8.48.13–15). Chapter 8.49 begins with Kṛṣṇa wanting to know the reason for Arjuna's fury. Arjuna tells him that he cannot forgive Yudhiṣṭhira's insolent words and that therefore he has vowed to behead him (8.49.1–12).

However, he concludes his speech by asking Kṛṣṇa—who knows the past and future—to tell him what he should do, saying that he will act as he commands (*tat tathā prakariṣyāmi yathā māṃ vakṣyate bhavān*; 8.49.13). The dialogue continues with Kṛṣṇa trying to calm down Arjuna with instructions on what a sensible human being should and should not do (*kārya, akārya*), pointing out how sages disregard those who are unable to choose the right conduct (*dharma*). Restraint from killing living beings is the highest action (8.49.20ab, *prāṇinām avadhas tata sarvajyāyān mato mama*): one should never kill (8.49.20d, *na ca hiṃyāt kathaṃcana*). Therefore, how could Arjuna kill his elder brother and wise king? This folly is counter to *dharma*. Kṛṣṇa concludes his instruction with an important insight into truthfulness (*satya*), above which nothing exists (8.49.27b, *na satyād vidyate param*), exemplifying it with the story of the hunter Balāka and the ignorant ascetic Kauśika (8.49.14–56).

Thanks to these words of Kṛṣṇa—who knows the supreme *dharma* (8.49.59)—Arjuna's wrath is dispelled and eventually he desists from his intent of killing Yudhiṣṭhira (8.49.57–71). Nonetheless, Arjuna cannot help reproaching his brother for his harsh words and many mistakes. After another enlightening speech of Kṛṣṇa, Arjuna bows down at Yudhiṣṭhira's feet recognizing his merits and states that he will either kill Karṇa or be killed by him. Finally, Arjuna asks for Yudhiṣṭhira's forgiveness. In turn, Yudhiṣṭhira admits all his faults and asks Arjuna to behead him or otherwise he will leave the kingdom to Bhīma and will retreat to the forest to lead the life of an ascetic. Once again, Kṛṣṇa intervenes and recalls Arjuna's vow, shifting his attention to the killing of Karṇa. In the end, Yudhiṣṭhira, too, desists from his intention and peace is restored between the two brothers. The next chapter begins with Saṃjaya's words: "Having so replied to Yudhiṣṭhira after Kṛṣṇa's words, the son of Pṛthā [= Arjuna] was dejected, as though he had committed a sin. (1) Then, with a hint of laughter (*prahasann iva*), Vāsudeva addressed the son of Pāṇḍu: 'O son of Pṛthā, pray, how would it be if you had killed the son of Dharma, established in justice, by means of your sharp-bladed sword?' " (2)[52] Kṛṣṇa often takes part in the quarrels between Yudhiṣṭhira and Arjuna, step by step instructing and advising them both. The hint of laughter is placed at the beginning of the chapter and marks the restored harmony between the two brothers. Kṛṣṇa's *prahasann iva* comes along with his admonition to Arjuna, in which he makes him think about the evil consequences that would have ensued had he killed Yudhiṣṭhira. The lord's hint of laughter reveals his grace and foreseeing wisdom, thanks to which he prevents a tragedy.

11) 12.3.29b = we are now in the *Śāntiparvan*, philosophically the most relevant book of the *MBh*. This is a dialogue between Rāma Bhārgava (i.e., the Brahmin Paraśurāma) and his disciple Karṇa, a *kṣatriya* in the guise of a Brahmin. The chapter narrates how Karṇa, who had obtained the mighty weapon *brahmāstra* from his *guru*, is punished by Paraśurāma. It so happens that Paraśurāma falls asleep on Karṇa's thigh and a flesh-devouring worm begins to eat Karṇa's leg. In order to allow his master to sleep peacefully, he bears the terrible pain without moving. When the blood begins to flow from Karṇa's thigh, Paraśurāma wakes up and, furious, says that only a non-Brahmin could have endured such pain without lamenting (12.3.25). Karṇa then discloses his true identity and begs for Paraśurāma's forgiveness (12.3.26–28):

> To that afflicted one, who was shaking and had fallen down on the ground with folded hands, the best among the Bhṛgus [= Paraśurāma], full of anger, with a hint of laughter (*prahasann iva*) said: (29) "Since for cupidity of the weapon you behaved deceitfully—o fool—when you will use it (30) in battle you will have at your disposal only something that resembles it, which will not have the same efficacy: indeed, the *brahmāstra* cannot ever stay with a non-Brahmin. (31) Now go! This is not the place for you, o liar! Anyway, there will be no warrior equal to you on this earth." (32)[53]

What is noteworthy here is that our stock expression occurs in a moment of anger: Paraśurāma punishes his deceitful disciple with a hint of laughter on his face, wishing to teach him a lesson.

12) 13.14.174d = this passage is in the context of a teaching that is offered by the dying Bhīṣma. At first declaring his utter incapacity, Kṛṣṇa narrates to all the assembled warriors and sages the extraordinary qualities of Śiva (13.14.1–9). Kṛṣṇa's story begins with queen Jāmbavatī[54] who asks him for a mighty and intelligent son. In order to satisfy her desire, Kṛṣṇa goes to the

hermitage of sage Upamanyu, son of Vyāghrapāda,[55] located on the Himālayas (13.14.10–43). As soon as Kṛṣṇa enters the hermitage, Upamanyu—radiant with ascetic power—bows down to him. Upamanyu assures Kṛṣṇa that, by the grace of Īśāna (= Śiva), Jāmbavatī will obtain a son similar to him (13.14.44–71).

Upamanyu then tells the story of how he himself obtained Śiva's favor. During the *kṛtayuga*, the first perfect era, he and his younger brother Dhaumya[56] once went to some sages' hermitage together with their mother and tasted something that they had never tasted before: the sweet milk of a cow. Consequently, Upamanyu asked his mother about this milk and she told him that without Śiva's grace no milk could be had by the ascetics who live in the forest: indeed, only by his grace (*tatprasādāt*) can all desires be satisfied. From that moment onward, Upamanyu's devotion to Śiva became unmovable, so much so that he won Mahādeva's favor by standing on top of his hallux for a thousand years, progressively reducing his diet to fruits, dry leaves, water and, finally, air alone (13.14.72–87).

Upamanyu goes on narrating to Kṛṣṇa that on such occasion Śiva took the form of Indra and appeared before him to test his steadiness by offering him a boon. Upamanyu respectfully refused any boon from him, affirming that his austerities were directed only at pleasing the supreme lord Śiva, the ultimate cause of the universe. Upamanyu also explained the reason why he would have accepted only Śiva's grace or judgment (13.14.88–104). Having heard his words, the three-eyed Śiva revealed himself to Upamanyu, sitting on his bull together with Pārvatī, armed with the tremendous *pāśupata* weapon and accompanied by Brahmā, Nārāyaṇa, Skanda and Indra together with many other sages and seers (13.14.105–49). Even before this wondrous vision, Upamanyu had composed a lengthy hymn in Śiva's honor, offering him various gifts. Extremely pleased, Śiva, in front of all the other deities, expressed his deep satisfaction for Upamanyu's firm devotion. Thus the gods asked Śiva to shower his grace on such a unique devotee (13.14.150–73): "Once addressed in this way by all the gods beginning with Brahmā, the glorious lord Śaṅkara (= Śiva), with a hint of laughter (*prahasann iva*), said to me: (174) 'O son Upamanyu, I am pleased! Look at me, o bull among silent sages! O priestly seer, you are a firm devotee, you have indeed been tested by me (175) and I am extremely pleased by such devotion of yours. Therefore, today I will fulfill all your wishes'" (176).[57] Immediately, Upamanyu experiences intense bliss which brings tears of joy to his eyes (13.14.177). Once again, a god's hint of laughter accompanies his intention of showering his grace upon a devotee by bestowing whatever boon he/she desires.

13) 14.19.46d = this verse is taken from the *Anugītā* or *Uttaragītā* (*MBh* 14.16–51), a philosophical poem similar to the *BhG* in which a Brahmin has a lengthy dialogue with Kṛṣṇa. Herein, the Brahmin narrates the insight he gave to a bright disciple of his who had questioned him regarding several issues concerning the body and the self (*ātman*). The presentation of his teaching continues up to the end of the chapter (14.19.42–47):

> Just as the mind of one who has placed a treasure in his own coffer stays in that box, in the same way one that has turned his mind inwardly must search for the self and completely avoid carelessness. (42) So, always zealously active and with a contented mind, before long he will reach *Brahman* and, having realized it, will become the knower of the universal [principle]. (43) But that [principle] is not perceivable by sight nor by the other senses. That pervasive [principle] can be seen within yourself only by means of that lantern which is the mind. (44) The living individual clearly perceives that self—which is separate from the body—as having hands and feet everywhere; with eyes, heads and mouths everywhere. (45) Hence, having left aside his own body and resolving only upon *Brahman*, he, with a hint of laughter (*prahasann iva*), realizes the self by means of the mind. (46) O best among the twice born, I have revealed to you the secret of secrets and so [now] I will leave! I feel the desire to realize [the truth] and you, o disciple, may go wherever you like." (47)[58]

Here *prahasann iva* is not related to a locutionary act but is meant to point out that by concentrating upon *Brahman* one can easily achieve the supreme goal of *mokṣa* or self-realization. This instance is akin to the cases analyzed in the previous section, where the hint of laughter signals the heroes' ease in accomplishing even the most difficult tasks.

14) 14.20.5b = Vāsudeva narrates an ancient story about a learned Brahmin and his wife (Vassilov 2002, 239–41). One day, while the Brahmin is sitting all alone, his wife asks him what will her posthumous destiny be like, given that she has served him her entire life while he sat (*āsīnam*) doing nothing (*nyastakarmāṇam*), niggard (*kīnāśam*), and without discernment (*avicakṣaṇam*). Since chaste wives are said to attain the same abode as their husbands, she worriedly asks him what will happen to her (14.20.1–4):

> Having spoken thus, that calm [Brahmin], with a hint of laughter (*hasann iva*), replied to her: "O virtuous one, I am not indignant at this statement of yours, o faultless. (5) Whether an action be visible or audible, those who perform actions know that it is [simply] an action. (6) Those who are devoid of knowledge because of [attachment to] action are deluded; and it is well-known that for an embodied being the absence of action cannot be attained in this world." (7)[59]

The husband goes on with his teaching up to the end of the chapter (14.20.27). What is remarkable is that his *hasann iva* accompanies a spiritual instruction meant to correct the wife's deluded perspective. The hint of laughter is the expression of the Brahmin's grace toward his spouse. This is confirmed by his gentle attitude, despite the wife's harsh words.

15) 14.54.17b = this is a dialogue between Kṛṣṇa and Uttaṅka (14.52–53), where the latter concludes that the former is the creator of the universe and—like Arjuna in *BhG* 11—asks Kṛṣṇa to manifest his majestic form to him (*rūpam aiśvaryam*; 14.54.1–3). Vaiśaṃpāyana, who narrates this story, says that Uttaṅka saw Kṛṣṇa's universal form (*viśvarūpa*) and was completely overwhelmed with wonder (*vismaya*). Uttaṅka then sings a hymn of praise to Kṛṣṇa, asking him to please retain his glorious form (14.54.4–8). At this juncture, Kṛṣṇa bestows a boon on Uttaṅka, who at first is so amazed by the wonderful vision that he does not want anything from him. However, at Kṛṣṇa's insistence he asks that he may find water whenever he desires, even in a desert (14.54.12; *toyam icchāmi*

yatreṣṭaṃ maruṣv etad dhi durlabham). Just before leaving, Kṛṣṇa assures Uttaṅka that whenever he will desire water he will just have to think of him. The story goes that once Uttaṅka found himself roaming in a desert, longing for water. He was then reminded of Kṛṣṇa's words and started thinking of him. At that very moment he saw a naked barbarian, covered with dust and armed with a tremendous sword, a bow and arrows, surrounded by a pack of dogs (14.54.13–16ab): "The best among the twice-born saw a flow of abundant water pouring out of the barbarian's lower parts [= the penis] (16cd) and the latter, with a hint of laughter (*prahasann iva*), said to him: 'O Uttaṅka, come! O scion of the Bhṛgus, accept [this] water from me! (17) I feel great compassion seeing you with such great thirst.' The sage, however, did not welcome that water" (18).[60] Here we have a peculiar occurrence of *prahasann iva*. As the rest of the chapter makes clear, the hint of laughter expresses a challenge, a test to which Kṛṣṇa puts his devotee. Though it may appear as a mocking laugh, nonetheless it proves the lord's favor toward Uttaṅka.

Rām

Among the fourteen instances of *prahasann iva* and *hasann iva* in the *Rām*, seven can be referred to this section. Here we focus attention on 7.4.11b.[61] In a dialogue between the seer Agastya and Rāma, the former replies to the latter's questions on Rāvaṇa's previous births. Agastya begins by telling him the story of Prajāpati, who created aquatic beings who are very hungry, thirsty, and fearful:

> Prajāpati, the subduer of the enemies' pride, with a hint of laughter (*prahasann iva*) addressed those creatures thus: "You should protect them [= the waters] with effort!" (11) Some of them, who were angry, replied: "We shall protect [them] (*rakṣāma*)!" while the others, who were not angry, [replied]: "We shall worship [them] (*yakṣāma*)!" Then the creator of beings stated: (12) "Those who said 'We shall protect' will be demons (*rākṣasa*) for you; those who said 'We shall worship' will be semi-divine beings (*yakṣa*) for you." (13)[62]

Once again, a god exhibits a hint of laughter just before speaking. Prajāpati's *prahasann iva* seems to indicate that he already knows what will be the consequences of his command.

Prahasann iva and *Hasann iva* as Expressions of Mockery, Delight and Surprise

We now focus on the third purport of *prahasann iva* and *hasann iva*. This is the most straightforward one since it has to do with the main meaning of root √*has* in which the value of the particle *iva* is either softened or neglected. In several loci, our stock expressions are strengthened by synonymous nouns and verbs. Herein, we examine thirteen occurrences from the *MBh* out of a total of twenty-six.[63]

MBh

1) 1.127.5d[64] = having seen Karṇa, and having ascertained that he is the son of a charioteer, Bhīma, with a hint of laughter (*prahasann iva*), addresses him thus: "O son of the carter, you are unworthy of being killed in battle by Pārtha [= Arjuna]! Quickly take the whip, (6) you are not worthy of enjoying the kingdom of Aṅga, o vilest among men: you are like a dog [and should not eat] the sacrificial cakes that are placed near the sacrificial fire!" (7)[65] Here *prahasann iva* precedes a locutionary act that is meant to ridicule Karṇa's humble origins.

2–3) 3.40.17 and 3.40.21b = the context of these occurrences is well known. Arjuna is trying to kill a wild boar[66] on top of a mountain and is stopped by Śiva who appears to him in the guise of a hunter (*kirāta*). Arjuna shoots an arrow against the wild boar and the hunter does the same. Both arrows hit the wild boar simultaneously and kill the animal: "Then Jiṣṇu[67] [= Arjuna] looked at the man with the radiance of gold, disguised in the dress of a mountain hunter, accompanied by women, o killer of enemies. The delighted Kaunteya [= Arjuna], with a hint of laughter (*prahasann iva*), addressed him thus: [. . .]."[68] Arjuna is amazed at seeing the *kirāta* and asks him who he is. He is astonished at his insulting behavior and resolves to kill him (*MBh* 3.40.18–20). The hero's *prahasann iva* expresses mixed feelings: his hint of laughter is tinged with wonder but primarily with mockery and desire for revenge. A few verses later, after Arjuna has harshly addressed the *kirāta* for having stolen his prey, there is a second occurrence of *prahasann iva*:

> Once addressed by the Pāṇḍava, the mountain hunter, with a hint of laughter, said these tender words to the ambidextrous archer Arjuna: (21) "I definitely targeted this prey and hit it before you did; mind you, I can kill you in one stroke. (22) You should not attribute your errors to others. You are proud of your own strength: o slow witted, you have offended me and will not escape alive from me! (23) Be brave! I will shoot arrows like thunderbolts and you too should shoot your arrows and fight." (24)[69]

Our formulaic expression immediately preceeds a definite challenge to Arjuna. The *kirāta*'s serene attitude proves his self-confidence, while his hint of laughter shows his sarcasm.

4) 3.97.5d = this chapter presents the story of the Brahmin demon Ilvala. The sage Lomaśa narrates that Ilvala had cooked his brother Vātāpi in order to kill the seer Agastya.[70] When the seer invited by Ilvala reaches his place and sees that Vātāpi has been well-cooked, he resolves to eat him:

> Then the great sage having reached the seat of honor seated himself [there] while Ilvala, the lord of demons, with a hint of laughter (*prahasann iva*), served him the food. (5) Agastya ate Vātāpi entirely and, once he had eaten him, Ilvala tried to call his brother back to life. (6) But a belch of the great soul Agastya made Ilvala realize that the demon had been fully digested and thus he became sad. (7) Along with his ministers, he uttered these words with folded hands: "What is the reason that brought you here? Tell me, what can I do for you?" (8)[71]

Here *prahasann iva* displays Ilvala's ill intentions. The demon's hint of laughter is both sarcastic, prefiguring the death of the sage, and horrific, due to the gruesome nature of the food he serves to him.

5) 3.294.9d = Vaiśaṃpāyana narrates that Karṇa addresses a Brahmin who is actually Indra in disguise and asks him what he desires, be it a golden necklace, women or densely populated villages, promising that he will grant these to him. The Brahmin asks Karṇa to give him the armor (*varman*) he has worn since birth, together with his earrings (*kuṇḍala*). Karṇa, however, refuses to donate these items to him:

> When the best among the twice-born did not choose another gift, the son of Rādhā [= Karṇa], with a hint of laughter (*prahasann iva*), said to him again: (9) "O sage, the armor was born along with me and the earrings were born from the nectar of immortality, thanks to which I am invulnerable in this world. This is why I will not give them away! (10) O virtuous bull among Brahmins, accept from me a huge kingdom on earth, prosperous and free from troubles. (11) Deprived of the earrings and of my armor, o best of the twice-born, I will be at the mercy of my enemies." (12)[72]

Here *prahasann iva* signals Karṇa's surprise and perhaps even embarrassment at the Brahmin's request. Somehow, the hint of laughter mitigates the hero's refusal of donating the armor and earrings that make him invulnerable. It may also conceal Karṇa's suspicion as to the Brahmin's true identity.

6) 4.23.22d = this chapter narrates that once Sairandhrī [= Draupadī in disguise during her exile at Virāṭa's court], having freed herself from her kidnappers, reached the hall where Bṛhannaḍā [= Arjuna in disguise as a eunuch] was dancing together with some girls. Bṛhannaḍā then asks Sairandhrī how she managed to free herself. To him, Sairandhrī replies: "O Bṛhannaḍā, what is the matter with you today regarding Sairandhrī? O good woman, you surely lead a happy life in the women's apartments. (21) Indeed, you don't suffer the sorrow Sairandhrī is experiencing! This is why you question me, who am so distressed, with a hint of laughter (*prahasann iva*)." (22)[73] Arjuna/Bṛhannaḍā's hint of laughter sharply contrasts with Draupadī/Sairandhrī's distress and this is the reason why the latter rebukes the former, judging his *prahasann iva* to be totally inappropriate (*anucita*), an effect of the happy life he enjoys in the women's apartments.

7) 4.53.14b = Arjuna approaches his *guru*, the mighty Droṇa, just before ordering his charioteer Uttara to attack him: "Having approached Droṇa's chariot, the vigorous great warrior Pārtha appeared delighted (*harṣayukta*) and, with a hint of laughter (*prahasann iva*), (14) after revering [him], the strong-armed Kaunteya, the slayer of enemies, gently uttered these tender words [to him] (15) [. . .]."[74] The use of *prahasann iva* expresses the joy of an exemplary *kṣatriya* like Arjuna of having the opportunity to fight a loyal combat with his *guru*. The hint of laughter is definitely a sign of Arjuna's delight.

8) 7.50.16d[75] = several chapters are dedicated to describe the killing of Abhimanyu, son of Arjuna and Subhadrā, Kṛṣṇa's sister (7.32–51). Toward the end of the narrative, when the valiant boy has already been killed by the Kauravas, an exceedingly distressed Arjuna utters a few words. He remarks that the smiling (*hasann iva*) Saubhadra [= Abhimanyu] will not be there to welcome him when he returns from the battlefield, as he used to do.

The expression *hasann iva* refers to Abhimanyu's joyful mood, that Arjuna remembers with touching words. Abhimanyu's cheerful personality contrasts with the tragic situation in which Arjuna laments his death.

9) 7.160.23b = impelled by Duryodhana, Droṇa promises that he will mercilessly kill all his enemies. Yet, Droṇa points out that if Duryodhana thinks that Arjuna can be defeated by any ordinary human being he is wrong and starts enumerating Arjuna's impressive deeds (7.160.1–20). At this eulogy of Arjuna, Duryodhana mounts in a rage and tells Droṇa that he, Duḥśāsana, and Karṇa along with his maternal uncle Śakuni will kill Arjuna in battle that very day: "Having heard those words of his, Bhāradvāja [= Droṇa], with a hint of laughter (*hasann iva*), followed the king and said [to him]: 'May fortune be with you! (23) Indeed, who is the warrior that can destroy the undecaying bull among warriors, the bearer of the *gāṇḍīva* [bow], blazing as if he were [lit] by fire?' " (24).[76] Here *hasann iva* opens a direct speech and bears a sarcastic meaning: Duryodhana's resolve is thought to be so hopeless that it causes Droṇa's hint of laughter.

10) 10.12.12d = Droṇa reveals to his son Aśvatthāman the secret of an extraordinary weapon called *brahmaśiras*. Knowing his

son's wicked nature, he warns him that it should never be used against humans. On listening to his father's words, Aśvatthāman loses the hope of obtaining his inheritance and begins wandering the earth till he reaches Dvārakā, Kṛṣṇa's capital (10.12.1–11):

> While he [= Aśvatthāman] was staying at Dvārakā, he approached me [= Kṛṣṇa] all alone on the seashore and, with a hint of laughter (*hasann iva*), said: (12) "O Kṛṣṇa, by practicing a most arduous penance the master of the Bhāratas, my truly brave father, received from Agastya (13) the weapon called *brahmaśiras*, honored by gods and *gandharvas*. As it belongs to my father, that weapon will [soon] be mine, o Dāśārha [= Kṛṣṇa]. (14) O best among the Yadus, when I will receive that divine weapon do give me [your] weapon also, the disc that annihilates all enemies in battle!" (15)[77]

Even in this case *hasann iva* opens a direct speech where the speaker displays a good deal of arrogance. Aśvatthāman's hint of laughter is meant to express his delight at the thought that he will soon inherit the *brahmaśiras* from his father. This is what he wants Kṛṣṇa to believe, since in fact the evil Aśvatthāman has lost all hope of securing the celestial weapon.

11) 12.24.8d = this is an occurrence from the *Śāntiparvan*, within a definitely philosophical context. Yudhiṣṭhira asks Vyāsa about the circumstances that brought King Sudyumna to attain supreme perfection (*paramāṃ saṃsiddhim*).[78] Vyāsa's reply begins with an old tale of two brothers, Likhita and Śaṅkha, who were ascetics.[79] Once, on returning to his hermitage, Śaṅkha saw his brother eating some fruits and asked him: "'Where did you find those fruits and why are you eating them?' (7cd) Reverently saluting him, Likhita, with a hint of laughter (*prahasann iva*), replied: 'I took them from there!' (8) To him, Śaṅkha said in an angry tone: 'This is a theft you have committed! You were not supposed to take those fruits! (9) Go to the king and confess your theft!'" (10ab)[80] Likhita's joyful hint of laughter proves his candor since he didn't think there was anything wrong in what he did: he didn't willingly steal the fruits but simply carried out a naïve action, without considering its consequences.

12) 14.73.6b = Vaiśaṃpāyana narrates that once Arjuna followed the roaming of a sacrificial horse during an *aśvamedha* ritual and that when the horse reached the Trigarta kingdom it was surrounded by well-armed enemies who tried to capture it. Though Arjuna tried to reason with them using kind words, they shot several arrows against him which he effectively countered (14.73.1–6): "Then, o Bhārata, Jiṣṇu [= Arjuna] said [to them], with a hint of laughter (*prahasann iva*): 'O people ignorant of the *dharma*, move backward [if] you care for your life!' "[81] Arjuna's *prahasann iva* expresses his resoluteness in front of the enemies. With his hint of laughter he scorns his opponents, being confident in his own superiority.

13) 14.93.39c = in this chapter, a mongoose illustrates to some Brahmins the supreme effect of the act of giving (*dānasya paramaṃ phalam*). The mongoose tells them of a period of famine, when a virtuous family received a Brahmin guest. Though both husband and wife offered him their *saktu*[82] the guest was still hungry (14.93.1–29). When their young son wished to offer him his *saktu* in order to safeguard his father's honor, the latter at first prevented him from doing so because of his tender age (14.93.30–36). The boy then told his father that a *putra,* that is a son, is so called because he protects.[83] Moreover, he argued that a son is the same as his father and therefore he should be allowed to offer his food since it will be like saving himself by himself (*trāhy ātmānam ihātmanā*; 14.93.37). The father then tells him: " 'I have examined you several times: you are similar to me in appearance, conduct and self-control. I myself will offer him your *saktu*!' (38) Having spoken thus, the best among twice-born took his *saktu* and, delighted, with a hint of laughter (*prahasann iva*), gave it to the Brahmin" (39).[84] The father's *prahasann iva* is linked to his generous act—prompted by the words of his son, who acts as his *guru*—and expresses pure joy. Indeed, his happiness is emphasized by the word "delighted" (*prītātman*).

Rām

7.80.3d = after listening to the story of the origin of the *kimpuruṣas,*[85] Lakṣmaṇa and Bharata are utterly astonished. Therefore, Rāma tells them the whole story again. Herein, the seer Budha addresses Ilā, the daughter of Kardama: "Having seen all those *kinnarīs* agitated, the best among seers, with a hint of laughter (*prahasann iva*), said to that beautiful woman: [. . .]."[86] The agitation of the *kinnarīs* contrasts with the joyful serenity of Budha in addressing Ilā, which is expressed through his reassuring hint of laughter.[87]

Prahasann iva and *hasann iva* as Ambiguous or Seemingly Incongruous Expressions

In the epics one is faced with a few ambiguous or seemingly incongruous occurrences of *prahasann iva* and *hasann iva*, which signal different psychological and/or psycho-physical attitudes. Here we examine two occurrences from the *MBh*.[88]

MBh

1) 5.7.9b[89] = this chapter describes the well-known episode of Duryodhana going to Dvārakā in order to persuade Kṛṣṇa—whom he finds sleeping—to side with the Kauravas against the Pāṇḍavas. Thus when Kṛṣṇa asks him the reason for his visit, Duryodhana, with a hint of laughter (*prahasann iva*), replies begging his help in the war. Here the use of *prahasann iva* is ambiguous. It might prefigure a positive reply, given that Duryodhana is so proud of himself that he is certain of the Kauravas' final victory, that is, from his viewpoint the clever Kṛṣṇa cannot but choose their side. More likely, however, his hint of laughter is tinged with nervousness and foreshadows a negative answer since Duryodhana is well aware of the special bond between Kṛṣṇa and Arjuna. Thus his *prahasann iva* may hide the conviction that his attempt is as necessary as much as it is useless. All in all, his hint of laughter may be interpreted either as a sign of Duryodhana's arrogance or as a sign of his embarrassment.

2) 12.142.41b = this chapter is part of a larger section concerning the rules and practices that are to be adopted in times of emergency (*āpaddharma*; 12.129–167). Bhīṣma narrates to a king the story of a pigeon (*kapota*) and his wife-dove (*kapotī*) who had been captured by a fowler. At a certain point, the *kapotī* suggests to her husband to honor the fowler as their guest. The pigeon follows her advice and addresses the fowler with sweet, merciful words (12.142.13–22). The latter confides to him that he is very cold and

so the pigeon lights a fire with dry leaves. The fowler then tells him that he is hungry, but the pigeon does not have any food left for him since forest dwellers—just like ascetics (*muni*)—only eat what is necessary to satisfy their hunger, without ever storing anything (12.142.23–37). Distressed at not being able to satisfy his guest's request, the pigeon starts thinking what he can do to solve the problem. At last, he arrives at a tragic resolution: he kindles a fire and, repeating what he had heard from deities, ancestors and sages, praises the great merit (*dharmo mahān*) that ensues from honoring one's guests (*atithipūjana*). Bhīṣma concludes his story by saying: "O king, then the bird, steady in his vow of truthfulness, having circumambulated the fire three times, threw himself into it with a hint of laughter (*prahasann iva*)."[90] In this touching story, the use of *prahasann iva* is seemingly out of place and must be understood as a counterpoint to the *kapota*'s tragic epilogue. The capacity to smile/laugh is transferred to a bird and is meant to ease the tension, highlighting the inner serenity of the pigeon who readily sacrifices his life in order to honor his guest.

Rām

2.63.9d = Bharata tells about a nightmare he had: "I have seen him [= Daśaratha, Bharata's father] floating in that lake of cow-dung while drinking sesame-oil with folded hands, repeatedly laughing (*hasann iva*)."[91] Being the description of a bad dream, this occurrence is inevitably ambiguous and surreal, even horror-like. The repeated, hysterical laughs of Daśaratha—where one might expect him to cry—amplify his miserable condition: they express his uncontrollable reaction to the traumatic situation he is immersed in.[92]

Concluding Remarks

Whereas the formulaic dictions *prahasann iva* and *hasann iva* are absent in Vedic and Upaniṣadic literature they are widely extant in the epics. In the *MBh* and *Rām* they are utilized in a broad range of ways which we have grouped in the sections listed above. Leaving aside their ambiguous usages, what emerges from this survey is that the expressions *prahasann iva*/*hasann iva* reveal three basic meanings:

1. The ease with which a great hero accomplishes the most difficult task;
2. The bestowal of grace/boons by deities, sages and *gurus*;
3. Mockery, delight, and surprise.

There are instances in which one can legitimately classify *prahasann iva*/*hasann iva* in more than one way. These formulaic expressions are found with *verba dicendi* just before or simultanously with—and, less frequently, after—a direct speech. In the majority of cases, however, they do not come along locutionary acts but are employed to highlight heroic deeds that are performed effortlessly. In one of these instances, it is Kṛṣṇa himself who kills a demon with nine arrows (*MBh* 6.107.2d).

With reference to *BhG* 2.10, the most relevant section is the one in which gods and sages have their teachings/insights preceded by a hint of laughter. Herein, seven occurrences of *prahasann iva* in the *MBh* see Kṛṣṇa as protagonist.[93] In six of these cases, Kṛṣṇa's hint of laughter is addressed to Arjuna either directly or indirectly.[94] He knows something that Arjuna and the people around him ignore and his *prahasann iva* anticipates that he is about to offer a most precious *upadeśa*. Kṛṣṇa's hint of laughter stands out as an expression of his grace: it opens a speech that is aimed at enlightening Arjuna and all his listeners on the right course of action, clearing their doubts and confused minds.[95]

Chapter 4

On Kṛṣṇa's Hint of Laughter in the Arts and in Devotional Literature

If in several languages of the world the word for "smile" is derived from the word for "laugh," as for instance in French and Italian in which *sourire* and *sorriso* mean "low laugh" (*sou-rire; sor-riso,* from Latin *sub-ridere*) and no other terms exist for laughter but *rire* and *riso/risata* respectively,[1] we have noted from the start that Sanskrit, on the other hand, distinguishes smile from laughter.[2] Thus its word for smile is *smita* derived from verbal root √*smi*—the English *smile* being its cognate—whereas its word for laughter is *hāsa,* derived from verbal root √*has*.[3] Even within the *Dhātupāṭha,* the lexicon of verbal roots annexed to the *Aṣṭādhyāyī* of Pāṇini (c. fourth century BCE), √*has* refers to "laugh" whereas √*smi* refers to "smile."[4] When prefixes are added to root √*has,* as in the terms *upahāsa* and *parihāsa,* the prevailing meaning is that of derision or mockery, whereas when prefixes are added to root √*smi,* as in *vismaya,* the usual meaning is that of amazement, bewilderment, or wonder.

The Aesthetic Experience of the Comic (*hāsyarasa*) in Bharata's *Nāṭyaśāstra*

To the aesthetic experience of the comic (*hāsyarasa*), the legendary sage and mythical first actor Bharata devotes chapter 6, verses 48–61, of his *Nāṭyaśāstra* or "Drama Manual" (first century BCE–

third century CE), the earliest surviving treatise on the origins, nature, and performance of the dramatic arts (i.e., theater, dance and music).[5] The *hāsyarasa*,[6] which has as its basis the dominant emotional mood (*sthāyibhāva*) of laughter (*hāsa*),[7] is classified in three pairs (i.e., six varieties) according to the rank of the laughing characters, themselves classified in three grades—the highest (*uttama*), the medium (*madhya*), and the lowest (*adhama*)—displaying a progressive hierarchy from the utmost serene smile of the noble people to the vile bursts of laughter of the village folk.[8]

The symbolic color ascribed to *hāsya* is white, which refers to the whiteness of the teeth that are revealed in smile/laughter,[9] whereas its presiding deities are the Pramathas, a collective group who are the retinue (*gaṇas*) of lord Śiva led by his son Gaṇeśa, the "lord of the *gaṇas*."[10] The six varieties of *hāsyarasa*—said to arise from the erotic sentiment (*śṛṅgārarasa*) and to be an imitation (*anukṛti*) of it (vv. 39–40)—are the following: smile (*smita*), slight laughter (*hasita*),[11] open laughter (*vihasita*), mocking laughter (*upahasita*), loud laughter (*apahasita*), and excessive laughter (*atihasita*). Although Bharata observes that *hāsyarasa* is to be found primarily among women and lower-class people, the first pair of *smita* and *hasita* is understood to be typical of noble persons such as Brahmins, kings, heroes as well as gods,[12] and he describes it with great precision by having recourse to the following verses (54–55):

> With cheeks slightly expanded, with glances of perfect qualities, not showing the teeth, stable, should be the smile (*smita*) of the highest characters. (*īṣadvikasitair gaṇḍaiḥ kaṭākṣaiḥ sauṣṭhavānvitaiḥ | alakṣitadvijaṃ dhīram uttamānāṃ smitaṃ bhavet ||*)
>
> That which blooms the mouth and the eyes, expands the cheeks, shows the teeth slightly, is prescribed as slight laughter (*hasita*). (*utphullānananetraṃ tu gaṇḍair vikasitair atha | kiṃcil lakṣitadantaṃ ca hasitaṃ tad vidhīyate ||*)

It must be noted that Bharata's technical vocabulary and his definitions are of crucial importance since they apply to all domains of fine arts in India, the *Nāṭyaśāstra* being the one established authority. Given such framework, it is our contention that Kṛṣṇa's *prahasann iva* in *Bhagavadgītā* 2.10 is to be understood as falling within the sphere of *hasita*. Indeed, we are persuaded that the *Nāṭyaśāstra* canons are applicable to the *Bhagavadgītā*'s setting.[13] The deity's hint of laughter illuminates his whole face, widening his eyes and expanding his cheeks,[14] the partial opening of his mouth making his glittering teeth slightly visible.[15] Kṛṣṇa's majestic, beaming face reveals him as the all-powerful god, welcoming Arjuna as his beloved *bhakta*. But before probing into the characterization of Kṛṣṇa's hint of laughter as *hasita*, we must contrast it with Bharata's definitions of the other two pairs of *hāsyarāsa*, that is, the ones applying to the medium/common and lowest characters respectively (vv. 56–59):

> Now for the common characters:
>
> In open laughter (*vihasita*) the eyes are slightly contracted and the cheeks fully distended. The sound of the laughter is soft. The laughter is appropriate to the occasion, and the face is colored. (*ākuñcitākṣigaṇḍaṃ yat sasvanaṃ madhuraṃ tathā | kālāgataṃ sāsyarāgaṃ tad vai vihasitaṃ bhavet ||*)
>
> In mocking laughter (*upahasita*) the nostrils are distended, the eyes squint and the shoulders and head are bent.[16] (*utphullanāsikaṃ yat tu jihmadṛṣṭinirīkṣitam | nikuñcitāṅgakaśiras tac copahasitaṃ bhavet ||*)
>
> Now for the lowest characters:
>
> In loud laughter (*apahasita*) one laughs out of place, with tears in one's eyes, and the shoulders and head are shaking (with laughter). (*asthānahasitaṃ yat tu sāśrunetraṃ tathaiva ca | utkampitāṃsakaśiras tac cāpahasitaṃ bhavet ||*)
>
> In excessive laughter (*atihasita*) the eyes are swollen and bathed in tears, and there are loud and violent cries and one holds one's sides with one's hands. (*saṃrabdhasāśrunetraṃ ca vikṛṣṭasvaram uddhatam | karopagūḍhapārśvaṃ ca tac cātihasitaṃ bhavet ||*)

These four characterizations of laughter constitute a *crescendo*, from open laughter (*vihasita*) to excessive laughter (*atihasita*). In particular, though *vihasita* comes immediately after *hasita* it does not seem to fit Kṛṣṇa's *prahasann iva*, it being a laughter that emits a soft sound and in which the teeth are fully visible and the face colored. Rather, Kṛṣṇa's *prahasann iva*, as the attenuating particle *iva* implies, is a mere hint of laughter and clearly falls within the sphere of *hasita*: it is revealing that Bharata pairs together *smita* and *hasita* given that with *hasita* we keep a reference to smile, it being the first level of intensification of *smita*, whereas the following two pairs concern open laughter in ascending degrees and are thus the object of a separate description.[17]

In *Nāṭyaśāstra* 6.48, Bharata tells us that *hāsyarasa* is of two kinds, "existing in oneself" or "self-centered" (*ātmastha*) and "existing in others" (*parastha*), so that when a person smile/laughs on his/her own it is of the *ātmastha* variety, whereas when it is determined by the smile/laughter of somebody else it is of the *parastha* variety. Kṛṣṇa's *hasita* in the *Bhagavadgītā* is clearly of the *ātmastha* kind since his hint of laughter spontaneously surges from within himself.

Moreover, it appears to us that inseparable from Kṛṣṇa's *ātmastha prahasann iva* is his "mood of compassion" (*karuṇarasa*) toward Arjuna. In other words, Kṛṣṇa's *hasita* simultaneously reveals his love toward the hero who has sought refuge in him since he looks compassionately at Arjuna who is utterly confused and despondent. Thus Kṛṣṇa's *ātmastha hasita* is inseparable from his *kāruṇya*, which is maximized as pure *preman* given Arjuna's act of devout surrender to him as his *guru*.

In turn, Kṛṣṇa's *ātmastha hasita cum kāruṇya* leads to the ineffable experience of *śāntarasa*, the "peaceful mood" that at this juncture envelops both Arjuna and all of the poem's listeners/readers: this is the καιρός, the silent climax and turning point of the *Bhagavadgītā*. It is out of this blissful suspended time, in which all action (*karman*) has come to a stop, that the cooling flow of Kṛṣṇa's grace (*prasāda*) can start springing from his slightly opened, contracted lips.

Interestingly, Abhinavagupta (tenth to eleventh century CE), in his commentary to the *Nāṭyaśāstra* known as *Abhinavabhāratī*, rejects Bharata's interpretation of *hāsyarasa* as consisting of six varieties hierarchically ordained one after the other and recognizes only three states of *hāsya*, arguing that each of the three pairs is a type of smile/laughter together with its communicated form. Thus in the case of the first pair of *smita* and *hasita*, he says: "That which is *smita* in the superior character becomes *hasita* when communicated" (*smitaṃ hi yad uttamaprakṛtau tat saṃkrāntaṃ hasitaṃ sampadyate*).[18]

Along these lines, he interprets the first type of each of the three pairs to be *ātmastha* and the second (i.e., its communicated form) to be *parastha*. What Abhinavagupta has in mind is theatrical performance and the communicability of smile and laughter.

The communicated or transmitted variety is thought to go up one grade from the grade of the original, though it always pertains to the same state: the idea is that when an actor on stage represents an *uttama* or noble character, he/she first expresses *smita* on his/her own, that is, as *ātmastha* or *svasamuttha*, but when he/she has to effectively convey it to the spectator, he/she expresses it at a higher degree of intensity as *hasita*, which therefore must be understood as *parastha* or *parasamuttha* (i.e., existing in another person).[19] The spectator is then thought to enter into a condition of veritable oneness/communion with the represented hero or god, and by the power of this communion he/she achieves an otherworldly (*alaukika*) experience that illustrates Abhinavagupta's conception of the transcendence of *rasa* in the beholder, though to be sure this sublime condition is only temporary.[20]

With regard to the *vibhāva*s or determinants that cause the insurgence of the comic *rasa*, Bharata in *Nāṭyaśāstra* 6.48–50 states:

> It arises from such *vibhāva*s as wearing clothes and ornaments that belong to someone else or do not fit (*vikṛta*), shamelessness (*dhārṣṭya*), greed (*laulya*), tickling certain sensitive parts of the body (*kuhaka*), telling fantastic tales (*asatpralāpa*), seeing some (comic) deformity (*vyaṅga*), and describing faults (*doṣodāharaṇa*). It should be acted out by [such *anubhāva*s or consequents as] puffing out the cheeks, the nose, the lips, widening and contracting one's eyes, sweating, coloring of the face, grabbing one's sides (in laughter) and so forth. The ephemeral emotions (*vyabhicārin*) (that accompany it) are: dissimulation, laziness, drowsiness (*tandrā*), sleep, dreaming, awakening, envy, etc. . . . On this subject there are the following two traditional *āryā* stanzas:
>
> One laughs because of misplaced ornaments, eccentric behavior, language and dress, and other peculiar actions (*arthaviśeṣa*), and the resulting aesthetic experience is known as the comic.

> Because one can make people laugh by eccentric actions, words, and bodily movements and dress, therefore the resulting sentiment (*rasa*) should be known as the comic.[21]

In the *Abhinavabhāratī*, Abhinavagupta convincingly argues that the essence of what causes and excites *hāsya* (its *vibhāva*) is the fault of inappropriateness/impropriety or *anaucitya*[22] and that such disproportion/disharmony can be operating through both its determinants and consequents in all *rasas* (*anaucityapravṛttikṛtam eva hi hāsyavibhāvatvam | tac cānaucityaṃ sarvarasānāṃ vibhāvānubhāvādau sambhāvyate ||*).[23] Following Bharata, who links *hāsyarasa* to the imitation of *śṛṅgārarasa*, Abhinavagupta in his *Dhvanyālokalocana*, a commentary to the *Dhvanyāloka* of Ānandavardhana (ninth century CE), states that when writers use the word "love" in situations where love is spurious or one-sided—as in the case of the demon Rāvaṇa's love for Sītā—it should be understood as only a semblance (*ābhāsa*) of true love.[24] It is precisely this nongenuineness (*amukhyatā*), this mere *ābhāsa* of *śṛṅgāra*, that reveals the *anaucitya* or inappropriateness of the whole situation and generates the mood of *hāsya*.

As pointed out in chapters 1 and 2, there is no doubt that it is Arjuna's *anaucitya* that triggers Kṛṣṇa's *prahasann iva*, given the inappropriateness of the hero's crisis and despondency at such a juncture vis-à-vis his own reputation as a great warrior. To this we may add his disobedience/disrespect toward Kṛṣṇa himself, that is, the *anaucitya* of Arjuna's stubbornness in saying that he will not fight despite just surrendering to Kṛṣṇa as his *guru* and lord, the same Kṛṣṇa who has told him to stop being a eunuch (*klība*), shake off his miserable weakness, and arise (*uttiṣṭha*). Although it is clear that Arjuna is lost in confusion (*moha*) and does not mean to be consciously disrespectful to his master, still the patent contradiction of his self-centered words and behavior—through which he claims to have reached a final, irrevocable decision—is in itself laughable. Among the commentators of *Bhagavadgītā* 2.10, Sadānanda Yogīndra, Madhusūdana Sarasvatī, Viśvanātha Cakravartī Ṭhākura and Bāladeva Vidyābhūṣaṇa highlight Arjuna's *anaucitya* precisely along these lines.

Nonetheless, even if we interpret Kṛṣṇa's *prahasann iva* to be solely or primarily an expression of mockery—though such sarcasm is mitigated by the *iva* particle—it is a hint of laughter that is not derogatory for the sake of being derogatory but is rather meant to elicit Arjuna's reaction and his return to his senses. In other words, even if understood as mockery, the underlying intention behind Kṛṣṇa's *prahasann iva* is to trigger Arjuna's discrimination (*viveka*) and therefore should be recognized as the outpouring of his grace (*kṛpā, prasāda*): a peculiar *upāya* or means of instruction utilized by the *guru* in order to stimulate a positive reaction in his pupil and bring about his transformation. Thus Madhusūdana Sarasvatī notes that the lord's derision (*prahāsa*), which he interprets to be only metaphoric due to the lack of its constitutive element (i.e., shame), is aimed at triggering Arjuna's discernment, he being the full receptacle of the lord's grace. Even Jñāneśvar in his commentary observes how the sweetness of nectar (i.e., Kṛṣṇa's grace) is hidden in the bitter taste of the medicine (i.e., his apparently angry or mocking expression), just as a mother's love is often concealed in anger.

On the other hand, it must be pointed out that Kṛṣṇa's *prahasann iva* may also be interpreted as a hint of laughter of amusement and pure joy, given that the *anaucitya* that triggers the lord's *prahasann iva* can lead to either mockery or mirth or even to a peculiar combination (*samuccaya*) of the two. Kṛṣṇa's facial expression could be interpreted as an initially derisive smile that in turn leaves place to a compassionate glance of pure joy and satisfaction at Arjuna's having sought refuge at his feet. The hint of laughter triggered by the hero's impropriety can go both ways and even allow for opposite sentiments to arise in rapid succession one after the other, and such in-built polysemy is part and parcel of Kṛṣṇa's unpredictable personality and precisely what makes him so fascinating. A few commentators such as Bhāskara and Jñāneśvar have explained the lord's reaction as one of pure astonishment (*vismaya*), given that the hero Arjuna is wholly unrecognizable in his being overwhelmed by pity toward his kith and kin. Be that as it may, what is certain is that Kṛṣṇa's *prahasann iva* is revelatory of the god's love and grace toward his *bhakta*.

Iconographic Representations of Kṛṣṇa Pārthasārathi

The iconographic translation in stone of Kṛṣṇa's smile/hint of laughter in the *Bhagavadgītā* is hard to assess. Its privileged locus is undoubtedly the so-called Pārthasārathi icon in which Kṛṣṇa is worshipped as the charioteer (*sārathi*)[25] of Pārtha, that is, of Arjuna as the son of Pṛthā.[26] The mention of this icon is found in the medieval *Vaikhānasāgama*, a South Indian Vaikhānasa work also known as *Marīcisaṃhitā* and *Vimānārcanakalpa*, possibly dating around the tenth century CE.[27] Basing himself upon this source, T. A. Gopinatha Rao describes it thus in his *Elements of Hindu Iconography*:

> In this image Kṛishṇa is represented as holding the reins in one hand and a cane in the other, and as in the act of mounting a chariot, the right leg resting on the floor and the left leg placed in front of the chariot. The chariot itself is made to carry a flag[28] on the dome above, and is shown to be yoked to excellent horses. Arjuna, with bow in hand,[29] stands on the ground with his hands in the *añjali* pose. The right hand of Kṛishṇa is held so as to be in the *vyākhyāna-mudrā*.[30]

The icon celebrates Kṛṣṇa at the decisive moment when he offered his teaching to Arjuna, the latter having just surrendered to him. This peculiar *mūrti* appears to have originated in South India and predates the *Vaikhānasāgama*'s attestation (though unfortunately we lack clear evidence for this). Its very designation as Pārthasārathi is significant since it is meant to be the term of reference for the *Bhagavadgītā* episode.[31] It highlights how Kṛṣṇa and Arjuna are an indissoluble, interrelated pair, reminding us of the fact that they are the incarnations of Nārāyaṇa and Nara respectively. In its representation of the two protagonists, the icon captures the very essence of the poem inaugurated by the lord's *prahasann iva* at *Bhagavadgītā* 2.10. As chariotteer, Kṛṣṇa is always ready to step in and provide the proper direction: as the well-wishing friend of his devotee Arjuna, he would never allow the surrendered soul to veer off the path of *dharma*.

Pārthasārathi is a well-known epithet—the great *vaiṣṇava* theologian Rāmānuja is popularly revered as an *avatāra* of Pārthasārathi—and a fairly common name.[32] One is reminded of the Pūrvamīmāṃsā teacher Pārthasārathi Miśra (eleventh and twelfth century CE), who belonged to the school of Kumārila.[33] However, despite the fact that there exist a number of Pārthasārathi temples in South India—the most well-known among them being the one in Thiruvallikeni or Triplicane near Chennai in Tamil Nadu, possibly dating to the eighth century CE, of which Rāmānuja himself was especially fond of—[34]we were able to identify only few specimens of this *mūrti*.[35] It should be noted that these sculptures do not necessarily follow all of the *Vaikhānasāgama* prescriptions—for instance, the chariot can be missing—and present many variations. Even the Pārthasārathi Temple in Thiruvallikeni shows an arrangement of images that is strikingly different from the abovementioned description.[36]

Perhaps the best preserved specimen of a Pārthasārathi icon is the one found on the outer wall of the Chennakesava Temple in the Kadapa District of Andhra Pradesh. This temple is part of the Puṣpagiri complex located on the banks of the Pennar River and dates to the fourteenth century CE or even earlier. Here Kṛṣṇa is represented seated in an upper position and with four hands, the two upper ones holding the conch and the discus while the lower right hand is in the *vyākhyāna* or teaching *mudrā*[37] and the lower left hand is hanging and points downward, the wrist resting on the knee. Arjuna is represented standing on the ground to his left, smaller and in a lower position. He is in the devoted *añjali* pose, holding his bow in his left arm and carrying arrows on his back, looking intently at his lord with a gaze full of expectation. As teacher of the *Gītā* (*gītācārya*), Kṛṣṇa is in the foreground in all his divine majesty, seated in a most relaxed pose with his legs wide open, his right leg resting on the ground (see fig. 4.1). His face is broad and bears a radiant countenance, serene and benign: with slightly open lips, he smiles protectively at his beloved *śiṣya*.[38]

In the rather ancient Kallazhagar Temple dedicated to Viṣṇu located in the Alagar Koyil village near Madurai in Tamil Nadu, Kṛṣṇa as Pārthasārathi is also represented with four hands but in *samapādasthānaka*, that is, with even feet in a perfectly straight posture with legs and arms close together, his radiant face exhibiting a benevolent gaze, indicative of his divine majesty. His two upper hands are in *kartarīmukhahasta* or scissors posture, with the index

Figure 4.1. Kṛṣṇa Pārthasārathi teaching the *Bhagavadgītā* to Arjuna. Chennakesava Temple, Puṣpagiri, Andhra Pradesh, fourteenth century. *Source*: H. Krishna Sastri, *South-Indian Images of Gods and Goddesses*. Madras: Madras Government Press, 1916.

and middle fingers stretched holding the conch and the discus, while his two lower hands are one in the *vyākhyāna* or teaching posture and one in the *kaṭakahasta* in which posture the tips of the fingers are loosely applied to the thumb so as to form a ring, a gesture (*abhinaya*) which is also used in teaching. To his side is Arjuna, devoutly holding the *añjali* posture.[39]

In an early Chola temple dating to the time of Parantaka I (c. 907–955 CE), the Tiru Alandurai Mahadevar Temple in Kilappaluvur in the Udaiyarpalaiyam *taluka* of the Trichinopoly district of Tamil Nadu, an arched gateway (*toraṇa*) over one of the niches for subordinate deities (*devakoṣṭa*) contains a sculpture of Kṛṣṇa with Arjuna.[40] Another specimen dated to the end of the twelfth century CE is part of a frieze representing the battlefield at Kurukṣetra and is found in the Hoysaleśvara Temple in Halebid, in present-day Karnataka: Arjuna, standing up bow in hand, is portrayed in his chariot fighting against Karṇa, with Kṛṣṇa as charioteer.[41]

On the whole, the representations in stone of the Pārthasārathi icon are rare and incomparable with the numerous carvings of Kṛṣṇa as drawn from Purāṇic mythology, especially the *Bhāgavata Purāṇa*.[42] The scant presence of the *Bhagavadgītā*'s teaching moment in sculpture is indeed striking.[43] We think that one of the reasons is that the dual Pārthasārathi icon of Kṛṣṇa and Arjuna was deemed to be too intellectual in its focus upon the lord's *upadeśa* and thus less appealing than the popular representations of the Purāṇic Kṛṣṇa celebrating his *līlā*s and miraculous feats. The embodiment of the *Bhagavadgītā* episode represented by the Pārthasārathi *mūrti*, in which Kṛṣṇa and Arjuna exemplify the *guru-śiṣya* relation, epitomizes epic theology and was in all likelihood perceived as something too abstract and speculative, akin to setting in stone an Upaniṣadic dialogue.

With regard to painting, we have no attestation of the *Bhagavadgītā* in the earliest surviving specimens. Therefore, one must focus attention on the early modern period (1526–1857), when a new style emerged in the Mughal era as a fusion of Persian miniature with older Indian traditions. Starting from around the seventeenth century, this style was diffused across the Indian princely courts, each developing its own peculiar methods and techniques.

In the well-known *Razmnamah* (Book of wars), the Persian translation in abridged form of the *Mahābhārata* sponsored in the late sixteenth century by the Mughal Emperor Akbar (1542–1605), none of the precious miniature paintings that illustrate the text represent the *Bhagavadgītā* episode. Herein, our poem occupies just a few pages and is not valued as the ethical climax of the epic. What is offered is merely a sketch of the dialogue between Kṛṣṇa and Arjuna, the interest of this Persian rendition being on the great war itself and not on Kṛṣṇa's abstract reflections.[44] If in the *Razmnamah*—both in its first copy carried out in 1584–86 and in its most elaborate second copy completed in 1598–99—one finds beautiful miniatures illustrating a variety of battle scenes in which the great warriors, among whom is Arjuna together with his charioteer, are represented with impressive accuracy, nonetheless the *Bhagavadgītā* teaching moment per se is never thematized.

A remarkable and possibly unique case is represented by the nearly five hundred paintings of the *Bhagavadgītā* by Allah Baksh, from late seventeenth-century Mewar (1680–1698), a region in the south-central part of Rājasthān, whose rulers cultivated painting as part of their project of resistance to Mughal rule.[45] Commissioned by the Maharana Jai Singh (1653–1698) of Udaipur, these works of the Mewar school[46] are part of an illustrated *Mahābhārata* folio of more than four thousand illustrations. Allah Baksh's paintings on the *Bhagavadgītā* are fairly large—37x24 cm—and have no precedent in the history of Indian miniature art, given that the poem had never been illustrated in such detail prior to this date. As Alok Bhalla and Chandra Prakash Deval remark:

> These *Gita* paintings are . . . exceptional because the great religious poem had never been illustrated in its entirety, shloka by abstract shloka. There is no other miniature artist who has engaged with the song's metaphysical argument with such calm intelligence and imaginative empathy. . . . Allah Baksh's works of visionary thoughtfulness deserve an honoured place in the history of Indian miniature art and in the great library of Indian scriptures and their interpretations. Unfortunately, very little attention has been paid to them.[47]

As the *Bhagavadgītā* has a total of seven hundred verses, we may assume that originally there must have been an equal number of paintings, one for every *śloka*. However, only one painting each has been located for chapters 1 and 17 and even for our *prahasann iva* verse of *BhG* 2.10 no painting has reached us. With reference to our topic the miniature of *BhG* 2.7, when Arjuna seeks refuge in Kṛṣṇa as his disciple and implores him to instruct him, deserves notice. The scene is lit by a serene blue-green light, suffusing the painting in an atmosphere of momentous silence. While Arjuna is represented down on his knees with folded hands and awaits everything from his lord, Kṛṣṇa, who is enveloped in a brilliant halo, is depicted on an elevated lotus-shaped seat, of a resplendent yellow like the chariot, which in turn rests on an inverted lotus thus forming an intersecting cone. He sits in a yogic posture with his right palm raised in the blessing gesture of fearlessness or *abhayamudrā*, assuring his devotee of his grace. The figures at the bottom left are mirror images of Kṛṣṇa and Arjuna on a white marble platform. The lord sits on a bright yellow seat whereas Arjuna stands before him with folded hands. Kṛṣṇa is beautifully dressed in a pale red robe laced with gold, while Arjuna wears a saffron garment.

To offer a second sample of Allah Baksh's art we can refer to his richly colored rendering of *BhG* 2.15, where the effulgent lord teaches Arjuna that only the wise one for whom pain and pleasure are alike is fit for immortality. Herein, Kṛṣṇa's right hand is raised in the *cinmudrā*, the gesture of consciousness where the joining of the index finger and thumb to form a circle signifies the oneness of *ātman* and *Brahman*, while his left hand is in the *varadamudrā* or wish-giving gesture. On his part, Arjuna reverently kneels down with folded hands, his head slightly bent down, imbibing the lord's *upadeśa*. The miniature seems to suggest that the warrior must incorporate the values of detachment (*vairāgya*) and equanimity (*samatva*) represented by the figure of the renunciant at the bottom.

Also deserving mention are the folk pictures of Paithani and Pinguli art whose evidence dates back to approximately the seventeenth century, still extant in Maharashtra and Karnataka, utilized by itinerant bards in their recitation of the *Mahābhārata* and *Rāmāyaṇa* episodes. This style of painting, known as Chitrakathi, is akin to the shadow puppets of the region and herein the scenes of the battle of Kurukṣetra with Kṛṣṇa acting as Arjuna's charioteer are familiar.[48]

On the whole, even in painting the emphasis is clearly on the representation of the Kṛṣṇa of devotional *bhakti* literature, celebrating his innumerable *līlā*s and his love for Rādhā and the *gopī*s, rather than on the epic Kṛṣṇa and his role as teacher to Arjuna. As Ursula King has noted, the iconography of the *Bhagavadgītā* with special reference to the pair of Kṛṣṇa and Arjuna did not belong to the popular repertoire of Hindu iconography and came to be thoroughly developed only from around the mid-eighteenth century at the courts of Hindu *rājas*: that is, by painters in the Rājput studios of North India. It is here that we witness the emergence of illustrated *Bhagavadgītā* manuscripts (in contrast with the illustrations of the *Mahābhārata* epic, which are found in earlier manuscripts).[49] The enterprise of Allah Baksh from late seventeenth-century Mewar must be viewed as its most significant antecedent, inaugurating this new phase.

What needs to be emphasized is that the *Bhagavadgītā*, much like the *Upaniṣads*, has been for centuries a more elitist text primarily meant for individual/collective recitation/memorization, meditation, and philosophical inquiry through its impressive, age-old exegetical tradition.[50] Significantly, in the colophons of its chapters the *Bhagavadgītā* is extolled as an *Upaniṣad* that concerns itself with the "knowledge of *Brahman*" (*brahmavidyā*) and the "doctrine of *yoga*" (*yogaśāstra*), and due to its sacredness in ancient times the reading and listening of the poem was proscribed to women and people of lower castes.[51] Thus it was devoutly recited[52] and learned by heart among educated Brahmins and within intellectual circles but had little appeal among the Hindu masses, with the one noticeable exception of the thirteenth-century Marāṭhī gloss written by Jñāneśvar (i.e., the *Jñāneśvarī*).[53]

Things take a new turn from around 1750, when we witness the transition of the *Bhagavadgītā* from elite status to popular work. This innovation was due to the attractiveness that the Kṛṣṇa/Arjuna pair, exemplifying *dharma* and *bhakti* and the paradigm of *kṣatriya*hood, exercised on the many Hindu princes who sought to define themselves as distinct from their Mughal rulers. Indeed, upholding the poem that represented the quintessence of the *Mahābhārata* was the best way to reclaim their self-identity and reinforce *kṣatriya* pride. This is the reason why the *Bhagavadgītā*'s teaching moment came to visual prominence around this time, the Hindu iconographic tradition conforming itself to the relevance accorded to it by the Brāhmaṇical commentarial tradition.

To be sure, it being a dialogue on a variety of religious and philosophical issues, the *Bhagavadgītā* provides little material for visualization, with only two noticeable exceptions: (a) the opening scene, showing Kṛṣṇa and Arjuna on their chariot amid the warring armies on the battlefield; and (b) the scene of the glorious theophany of Kṛṣṇa as potently described in chapter 11 of the poem. In their portrayals, artists have focused special attention on these two motifs, the first allowing for a number of variations among which the one where Kṛṣṇa starts offering his *upadeśa* to Arjuna who surrenders to him as his *bhakta* in the *añjali* pose is the most noteworthy, it being acknowledged as the unmistakable guiding force in the interpretation of the text. Chapter 85 of the *Viṣṇudharmottara* gives the following prescriptions with regard to the iconographic depictions of Kṛṣṇa and Arjuna: "Arjuna should be made beautiful, adorned by all ornaments, wearing *kirīṭa*[54] and red armlets, green like the *dūrvā*[55] and carrying a bow and arrow. . . . Krishna should be very beautiful resembling in colour the blue lotus-leaf."[56]

It is the interdependence/inseparability of both figures that makes the symbolic value of their iconographic representation so powerful. In this regard, a fine specimen is an early nineteenth-century Kangra painting that P. Banerjee in his book *The Life of Krishṇa in Indian Art* appropriately titles *Krishṇa Delivering the Message of the Gītā to Arjuna in the Battle-field*.[57] With his left hand raised in the act of delivering his teaching, Kṛṣṇa wears a beautiful ochre dress and is comfortably seated on top of the chariot, which is drawn by four white horses while Arjuna, fully equipped as a warrior with his armor and sword, sits kneeling in the *añjali* pose and facing him from a lower position within the seat of the chariot (see fig. 4.2). With a dark-blue complexion and lotus-petal eyes,[58] encircled by a divine halo and wearing a majestic crown surmounted by a peacock feather, Kṛṣṇa exhibits a serene, compassionate gaze.

Another noticeable example of this same motif can be seen in an eighteenth-century Kishangarh painting that J. Leroy Davidson in his *Art of the Indian Subcontinent from Los Angeles Collections* titles "Krishna delivering the sermon of the *Bhagavad Gita* to Arjuna."[59] The scene is the field of Kurukṣetra on the eve of the battle and Kṛṣṇa as charioteer stands in the foreground with his head turned toward Arjuna who sits in the *añjali* pose in the back of the chariot (see fig. 4.3). The focus of the painting is Kṛṣṇa's head, distinguished by a radiant halo: the divine *sārathi* bears a benevolent gaze, the painting capturing the moment when he starts imparting his salvific

Figure 4.2. Kṛṣṇa Pārthasārathi teaching the *Bhagavadgītā* to Arjuna. Kangra painting, early nineteenth century. Presently kept at the National Museum in Delhi. *Source*: Public domain.

Figure 4.3. Kṛṣṇa Pārthasārathi teaching the *Bhagavadgītā* to Arjuna. Kishangarh painting, eighteenth century. *Source*: J. Leroy Davidson, *Art of the Indian Subcontinent from Los Angeles Collections*. Los Angeles: The Ward Ritchie Press, 1968.

teaching to Arjuna. With his right hand he holds a staff and the reins through which he commands two beautiful white horses, while his left hand is turned toward Arjuna, his fingers being kept in the *vyākhyāna* or teaching *mudrā*. In the background are the armies of the Pāṇḍavas and Kauravas confronting each other, while all the gods descend from the heavens on their golden vehicles in order to behold the imminent conflict.

In addition, the dialogue between Kṛṣṇa and Arjuna has been illustrated also through the so-called terrace scene, an imaginary visualization in which the two sit opposite each other on some cushions on a terrace with no one else around. The divine *guru* exhibits a serene, benevolent gaze toward his pupil, and the *bhakti* element is highlighted by Arjuna's *añjali* posture. Ursula King argues that this terrace motif had its earlier precedents in Mughal portraits and later in the representations of Guru Nānak (1469–1539) as teacher.[60]

These various depictions of Kṛṣṇa and Arjuna on their chariot amid the warring armies on the battlefield were later carried over in the print versions of the *Bhagavadgītā* when the poem became more and more popular among India's urban middle classes and was made known to the West through Charles Wilkins's first English translation published in 1785.[61] Inspired by the illustrations present in the manuscript tradition, in India the drawings in the Sanskrit and vernacular printed versions of the text started appearing after 1850 (the first printed Sanskrit specimens of the poem having appeared in 1805 and 1808). In modern times, the printed illustrations of this motif, either emphasizing an activist interpretation in which Kṛṣṇa calls Arjuna to fight—providing a powerful inspiration for the development of Hindu nationalism—or a quieter interpretation emphasizing the *bhakti* element, became extremely popular (see fig. 4.4).

The so-called *Gītācārya* representation in which Kṛṣṇa, bearing a compassionate smile, teaches the *Bhagavadgītā* to Arjuna has nowadays become ubiquitous, being found not only in innumerable cover illustrations of the poem[62] but also in many different medias such as oleographs, sandalwood and ivory carvings, posters and calendar pictures.[63] Even in the popular *Amar Chitra Katha* collection of children's comics and storybooks, the illustration of Arjuna kneeling at Kṛṣṇa's feet on the Kurukṣetra battlefield is prominent in its *Mahābhārata* mini-series.[64]

Figure 4.4. Illustration taken from Lionel D. Barnett's translation of the *Bhagavadgītā* (London: J. M. Dent, 1928 [1905]). *Source*: Barnett, Lionel D., trans. *Bhagavad-Gītā or The Lord's Song*. London: J. M. Dent & Sons, 1928 (1905).

The chariot scene can be found painted, carved in wood and even sculpted in various contemporary temple complexes throughout the subcontinent, such as at the Birla Mandir in Delhi and of course at the holy site of Kurukṣetra and its attached Shri Krishna Museum (see fig. 4.5).[65]

As Agehananda Bharati noted, in contemporary urban India Kṛṣṇa as the mentor of Arjuna has become a ubiquitous icon pretty much in its own right, quite independently from the text of the *Bhagavadgītā* and its teachings.[66] The image is found in both sacred and secular settings, from greeting cards and ornaments to commercial advertisements, and its relocation and revalorization over time by different communities confirms its vitality and appeal (see fig. 4.6).[67]

Kṛṣṇa's *prahasann iva* in Theater and Dance

Historically, the *Bhagavadgītā* appears to have been under-represented in theatrical plays and classical dance performances such as the ones in the Bharatanāṭyam, Kūchipūḍi, and Odissi styles.[68] If the

Figure 4.5. Outer View of the Shri Krishna Museum, Kurukṣetra. *Source*: Public domain.

Figure 4.6. Kṛṣṇa Pārthasārathi blessing Arjuna, contemporary image. *Source*: Public domain.

theatrical representation of the *Mahābhārata* was always quite popular and was even exported to Southeast Asia, for instance, through its appearance in Indonesian shadow plays, the *Bhagavadgītā* episode did not receive the same attention.[69] Nonetheless, it is remarkable that in verse 10.9 of the poem Kṛṣṇa tells Arjuna that the wise men (*budhā*)

> With thoughts on Me, with life concentrated on Me,
> Enlightening one another, (*bodhayantaḥ parasparam*)
> And telling constantly of Me, (*kathayantaś ca māṃ nityam*)
> [they] find contentment and joy.

The narration (*kathā*) of Kṛṣṇa's nectarine words and deeds in the setting of a *satsaṅga* (lit. "association with the good") (i.e., a gathering of like-minded devotees) is an experience of pure bliss and is thought to be conducive to the attainment of liberation (*mokṣa*). Already half a century ago, Norvin Hein noted the significance of such practice, observing that "the recitative dance drama, which was already in use, may have been among the customs here suggested whereby the devout told Krishna's story."[70] Though we have no evidence that the *Bhagavadgītā* was represented through dance or theatrical staging, it is reasonable to assume that among the communities of *bhakta*s the poem or parts of it were subject to some form or other of public performance.[71] Indeed, we should never forget that the word *gītā* means "song"—being derived from verbal root √*gai*, meaning "to sing," "to speak or recite in a singing manner"[72]—and that in *BhG* 9.14 Kṛṣṇa himself states that the great-souled men are the ones who constantly sing his praises (*satataṃ kīrtayanto mām*).[73]

The *Bhagavadgītā* is certainly not easy to stage since apart from the *viśvarūpa* episode, which in time developed its own choreographic conventions,[74] it is but a conversation (*saṃvāda*) on abstract religious and philosophical concepts in which action has come to a complete standstill. It thus constitutes a veritable challenge for any actor and dancer. Moreover, there are few detectable emotional variances occurring during the dialogue between Kṛṣṇa and Arjuna and thus inevitably a limited narrative-focused vocabulary of gestures for the performers to work with.[75] Nonetheless, Arjuna's despondency/devout surrender to Kṛṣṇa and the latter's response to him through his *prahasann iva*, which introduces his *upadeśa*, lends itself very well to theatrical representation. Because *BhG* 2.1–10 are the crucial verses that occasion the dialogue, it is natural to infer that all dramatic enactments of the poem must have begun from here: even if the *Bhagavadgītā* was not represented in its entirety certainly this essential triggering moment must have been part of the repertoire of *kīrtankārs*, actors, and dancers.[76] Even nowadays in the *Vividavadham* ("Slaying of Vivida") play of Kṛṣṇāṭṭam, the ritualistic dance-theater of Kerala, what is staged in its sixth scene is Arjuna's initial despondency and Kṛṣṇa's teaching to him in order to convince him to fight, centered upon the immortality of the soul as opposed to the body's impermanence (see fig. 4.7).[77]

Significantly, in traditional Bharatanāṭyam dance, there are some basic recommendations with regard to the portrayal of Kṛṣṇa as Pārthasārathi. Thus the god should be represented in *samapādasthānaka*: with the feet evenly placed standing straight with all parts of the body aligned from head to toe, and bearing four hands. The two upper hands should be in the *kartarīmukhahasta* or scissors posture, while the two lower hands should be kept one in the *haṃsāsyahasta,* with the forefinger and thumb kept together

Figure 4.7. Kṛṣṇa and Arjuna in a contemporary Kṛṣṇāṭṭam play. *Source*: Public domain.

without any gap and the remaining fingers stretched out, and the other one in the *kapitthahasta*, with the thumb stretched by the side of the palm and capped with the pad of the index finger above the thumb's tip—while the little, ring, and middle fingers stay curled into the palm.[78] The positions of the feet and hands are indicative of Kṛṣṇa's divinity and of his teaching function.

A fine rendering of the *Bhagavadgītā* episode in Odissi dance is the one offered in July 2017 by Ileana Citaristi[79] (playing the part of Kṛṣṇa) and Saswat Joshi (playing the part of Arjuna) in their brilliant performance titled *Parthasarathi*.[80] Between minutes 5:48 and 6:12 of their dance, one can savor the talent of Ileana Citaristi in representing Kṛṣṇa's hint of laughter toward Arjuna. The spectator can appreciate the various nuances of the god's *prahasann iva*, which she transmits most effectively through her gestures and facial expressions: in rapid sequence, she is able to express in an emotional continuum the god's surprise and slightly mocking irony at Arjuna's dejection, which she then transmutes into a benevolent smile of pure grace, inviting the hero to stand up and regain his dignity (see fig. 4.8).

When I asked the artist if in the Odissi dance there is any specific rule with regard to this peculiar smile/hint of laughter, she told me that "it is left to the dancer's interpretation, there being no fixed codification for its representation." She emphasized that

Figure 4.8. Ileana Citaristi (right) and Saswat Joshi (left) performing *Parthasarathi*, Odissi dance, July 2017. *Source*: Public domain.

in her own rendering of Kṛṣṇa's *prahasann iva* "what she wished to convey was his paternal benevolence toward Arjuna, in order to inspire confidence in him."[81]

It should be remembered that some of the major criticisms of Peter Brook's staging of the *Mahābhārata* focused on his elliptical, cursory "five-minute encapsulation" of the *Bhagavadgītā,* which was "rendered into whispered words never revealed to the audience."[82] In chapter 1, we highlighted how Alf Hiltebeitel especially criticized the absence of Kṛṣṇa's smile, of his "subtle grin," which reveals a *bhakti* mode, it being "one of the things that you can't miss if you know what the iconography looks like."[83] This failure to emphasize such a turning point was a serious flaw, its absence being immediately felt by an Indian audience well acquainted with the text and its traditional portrayal.

Kṛṣṇa's *prahasann iva* in Film

With regard to the representation of the *Bhagavadgītā* through the medium of film, worthy of attention is the 1993 Sanskrit movie produced by T. Subbarami Reddy and directed by G. V. Iyer (1917–2003), the so-called barefoot director, famous for his films on spiritual subjects both mythological and historical. Titled *Bhagvad Gita: Song of the Lord,* it was the recipient of the National Film Award.[84] Herein, at minutes 26–27, at the crucial juncture of Arjuna's crisis and refusal to fight, Kṛṣṇa's smile/hint of laughter is inherently polysemic (see fig. 4.9). Gopi Manohar, the actor playing the part of the lord, exhibits a facial expression that, though slightly mocking at first—when pronouncing the words of *BhG* 2.2–3, rebuking Arjuna for his faintheartedness and unmanliness—rapidly transmutes itself into a radiant, benevolent smile indicative of his grace toward his friend.

Herein, the nuances of Kṛṣṇa's facial expressions toward Arjuna—expressed by G. V. Ragavendra—are effectively conveyed by *extending* the *prahasann iva* through a much wider sequence than the single verse of *BhG* 2.10, similar to the way Ileana Citaristi did through her Odissi dance. To be sure, a director such as G. V. Iyer could not miss the opportunity to give prominence to the god's smile/hint of laughter.

Figure 4.9. A scene of the film *Bhagvad Gita: Song of the Lord* (1993), directed by G. V. Iyer. *Source*: https://www.youtube.com/watch?v=eAOxV8u402o.

In Hindī, the poem was communicated to a mass audience through B. R. Chopra's and his son Ravi Chopra's serialization of the *Mahābhārata* on Doordarshan, the Indian national television, which devoted three episodes to the *Bhagavadgītā*. The whole epic was broadcast from October 2, 1988, to June 24, 1990, each episode lasting approximately forty-five minutes. This series has enjoyed and still enjoys a powerful afterlife on DVDs, especially among the South Asian diaspora throughout the world. Nitish Bharadwaj played the role of Kṛṣṇa and Firoz Khan that of Arjuna.[85]

In the *Bhagavadgītā*'s first episode at minutes 17–20 and 23–24[86]—both before Hṛṣīkeśa's *prahasann iva*, when a despondent Arjuna states that he will not fight, and immediately after it, when Kṛṣṇa starts delivering his teaching on the immortality of the self—the lord exhibits a smile/hint of laughter that is both ironic and graceful in the sense that the actor Nitish Bharadwaj very ably displays a facial expression that though initially mocking at Arjuna soon opens itself into a wide smile filled with love for his dearest pupil (see fig. 4.10).

Even here, the secret for acknowledging the richness and plural meanings inherent in the lord's *prahasann iva* is to expand it through a longer sequence that starts much earlier, from Kṛṣṇa's

Figure 4.10. A scene of the *Bhagavadgītā* episode televised by Doordarshan. *Source*: https://www.youtube.com/watch?v=PwFDQWauIJw.

very first words in the poem: from *BhG* 2.2–3, when he sarcastically criticizes Arjuna's faintheartedness and calls him a eunuch, to *BhG* 2.11 and beyond, when he benevolently starts offering him his teaching. To be sure, Kṛṣṇa's mocking expression is perfectly attuned to the words he addresses to Arjuna at *BhG* 2.2–3, whereas from 2.10, after Arjuna has taken refuge at his feet at 2.7, what is given prominence is the lord's loving smile toward his *bhakta*.

What these contemporary enactments show—which are no doubt indebted to a much older tradition of theatrical performance—is that the polysemy of *prahasann iva* that in the textual narrative is condensed at *BhG* 2.10 and raises even opposite understandings that are inevitably hard to accommodate, in the performative arts is convincingly and more easily conveyed *by expanding it throughout a longer sequence,* which extends itself from *BhG* 2.2 to 2.11 and even beyond. This is a most important point, since the embodied form of the poem represented by dance, theater, and film offers precious interpretations that add unique, revealing perspectives. The simple reading of the text—though reputed to be highly meritorious, as in the individual and collective practice of *pothīpārāyaṇa*—shows its limits and is hermeneutically insufficient: in order to be fully understood, the poem must be approached in broader terms, that is, through a performative enactment (*kathā*). We have noted that Kṛṣṇa himself tells Arjuna that this is precisely what "wise men" (*budhā*) do (*BhG* 10.9).[87]

It must also be pointed out that in the many videos on the *Bhagavadgītā* that circulate on the internet, the image of Kṛṣṇa benevolently smiling to Arjuna from within the chariot is one of the most recurrent, being a stock icon: one fine example is an image at minute 3:04 of a video on the *prahasann iva* juncture sponsored by the International Society for Krishna Consciousness, i.e., the Hare Krishna movement (see fig. 4.11).[88]

The benevolence of the lord's smile is thus to be appreciated as the conclusive meaning of his polysemic *prahasann iva,* which needs to be acknowledged not so much as a discrete event but rather as a dynamic process in which the mark of love/grace constitutes its final signification, its climax. Far from being a recent convention, this hermeneutical approach characteristic of the performative arts has a long story behind it, the contemporary performers and the new media being the heirs of a time-honored tradition.

Figure 4.11. Kṛṣṇa Pārthasārathi benevolently smiling at Arjuna. *Source*: Public domain.

Kṛṣṇa's Smile and Hint of Laughter Beyond *Bhagavadgītā* 2.10

In fine arts, it appears that god Śiva smiles more than Viṣṇu, who is commonly represented as a hieratic, impassible deity. Śiva also exhibits a loud laugh (*aṭṭahāsa*), which is a special feature of his terrifying form—as in his south-facing Aghora *mūrti*—in which the mouth is wide open, the teeth are visible, and their brightness is a standard of comparison for whiteness. But even though Viṣṇu does not often smile,[89] the images of Kṛṣṇa are typically characterized by a smiling face to the point that Bharata's definitions of both *smita* and *hasita* find an exemplary illustration in many of his icons. To be sure, there is a privileged relation between smile and youth,[90] and if it is true that gods in general are believed to enjoy youth forever the case of Kṛṣṇa's youth and smile is paradigmatic being celebrated in literature as well as in the arts.

Scholars have underlined the difference between the more intellectual *bhakti* of the *Bhagavadgītā*, associated with knowledge (*jñāna*) and detachment (*vairāgya*), and the later emotional *bhakti* of the *Purāṇas*. In trying to reconstruct Kṛṣṇa's complex, multi-layered figure in a historical perspective, they have differentiated between the early clan god, the epic hero—whose identification with Viṣṇu as one of his embodiments (*avatāra*) in the *Bhagavadgītā* is understood to be a later development—[91]and his portrait in the *Viṣṇu Purāṇa* (c. third to fourth century CE), *Bhāgavata Purāṇa* (c. ninth century CE) and later devotional poems such as Jayadeva's *Gītagovinda*[92] (twelfth century CE).[93] This notwithstanding, the Hindu tradition has always acknowledged Kṛṣṇa as being one and the same, without ever distinguishing the early clan god from the epic hero and the god of the *Bhagavadgītā* from the one extolled in the *Bhāgavata Purāṇa* detailing his *līlās* in Vraja[94] and Dvārakā.[95]

It is noteworthy that the *Bhāgavata Purāṇa*—which appears to have been written in southern India—begins by establishing a narrative frame that explicitly links it to the *Mahābhārata*. Thus King Parīkṣit, who had been rescued by Kṛṣṇa in the epic, is the listener of the text that is recited to him by Śuka, one of the sons of Vyāsa who is traditionally revered as the composer of the *Mahābhārata*. As a whole, the *Bhāgavata Purāṇa* offers its own account of the

Mahābhārata by focusing on the episodes that emphasize Kṛṣṇa's divinity though with no explicit allusions to the *Bhagavadgītā* (despite some quotations from it), rather presenting its own *Gītā* in the eleventh book (the *Uddhavagītā*), in which Kṛṣṇa offers instruction to sage Uddhava.

It is indisputable that along the centuries the devotional centers and *sampradāya*s spread throughout the subcontinent that recognized Kṛṣṇa as their "chosen deity" (*iṣṭadevatā*) aimed at offering a unified picture of him. This they did by operating an accommodation and mutual reinforcement of kṛṣṇaite narratives present in diverse textual sources. In this regard, especially revealing are the devotional retellings of the Sanskrit *Mahābhārata* in the vernacular languages of both the south and north of India in which the focus is Kṛṣṇa.[96] Through its *Kṛṣṇacarita*s, the Hindu tradition articulated the richness of the god's plural aspects into a grand unified canon, simultaneously acknowledging him as darling infant, cowherd, flute player, lifter of the Govardhana[97] mountain, vanquisher of demons, favorite of the *gopī*s with whom he seductively sports and dances, prince, wise counsellor, youthful hero, etc. Over a period of a thousand years or more, many different strands coalesced to form the god's multifaceted character, the mythical, theological, and ritual dimensions of Kṛṣṇa *bhakti* having influenced aesthetic theories and artistic expressions.

Along these lines, Kṛṣṇa's *prahasann iva* of *Bhagavadgītā* 2.10 must be appreciated as one of the earliest specimens of the god's smile/hint of laughter—if not the very first, undoubtedly the most meaningful one within the Sanskrit epic—which the kṛṣṇaite tradition in its manifold dimensions has come to envision as a distinguishing feature of Kṛṣṇa's supreme personality, it being celebrated in both literature and the arts. If the laughter of Kṛṣṇa in the *Mahābhārata* is often a prelude to some catastrophic event,[98] his smile comes to be acknowledged as the hallmark of his benevolence, it being the sure sign of his divine play.[99]

In order to sketch an overview of Kṛṣṇa's smile/hint of laughter after *Bhagavadgītā* 2.10, we shall point out a few select episodes and iconographical representations of the god that are by all standards significant. We will necessarily content ourselves to present their main characteristics through a cursory outline, bringing attention to some notable examples so as to show how Kṛṣṇa's smile/hint of laughter is a constitutive feature of his throughout the centuries and throughout the subcontinent and even beyond, the god's iconography having diffused itself in Southeast Asia and in the whole world through the Hindu diaspora.[100] Herein, the *smita* and *hasita* of Kṛṣṇa in his various embodiments indicates the outpouring of his grace.

The natural starting point is the mischievous form of Kṛṣṇa as a child (*bāla*),[101] undoubtedly one of the most endearing representations of the god in art and devotional literature. In particular, the episode of the child Kṛṣṇa as butter thief (*navanītacora*) is of prime significance in the narrative of the *Bhāgavata Purāṇa* and even prior to it in the vernacular literatures of South India such as in the Tamil poems of the Āḻvār saints (sixth to ninth century CE). Its tradition in sculpture is widespread and old, dating from around the fourth to fifth century CE and is also widely attested to in *rāsalīlā*s performances, painting, and modern and contemporary devotional images.[102] In the iconography that portrays child Kṛṣṇa as butter thief, both old and new, he typically exhibits a naughty, captivating smile, as John Stratton Hawley chose to emphasize by selecting a "calendar art" image of *navanītacora* Kṛṣṇa, with his right hand sunk in the butter bowl, for the frontispiece of his 1983 monograph *Krishna, the Butter Thief.*

In a fine Tanjore painting dating to the end of the eighteenth century, the child Kṛṣṇa tightly holds a big pot of fresh butter under his left arm and a ball of butter in his right hand. His smile and wide eyes highlight his joy of savoring the stolen delicacy, successfully playing a prank on his foster-mother Yaśodā who is depicted on his left side in the act of slightly reprimanding him. On the opposite side, a *gopī* stands in sheer contemplation of him. Though Yaśodā and the *gopī* do not openly smile, they exhibit a tender look of love toward the mischievous child (see fig. 4.12).

In similar icons one also finds eminent figures such as kings and dignitaries who stand on the side of *bāla* Kṛṣṇa with their hands joined in the *añjali* pose. The latter's divine status is always conveyed by his central, larger size vis-à-vis the smaller size of the adult figures surrounding him, and by the jewels and flowers that enrich his persona. This peculiar smile is at one and the same time a mischievous one, celebrating the child Kṛṣṇa as the thief of

Figure 4.12. Child Kṛṣṇa as *navanītacora*. Tanjore painting, late eighteenth century. *Source*: Public domain.

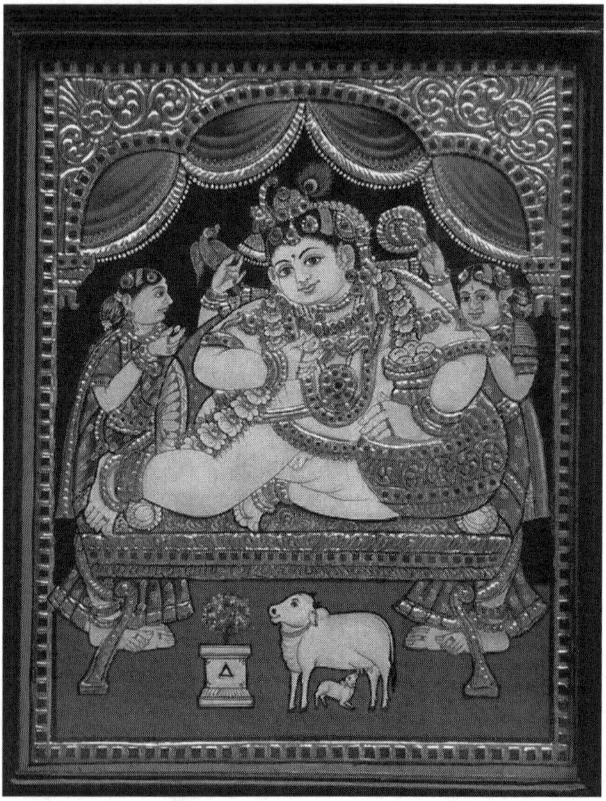

the fresh, delicious butter of Yaśodā, as it is a transcendent smile that points at his being the supreme *cittacora*, that is, the stealer of the minds and hearts of all creatures (see fig. 4.13).

When Bālakṛṣṇa succeeds in stealing the butter from his foster-mother, he is described dancing joyously, and this lighthearted dance of his is represented in the icon known as *navanītanṛttamūrti*.[103] Standing on a lotiform base and putting his weight on his left leg with his right leg bent and raised, the smiling god performs a dance step, his left arm being extended in a graceful movement known as *gajahasta*, representing an elephant's trunk, while his

Figure 4.13. Child Kṛṣṇa as *navanītacora,* contemporary poster. *Source*: Public domain.

right hand is held in the *abhayamudrā,* that is, the fear-allaying gesture (see fig. 4.14).

Precisely the episode of the child Kṛṣṇa stealing the butter results in his foster-mother being granted a vision of the cosmos (*brahmāṇḍa*) in his mouth (see fig. 4.15). The story goes that when it was reported to her from Kṛṣṇa's elder brother Balarāma and other children that Kṛṣṇa had eaten dirt, she got mad at him and started scolding him. The child, however, protested his innocence, insisting that the other boys had lied to her and that she should look at his mouth herself. Thus, when Yaśodā asked him to open

Figure 4.14. Bālakṛṣṇa as *navanītanṛttamūrti*. Chola style, fourteenth century. *Source*: Public domain.

his mouth she was astonished to see the whole universe within it (*Bhāgavata Purāṇa* 10.8.21–45).[104]

In his *Kṛṣṇakarṇāmṛta*, the fourteenth-century poet Līlāśuka Bilvamaṅgala beautifully describes this episode in verse 64 of his second canto:

> "When Kṛishna went forth to play, today, He swallowed mud to His heart's content."—"Is this true, Krishna?"—"Who said thus?"—"Balarama"—"Quite false, mother; look at my mouth!"—"Open!" Forth-with when the (seeming) Child's mouth was wide opened, His mother beheld therein all the universe, and was struck with wonder (*vismaya*): may such Keśava[105] protect us![106]

Figure 4.15. Child Kṛṣṇa granting vision of the universe to his foster-mother Yaśodā, contemporary poster. *Source*: Public domain.

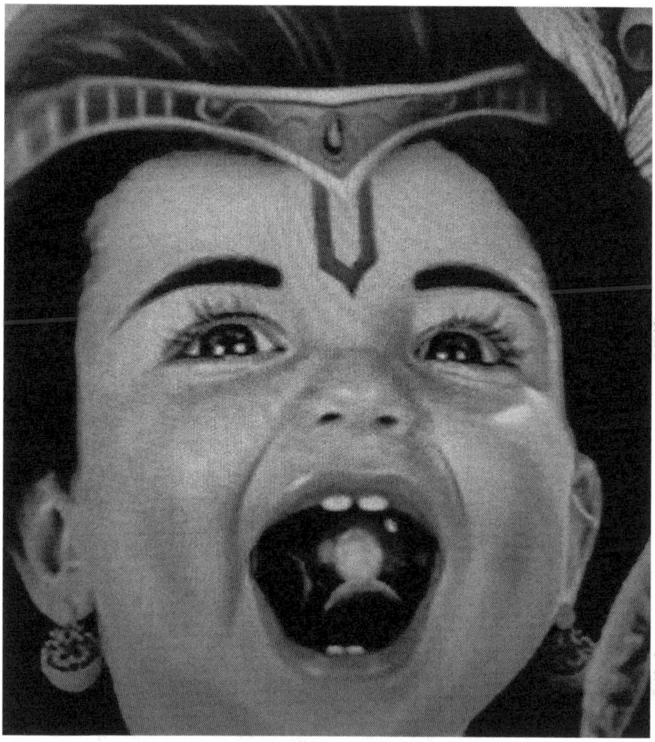

This tale of the mischievous child Kṛṣṇa who cheerfully opens his mouth wide immediately calls to mind the god's glorious manifestation narrated in chapter 11 of the *Bhagavadgītā*, when Arjuna sees within his mouths a doomsday fire that swallows up throngs of warriors and all beings, crushing them between his jaws (*BhG* 11.26–30). Yaśodā and Arjuna are both granted a vision that stuns them in *vismaya* (i.e., bewilderment and terror), this being the instinctive reaction when confronted with the transcendent reality of the supreme being. Just as Arjuna's *vismaya* is the human response to Kṛṣṇa's revelation of his supernal form—who in his human form had displayed a benevolent smile to his *bhakta*—Yaśodā's *vismaya* is the inevitable reaction at *bāla* Kṛṣṇa's widely opening his mouth in a prankish, naughty smile: the two divine smiles respond to one another, the *prahasann iva* anticipating Arjuna's extraordinary vision which is the acme of Kṛṣṇa's grace toward him, the lord having endowed him with a supernatural eye (*divyacakṣus*). And just like Arjuna begs Kṛṣṇa to revert to his usual form, so as to be like a father with a son, similarly Yaśodā cannot live long on the plane of metaphysics and must lapse back into her ordinary emotional involvement, that of a mother tendering her dear child.

Another paradigmatic icon is the one of Kṛṣṇa as Veṇugopāla, that is, the young cowherd playing the flute (*veṇu, muralī*), which is an extension of his beauty and exquisite charm through which he attracts to himself the *gopīs* and all souls (see fig. 4.16).[107] Typically, Kṛṣṇa stands erect with the left leg resting on the ground while his right leg is crossed against the left so as to touch the ground with the toes. The flute is held in both hands.

Figure 4.16. Kṛṣṇa Veṇugopāla with attendant cow. Shirdi Sai Baba temple, Guindy, Chennai. *Source*: Public domain.

Through the melody of his *veṇu*, a smiling Kṛṣṇa summons everyone to come to him, to join in his symphony of pure delight saturated with love. A popular Beṅgālī saying states that "without Kṛṣṇa there is no song" (*kānu binā gīta nāhi*), and indeed each and every soul is believed to long for the lord's *darśan* and the irresistible melody of his flute.[108] As Līlāśuka Bilvamaṅgala passionately sings in his *Kṛṣṇakarṇāmṛta* (1.44), craving to behold his beloved *iṣṭa*:

> When shall I see your lotus face
> With its always smiling (*aśrāntasmitam*) dawn-red lips,
> Joyously swelling the charming flute song
> Which is sweetly accompanied by half closed eyes that widen and dance?[109]

Kṛṣṇa's radiant, smiling face and his flute are inseparable: as T. A. Gopinatha Rao observes in his *Elements of Hindu Iconography*: "In the case of these images, the rapture of music has to be clearly depicted on the face; and they are in consequence generally so very pretty as to attract attention wherever they may be."[110] In the hands of their lord, all *bhakta*s should long to be just like his *veṇu*, "for then the Lord will come to you, pick you up, put you to His lips, and breathe through you and out of the hollowness of your heart, due to the utter absence of egoism that you have developed, He will create captivating music for all creation to enjoy. Be straight without any will of your own, merge your will in the will of God. Inhale only the breath of God."[111] In all of his actions, the underlying theme that the cowherd Kṛṣṇa exhibits and that his hint of laughter graciously reveals is *līlā*: the god's gratuitous play.[112] His entire life among the cowherds of Vṛndāvana[113] is but an ongoing, unpredictable, and spontaneous sport since indeed there is nothing that the god needs to do, he being totally free from the constraints of human condition. As Kṛṣṇa's veritable playground, Vṛndāvana is the stage of the frolicking child and adolescent god, of his feats against demons and of his pranks with the *gopī*s, of his ecstatic dance at the rapturous melody of his flute and of his communion with all individual souls as the ocean of bliss (see fig. 4.17).

The *rāslīlā* (lit. "dance pastime"), Kṛṣṇa's dance with the *gopī*s, typifies one's personal relationship with god (see fig. 4.18). As described in *Bhāgavata Purāṇa* 10.29–33, the female cowherds dance

Figure 4.17. Kṛṣṇa in Vṛndāvana riding the swing (*jhūlā*) surrounded by two *gopīs*, contemporary silk painting. *Source*: Author's private collection.

in a circle and Kṛṣṇa inserts himself between each pair, so that each one perceives that he is attending to her alone. In a wider sense, the *rāslīlā* refers to the full extent of Kṛṣṇa's divine play with the milkmaids, that is, their love, union, incomprehensible separation and final reunion. One of the *gopīs* in particular, Rādhā,[114] is the favorite of young Kṛṣṇa and their love, transcending all conventions, mirrors the ultimate form of unconditional love of god.

A major subject for visual artists and performers, along the centuries the *rāslīlā* has inspired several classical dance forms that remain popular today and are constantly enacted.[115] In such performances Kṛṣṇa's face is captivating and radiant, being characterized by a benign, seductive smile as well as by outbursts of joyful laughter, especially when he delights himself by playing tricks on the female cowherds.

Even in other prominent iconographical representations of Kṛṣṇa, as when he is depicted vanquishing the five-headed serpent-demon Kāliya[116] by dancing upon his middle head (*Bhāgavata Purāṇa* 10.1.16; *Viṣṇu Purāṇa* 5.7.1–83) or when he is portrayed lifting mountain Govardhana on his little finger for seven days (see

Figure 4.18. The *rāslīlā*, Kṛṣṇa dancing with all the *gopīs*. Basohli painting, Punjab Hills, c. 1750. *Source*: Public domain.

fig. 4.19), thus protecting the cowherds and their cattle from a storm that had been summoned by the Vedic god Indra—angry because the cowherds had shifted their devotion from him to Kṛṣṇa (*Viṣṇu Purāṇa* 5.11.1–25)—the young god exhibits a radiant countenance that is meant to highlight his gracious *līlā*, the unfathomable ease with which he performs such extraordinary feats.[117]

On the occasion of his victory over Kāliya, the *Viṣṇu Purāṇa* narrates: "When Kṛṣṇa was called to mind by the cowherds, the petals of his lips blossomed into a smile, and he split open that snake, freeing his own body from the coils. Using his two hands

Figure 4.19. Kṛṣṇa lifts the Govardhana mountain, contemporary poster. *Source*: Public domain.

to bend over the middle head of that serpent with curving hoods, the wide-striding Kṛṣṇa mounted that head and began to dance on it" (see fig. 4.20).[118]

The Application of the Classical *rasa* Theory to the Practice of Kṛṣṇa *bhakti*

The gaiety of Kṛṣṇa has been a constant source of inspiration for all kṛṣṇaite *sampradāya*s and an exemplary model for countless saints. Caitanya (c. 1486–1533), the founder of Gauḍīya (Bengal) Vaiṣṇavism who in time came to be revered as an *avatāra* of both Kṛṣṇa and Rādhā, was continuously immersed in ecstatic moods and would often laugh, dance, and sing. Acting spontaneously and unashamedly, reveling in the ecstasy of bliss, his overwhelming *bhakti* was an end in itself and his whole life is referred to as *līlā*. As David R. Kinsley writes:

Figure 4.20. Kṛṣṇa overcoming the serpent-demon Kāliya and dancing upon him. Bronze statue, South India, c. 1300. *Source*: Public domain.

> Caitanya often played both by himself and with his devotees . . . he laughed, joked, and sported with his friends. . . . [F]or [him] devotion, or religious activity generally, was fun, that he enjoyed . . . immensely, that . . . amused him. Caitanya was particularly prone to play when he was overcome by the *bhāva* or emotion of a boy or child, as in this passage:
>
> For a moment he fell under the spell of boyishness and became restless. Imitating boyish pranks, he made sounds in imitation of musical instruments. He moved his feet in various ways and laughed loudly. Under this spell, he crawled on all fours like a child.[119]

Kṛṣṇa's graceful smile in particular has been a constant source of inspiration for devotees and theologians,[120] being regarded as the sweetest (*madhura*) of his characteristics, even sweeter (i.e., more precious and desirable) than his beautiful body and face. As we read in *Kṛṣṇakarṇāmṛta* 1.92:

> Sweet, sweet the body (*vapus*) of this god.
> Sweet, sweet, the face (*vadana*). Very sweet.
> Oh, this gentle smile (*mṛdusmita*) with the smell of honey (*madhugandhin*):
> Sweet, sweet, sweet, sweet.[121]

Even beyond the kṛṣṇaite paradigm, the smile of deities[122] as well as saints is universally regarded as the special token of their favor and grace (*prasāda*): "A gracious look from the saints; sweet words from the saints' mouth, their smiling countenance—these alone bring great good fortune to the devotees."[123]

The poet and theologian Rūpa Gosvāmin (c. 1470–1557),[124] one of the six Gosvāmīs (lit. "lord of cows") who helped to establish the Gauḍīya tradition at the behest of Caitanya, in one of his major works titled *Bhaktirasāmṛtasindhu* or "The Ocean of the Essence of Devotional *rasa*" (*Uttara Vibhāga, Hāsyabhaktirasākhyā Prathamalaharī*) applies the classical *rasa* theory of Sanskrit poetics to the practice of Kṛṣṇa *bhakti*.[125] As he states:

> When Humorous Love (*hāsarati*) becomes fully developed by the Excitants (*vibhāva*) and other aesthetic components that are about to be described, the wise call it the Rasa of Humorous Devotion (*hāsyabhaktirasa*). Kṛṣṇa and those associated with him are the Substantial Excitants of this Rasa. The wise say that old people and children are usually the vessels of this type of love, but sometimes serious people are considered to be vessels under special conditions determined by the Excitants and other aesthetic components. An illustration of Kṛṣṇa: "I will not go near that terrifying withered up old man, Mother! He will trick me and put me in his bag and take me away." When the wonderful boy Hari said these words while looking around with frightened eyes, the sage Nārada[126] laughed openly, even though he was very skilled at suppressing his laughter.[127]

Following Bharata, Rūpa Gosvāmin says that laughter in ecstatic love (*hāsyabhaktirasa*) can be broken down into the six states of *smita, hasita, vihasita, avahasita, apahasita,* and *atihasita.*[128] In accordance with Bharata's hierarchical pattern, he notes that while the highest states of *smita* and *hasita* are a characteristic of the highest *bhakta*s, *vihasita* and *avahasita* are found in the middle devotees, and *apahasita* and *atihasita,* the lowest states, are found among the lowest *bhakta*s. This notwithstanding, he observes that "because of the diverse and special nature of the Excitants and other aesthetic components, knowers of emotions say that the other states are also sometimes found even in the highest devotees."[129] Notably, he illustrates each of these six states by telling stories about Kṛṣṇa in which the god, through his mischievous words and actions, elicits the smiling and/or laughing response of the ones who witness his *līlā*s:

1. *Smita,* a smile in which the eyes are widened and the cheeks raised but the teeth are not visible. Illustration: "Hey, where can I hide, Subala[130]? A nasty old woman is chasing after me, trying to catch me for stealing her yogurt. Quick, save me!" Seeing Hari running away saying these words with an agitated voice, the lotus faces of the group of sages in heaven blossomed with gentle smiles.

2. *Hasita,* a slight laughter in which just the tips of the teeth are visible. Illustration: [Kṛṣṇa has sneaked into the house of Rādhā's husband Abhimanyu[131], disguising himself as Abhimanyu. Seeing the real Abhimanyu approaching, he says to Abhimanyu's mother Jaṭilā:] "There comes Hari disguised in my clothes. But I am your son." Seeing her own son approaching, but believing the words of Kṛṣṇa, Jaṭilā became filled with anger, and grabbing hold of Abhimanyu, who was shouting with terror "Ma! Ma!" she threw him out of his own courtyard. Seeing this, Rādhā's group of girlfriends laughed slightly, revealing the tips of their bright teeth.

3. *Vihasita,* full laughter in which the sound of laughter is heard clearly and the teeth are fully visible. Illustration: [Kṛṣṇa says to a friend:] "Enter the house and steal the thick yogurt without fear, for Jaṭilā is sleeping soundly and snoring loudly." Hearing Keśava speak these words, Jaṭilā, who was only pretending to be asleep, laughed out loud in a manner that revealed her decaying teeth.

4. *Avahasita,* open laughter in which the nose becomes puffed and the eyes squint. Illustration: [After Kṛṣṇa had just returned home from spending the entire night in the love bower, Yaśodā, thinking he had slept in his own bed, says to him:] "Son, why are your eyes so red so early in the morning? And why are you wearing Balarāma's dark blue clothing (also the color of Rādhā's clothing)?" Hearing these words spoken by Yaśodā, the female messenger was unable to check her laughter as her nostrils flared and her eyes contracted.

5. *Apahasita,* raucous laughter in which tears fill the eyes and the shoulders shake. Illustration: When the great sage Nārada saw the divine child of Vraja clearly dancing the dance of the gods for the old cowherd women, his eyes filled with tears and his head and arms flew about in all directions as he turned the clouds white with the brightness of his teeth.

6. *Atihasita,* boisterous laughter in which the hands are clapped together and the limbs are thrown about wildly. Illustration: [Kṛṣṇa to Mukharā[132]:] "Hey old woman, your wrinked face looks like a monkey's! After seeing you, the best of the monkeys will be anxious to marry and unite with you, and will force me to help him secure you." [Mukharā to Kṛṣṇa:] "My mind has become confused with all this monkey business; therefore I will marry no one except you, since you are the destroyer of the king of monkeys." Hearing these words of Mukharā, the girls laughed wildly while clapping their hands.

> Even if the subject of laughter is not indicated directly, still it can be ascertained by the reference shared with the Excitants and other aesthetic components. An illustration: "Hey Kuṭilā,[133] your breasts look like long pea pods, your nose looks like a frog, your eyes look like an old turtle, your lips look like charcoal, and your stomach looks like a drum. What woman could possibly be more beautiful than you, O daughter of Jaṭilā? Why then is my flute unable to overcome your resistance, as it has had the good fortune of doing with the other beautiful women of Vraja?"[134]

To sum up, there is no doubt that a constitutive characteristic of Kṛṣṇa's figure, notwithstanding its extraordinary richness and plural dimensions along the centuries, is its multidimensional smile and laughter: sometimes ironic, sometimes enigmatic, sometimes purely mischievous but always inherently blissful. Even when his laughter announces some impending disaster, as it happens at some crucial points in the *Mahābhārata,* it is theologically understood as the darker, transcendent aspect of his divinity (i.e., his unfathomable *mysterium tremendum* beyond human comprehension), which in the *Bhagavadgītā* finds its culminating expression in the glorious theophany of chapter 11.[135] Nonetheless, Kṛṣṇa's smile/hint of laughter has predominantly been conceptualized as the essential characteristic of his *fascinans* aspect, of his irresistible power of attraction which fuses together beauty, love, and grace.[136]

Just as the various Kṛṣṇas are integrated into a unified portrayal, in the same way his smile/laughter is extolled as one of the most prominent features of his personality. As verse 4 of the popular *Kṛṣṇāṣṭaka* hymn proclaims:

> To the one who has the fragrance of a coral tree flower, a beautiful laughter (*cāruhāsa*), four arms [as Viṣṇu], and who wears a peacock feather on his head: to Kṛṣṇa I bow down, the master of the universe.
> (*mandāragandhasaṃyuktaṃ cāruhāsaṃ caturbhujam | barhipicchāvacūḍāṅgaṃ kṛṣṇaṃ vande jagadgurum ||*).

What is central in the god's portrayal is the benign character of his *smita* and *hasita*, which is first and foremost an expression of his amazing grace (*kṛpā*) toward his *bhaktas*. His smile communicates his *ānanda*,[137] which he partakes with his devotees in a communion of love, as part and parcel of his ongoing cosmic play, and is inherently transformative. Along these lines, the sensuous and at the same time otherworldly beauty of Kṛṣṇa's persona is conveyed in countless devotional hymns (*bhajans*). Here is a contemporary example:

> Worship the dark-blue complexioned and enchanting flute player, Lord Kṛṣṇa, who has a beautiful smiling lotus face, is dressed in yellow and is adorned with a peacock feather on his head and who, while walking, makes the melodious sound of *jhum jhum jhum* through his anklets.
> (*ghana ghana nīla baṅsī ādhāriyā | madhura madhura smita vadana savāriyā | mora mukuṭa pītāmbara ghātiyā | jhumaka jhumaka jhuma bhaja ghuṅghāriyā ||*)[138]

All in all, Kṛṣṇa's *prahasann iva* of *Bhagavadgītā* 2.10 must be appreciated as the most significant hint of laughter in the god's mission as *avatāra*, whose programmatic task, as he reveals to Arjuna, is "the protection of the good and the destruction of evil-doers, making a firm footing for the right, age after age" (*paritrāṇāya sādhūnāṃ vināśāya ca duṣkṛtām | dharmasaṃsthāpanārthāya saṃbhavāmi yuge yuge ||* *BhG* 4.8). Kṛṣṇa's graceful *prahasann iva* is the sublime prelude to the outpouring of his *upadeśa* to Arjuna and to all mankind, meant to transmute everyone's heart and mind and lead to blissful union with himself, the supreme lord.

The god's smile/hint of laughter is to be understood as a most powerful *darśana* that he bestows upon Arjuna and all the hearers and readers of the *Bhagavadgītā*, which has an inexhaustible creative, transformational force. Kṛṣṇa's *prahasann iva* "touches" the *bhaktas*' eyes and hearts, instantly purifying them and making absolutely easy what Arjuna and all men thought and think to be insurmountably difficult: in a flash, his hint of laughter brings joy and levity where there was gloom and utter despair (see fig. 4.21).

The idea is that whoever is touched by the deity's smiling glance and takes refuge at his feet is blessed beyond measure and

Figure 4.21. Kṛṣṇa gracefully smiles to Arjuna, blessing him through his *abhāyamudrā*. Contemporary poster. *Source*: Public domain.

will achieve the supreme goal of life. In his *Bhāmatī*, a subcommentary on Śaṅkara's *Brahmasūtrabhāṣya*, the great philosopher Vācaspati Miśra (tenth century CE) magnifies the Absolute *Brahman* with these words:

> The *Veda*s are his breath; the five elements are his glance; the animate and inanimate beings are his smile; and the great dissolution is his sleep.
> (*niḥsvasitam asya vedāḥ vīkṣitam etasya pañcabhūtāni | smitam etasya carācaram asya ca suptaṃ mahāpralayaḥ ||*)[139]

In this series of metaphors, breathing, glancing, and smiling are the minimal efforts one can make, smiling being the greatest of them. Thus, all beings are but the smile of the supreme godhead.[140] By the same token, Krsna's smile/hint of laughter brings about liberation (i.e., blissful communion [*sayujyatā*] with him), freeing all creatures from their blinding ignorance (*avidyā*) and allowing the recognition of the Bhagavat's omnipresence and of the entire world as the field (*kṣetra*) of his ongoing *līlā*.

Notes

Introduction

1. On the typology of laughter, see the classic work of H. Bergson, *Laughter: An Essay on the Meaning of the Comic* (New York: Macmillan, 2018 [Paris 1900]). For an overview, see H. Plessner, *Laughing and Crying: A Study of the Limits of Human Behavior*, trans. J. Spencer Churchill and M. Grene (Evanston, IL: Northwestern University Press, 2020); P. L. Berger, *Redeeming Laughter: The Comic Dimension of Human Experience* (New York and Berlin: Walter De Gruyter, 1997); M. L. Apte, *Humor and Laughter: An Anthropological Approach* (Ithaca and London: Cornell University Press, 1985). On laughter in the history of religions and in Greek and Roman antiquity, see S. Halliwell, *Greek Laughter: A Study of Cultural Psychology from Homer to Early Christianity* (Cambridge: Cambridge University Press, 2008); M. Beard, *Laughter in Ancient Rome: On Joking, Tickling, and Cracking Up* (Berkeley: University of California Press, 2014). For an anthology of sources on humor and laughter from antiquity to late modernity, see J. Figueroa-Dorrego and C. Larkin-Galiñanes, eds., *A Source Book of Literary and Philosophical Writings about Humour and Laughter: The Seventy-Five Essential Texts from Antiquity to Modern Times* (Lewiston, NY: Edwin Mellen, 2009).

2. On laughter as a lexically and phrasally produced import, see J. Ginzburg, E. Breitholtz, R. Cooper, J. Hough, and Y. Tian, "Understanding Laughter," Proceedings of the 20th Amsterdam Colloquium, 2015, https://hal-univ-diderot.archives-ouvertes.fr/hal-01371396. For an overview of the various theories on humor and laughter, see A. J. Chapman, H. C. Foot, and P. Derks, eds., *Humor and Laughter: Theory, Research, and Applications* (New York: Routledge, 1996); J. Morreall, ed., *The Philosophy of Laughter and Humor* (Albany: State University of New York Press, 1986).

3. See K. Gift, "Sarah's Laughter as Her Lasting Legacy: An Interpretation of *Genesis* 18:9–15," Coe College, 2012, http://research.monm.

edu/mjur/files/2019/02/MJUR-i02-2012-7-Gift.pdf; D. J. Zucker, "Isaac: A Life of Bitter Laughter," *Jewish Bible Quarterly*, https://jbqnew.jewishbible.org/assets/Uploads/402/jbq_402_isaaclaughter.pdf.

4. Even in the *Nāṭyaśāstra* of Bharata it is said that "laughter arises from the imitation of the actions of other people" (7.10; *paraceṣṭānukaraṇād dhāsas samupajāyate*); see R. Gnoli, *The Aesthetic Experience According to Abhinavagupta* (Varanasi: The Chowkhamba Sanskrit Series Office, 1985[3]), 90, 98.

5. A touch of humor is a characteristic of many Hindu gods and *gurus*; see for instance K. Narayan, *Storytellers, Saints, and Scoundrels: Folk Narrative in Hindu Religious Teaching* (Philadelphia: University of Pennsylvania Press, 1989). A contemporary *guru* such as Sathya Sai Baba (1926–2011) had a good sense of humor; see P. Mason, S. Lévy, and M. Veeravahu, eds., *Sai Humour* (Prasanthi Nilayam: Sri Sathya Sai Towers Hotels, 1999). His hagiographer Narayan Kasturi (1897–1987) was himself a noted humorist; see A. Rigopoulos, *The Hagiographer and the Avatar: The Life and Works of Narayan Kasturi* (Albany: State University of New York Press, 2021). We are also reminded of Meher Baba (1894–1969), who often used the expression "Don't worry, be happy"; see https://www.youtube.com/watch?v=xSqM7Qw3HlM.

6. U. Eco, *Il nome della rosa* (Milan: Bompiani, 1980). For an English translation, see *The Name of the Rose*. Translated from the Italian by W. Weaver (New York: Warner Books, 1983).

7. On these issues, see G. Stroumsa, *Le rire du Christ. Essais sur le christianisme antique* (Paris: Bayard, 2006). A saying falsely attributed to Saint Augustine of Hippo (354–430 CE) but actually of medieval origin (*Patrologia Latina* XL, 1290) concisely states: *Dominum numquam risisse sed flevisse legimus*, "We read that the Lord never laughed but cried." The classic work of Elton Trueblood, *The Humor of Christ* (New York: Harper & Row, 1964), offers a challenge to the traditional stereotype of a somber, gloomy Christ.

8. On these issues, see W. Watson, *The Lost Second Book of Aristotle's "Poetics"* (Chicago and London: University of Chicago Press, 2012).

9. On the development of the ideas on laughter in the Middle Ages and Early Modern times, see A. Classen, ed., *Laughter in the Middle Ages and Early Modern Times: Epistemology of a Fundamental Human Behavior, Its Meaning, and Consequences* (Berlin: De Gruyter, 2010).

10. See https://blog.cancellieri.org/umberto-eco-sul-riso-e-la-comicita

11. See M. Parodi, "Disarmonia. Una causa del riso da Umberto Eco al Medioevo," *I castelli di Yale online* V, 2 (2017): 267–77, https://cyonline.unife.it/article/view/1540.

12. B. K. Matilal, "Kṛṣṇa: In Defense of a Devious Divinity," in *The Collected Essays of Bimal Krishna Matilal. Philosophy, Culture and Religion. Ethics and Epics*, ed. J. Ganeri (New York: Oxford University Press, 2002), 91.

13. On the Buddha's smile in a comparative perspective, see P.-S. Filliozat and M. Zink, *Sourires d'Orient et d'Occident* (Paris: Académie des Inscriptions et Belles-Lettres, 2013). See also R. Panikkar, *Myth, Faith and Hermeneutics: Cross-cultural Studies* (Toronto: Paulist, 1979), 257–76; A. Rigopoulos, "Sorrisi e silenzi nell'Induismo e nel Buddhismo. Dimensioni apofatiche a confronto nella riflessione di Raimon Panikkar," in *Le pratiche del dialogo dialogale. Scritti su Raimon Panikkar*, ed. M. Ghilardi and S. La Mendola (Udine: Mimesis, 2020), 287–304.

14. Following the *vaiṣṇava* philosopher Rāmānuja (1017–1137 CE), Richard H. Davis notes how in Kṛṣṇa coexist "supremacy" (*paratva*) and "easy accessibility" (*saulabhya*); see R. H. Davis, *The Bhagavad Gita: A Biography* (Princeton, NJ: Princeton University Press, 2015), 25, 60–61.

15. The same is true in Pāli, where from root √*smi* we have *sita* and *mihita* for "smile" and from roots √*has* and √*hṛṣ* we have *hasita/hassa/hāsa* for "laughter;" see T. W. Rhys Davids and W. Stede, eds., *The Pali Text Society's Pali-English Dictionary* (Boston: Routledge & Kegan Paul, 1986 [1921–25]), 534, 709, 730–31. In the vernacular languages of India such a differentiation is not always maintained. For instance, though in Hindī the verbs "to laugh," *haṅsnā*, and "to smile," *muskarānā*, are clearly distinguished one from the other, in cognate Indo-Aryan languages such as Marāṭhī ("to laugh," *haṅsaṇe*; "to smile," *hasaṇe*) and in South Indian Dravidian languages such as Telugu ("to laugh," *navvaḍam/navvaḍāniki*; "to smile," *chirunavvu navvaḍam*) there is an overlapping between the two. In Telugu, *chirunavvu* is a gentle smile and is thus akin to Kṛṣṇa's *prahasann iva*.

16. M. Monier-Williams, *Sanskrit-English Dictionary* (New Delhi: Munshiram Manoharlal, 1988^{3} [Oxford: Clarendon Press, 1899]), 700.

17. V. S. Apte, *The Practical Sanskrit-English Dictionary*. Rev. ed. (Kyoto: Rinsen Book Company, 1986), 1122.

18. See V. R. Jhalakikar, ed., *Kāvyaprakāśa of Mammaṭa. With the Sanskrit Commentary Bālabodhinī* (Poona: Bhandarkar Oriental Research Institute, 1983^{8}), 6–10 (chap. 1, *kārikā* 2).

19. See E. A. Cecil, "Mapping the Pāśupata Landscape: Narrative, Tradition, and the Geographic Imaginary," *The Journal of Hindu Studies* 11, no. 3 (2018): 285–303.

20. See for instance V. Chitluri, *Baba's Divine Symphony* (New Delhi: Sterling, 2014), 40, 69. As the *Shri Sai Satcharita* states (chap. 10, v. 27): "Sometimes he [= Sai Baba of Shirdi] treated people with great affection;

sometimes he charged at them, stone in hand. There was a volley of curses and abuses, on occasions, as there was an embrace of blissful joy on other occasions;" see G. R. Dabholkar (Hemad Pant), *Shri Sai Satcharita: The Life and Teachings of Shirdi Sai Baba,* trans. Indira Kher (New Delhi: Sterling, 1999), 150–51. See also the story of Siddique Phalake, a Muslim resident of Kalyan, in ibid., 172–75 (chap. 11, vv. 77–113). On the *faqīr* of Shirdi, see A. Rigopoulos, *Oral Testimonies on Sai Baba. As Gathered During a Field Research in Shirdi and Other Locales in October-November 1985* (Venice: Edizioni Ca' Foscari, 2020); also see *The Life and Teachings of Sai Baba of Shirdi* (Albany: State University of New York Press, 1993).

21. *na prayojanavattvādhikaraṇa* ||. See *Brahmasūtrabhāṣya* 2000, 404–6.

22. The subject of the omniscience of *Brahman* is dealt with in Śaṅkara's *Brahmasūtrabhāṣya ad* 1.1.2–3.

23. Though in his gloss *ad Brahmasūtrabhāṣya* 2.1.33 Vācaspati Miśra distinguishes three reasons for the Bhagavat's manifestation of the universe—chance (*yadṛcchā*), intrinsic nature (*svabhāva*) and gratuitous play (*līlā*)—thus differentiating between *svabhāva* and *līlā,* yet for Śaṅkara such distinction is much more nuanced since in his commentary he alludes to a cause-and-effect relationship between them. Indeed, on Īśvara's part there is no other reason for the manifestation of the universe than his intrinsic nature, which manifests itself in a propensity to create as a form of pure amusement (*līlārūpā pravṛttir bhaviṣyati*); see A. K. Śastri and V. L. S. Pansīkar, eds., *The Brahmasūtra Śankara Bhāshya with the Commentaries Bhāmatī, Kalpataru and Parimala* (Bombay: Nirnaya Sagar Press, 1917), 480–81.

24. As it will be seen in chapter 3, one of the chief meanings of *prahasann iva* in the epics is precisely that of ease.

25. F. Edgerton, trans., *The Bhagavad Gītā* (New York: Harper Torchbooks—The Cloister Library, 1964 [1944]), 89.

26. See M. Piantelli, *Śaṅkara e la rinascita del brāhmanesimo* (Fossano: Editrice Esperienze, 1974), 103–4.

27. On the adjective *gambhīra*, see A. Nikolaev, "Deep Waters: The Etymology of Vedic *gabhīrá-*," *Historische Sprachforschung* 132 (2019 [2021]): 191–207.

28. On laughter in the Bible and in early Christianity, see P. J. Achtemeier, ed., *Harper's Bible Dictionary* (San Francisco: Harper & Row, 1985). See also R. Gallaher Branch, "Laughter in the Bible? Absolutely!," https://www.biblicalarchaeology.org/daily/biblical-topics/bible-interpretation/laughter-in-the-bible-absolutely/.

29. *The Bible. New Revised Standard Version* (NRSV), https://www.biblestudytools.com/nrs/.

30. In 1979, in the archaeological site of Ketef Hinnom southwest of the Old City of Jerusalem, two tiny silver scrolls were found on which

portions of this prayer are inscribed. They were in a burial chamber and apparently were used as amulets. These scrolls contain what may be the oldest surviving texts from the Hebrew Bible, dating from around the late seventh to early sixth century BCE prior to the Babylonian exile. They are now preserved at the Israel Museum. On the priestly blessing, see J. D. Smoak, "The Priestly Blessing in Inscription and Scripture: The Early History of *Numbers* 6:24–26," *Oxford Scholarship Online*, October 2015, https://academic.oup.com/book/10129; K. Seybold, M. Jacobs, and D. E. Saliers, "Aaronic Blessing," in *Religion Past and Present. Encyclopedia of Theology and Religion* (Brill Online 2011), http://dx.doi.org/10.1163/1877-5888_rpp_COM_00010.

31. On this episode, see J. M. Philpot, "*Exodus* 34:29–35 and Moses' Shining Face," *Bulletin for Biblical Research* 23, no. 1 (2013): 1–11.

32. On the body of god in Jewish and Christian traditions, see F. Stavrakopoulou, *God: An Anatomy* (New York: Alfred A. Knopf, 2021); C. Markschies, *God's Body: Jewish, Christian, and Pagan Images of God* (Waco, TX: Baylor University Press, 2019).

33. Within the patristic tradition, the splendor of Moses' face is related to the episode of Jesus' transfiguration (*Matthew* 17:1–8; *Mark* 9:2–8; *Luke* 9:28–36).

34. On the cross-cultural resonances among the Judaic and Hindu traditions, see H. Goodman, ed., *Between Jerusalem and Benares: Comparative Studies in Judaism and Hinduism* (Albany: State University of New York Press, 1994). On differences and similarities in comparative perspective, see C. W. Bynum, *Dissimilar Similitudes: Devotional Objects in Late Medieval Europe* (Princeton, NJ: Princeton University Press, 2020); O. Freiberger, *Considering Comparison: A Method for Religious Studies* (New York: Oxford University Press, 2019). See also G. J. Larson and E. Deutsch, eds., *Interpreting Across Boundaries: New Essays in Comparative Philosophy* (Princeton, NJ: Princeton University Press, 1988).

35. The three fundamental steps one must follow in order to achieve self-realization in nondual Vedānta. On the stages of *śravaṇa, manana* and *nididhyāsana*, see Piantelli, *Śaṅkara e la rinascita del brāhmanesimo*, 160–63.

Chapter 1

1. F. Wilson, ed., *The Love of Krishna*. The *Kṛṣṇakarṇāmṛta* of Līlāśuka Bilvamaṅgala (Philadelphia: University of Pennsylvania Press, 1975), 110.

2. The Sanskrit verse of *BhG* 2.10 is the same in the vulgate edition, the Kashmirian recension, and the critical edition. For the critical edition of the *BhG*, see S. K. Belvalkar, *The Bhagavadgītā, Being Reprint of Relevant Parts of Bhīṣmaparvan* (Poona: Bhandarkar Oriental Research Institute, 1945).

3. The following are the eighty-four *loci* of *prahasann iva* in the *MBh*: 1.127.5d, 1.141.1b, 1.147.21c, 1.151.7b, 1.151.14d, 1.152.15d, 1.181.2b, 1.206.16c, 1.211.16b, 2.54.11b, 3.38.36b, 3.38.39b, 3.40.17f, 3.40.21b, 3.77.11b, 3.97.5d, 3.186.116b, 3.294.9d, 4.13.5c, 4.23.22d, 4.52.23b, 4.53.14b, 5.7.9b, 5.73.1b, 5.89.23d, 5.179.1b, 6.24.10b, 6.41.16d, 6.43.21d, 6.54.15d, 6.75.39f, 6.79.36b, 6.79.48e, 6.107.2d, 6.115.34b, 7.21.10d, 7.37.13b, 7.47.26b, 7.57.46b, 7.77.29c, 7.82.14d, 7.82.20d, 7.90.28d, 7.91.32b, 7.91.35d, 7.91.43d, 7.96.13d, 7.99.16b, 7.102.98c, 7.103.4b, 7.111.3b, 7.114.50f, 7.130.29b, 7.137.18d, 7.137.26d, 7.141.7b, 7.142.6d, 7.142.16d, 7.144.16d, 7.146.28d, 7.148.39d, 7.169.20d, 7.173.48b, 8.9.26d, 8.33.14d, 8.34.16d, 8.40.85b, 8.50.2b, 9.27.51d, 9.30.15f, 12.3.29b, 12.24.8d, 12.125.18d, 12.142.41b, 12.151.10b, 12.310.27b, 13.14.174d, 14.19.46d, 14.54.17b, 14.73.6b, 14.83.8b, 14.93.39c, 16.8.49d, 18.1.11b; see the electronic text of the Bhandarkar Oriental Research Institute's critical edition, available at http://bombay.indology.info/mahabharata/welcome.html.

4. The following are the thirty-nine *loci* of *hasann iva* in the *MBh*: 1.141.18d, 2.60.37d, 3.227.21d, 3.290.8b, 5.194.16d, 6.49.15d, 6.60.13d, 6.60.31b, 6.65.22d, 7.50.16d, 7.82.5b, 7.90.13d, 7.90.26b, 7.92.14d, 7.110.31d, 7.117.14b, 7.134.43b, 7.141.10d, 7.144.6b, 7.160.23b, 7.164.45b, 8.10.21d, 8.17.39d, 8.17.84d, 8.24.94c, 8.35.23b, 8.44.42d, 8.45.5b, 8.55.52d, 9.11.48d, 9.25.9b, 9.26.42d, 9.26.47d, 9.27.24f, 9.27.35d, 9.27.38d, 10.7.59d, 10.12.12d, 14.20.5b.

5. *prahasann iva*: 1.38.3b, 1.51.12d, 2.30.22b, 2.85.3b, 3.27.28f, 4.8.19d, 4.10.26d, 5.1.118d, 6.95.21c, 7.4.11b, 7.17.3d, 7.60.13b, 7.80.3d; *hasann iva*: 2.63.9d; see the electronic text of the Baroda critical edition, available at https://sanskritdocuments.org/mirrors/ramayana/valmiki.htm.

6. For a comparison of select English translations of the *BhG*, see G. J. Larson, "The Song Celestial: Two Centuries of the *Bhagavad Gītā* in English," *Philosophy East and West* 31, no. 4 (1981): 513–41. For a survey of *BhG* translations in Indian and non-Indian languages, see W. M. Callewaert and S. Hemraj, *Bhagavadgītānuvāda: A Study in Transcultural Translation* (Ranchi: Satya Bharati Publication, 1982).

7. C. Wilkins, trans., *The Bhagvat-Geeta or Dialogues of Kreeshna and Arjoon* (London: C. Nourse, 1785), 35.

8. E. Arnold, trans., *The Song Celestial or* Bhagavad-Gita *(From the* Mahabharata*). Being a Discourse Between Arjuna, Prince of India, and the Supreme Being Under the Form of Krishna* (New York: Truslove, Hanson & Comba, 1900), available at https://www.unodc.org/pdf/india/Bhagavad.pdf.

9. Edgerton, *Bhagavad Gītā*, 10.

10. S. Radhakrishnan, trans., *Bhagavadgītā. With an Introductory Essay, Sanskrit Text, English Translation and Notes* (London: George Allen & Unwin, 1963[7] [1948]), 102.

11. R. C. Zaehner, trans., *The Bhagavad-Gītā. With a Commentary Based on the Original Sources* (New York: Oxford University Press, 1973 [1966]), 124.

12. E. Deutsch, trans., *The Bhagavad Gītā. Translated, with Introduction and Critical Essays* (San Francisco: Holt, Rinehart and Winston, 1968), 37.

13. J. A. B. van Buitenen, trans., *The Bhagavadgītā in the Mahābhārata: Text and Translation* (Chicago and London: University of Chicago Press, 1981), 75. In his introduction, van Buitenen observes: "Arjuna's dilemma is both a real one and, despite Kṛṣṇa's sarcasm, an honorable one"; ibid., 3.

14. W. Sargeant, trans., *The Bhagavad Gītā: Twenty Fifth Anniversary Edition*, ed. Christopher Key Chapple, foreword by Huston Smith (Albany: State University of New York Press, 2009 [1984]), 95.

15. B. Stoler Miller, trans., *The Bhagavad-Gita: Krishna's Counsel in Time of War* (New York: Bantam, 1986), 31.

16. A. Malinar, *The Bhagavadgītā: Doctrines and Contexts* (Cambridge: Cambridge University Press, 2007), 64.

17. A. Cherniak, trans., *Mahābhārata. Book Six. Bhīṣma, Volume 1. Including the 'Bhagavad Gītā' in Context*, foreword by Ranajit Guha (New York: Clay Sanskrit Library—New York University Press and the JJC Foundation, 2008), 183.

18. G. Feuerstein and B. Feuerstein, trans., *The Bhagavad-Gītā: A New Translation* (Boulder: Shambhala, 2014 [2011]), 95. On the "important qualifying remark" that Hṛṣīkeśa imparted his teaching "laughingly, as it were," the authors note: "We could understand this easily in the sense that he was benignly mocking Arjuna. In order to create a mind of clarity (*sattva*) in a student, the teacher first has to dynamize a lethargic mind by introducing the quality of *rajas* into it. The progression, then, is *tamas* → *rajas* → *sattva*. Ultimately, of course, all three primary-qualities (*guṇa*) must be transcended in order to bring about spiritual liberation. From the highest perspective, even *sattva*, the principle of lucidity, represents a limitation;" ibid., 105 n. 36.

For a broader overview, here are more examples of English translations of *prahasann iva* in chronological order: Kāshināth Trimbak Telang (1882) "with a slight smile"; see K. T. Telang, trans., *The Bhagavadgītā with the Sanatsujātīya and the Anugītā* (Oxford: Clarendon Press, 1908[2] [1882]), 43; Alladi Mahadeva Sastry (1897) "as if smiling"; see A. Mahadeva Sastry, trans., *The Bhagavad Gita with the Commentary of Sri Sankaracharya* (Madras: Samata Books, 1977[7] [1897]), 22; Lionel D. Barnett (1905) "with seeming smile"; see L. D. Barnett, trans., *Bhagavad-Gītā or The Lord's Song* (London: J. M. Dent & Sons, 1928 [1905]), 88; Annie Besant and Bhagavân Dâs (1905) "smiling"; see A. Besant and Bhagavân Dâs, trans., *The Bhagavad-Gîtâ*. With Saṃskrit Text, free translation into English, a word-for-word translation, and an Introduction on Saṃskrit Grammar (London and Benares: Theosophical Publishing Society, 1905), 28; Swami Swarupananda (1909) "as if smiling"; see Swami Swarupananda, trans., *Srimat-Bhagavad-Gita*. With Text, Word-for-Word Translation, English Rendering, Comments and Index (Calcutta: Advaita Ashrama, 1967[10] [1909]), 34; W. Douglas P. Hill (1928) "as one smiling"; see W. D. P. Hill, trans., *The Bhagavad-gītā: An English Translation and Commentary* (Madras: Oxford University Press, 1953[2] [1928]), 84; Sri Aurobindo (1938) "smiling as it were"; see Sri Aurobindo, trans., *The Bhagavad Gita*, available at https://www.auro-ebooks.com/bhagavad-gita; Swami Nikhilananda (1944) "smiling"; see Swami Nikhilananda, trans., *The Bhagavad Gita* (New York: Ramakrishna-Vivekananda Center, 1944), 71; Swami Prabhavananda and Christopher Isherwood (1944) "smiling"; see Swami Prabhavananda and C. Isherwood, trans., *The Song of God: Bhagavad-Gita*, introduction by Aldous Huxley (New York: The New American Library, 1958[5] [1944]), 36; Swami Vireswarananda (1948) "as if smiling"; see Swami Vireswarananda, trans., *Srimad-Bhagavad-Gita*. Text, Translation of the Text and of the Gloss of Sridhara Swami (Mylapore: Sri Ramakrishna Math, 1948), 33; Venkataraman Raghavan (1949) "gently smiling"; see V. Raghavan, *Readings from the Bhagavadgītā* (Adyar, Chennai: Dr. V. Raghavan Centre for Performing Arts, 2010 [1949]), 6; Nataraja Guru (1961) "with a semblance of smiling"; see Nataraja Guru, trans., *The Bhagavad Gita* (Bombay: Asia Publishing House, 1961), 116; Juan Mascaró (1962) "smiled"; see J. Mascaró, trans., *The Bhagavad Gita* (New York: Penguin Books, 1978 [1962]), 49; Swami Chidbhavananda (1965) "smiling, as it were"; see Swami Chidbhavananda, trans., *The Bhagavad Gita* (Tirupparaitturai: Sri Ramakrishna Tapovanam, 1972[6] [1965]), 127; Abhay Caranaravinda Bhaktivedanta Swami Prabhupāda (1968) "smiling"; see A. C. Bhaktivedanta Swami Prabhupāda, trans., *Bhagavad-gītā As It Is* (New York: The Bhaktivedanta Book Trust, 1976 [1968]), 21; Swami Venkatesananda (1972) "as if smiling"; see Swami Venkatesananda, trans., *The Song of God (Bhagavad Gita)* (Elgin, South Africa: The Chiltern Yoga Trust, 1984[4] [1972]), 109; Keyes W. Bolle (1979) "seemed to smile"; see K. W. Bolle, trans., *The Bhagavadgītā: A New Translation* (Berkeley: University of California Press, 1979), 21; Swami Sivananda (1979) "as if smiling"; see Swami Sivananda, trans., *The Bhagavad Gita* (Shivanandanagar: The Divine Life Society, 1996[3] [1979]), 9; Robert N. Minor (1982) "with a semblance of a laugh"/"faint smile"; see R. N. Minor, trans., *Bhagavad-Gita: An Exegetical Commentary* (Columbia, Missouri: South Asia Books, 1982), 33; Eknath Easwaran (1985) "smiled"; see E. Easwaran, trans., *The Bhagavad Gita* (Tomales, CA: Nilgiri Press, 2007[2] [1985]), 89; Swami Chinmayananda (2000) "as if smiling"; see Swami Chinmayananda, trans., *The Bhagavad Geeta* (Langhorn, PA: Chinmaya, 2000), 63 (https://factmuseum.com/pdf/upaveda/Holy-Geeta-by-Swami-Chinmayananda.pdf); Stephen Mitchell (2000) "smiled"; see S. Mitchell, trans., *Bhagavad Gita: A New Translation*

(New York: Harmony Books, 2000), 47; Lars Martin Fosse (2007) "with a hint of derision"; see L. M. Fosse, trans., *The Bhagavad Gita* (Woodstock, NY: YogaVidya, 2007), 13; Graham Schweig (2007) "as if about to laugh"; see G. Schweig, trans., *Bhagavad Gita: The Beloved Lord's Secret Love Song* (San Francisco: Harper, 2007), 45; Walter Harding Maurer (2009) "almost bursting into laughter"; see W. H. Maurer, *The Sanskrit Language: An Introductory Grammar and Reader*, rev. ed. (London and New York: Routledge, 2009), 419; Swami B. V. Tripurari (2010) "smiling"; see Swami B. V. Tripurari, trans., *Bhagavad Gita: Its Feeling and Philosophy* (San Rafael, CA: Mandala Publishing, 2010), 40; Gavin Flood and Charles Martin (2013) "while laughing at him, as it were"; see G. Flood and C. Martin, trans., *The Bhagavad Gita: A New Translation* (New York: W. W. Norton, 2013), 13; Swami Mukundananda (2014) "smilingly"; see Swami Mukundananda, trans., *Bhagavad Gita: The Song of God*, 2014 (https://www.holy-bhagavad-gita.org/chapter/2/verse/10); James L. Fitzgerald (2018) "smiling"; see J. L. Fitzgerald, "*Mahābhārata*," in *Brill's Encyclopedia of Hinduism Online*, eds. K. A. Jacobsen, H. Basu, A. Malinar, and V. Narayanan (Leiden: Brill, 2018; https://referenceworks.brillonline.com/browse/brill-s-encyclopedia-of-hinduism). Fitzgerald adds that *prahasann iva* could even be translated as "grinning," though often the smile seems ironic.

19. The doubling of *n* in *prahasann iva* is due to a rule of external *sandhi*, which takes place when the *n* occurs as a final after a short vowel before any initial vowel. In Sanskrit, present participles are normally reserved for actions that are contemporaneous with those of the main verb, as in this case. They function as verbal adjectives and must agree in case, number, and gender with the noun they modify. On the present participle in Sanskrit, see R. P. Goldman and S. J. Sutherland Goldman, *Devavāṇīpraveśikā: An Introduction to the Sanskrit Language* (Berkeley: Center for South Asia Studies, University of California, 2002), 255–72.

20. Its use is indeed very common; see S. Sellmer, *Formulaic Diction and Versification in the Mahābhārata* (Poznań: Adam Mickiewicz University Press, 2015), 198.

21. Typically, this *upasarga* denotes expansion, a broadening. Among the many examples of the prefix *pra* meaning "forward" we may mention the nouns *prajā*, "procreation"/"propagation," *pravṛtti*, "moving onward"/"coming forth," *prakāśa*, "light"/"manifestation," and *prajñā*, "wisdom"/"intelligence."

22. Monier-Williams, *Sanskrit-English Dictionary*, 700.

23. Apte, *The Practical Sanskrit-English Dictionary*, 1121.

24. On the *prahasana* genre, see D. P. Pierdominici Leão, *The* Somavallīyogānandaprahasana *of Aruṇagirinātha Ḍiṇḍimakavi (critical text, translation and study)*, PhD thesis (Rome: Università "La Sapienza," 2018), 58–75.

See also D. Rossella, "Satire, Wit and Humour on Kings and Ascetics in *kāvya* Literature. «He who laughs last, laughs best»," in *Kings and Ascetics in Indian Classical Literature,* ed. P. M. Rossi and C. Pieruccini, International Seminar Proceedings, 21–22 September 2007 (Milan: Cisalpino, 2009), 117–33. For an overview on India's comic tradition, see L. Siegel, *Laughing Matters: Comic Tradition in India* (Delhi: Motilal Banarsidass, 1989 [Chicago, 1987]). On humor in South Asian religions, see the collection of articles in *Sacred Play: Ritual Levity and Humor in South Asian Religions,* ed. S. J. Raj and C. G. Dempsey (Albany: State University of New York Press, 2010).

25. Monier-Williams, *Sanskrit-English Dictionary,* 700.

26. As Raimon Panikkar noted: "There are three realms of reality: these domains are expressed in an already irreducible way in language and clearly evidenced in the so-called personal pronouns. I must immediately add that 'pro-noun' does not necessarily mean 'in place' of the name, a substitution. It can also mean 'prior,' that is, more important than the name. A pronoun is truly a primordial word. The Sanskrit grammarians called it *sarvanāman,* a name for everything (the fullness of a name);" R. Panikkar, *Lo spirito della parola* (Turin: Bollati Boringhieri, 2021), 96 (our translation).

27. Monier-Williams, *Sanskrit-English Dictionary,* 652; Apte, *The Practical Sanskrit-English Dictionary,* 1052. The *Viṃśatyupasargavṛtti* traditionally ascribed to Candragomin (seventh century CE) lists thirteen different meanings of *pra*: excellence/eminence (*udīrṇa*), multiplicity (*bhṛśārtha*), supremacy (*aiśvarya*), birth (*saṃbhava*), use/application (*niyoga*), satisfaction (*tṛpti*), purity (*śuddhi*), desire (*icchā*), power (*śakti*), peace (*śānti*), worship (*pūjā*), culmination (*agra*), and vision (*darśana*); see D. Dimitrov, ed., *Lehrschrift über die Zwanzig Präverbien im Sanskrit. Kritische Ausgabe der* Viṃśatyupasargavṛtti *und der tibetischen Übertzung* Ñe bar bsgyur ba ñi śu pa'i 'grel pa (Marburg: Indica et Tibetica Verlag, 2007), 24–27. Moreover, Kṣīrasvāmin (eleventh century CE) in his *Nipātāvyayopasargavṛtti* lists twenty-six meanings of *pra* of which only eight are in common with the *Viṃśatyupasargavṛtti*. The other eighteen are: cessation (*uparama*), direction (*digyoga*), amusement (*narman*), love (*preman*), knowledge (*jñāna*), ornament (*bhūṣaṇa*), defect (*doṣa*), occasion (*avasara*), service (*sevā*), haste (*sāhasa*), application (*upayoga*), proclamation (*prakathana*), negligence (*anavadhāna*), measure (*māna*), violence (*hiṃsā*), titling (*śāstranāman*), cheat (*vañcanā*), and opposite meaning (*arthaviparyaya*); see S. A. Śarmā, ed., *Nipātāvyayopasargavṛttiḥ*. Śrīveṅkaṭeśvaraprācyamahāvidyālayavyākaraṇopādhyāyena "vyākaraṇāsāhityavidyāpravīṇā"—dyupādhibhjā kautsena Appala Someśvaraśarmā, ity anena saviśeṣaṃ pariṣkṛta. Śrīveṅkaṭeśvaraprācyagranthāvalī (Tirupati: Tirupati Devasthānamudrālaya, 1951), 36.

28. The expression *prahasann iva* could even be viewed as a particular kind of compound, that is, a *kevalasamāsa,* as per Kātyāyana's *Vārtika* to Pāṇini's *Aṣṭādhyāyī* 2.2.18: "There is a [type of] compound [that forms itself] with [the particle] *iva* and the not dropping of the case ending [of its preceding word]" (*ivena saha samāso vibhaktyalopaś ca*). The example offered by grammarians is the famous *incipit* of Kālidāsa's *Raghuvaṃśa* 1.1: *vāgarthāviva* (= *vāg-arthau-iva*) *saṃpṛktau* . . . , "as speech and meaning are joined together . . ." However, there is no textual evidence for the interpretation of *prahasann iva* as a *kevalasamāsa* or *ivasamāsa* and overall it seems unlikely. On *kevalasamāsa*s, see G. A. Tubb and E. R. Boose, *Scholastic Sanskrit: A Handbook for Students* (New York: American Institute of Buddhist Studies, Columbia University Press, 2007), 88–89.

29. J. P. Brereton, "The Particle *iva* in Vedic Prose," *Journal of the American Oriental Society* 102, no. 3 (1982): 446. See also the recent article of E. Biagetti, O. Hellwig, and S. Sellmer, "Hedging in Diachrony: The Case of Vedic Sanskrit *iva*," *Proceedings of the 21st International Workshop on Treebanks and Linguistic Theories, March 9–12, 2023, Association for Computational Linguistics* 2023, 21–31; https://www.academia.edu/98485196/Hedging_in_diachrony_the_case_of_Vedic_Sanskrit_iva. On the particle *iva* in the hymns of the *Ṛgveda,* see G.-J. Pinault, "On the Usages of the Particle *iva* in the Ṛgvedic Hymns," in *The Vedas: Texts, Language and Ritual. Proceedings of the Third International Vedic Workshop Leiden 2002,* ed. A. Griffiths and J. E. M. Houben (Groningen: Egbert Forsten, 2004), 285–306. On *iva* clauses, see M. Hale, "Some Notes on the Syntax of *iva* clauses in Vedic;" https://www.researchgate.net/profile/Mark_Hale/publication/286626021_Some_Notes_on_the_Syntax_of_iva_Clauses_in_Vedic_Handout/links/566c9c0408ae1a797e3d9d85/Some-Notes-on-the-Syntax-of-iva-Clauses-in-Vedic-Handout.pdf.

30. Nataraja Guru notes: "The term *iva* (as if) applied to the smile of Krishna is a peculiarity of the *lingua mystica* familiar in the *Upanishads* . . . by which the edge is, as it were, taken off the actuality of the description, tending to make it more perceptual and thus more in keeping with a contemplative text;" Nataraja Guru, *The Bhagavad Gita,* 118.

31. Maurer, *The Sanskrit Language: An Introductory Grammar and Reader,* 419.

32. Dhṛtarāṣṭra's charioteer and bard, son of Gavalgaṇa, to whom he narrates the events of the great battle. He is the eyes—and ears—of the blind king Dhṛtarāṣṭra, having been granted divine vision by sage Vyāsa.

33. An epithet of Kṛṣṇa meaning "he whose hair is splendid"/"the bristling haired one" (*hṛṣī-keśa*) as well as "lord of the sense-organs" (*hṛṣīka-īśa*); see 1.15, 1.21, 1.24, 2.9, 2.10, 11.36, 18.1. For an overview of

Kṛṣṇa's names and epithets in the *BhG*, see P. L. Bhargava, "Names and Epithets of Kṛṣṇa in the *Bhagavadgītā*," *Indologica Taurinensia* 7 (1979): 93–96. Analogously, Arjuna is referred to as "the thick-haired one" (*guḍā-keśa*); see 1.24, 2.9, 10.20.

34. Dhṛtarāṣṭra, husband of Gāndhārī and father of Duryodhana and of ninety-nine other sons (i.e., the Kauravas). He was born blind as a result of his mother, Ambikā, closing her eyes during intercourse with his father, Kṛṣṇa Dvaipāyana Vyāsa.

35. Lit. "son of Vasudeva," a patronymic of Kṛṣṇa.

36. Mahadeva Sastry, *The Bhagavad Gita with the Commentary of Sri Sankaracharya*, 22–23. We have slightly modified his translation in a few points.

37. For a fine introduction to the *BhG*, see Davis, *The Bhagavad Gita*. See also I. Theodor, *The Bhagavad-gītā: A Critical Introduction* (London and New York: Routledge, 2021); A. Rigopoulos, "La *Bhagavadgītā*," in F. Sferra, ed., *Hinduismo antico. Volume primo. Dalle origini vediche ai Purāṇa* (Milan: Mondadori, 2010), CLXXIII–CXCII, 1500–1504. For an excellent contextualization of the *BhG* within the *MBh*, see Malinar, *The Bhagavadgītā: Doctrines and Contexts*. By the same author, see also "*Bhagavadgītā*," in *Brill's Encyclopedia of Hinduism Online*, eds. K. A. Jacobsen, H. Basu, A. Malinar, and V. Narayanan (Brill: Leiden, 2018; https://referenceworks.brillonline.com/browse/brill-s-encyclopedia-of-hinduism). For an overview on Kṛṣṇa in the *BhG*, see R. N. Minor, "Krishna in the *Bhagavad Gita*," in *Krishna: A Sourcebook*, ed. E. F. Bryant (New York: Oxford University Press, 2007), 77–94. On Kṛṣṇa's place within the *MBh*, see A. Hiltebeitel, "Kṛṣṇa and the *Mahābhārata* (A Bibliographical Essay)," *Annals of the Bhandarkar Oriental Research Institute* 60, 1/4 (1979): 65–107; A. Hiltebeitel, "Krishna in the *Mahabharata*: The Death of Karṇa," in *Reading the Fifth Veda. Studies on the Mahābhārata*, ed. V. Adluri and J. Bagchee. *Essays by Alf Hiltebeitel* (Leiden: Brill, 2011), 411–59.

38. Even though he is here referring to Śiva's smile, not Kṛṣṇa's; see A. Hiltebeitel, "The Two Kṛṣṇas on One Chariot: Upaniṣadic Imagery and Epic Mythology," *History of Religions* 24, 1 (1984): 19.

39. S. J. Rosen, ed., *Vaiṣṇavism: Contemporary Scholars Discuss the Gauḍīya Tradition*. Foreword by Edward C. Dimock, Jr. (New York: FOLK Books, 1992), 54. In Brook's *Mahābhārata*, the role of Kṛṣṇa was played by Bruce Myers (1942–2020) and that of Arjuna by Vittorio Mezzogiorno (1941–1994); on these actors' ideas about Kṛṣṇa and Arjuna, see V. Di Bernardi, *Mahābhārata. L'epica indiana e lo spettacolo di Peter Brook* (Rome: Bulzoni, 1990[2]), 151–60. For a shortened, modern prose version of the great epic, see R. K. Narayan, *The Mahabharata: A Shortened Modern Prose Version of the Indian Epic* (London: Mandarin, 1978). For a critical examination of modern *Mahābhārata*s, see R. E. Goldman, "'*The Great War and Ancient*

Memory:' Modern *Mahābhāratas* and the Limits of Cultural Translation," *Visual Anthropology* 5, no. 1 (1992): 87–96.

40. D. D. Shulman, *The King and the Clown in South Indian Myth and Poetry* (Princeton: Princeton University Press, 1985), 384.

41. For an overview on Arjuna in the *MBh*, see R. C. Katz, *Arjuna in the Mahabharata: Where Krishna Is, There Is Victory*. Foreword by Daniel H. H. Ingalls (Columbia: University of South Carolina Press, 1989).

42. In *BhG* 1.14, this war chariot "yoked with white horses" (*śvetair hayair yukte*) is called *syandana*. It was a gift from god Agni, who in turn had obtained it from god Varuṇa. In *BhG* 1.24, it is praised as the "highest chariot" (*rathottamam*).

43. See M. B. Emeneau, "*Bhagavadgītā* Notes," in *Mélanges d'indianisme à la mémoire de Louis Renou* (Paris: Éditions E. de Boccard, 1968), 276–77.

44. On the imagery of the *ātman* as the traveler in the chariot, the body as the chariot, the intellect as the charioteer, the mind as the reins, and the senses as the horses, see *Kaṭha Upaniṣad* 3.3–6, 9. On the Vedic chariot as a living prismatic metaphor, see E. Mucciarelli, "The Steadiness of a Non-steady Place: Re-adaptations of the Imagery of the Chariot," in *Adaptive Reuse: Aspects of Creativity in South Asian Cultural History*, ed. E. Freschi and P. A. Maas (Wiesbaden: Harrassowitz, 2017), 169–94.

45. "Equanimity is *yoga*," as per Kṛṣṇa's definition in *BhG* 2.48: *samatvaṃ yoga ucyate*. The wise considers pain and pleasure as being the same (*samaduḥkhasukha*; *BhG* 2.15, 14.24). There are twenty-two occurrences of *sama*/*samatva*/*samatā* in the *BhG*, which proves its relevance: see 1.4, 2.15, 2.38, 2.48, 4.22, 5.18, 5.19, 6.8, 6.9, 6.13, 6.29, 6.32, 9.29, 10.5, 12.4, 12.13, 12.18, 13.9, 13.27, 13.28, 14.24, 18.54.

46. The term *vairāgya* is found at *BhG* 6.35, 13.8, and 18.52; see also the cognate terms *asaṅga* at 15.3 and *tyāga* at 16.2 and 18.1–11.

47. Within the *Bhīṣmaparvan* itself, see 6.1.33, 6.19.3, 6.21.1, 6.41.6.

48. Master archer and teacher of the military art, Droṇa was especially fond of Arjuna whom he considered his best pupil.

49. In *Nāṭyaśāstra* 6.62, one of the reasons for the arising of the sentiment of compassion (*karuṇarasa*) is seeing the killing of one's beloved.

50. Initially this divine bow was given by Soma to Varuṇa. Agni, however, persuaded Varuṇa to part with it and presented it to Arjuna to enable him to burn the Khāṇḍava forest.

51. In the *Bhīṣmaparvan*, even sage Vyāsa makes an appeal to stop the battle after the enumeration of adverse omens (6.2.16, 6.4.43). But Dhṛtarāṣṭra considers Vyāsa's words to be futile, as he viewed war as a matter of fate (6.4.44–46).

52. Arjuna's refusal to fight is traditionally motivated by the prevalence of the lower *guṇa*s of *rajas* and *tamas*: the thought of the painful consequences (*śoka*) of having to fight against his *ācārya*s and *bandhus*

(said to be due to *rajas*) and his confusion (*moha*) about *dharma* (said to be due to *tamas*).

53. In *MBh* 5.131.36 and 5.133.3, Vidurā's son questions the value (*artha*) of a warrior's *svadharma* by putting forward views that are quite similar to those of Arjuna. Just like *BhG* 1.32, both verses end with the refrain: "What is the use of enjoyments or life?" (*kiṃ bhogair jīvitena vā*).

54. Back from their fourteen-year exile, the Pāṇḍavas had demanded the Kauravas return their half of the kingdom, but Duryodhana had adamantly refused. All the Pāṇḍavas's efforts toward compromise and peace were rejected by their cousins: even when Yudhiṣṭhira said that he and his brothers would content themselves with just five villages the Kauravas had dismissed such a solution. War had thus become unavoidable.

55. An epithet of Kṛṣṇa meaning "tender of cattle."

56. Edgerton, *The Bhagavad Gītā*, 6.

57. Lit. "difficult to conquer." He was the eldest son of Dhṛtarāṣṭra and Gāndhārī, the leader of the Kauravas in their struggle against the Pāṇḍavas.

58. An epithet of Kṛṣṇa meaning "destroyer of [the demon] Madhu."

59. Edgerton, *The Bhagavad Gītā*, 7.

60. On evil/sin (*pāpa*) in the *BhG*, see D. Hudson, "Arjuna's Sin: Thoughts on the *Bhagavad-gītā* in Its Epic Context," *Journal of Vaiṣṇava Studies* 4 (1996): 65–84.

61. On these issues, see C. K. Chapple, "Arjuna's Argument: Family Secrets Unveiled," *Journal of Vaiṣṇava Studies* 9, no. 2 (2001): 23–31.

62. Vṛṣṇi was a descendant of Yadu. Kṛṣṇa as well as other figures such as Sātyaki and Kṛtavarman belonged to this clan.

63. Another name of Kṛṣṇa, meaning "people-agitator."

64. Edgerton, *The Bhagavad Gītā*, 7–8.

65. On the religious significance and function of crying, see J. S. Hawley and K. C. Patton, eds., *Holy Tears: Weeping in the Religious Imagination* (Princeton: Princeton University Press, 2005).

66. Long ago Hermann Jacobi noted that Kṛṣṇa's reply lists topics that are used elsewhere in the *MBh* when a warrior refuses to fight and gives the example of Arjuna's reply to Uttara in 4.36.17–23; H. Jacobi, "Über die Einfugüng der *Bhagavadgītā* im *Mahābhārata*," *Zeitschrift der Deutschen Morgenländischen Gesellschaft* 72 (1918): 325. Other examples are Kṛṣṇa's reply to Bhīma joining the peace party (5.73) and Vidurā's speech to her son (5.131–34).

67. On the fruitlessness and bad reputation of the *klība*, see *Mānavadharmaśāstra* 2.158, 4.211.

68. See Vidurā's speech to her son (5.131.5–7). See also *MBh* 2.34.21, 2.38.24, 5.73.17. A hero is required to be a man (*puruṣo bhava*; see *MBh* 5.167.6, 5.167.13–15).

69. The story is told in the *Virāṭaparvan*, the fourth book of the *MBh* (4.23.22). Dressed as a woman, Arjuna presents himself as the eunuch Bṛhannalā/Bṛhannaḍā and disguises himself as a dance teacher in the king's harem. On this episode and Arjuna's incongruous, grotesque appearance as an androgynous clown, see Shulman, *The King and the Clown in South Indian Myth and Poetry*, 256–76. In a self-conscious, ludicrous reversal of roles with respect to the opening chapter of the *BhG*, Bṛhannalā/Arjuna acts as the brave charioteer of Uttara—a coward who panics when he sees the Kaurava army—and asks him why he does not wish to fight against the enemy; see ibid., 262.

70. On these issues, see A. Hejib—K. K. Young, "*Klība* on the Battlefield: Towards a Reinterpretation of Arjuna's Despondency," *Annals of the Bhandarkar Oriental Research Institute* 61 (1980): 235–44. See also Malinar, *The Bhagavadgītā: Doctrines and Contexts*, 38–42.

71. In chapter 2 of the *BhG* the meter changes from *śloka* to *triṣṭubh* in three other places, which again is meant to highlight their importance: at 2.20, 2.29, and 2.70. Each of the four lines of the *triṣṭubh* verse is made up of eleven syllables whereas the *śloka* verse has eight.

72. This is the same solution that Saṃjaya, acting as Duryodhana's ambassador, recommends to Yudhiṣṭhira in the *Udyogaparvan*: "I think it is better to live on alms in the kingdom of the Andhaka-Vṛṣṇis" (*bhaikṣācaryam andhakavṛṣṇirājye śreyo manye*; 5.27.2). On the other hand, Kṛṣṇa in a speech to Yudhiṣṭhira states that victory or death is the "alms" a *kṣatriya* lives on; see 5.71.3–4.

73. The Kashmirian recension of *BhG* 2.11 especially emphasizes the issue of *kārpaṇyadoṣa*.

74. The *BhG* author seems to have in mind *Kaṭha Upaniṣad* 2.1 where Yama, the god of death, instructs the Brahmin boy Naciketas thus: "The good (*śreyas*) is one thing, the gratifying (*preyas*) is quite another; their goals are different, both bind a man. Good things await him who picks the good; by choosing the gratifying, one misses one's goal;" P. Olivelle, trans., *Upaniṣads* (New York: Oxford University Press, 1998), 235. Besides 2.7, the term *śreyas* is found in *BhG* 1.31, 2.5, 2.31, 3.2, 3.11, 3.35, 5.1, 5.2, 12.12, 16.22.

75. Kṛṣṇa claims authority as supreme teacher both at the beginning of chapter 3, where he declares he has taught the doctrines of *jñānayoga* and *karmayoga* long ago (*purā*; 3.3), and at the beginning of chapter 4, where he proclaims himself to be the original teacher of *yoga* (4.3). On the *guru*'s foundational role in Indian culture, see R. M. Steinmann, *Guru-śiṣya-sambandha. Das Meister-Schüler-Verhältnis im Traditionellen und Modernen Hinduismus* (Stuttgart: Steiner Verlag Wiesbaden GMBH, 1986); A. Rigopoulos, *Guru. Il fondamento della civiltà dell'India.* Con la prima traduzione italiana del "Canto sul Maestro" (Rome: Carocci, 2009).

76. On these issues, see L. Minnema, *Tragic Views of the Human Condition: Cross-Cultural Comparisons Between Views of Human Nature in Greek and Shakespearean Tragedy and the Mahābhārata and Bhagavadgītā* (New York: Bloomsbury, 2013), 51–62, 101–14, 241–54, 307–44.

77. Along these lines, Franklin Edgerton points out that in *MBh* 2.61.38 the expression *prajñāvādikaḥ* means "talking as (pretending to be) wise;" Edgerton, *The Bhagavad Gītā*, 92. Significantly, the Kashmirian recension has the variant *prajñāvān nābhibhāṣase,* "you don't speak as a sage." For an overview, see T. Kato, "A Note on the Kashmirian Recension of the *Bhagavadgītā*: *Gītā* Passages in Bhāskara's *Gītābhāṣya* and *Brahmasūtrabhāṣya*," *Journal of Indian and Buddhist Studies* 62, no. 3 (2014): 1144–50; T. Kato, "Interpretation of the *Bhagavadgītā* II.11," *Journal of Indian and Buddhist Studies* 64, no. 3 (2016): 1106–12. See also S. Piano, ed., *Bhagavad-gītā. Il canto del glorioso Signore* (Cinisello Balsamo: Edizioni San Paolo, 1994), 100–101, n. 11b.

78. It draws on the style of funeral orations. These verses are included in the *Viṣṇusmṛti* (19.24) as words of consolation which should be addressed to mourners. For the recurrent and parallel passages in the *BhG* and other Sanskrit texts, see G. C. O. Haas, "Recurrent and Parallel Passages in the Principal *Upanishads* and the *Bhagavad-gītā* with References to Other Sanskrit Text," in *The Thirteen Principal Upanishads Translated from the Sanskrit. With an Outline of the Philosophy of the Upanishads and an Annotated Bibliography* (Madras: Geoffrey Cumberlege, Oxford University Press, 1949^2), 560–62. For other speeches of consolation in the *MBh*, see 11.2.3. On the hour of death, see F. Edgerton, "The Hour of Death: Its Importance for Man's Future Fate in Hindu and Western Religions," *Annals of the Bhandarkar Oriental Research Institute* 8, 3 (1926–27): 219–49.

79. On the parallelism between *BhG* 2.20 and *Kaṭha Upaniṣad* 2.18, see L. Rocher, "*Bhagavadgītā* 2.20 and *Kaṭhopaniṣad* 2.18: A New Interpretation," *The Adyar Library Bulletin* 27 (1963): 45–58.

80. At 2.38, Kṛṣṇa reiterates to him that he must not be attached to what will be the outcome of battle: "Holding pleasure and pain alike (*sama*), / Gain and loss, victory and defeat, / Then gird thyself for battle: / Thus thou shalt not get evil;" Edgerton, *The Bhagavad Gītā*, 13.

81. See also *MBh* 11.3.6. This idea is probably derived from *Bṛhadāraṇyaka Upaniṣad* 4.4.5. Death is not to be understood as nonbeing (*asat*) but as a mere change in appearance given that what truly is (*sat*) cannot vanish into nonbeing. On the metaphor of the soul's "changing clothes" in a comparative vein, noteworthy is a passage from *Psalm* 102:26: "They [= the earth and the heavens, all creatures] will perish, but you [= Yhwh] endure; they will all wear out like a garment. You change them like clothing, and they pass away;" *The Bible. New Revised Standard*

Version (NRSV), https://www.biblestudytools.com/nrs/. See also *Isaiah* 51:6. On the rebirth of the soul in ancient Greek philosophy, see Plato's *Phaedo* (70a–75e).

82. In contrast to other parts of the *MBh*, Kṛṣṇa does not view fighting against one's relatives as an emergency situation, a calamity that allows the application of *āpaddharma*, that is, special rules in times of distress.

83. As Arjuna himself observes in *BhG* 1.36, it is the Kauravas who are the *ātatāyinaḥ* (lit. "the ones whose bow is drawn") (i.e., the aggressors) and according to the authority of *Mānavadharmaśāstra* 8.348–51 whoever is attacked has the right to defend himself/herself:

> Twice-born men may take up arms when the Law is thwarted or when the vicissitudes of time bring calamity upon twice-born classes. When a man kills in accordance with the Law to protect his life, in a conflict over sacrificial fees, or in defense of women or Brahmins, he remains untainted. When an assailant attacks with the intent to kill—whether he is an elder, a child, an old person, or a learned Brahmin—one may surely kill him without hesitation. In killing an assailant, the killer incurs no fault; whether it is done openly or in secret, wrath there recoils on wrath. (P. Olivelle, ed., trans., *Manu's Code of Law: A Critical Edition and Translation of the Mānava-Dharmaśāstra* [New York: Oxford University Press, 2005], 185–86)

84. As Duryodhana states in *MBh* 5.125.19: "He [= the warrior] must stand erect; never must he submit. Manliness means steadfastness! Even if he feels like falling apart, he should never here on earth bow to anybody!" In the *Śāntiparvan*, Bhīṣma gives the same advice to Yudhiṣṭhira (12.131.9). In the epic even women formulate the rules of manliness: for instance, Pṛthā/Kuntī to her son Yudhiṣṭhira and Vidurā to her son Vidura (5.132.36–38).

85. Here Kṛṣṇa makes it clear that Arjuna's entitlement (*adhikāra*) is only to the ordained act.

86. Edgerton, *The Bhagavad Gītā*, 14.

87. Other possible translations of this compound which is synonymous of *mokṣa* ("liberation"/"release") are "the extinction in *Brahman*" or even "the inexpressible [state] of *Brahman*." Besides 2.72, *brahmanirvāṇa* is found in *BhG* 5.24, 5.25, and 5.26. The use of the term *nirvāṇa* indicates Buddhist influence.

88. See for instance Malinar, *The Bhagavadgītā: Doctrines and Contexts*, 77. See also M. Jĕzić, "Textual Layers of the *Bhagavadgītā* as Traces

of Indian Cultural History," in W. Morgenroth, ed., *Sanskrit and World Culture. Proceedings of the Fourth World Sanskrit Conference, Weimar, May, 23–30, 1979* (Berlin: Akademie Verlag, 1986), 628–38.

89. Besides 2.7, the verb *pra* + √*pad* occurs in *BhG* 4.11, 7.14, 7.15, 7.19, 7.20, 15.4. On the notion of *prapatti* in Śrīvaiṣṇavism, see S. Raman, *Self-Surrender (prapatti) to God in Śrīvaiṣṇavism: Tamil Cats and Sanskrit Monkeys* (London and New York: Routledge, 2007); R. C. Lester, "Rāmānuja and Śrī-vaiṣṇavism: The Concept of *prapatti* or *śaraṇāgati*," *History of Religions* 5, no. 2 (1966): 266–82. The *prapanna* goes through six stages, the final one being *kārpaṇya* or *akiṃcanya* which is the perfection of *prapatti*; see M. Piantelli, "Lo Hinduismo. I. Testi e dottrine," in *Storia delle religioni. 4. Religioni dell'India e dell'Estremo Oriente*, ed. G. Filoramo (Bari: Laterza, 1996), 109–10.

90. *Śraddhā* can be understood to mean "putting one's heart in someone/something," *śrad* being probably allied to Latin *credo* and *cor/cordis*; see Monier-Williams, *Sanskrit-English Dictionary*, 1095. As Kṛṣṇa teaches to Arjuna in *BhG* 17.3: "Man here is made up of faith; As a man's faith is, just so he is." The term also recurs in *BhG* 3.31, 4.39, 6.37, 6.47, 7.21, 7.22, 9.23, 12.2, 17.2, 17.3, 17.17, 17.28, 18.71. On *śraddhā*, see M. Hara, "Note on Two Sanskrit Religious Terms: *bhakti* and *śraddhā*," *Indo-Iranian Journal* 7, no. 2/3 (1964): 132–45. According to David Shulman, however, the primary meaning of *śraddhā* is "a mental function that tends to involve focusing and seeing clearly, which is to say, paying attention." Along these lines, he translates *BhG* 17.3 as follows: "You are what you pay attention to;" D. D. Shulman, *More than Real: A History of the Imagination in South India* (Cambridge, MA: Harvard University Press, 2012), 139.

91. On the various forms of Hindu prayer, see M. Piantelli, "Aspetti della preghiera dell'India," in *L'uomo davanti a Dio. La preghiera nelle religioni e nella tradizione cristiana*, ed. E. Guerriero (Cinisello Balsamo: Edizioni San Paolo, 1998), 34–89.

92. On the term *bhakti*, see Hara, "Note on Two Sanskrit Religious Terms: *bhakti* and *śraddhā*," 124–32. For an overview of *bhakti* theology and its nine characteristics, see A. Rigopoulos, *Hindūismo* (Brescia: Queriniana, 2005), 191–211. On Kṛṣṇa *bhakti*, see B. Holdrege, *Bhakti and Embodiment: Fashioning Divine Bodies and Devotional Bodies in Kṛṣṇa Bhakti* (New York: Routledge, 2015).

93. Olivelle, *Upaniṣads*, 265.

94. Thus the compound *prasannamukha* means "with a pleased countenance"/"smiling;" see Monier-Williams, *Sanskrit-English Dictionary*, 696–97; Apte, *The Practical Sanskrit-English Dictionary*, 1115. Within the *BhG*, *prasāda* is found at 2.64, 2.65, 17.16, 18.37, 18.56, 18.58, 18.62, 18.73, 18.75. On grace in Hinduism, see N. M. Martin, "Grace and Compassion," in

Brill's Encyclopedia of Hinduism Online, eds. K. A. Jacobsen, H. Basu, A. Malinar, and V. Narayanan (Leiden: Brill, 2013), https://referenceworks.brillonline.com/browse/brill-s-encyclopedia-of-hinduism.

95. See M. Hara, "Words for Love in Sanskrit," *Rivista degli Studi Orientali* 80, no. 14 (2007): 81–106. Kṛṣṇa's feet represent his infinite grace and compassion. In devotional circles they are compared to a ten-petalled blue lotus of exquisite fragrance and soft freshness.

96. Descendants of Yadu, one of the sons of Yayāti, the Yādavas were the pastoral tribe in which Kṛṣṇa was born. Under his princely leadership, they had established a kingdom at Dvārakā (lit. "the gated"), in the Saurāṣṭra peninsula of Gujarāt on the coast of the Arabian Sea. All the Yādavas that were present in Dvārakā after the death of Kṛṣṇa perished in it when it was submerged by the ocean.

97. With Kṛṣṇa on Arjuna's side, victory is assured as Saṃjaya solemnly states in the last verse of the poem (*BhG* 18.78).

98. M. Piantelli, "Nota sulla '*Bhagavadgītā*,'" in *Bhagavadgītā*, ed. A.-M. Esnoul (Milan: Adelphi, 1996[4] [1976]), 191 (our translation). For an analysis of this episode, see A. Hiltebeitel, *The Ritual of Battle: Krishna in the Mahābhārata* (Albany: State University of New York Press, 1990), 102–13. Arjuna's choice calls to mind the words of *Psalm* 20:7: "Some take pride in chariots, and some in horses, but our pride is in the name of the Lord our God;" *The Bible. New Revised Standard Version* (NRSV), https://www.biblestudytools.com/nrs/. See also *Psalm* 33:16–17: "A king is not saved by his great army; a warrior is not delivered by his great strength. The war horse is a vain hope for victory, and by its great might it cannot save;" ibid. Along these lines, in the Christian tradition Roberto Bellarmino (1542–1621) wrote: "With Christ, our leader and king, it is not anymore in chariots and horses that we place our faith but in the devoutly invoked name of God;" G. Ravasi, *I salmi. Introduzione, testo e commento* (Cinisello Balsamo: Edizioni San Paolo, 2006[3]), 105 (our translation).

99. Malinar, *The Bhagavadgītā: Doctrines and Contexts*, 135. Although Kṛṣṇa transcends the cosmos he also encompasses it and is keen to preserve it. As Kṛṣṇa cares for the world's welfare, in the same way Arjuna and his *bhakta*s must care for it. Kṛṣṇa unifies the conflicting values of social responsibility and world renunciation, blending in himself the characteristics of both the king and the ascetic.

100. See Hiltebeitel, *The Two Kṛṣṇas on One Chariot*, 1–26. Their association is mentioned already in the *Aṣṭādhyāyi*, Pāṇini's grammar, dating back to the fourth century BCE (*sūtra* 4.3.98). Arjuna was the son of Pṛthā/Kuntī and thus Kṛṣṇa's cousin, she being Kṛṣṇa's aunt. Moreover, Kṛṣṇa was also Arjuna's brother-in-law and groomsman: Arjuna married Subhadrā, Kṛṣṇa's sister, by abduction (*haraṇa*), and the couple had a

son, Abhimanyu. When in the *Mausalaparvan* Kṛṣṇa dies by means of a hunter's arrow piercing his heel—the only vulnerable part of his body, as in Achilles' legend—Arjuna instantly loses his strength, a premonitory sign of his impending death.

101. The sons of Dharma and Ahiṃsā, they are an ancient pair of warriors and seers (*ṛṣis*) who undertook asceticism at the Himālayan site of Badrīnāth. On the indissoluble couple of Nara and Nārāyaṇa, see M. Biardeau, "Nara et Nārāyaṇa," *Wiener Zeitschrift für die Kunde Südasiens* 35 (1991): 75–108. On Kṛṣṇa and Arjuna being viewed from the perspective of the twin myth in Indo-European mythology, see D. Frame, "Echoes of the Indo-European Twin Gods in Sanskrit and Greek Epic: Arjuna and Achilles;" https://chs.harvard.edu/CHS/article/display/5901.

102. On the interplay of these opposite motifs in Indian literature, see M. Bloomfield, "On Recurring Psychic Motifs in Hindu Fiction, and the Laugh and Cry Motif," *Journal of the American Oriental Society* 36 (1916): 54–89. See also Plessner, *Laughing and Crying: A Study of the Limits of Human Behavior*.

103. Such opposition is reminiscent of the iconographic contrast between the two philosophers Democritus of Abdera (c. 460–370 BCE) and Heraclitus of Ephesus (c. 535–475 BCE), the first being represented as laughing and the latter being represented as weeping. In his *De tranquillitate animi*, the Stoic philosopher Seneca (4 BCE–65 CE) sides with Democritus affirming that "laughing down life" (15.2) is the way through which humans can effectively distance themselves from the world and achieve cheerfulness (*euthymia*). Democritus's laughter is interpreted as revelatory of his serene wisdom, of his indifference toward the world and the vanity of human endeavors.

104. As Maharishi Mahesh Yogi (1918–2008) aptly observes in his commentary to *BhG* 2.10: "'Hrishikesha smilingly spoke': this expression is used to indicate that lifting Arjuna out of his state of silence and hesitancy and releasing him from the benumbed condition of the senses was not a big task for one who is the Lord of the senses. . . . The disheartened seeker becomes uncouraged by the first sign of the master's smile, which shows him without a word that his problems are neither so serious as he thinks nor so difficult as to be insurmountable. The contrast brought out is significant. It shows Arjuna in despair, while Lord Krishna smiles in His usual divine, playful, blissful mood;" Maharishi Mahesh Yogi, *On the Bhagavad-Gita: A New Translation and Commentary. Chapters 1 to 6* (New York: Penguin, 1969), 89.

105. On the concept of *avatāra*, see A. Couture, "*Avatāra*," in *Brill's Encyclopedia of Hinduism Online*, eds. K. A. Jacobsen, H. Basu, A. Malinar, and V. Narayanan (Leiden: Brill, 2018), https://referenceworks.brillonline.

com/browse/brill-s-encyclopedia-of-hinduism. The term *avatāra*, however, is never used in the *Bhagavadgītā*.

106. On these issues, see V. M. Tschannerl, *Das Lachen in der altindischen Literatur* (Frankfurt: Peter Lang, 1992), 101–12. The laughter of Homeric heroes was also aggressive, charged with sarcasm. In ancient Greece the warriors' laughter was personified as a god, Γέλως, and the Spartans had erected a sanctuary to him which stood side by side to the ones dedicated to the personification of terror and the personification of death; see R. Vollkommer, "Gelos," in *Lexicon Iconographicum Mythologiae Classicae* (Zürich-München: Artemis, 1988), 4: 179. On the etymology of Γέλως, see R. Beekes, *Etymological Dictionary of Greek* (Leiden: Brill, 2010), 1:264–65. On the warriors' laughter, see L. Tritle, "Laughter in Battle," in *The Many Faces of War in the Ancient World*, eds. W. Heckel, S. Müller, and G. Wrightson (Cambridge: Cambridge Scholars Publishing, 2015), 117–34. In Hinduism, the warrior goddess Kālī laughs on the battlefield: her solitary laughter when everyone has been killed and everything has been destroyed makes her the embodiment of terror. In the *Sauptikaparvan* of the *Mahābhārata* (10.8.65), in the context of Aśvatthāman's night attack on the Pāṇḍava camp, Kālī is described as smiling/laughing derisively (*smayamānām*); see T. B. Coburn, *Devī-Māhātmya: The Crystallization of the Goddess Tradition* (Delhi: Motilal Banarsidass, 1988), 111–12. For an introduction to Kālī, see J. E. McDaniel, "Kālī," in *Brill's Encyclopedia of Hinduism*. Vol. 1: *Regions, Pilgrimages, Deities*, eds. K. A. Jacobsen, H. Basu, A. Malinar, and V. Narayanan (Leiden: Brill, 2009), 587–604. We are also reminded of the transgressive laughter of the adepts of the ancient movement of the Pāśupatas, in imitation of the "loud laughter" (*aṭṭahāsa*) of their chosen deity Rudra ("Roarer," "Howler"), the wild and terrible form of Śiva; see *Pāśupatasūtra* 1.8. With his ghastly laughter, Rudra-Śiva breaks the shell of Brahmā's egg (*brahmāṇḍa*), that is, transcends the limits of our finite universe; see *Kālabhairavāṣṭaka* 7. On the Pāśupatas' practice of courting dishonor, see D. N. Lorenzen, *The Kāpālikas and Kālāmukhas: Two Lost Śaivite Sects* (Berkeley and Los Angeles: University of California Press, 1972), 185–92; D. H. H. Ingalls, "Cynics and Pāśupatas: The Seeking of Dishonor," *Harvard Theological Review* 55 (1962): 281–98.

107. Edgerton, *The Bhagavad Gītā*, 12–13.

108. See for instance Yudhiṣṭhira's predicament in *MBh* 5.70.75.

109. Swami Swarupananda, *Srimat-Bhagavad-Gita*, 34.

110. Kṛṣṇa's *prahasann iva* may be compared to Aphrodite's smile, which strikes us as a mixture of tender kindness and mockery; see A. Wacławczyk and A. Mickiewicz, "What is Aphrodite Laughing at? An Attempt at Interpretation of the Epithet φιλομμειδής in the Archaic

Greek Poetry," in *Święto — Zabawa — Uroczystość w świecie starożytnym. Feast — Play — Celebration in the Ancient World*, ed. L. Ożarowska, K. Sekita and J. Simo (Warsaw: Wydawniktwo Naukowe Sub Lupa: 2011), 133–41. On Aphrodite's smile in Sappho's *Prayer to Aphrodite* (Fragment 1), see "The Descent of the Goddess: Ritual and Difference in Sappho's Prayer to Aphrodite;" http://nrs.harvard.edu/urn-3:hul.ebook:CHS_TravisR.The_Descent_of_the_Goddess.1990. Kṛṣṇa's hint of laughter can also be compared to the enigmatic smile of many statues of Greek deities, expressing their detachment and Olympian serenity.

111. See K. Lorenz, *On Aggression*, trans. M. K. Wilson (London and New York: Routledge, 1966), 172–73, 269, 284–87. And yet bearing one's teeth is not always a threat: in primates showing the teeth, especially if they are clenched together, is usually a sign of submission, and the human smile may have evolved from that. In any given culture, the variety of smiles is due to the simple fact that there are many different ways to smile and reasons for smiling; see http://www.bbc.com/future/story/20170407-why-all-smiles-are-not-the-same.

112. Fitzgerald, "*Mahābhārata*." On Kṛṣṇa's unfathomable personality within the *MBh*, see Matilal, "Kṛṣṇa: In Defense of a Devious Divinity," 91–108.

113. One is reminded of the first verse of the poem "The Smile" of William Blake (1757–1827): "There is a Smile of Love / And there is a Smile of Deceit / And there is a Smile of Smiles / In which these two Smiles meet."

114. Monier-Williams, *Sanskrit-English Dictionary*, 682.

115. As Govindanātha states in *Śrīśaṅkarācāryacarita* 1.3: "May the charioteer of the son of Pṛthā, of whom men and gods are the cushion of his lotus feet in which all beings seek refuge, fulfill all my desires for good!" Govindanātha, *Il Poema di Śaṅkara:* Śrīśaṅkarācāryacarita. Edited by M. Piantelli (Turin: Promolibri, 1994), 23 (our translation).

116. On the concept of *tejas*, see P. Magnone, "The Development of *tejas* from the Vedas to the Purāṇas," *Wiener Zeitschrift für die Kunde Südasiens* 36 (1992): 137–47. By the same author, see "*Tejas* Transactions in the Itihāsa-Purāṇa," in *The Churning of the Epics and Purāṇas*, eds. S. Brodbeck, A. Bowles, and A. Hiltebeitel (New Delhi: Dev Publishers, 2018), 341–65.

117. Significantly, in *BhG* 10.41 Kṛṣṇa declares that whatever is endowed with beauty is born of a particle of his own splendor (*yad-yad vibhūtimat sattvaṃ śrīmad ūrjitam eva vā | tat-tad evā 'vagaccha tvaṃ mama tejoṃśasaṃbhavam ||*). On the concept of beauty, see R. Torella, "Beauty," in *Burlesque of the Philosophers: Indian and Buddhist Studies in Memory of Helmut Krasser*, eds. V. Eltschinger, J. Kramer, P. Patil, Ch. Yoshimizu (Hamburg:

Numata Center for Buddhist Studies, 2023), 2:755–80; V. Raghavan, *The Concept of the Beautiful in Sanskrit Literature* (Chennai: The Kuppuswami Sastri Research Institute, 2008 [1988]).

118. The famous tale narrated in *Bhāgavata Purāṇa* 10.8 comes to mind, in which the boy Kṛṣṇa gives the vision of the entire universe in his mouth to his foster-mother Yaśodā.

119. See *Kalyana-Kalpataru. Gita-Tattva Number 1* (Gorakhpur: Gita Press, 1946), 57. Bhagwan Shree Rajneesh/Osho argues that Kṛṣṇa's laughter is due to the fact that though Arjuna is in such an indecisive state he still makes such a decisive statement (i.e., that he will not fight). The idea is that Kṛṣṇa would laugh at Arjuna's self-deception; see Osho, *Inner War and Peace: Timeless Solutions to Conflict from the Bhagavad Gita* (London: Watkins, 2005 [1970]), 170–71.

120. In his commentary to *BhG* 2.10, Sarvepalli Radhakrishnan writes: "The smile indicates that he [= Kṛṣṇa] saw through Arjuna's attempt at rationalization or what is now known as wishful thinking. The attitude of the saviour God who knows all the sins and sorrows of suffering humanity is one of tender pity and wistful understanding;" Radhakrishnan, *Bhagavadgītā*, 102.

121. D. R. Brooks, *Poised for Grace: Annotations on the Bhagavad Gita from a Tantric View* (The Woodlands, TX: Anusara, 2008), 47.

122. Swami Chidbhavananda, *The Bhagavad Gita*, 127–28.

123. On the Śiva Dakṣiṇāmūrti icon and its resemblance to the iconography of the enlightened Buddha, see M. Geetha, "Image of Siva Dakshinamurti in the Early Chola Temples: A Glance," *The Quarterly Journal of the Mythic Society* 103, no. 2 (2012): 74–85; A. J. Gail, "The Enlightened Buddha and the Preaching Śiva: More Light on the Dakṣiṇāmūrti Icon," in *South Asian Archaeology 1999*. Proceedings of the Fifteenth International Conference of the European Association of South Asian Archaeologists, held at the Universiteit Leiden, 5–9 July, 1999, ed. E. M. Raven (Leiden: Brill, 2008), 457–62; H. Bakker, "Dakṣiṇāmūrti," in *Vidyārṇavavandanam: Essays in Honour of Asko Parpola*, ed. K. Karttunen and P. Koskikallio (Helsinki: Finnish Oriental Society, 2001), 41–53. On silence and its eloquence, see A. Rigopoulos, "Negazioni e silenzi sotto i cieli dell'India. Orizzonti upaniṣadici e buddhisti a confronto," in *Forme della negazione: Un percorso interculturale tra Oriente ed Occidente*, ed. L. Marcato (Milan: Mimesis, 2015), 101–17. As the South Indian mystic Ramaṇa Maharṣi (1879–1959) once said: "Silence, the universal language, which always springs out from the heart, is the state of grace;" Sri Ramana Maharshi, *Opere* (Rome: Ubaldini, 2012), 157 (our translation).

124. *Śrīśāṃkaragranthāvaliḥ, sampuṭaḥ* 11, *stotrāṇi laghuprakaraṇāni ca* (Śrīrangam: Śrīvāṇīvilāsasamudraṇālaya, 1972[4]), 257–58 (our translation).

In medieval Europe, a parallel is represented by the "compassionate eyes" (*misericordes oculi*) of the Virgin Mary, the "Gracious Queen."

125. See Swami Nikhilananda, trans., *Self-Knowledge: An English Translation of Śaṅkarācārya's Ātmabodha with Notes, Comments, and Introduction* (Madras: Sri Ramakrishna Math, 1947[10]), 201–2.

126. Doubts (*saṃśaya, saṃdeha*) must be dissolved since they confuse the mind and paralyze action. Given two or more alternatives, the wise must cultivate discrimination (*viveka*) in order to establish what is right and wrong and decide his/her course of action.

127. On these issues, see K. P. Prentiss, *The Embodiment of Bhakti* (New York and Oxford: Oxford University Press, 2000). Tranquility of mind is a fundamental virtue: at *BhG* 2.65, Kṛṣṇa points out that the intellect (*buddhi*) of the tranquil-minded (*prasannacetaso*) quickly becomes steady.

128. The sacredness of the *guru*'s feet is sung in countless devotional hymns, past and present, as in this solemn *incipit*: *mānasa bhajare gurucaraṇam | dustarabhavasāgarataraṇam |* "Worship in thy mind the *guru*'s feet: [these alone] carry over the ocean of existence, hard to overcome." *Gurugītā* 76 proclaims: *pūjāmūlaṃ guroḥ padam*, "The root of worship is the foot of the *guru*." To Śaṅkara is attributed a hymn of eight verses in praise of the *guru*'s lotus feet (*guror aṅghripadme*), the *Gurvaṣṭakam*; see T. M. P. Mahadevan, *The Hymns of Śaṅkara* (Madras: Ganesh & Co. Private, 1970), 28–35. For an appreciation of the religious significance of feet in Indian culture, see J. Jain-Neubauer, *Feet & Footwear in Indian Culture* (Toronto: Bata Shoe Museum Foundation, 2000).

129. See K. Valpey, "*Pūja* and *darśana*," in *Brill's Encyclopedia of Hinduism*. Vol. 2: *Sacred Texts and Languages, Ritual Traditions, Arts, Concepts*, eds. K. A. Jacobsen, H. Basu, A. Malinar, and V. Narayanan (Leiden: Brill, 2010), 380–94. See also D. L. Eck, *Darśan: Seeing the Divine Image in India* (New York: Columbia University Press, 1998[3]); L. A. Babb, "Glancing: Visual Interaction in Hinduism," *Journal of Anthropological Research* 37, no. 4 (1981): 387–401.

130. A disciple must always approach the *guru* by reverently prostrating himself/herself to him. As Kṛṣṇa says to Arjuna in *BhG* 4.34:

> Learn to know this (*tad* = *jñāna*) by obeisance
> (*praṇipātena*) (to those who can teach it),
> By questioning (them), by serving (them);
> They will teach thee knowledge (*jñānam*),
> Those who have knowledge, who see the truth.
> (Edgerton, *The Bhagavad Gītā*, 26)

131. On divine visions in the *MBh,* see J. W. Laine, *Visions of God: Narratives of Theophany in the Mahābhārata* (Vienna: Publications of the De Nobili Research Library, 1989).

132. Kṛṣṇa had already revealed himself in his cosmic form as Viśvarūpa to Duryodhana in the *Udyogaparvan,* anticipating the *BhG* theophany. Duryodhana, however, had refused to accept Kṛṣṇa's divinity.

133. Edgerton, *The Bhagavad Gītā,* 59.

134. Monier-Williams, *Sanskrit-English Dictionary,* 106. It should be noted that the expression *avahasann iva* occurs only once in the whole epic (*MBh* 12.96.19b). The context is as follows: Yudhiṣṭhira questions Bhīṣma on how a warrior should fight against another warrior. Bhīṣma answers by recalling the various norms of conduct and points out that a warrior must win following the rules of *dharma* since it is preferable to die following *dharma* than to win by deception. The evil-doer rejoices in unrighteousness and, by doing so, sinks in sin (*pāpa*): "Making fun (*avahasann iva*) of the virtuous ones, he thinks that *dharma* doesn't exist and consequently, due to his faithlessness, he goes to destruction" (*na dharmo 'stīti manvānaḥ śucīn avahasann iva | aśraddhadhānabhāvāc ca vināśam upagacchati ||*).

135. In a *BhG* manuscript by Kariccaṅkāl Śrīnivāsan (end of eighteenth century, *ms.* GOML R3507) written in the hybrid *manipravalam* language combining Sanskrit lexicon and Tamil morpho-syntax, *avahāsārtham* is explained as *ammāṉ kumāraṉum attai kumāraṉum ceyituk koḷḷukuṟa parihā-sa-muṟaiyāl* (93v1–2), that is, "In the way an aunty and her nephew or an uncle and his nephew may have laughed together;" Giovanni Ciotti, personal communication, October 3, 2022.

136. See Apte, *The Practical Sanskrit-English Dictionary,* 238.

137. Though etymologically the opposite of *ava* is *ud,* meaning "up"/"above," our contention is that here *pra* fulfils the same function.

138. Hiltebeitel, *The Ritual of Battle,* 258.

139. Malinar, *The Bhagavadgītā: Doctrines and Contexts,* 184.

140. See *Bhāgavata Purāṇa* 7.5.23. On the other hand, the meaning of *sakhya* in the *Bhāgavata Purāṇa* itself is unclear. In the story of King Puraṃjana in book 4, it means realizing that the lord is one's friend in the manner of the other bird in the famous passage of *Muṇḍaka Upaniṣad* 3.1.1–2 (first found in *Ṛgveda* 1.164.20–22 and reiterated in *Śvetāśvatara Upaniṣad* 4.6–7): "Two birds, companions and friends (*sakhāyā*), nestle on the very same tree. One of them eats a tasty fig; the other, not eating, looks on. Stuck on the very same tree, one person grieves, deluded by her (= *prakṛti,* the female cosmic power) who is not the Lord; but when he sees the other, the contented Lord—and his majesty—his grief disappears;"

Olivelle, *Upaniṣads,* 274. For an introduction to the *Bhāgavata Purāṇa,* see J. Edelman, "*Bhāgavatapurāṇa*" in *Brill's Encyclopedia of Hinduism Online,* eds. K. A. Jacobsen, H. Basu, A. Malinar, and V. Narayanan (Leiden: Brill, 2018; https://referenceworks.brillonline.com/browse/brill-s-encyclopedia-of-hinduism). On *bhakti* in the *Bhāgavata Purāṇa,* see D. P. Sheridan, *The Advaitic Theism of the Bhāgavata Purāṇa* (Delhi: Motilal Banarsidass, 1986); A. J. Gail, *Bhakti im Bhāgavatapurāṇa. Religionsgeschichtliche Studie zur Idee der Gottesliebe in Kult und Mystik des Viṣṇuismus* (Wiesbaden: Otto Harrassowitz, 1969).

141. The noun *sakhi* ("friend," "companion") occurs in *BhG* 1.26, 4.3, 11.41, 11.44.

142. Edgerton, *The Bhagavad Gītā,* 59.

143. See Piano, *Bhagavad-gītā. Il canto del glorioso Signore,* 89 n. 21c. On Kṛṣṇa as *acyuta,* see R. Balkaran, "Arjuna and Acyuta: The Import of Epithets in the *Bhagavad-gītā,*" in Theodor, *The Bhagavad-gītā: A Critical Introduction,* 137–44. If *acyuta* is a well-known epithet of Viṣṇu-Kṛṣṇa, in the epic it is also the epithet of great warriors such as Yudhiṣṭhira.

144. Edgerton, *The Bhagavad Gītā,* 91.

145. Interestingly, the name of a particular kind of jasmine with fragrant flowers is *prahasantī,* also known as *vāsantī.* Jasmine flowers are widely used in Kṛṣṇa's worship: their delicate white petals are associated with purity and symbolize love and devotion.

146. This *ānanda* is reminiscent of the perfect joy exalted by Saint Francis of Assisi (1181/1182–1226), the *ioculator Domini;* see M. Benedetti, "«Ma qual è la vera letizia?» Realtà e metamorfosi di Francesco," in *Francesco da Assisi. Storia, arte, mito,* ed. M. Benedetti and T. Subini (Rome: Carocci, 2019), 29–40.

147. Theologically, the concept of *līlā* develops with the rise of the great monotheistic systems as an expression of god's joyful and spontaneous creative power and is a corollary of his omnipotence and freedom. On the concept of *līlā,* see J. J. Lipner, "A God at Play? Reexamining the Concept of *Līlā* in Hindu Philosophy and Theology," *International Journal of Hindu Studies* 26 (2022): 283–326; C. Olson, "*Līlā,*" in *Hinduism and Tribal Religions. Encyclopedia of Indian Religions,* ed. J. D. Long, R. D. Sherma, P. Jain, and M. Khanna (Dordrecht: Springer, 2022), https://doi.org/10.1007/978-94-024-1188-1_87K; G. Schweig, "*Līlā,*" in *Brill's Encyclopedia of Hinduism Online,* eds. K. A. Jacobsen, H. Basu, A. Malinar, and V. Narayanan (Leiden: Brill, 2018), https://referenceworks.brillonline.com/browse/brill-s-encyclopedia-of-hinduism. See also Narayan, *Storytellers, Saints, and Scoundrels,* 181–82.

148. https://www.holy-bhagavad-gita.org/chapter/2/verse/10.

149. A name of Arjuna, meaning "wealth-conqueror."

150. Edgerton, *The Bhagavad Gītā*, 56.

151. On this glorious manifestation of the divine as *mysterium tremendum et fascinans*, see the classic study of R. Otto, *The Idea of the Holy. An Inquiry into the Non-Rational Factor in the Idea of the Divine and Its Relation to the Rational*. Translated by J. W. Harvey (London: Oxford University Press, 1950[2] [1923]).

152. Monier-Williams, *Sanskrit-English Dictionary*, 1002, 1271.

153. The *añjalimudrā* involves placing the hands together, palms slightly hollowed, and holding them in front of one's chest. As a mark of supplication, the hands may be raised to the forehead, a gesture known as *añjalibandhana*.

154. Monier-Williams, *Sanskrit-English Dictionary*, 953.

155. The experience of *vismaya* calls to mind the Greek notion of θαῦμα (i.e., "wonder," "awe"). In Plato's *Theaetetus* 155d we read: "This experience—wondering—is very much the characteristic of the philosopher. There is no other beginning to philosophy than this." For both Plato and Aristotle, without θαῦμα philosophical inquiry would have never started. On these issues, see J. Lightfoot, *Wonder and the Marvellous from Homer to the Hellenistic World* (Cambridge: Cambridge University Press, 2021).

156. Along these lines, *sūtra* 1.12 of Vasugupta's *Śivasūtra* (ninth century CE) immediately comes to mind: *vismayo yogabhūmikāḥ*, i.e., "The stages of Yoga are amazement." For Kṣemarāja's commentary on it, see Vasugupta, *Gli aforismi di Śiva con il commento di Kṣemarāja (Śivasūtravimarśinī)*, ed. R. Torella (Milan: Adelphi, 2013), 126–27. The intriguing saying attributed to Jesus in the *Gospel of Thomas* is also worth remembering: "Let him who seeks continue seeking until he finds. When he finds, he will be amazed. And when he becomes amazed, he will rule. And once he has ruled, he will attain rest;" https://letterepaoline.files.wordpress.com/2013/12/ev-th-comm.pdf (pp. 6–7).

157. Edgerton, *The Bhagavad Gītā*, 60.

158. Ibid., 61.

159. As Kṛṣṇa says in *BhG* 9.26:

A leaf, a flower, a fruit, or water,
Who presents to Me with devotion,
That offering of devotion I
Accept from the devout-souled (giver).
(Ibid., 48)

Leaf, flower, fruit and water are interpreted as symbols of the *bhakta*'s body, heart, mind, and tears respectively.

160. Ibid., 90. See also Malinar, *The Bhagavadgītā: Doctrines and Contexts*, 222. On Śaṅkara's commentary to this verse, see S. Marchignoli, "*Bhagavadgītābhāṣya* di Śaṅkara *ad* 18.66," in *Filosofie dell'India. Un'antologia di testi*, ed. F. Sferra (Rome: Carocci, 2018), 233–35, 355–56, and F. Sferra, "Introduzione," in ibid., 68–70.

161. Significantly, in Śrī Vaiṣṇava circles the theology of *prapatti* is understood as a development of *BhG* 18.66.

162. As per the insightful comment made by the famous *guru* and mystic Rāmakṛṣṇa (1836–1886) in M. Gupta, *The Gospel of Sri Ramakrishna (Sri Sri Ramakrishna Kathamrita)*. Translated from the Bengali by Swami Nikhilananda (New York: Ramakrishna-Vivekananda Center, 1942), 406, available at http://www.vedanta-nl.org/GOSPEL.pdf.

163. Here we follow a popular interpretation that goes back to the *Gītārthasaṃgraha* of Yāmunācārya (trad. 918–1038), the teacher of Rāmānuja, according to whom the poem can be subdivided into three portions, each of them comprising six chapters: *adhyāya*s 1–6 are said to be dedicated to the discipline of action (*karmayoga*), *adhyāya*s 7–12 to the discipline of devotion (*bhaktiyoga*), and *adhyāya*s 13–18 to the discipline of knowledge (*jñānayoga*). Nonetheless, it should be noted that this subdivision is a simplification that is only partially true since the *Bhagavadgītā* aims at offering a synthesis of the three paths of *karman, bhakti,* and *jñāna* throughout its chapters.

164. See van Buitenen, *The Bhagavadgītā in the Mahābhārata*, 13–23; Deutsch, *The Bhagavad Gītā*, 161–69. On these issues, see also K. H. Potter, *Presuppositions of India's Philosophies* (Delhi: Motilal Banarsidass, 1991), 11–24.

165. Apparently, Swami Vivekānanda (1863–1902) interpreted Kṛṣṇa's *prahasann iva* precisely along these lines; see https://www.youtube.com/watch?v=tONcYzfW8hQ (minutes 1:02:25–1:04:55). On his interpretation of the *Bhagavadgītā*, see Swami Vivekananda, *Thoughts on the Gita* (Calcutta: Advaita Ashrama, 1995^{14}); Swami Madhurananda, ed., *Bhagavad Gita. As Viewed by Swami Vivekananda* (Kolkata: Advaita Ashrama, 2022^{10}).

166. Still the epic antecedents of Kṛṣṇa's playful attitude as Veṇugopāla (i.e., player of the flute) and his link with Arjuna as master of music and dance are noteworthy; see M. Biardeau, *Études de mythologie hindoue. 2. Bhakti et avatāra* (Pondichéry: Publications de l'École Française d'Extrême-Orient, 1994), 285–86. On *līlā* in early Vaiṣṇavism, see C. Hospital, "*Līlā* in Early Vaiṣṇava Thought," in *The Gods at Play: Līlā in South Asia*, ed. W. Sax (New York: Oxford University Press, 1995), 21–34.

167. On these issues, see A. Pelissero, *Il riso e la pula. Vie di salvezza nello śivaismo del Kaśmīr* (Alessandria: Edizioni dell'Orso, 1998), 47.

168. Pārtha or "son of Pṛthā" is the most common epithet of Arjuna in the *Bhagavadgītā*: it recurs forty-one times, the first at *BhG* 1.25 and the last at *BhG* 18.78. Pṛthā, better known as Kuntī, was the daughter of the

Yādava prince Śūra, king of the Śūrasenas, whose capital was Mathurā. Sister of Vasudeva, she was the wife of Pāṇḍu whom she chose at a *svayaṃvara* and bore three sons, Yudhiṣṭhira, Bhīma and Arjuna, who were called "Pāṇḍavas" although they were actually the sons of the gods Dharma, Vāyu, and Indra respectively. Indeed, Pāṇḍu could have no sons since he had been cursed by a seer that he would die if he ever tried to have intercourse with a woman. Kuntī, however, had received from sage Durvāsas a *mantra* through which she could attract to herself any god and be impregnated by him.

169. Edgerton, *The Bhagavad Gītā*, 20.

170. Ibid., 23, 39.

171. See for instance *Śrīmadbhagavadgītā, padaccheda-anvaya aur sadharaṇa-bhāṣāṭīkāsahita* (Gorakhpur: Gītā Press, 1974[27] [1922]), *ad BhG* 10.14. In devotional circles, Kṛṣṇa is referred to as *līlāmaya*, "the one who is full of pleasing pastimes" and *līlāmānuṣavigraha*, "the one who takes a human form merely for amusement."

172. Mahadeva Sastry, *The Bhagavad Gita with the Commentary of Sri Sankaracharya*, 497. Śaṅkara refers twice to *BhG* 18.61 in *Brahmasūtrabhāṣya* 1.2.6 and 2.1.14. The concepts of *līlā* and *māyā* are related and sometimes they are understood as being synonymous. For an example from the *Mahābhārata*, see Biardeau, *Études de mythologie hindoue*, 168, 250–51.

173. On the "doctrine of time" (*kālavāda*) as being constitutive for the epic, see A. Hiltebeitel, *Rethinking the Mahābhārata: A Reader's Guide to the Education of the Dharma King* (Chicago and London: University of Chicago Press, 2001), 36–40. See also M. Piantelli, "La concezione del tempo nell'esperienza dell'Induismo. Spunti di riflessione," *Tempo e Apocalisse.* Atti dell'incontro del 19–20 settembre 1981 al monastero di Montebello, ed. S. Quinzio (Milazzo: SPES, 1985), 117–56.

174. Edgerton, *The Bhagavad Gītā*, 58.

175. See A. Malinar, "Yoga Powers in the *Mahābhārata*," in *Yoga Powers: Extraordinary Capacities Attained Through Meditation and Concentration*, ed. K. A. Jacobsen (Leiden: Brill, 2012), 47–59.

176. Noteworthy in this regard is *BhG* 9.32:

> For if they take refuge in Me, son of Pṛthā,
> Even those who may be of base origin,
> Women, men of the artisan caste, and serfs too,
> Even they go to the highest goal.
> (Edgerton, *The Bhagavad Gītā*, 49)

On these issues, see D. N. Lorenzen, *Praises to a Formless God: Nirguṇī Texts from North India* (Albany: State University of New York Press, 1996), 31–32.

177. This image is often found in the epic; see for instance *MBh* 12.46.6, 12.316.19.

178. The body's luminosity and the golden color of the skin are a characteristic of *yogins*, saints and "great beings" (*mahāpuruṣa*) such as the Buddha; see E. Burnouf, "Sur les trente-deux signes caractéristiques d'un grand homme," in *Le lotus de la bonne loi: Traduit su sanscrit, accompagné d'un commentaire et de vingt et un mémoires relatifs au buddhisme*. Nouvelle édition avec une Préface de Sylvain Lévi (Paris: Maisonneuve, 1925), 568–69, 579–80.

179. This doctrine finds its *locus classicus* in the *Upaniṣads*; see *Bṛhadāraṇyaka Upaniṣad* 6.2.9–16 and *Chāndogya Upaniṣad* 5.4–10.

180. Edgerton, *The Bhagavad Gītā*, 16. When George L. Hart observes that Kṛṣṇa at the beginning of the *Bhagavadgītā* "seems extremely distant," he fails to recognize that the lord's attitude is revelatory of his *prasāda*, of his divine serenity and equanimity, which is not to be confused with indifference or lack of love for his *bhakta* Arjuna; see G. L. Hart, "Archetypes in Classical Indian Literature and Beyond," in *Syllables of Sky: Studies in South Asian Civilization in Honour of Velcheru Narayana Rao*, ed. D. Shulman (Delhi: Oxford University Press, 1995), 175–76.

181. Edgerton, *The Bhagavad Gītā*, 80.

182. Ibid., 89.

183. On yogic silence, see Y. Grinshpon, *Silence Unheard: Deathly Otherness in Pātañjala-Yoga* (Albany: State University of New York Press, 2001).

184. Edgerton, *The Bhagavad Gītā*, 15.

185. Ibid., 31.

186. Ibid., 32.

187. Ibid., 56. The theme of Kṛṣṇa's dazzling splendor is a veritable leitmotif in devotional circles. In one of his lyrics (*abhaṅg*), Jñāneśvar writes: "Who has dispelled the darkness of ignorance from my mind? Before whose radiance has the sun's splendour grown pale? O enchanting Śrī Kṛṣṇa! Thou alone hast done it! Is not Lord Śrī Kṛṣṇa like a full moon appearing after the period of dark nights to make the bird '*cakora*' feed on the nectarine juice drizzling from its rays and to blossom the night-blooming lotus? To talk about Thy form is so very mysterious indeed!" P. V. Bobde, trans., *Garland of Divine Flowers: Selected Devotional Lyrics of Saint Jñāneśvara* (Delhi: Motilal Banarsidass, 1999), 15–16.

188. Edgerton, *The Bhagavad Gītā*, 68.

189. Ibid., 91.

190. Ibid., 62.

191. On compassion in the *Bhagavadgītā*, see A. Rigopoulos, "Declinazioni della compassione nella *Bhagavad-gītā*: da vile debolezza

del cuore a virtù suprema," in *Religioni e compassione*, ed. M. Dal Corso (Villa Verucchio: Pazzini, 2023), 71–97.

192. Edgerton, *The Bhagavad Gītā*, 72.

193. The Upaniṣadic reference is *Kaṭha Upaniṣad* 6.1.

194. Edgerton, *The Bhagavad Gītā*, 74.

195. Ibid., 73.

196. Ibid.

197. Ibid., 80.

198. On the *Bhagavadgītā*'s understanding of *saṃnyāsa*, see P. Olivelle, "Contributions to the Semantic History of *saṃnyāsa*," in *Collected Essays II. Ascetics and Brahmins: Studies in Ideologies and Institutions* (Florence: Firenze University Press, 2008), 132–35.

199. Edgerton, *The Bhagavad Gītā*, 87–88.

200. Two verses later, in *BhG* 18.75, Saṃjaya states that it is by the grace of sage Vyāsa (*vyāsaprasādāc*) that he has been able to hear this supreme and most secret *yoga* taught by Kṛṣṇa to Arjuna.

201. Edgerton, *The Bhagavad Gītā*, 89.

Chapter 2

1. It appears that Arjuna developed the required attitude for the reception and retention of Kṛṣṇa's teaching only when faced with the tragedy of the impending bloodshed.

2. All translations from the Sanskrit unless otherwise specified are of Gianni Pellegrini.

3. Actually, we know of several pre-Śaṅkara commentaries on the *BhG* but Śaṅkara's is the earliest extant one (Saha 2017, 259–61).

4. Here are the passages from Śaṅkara's *BhGBh* that concern Arjuna's anguish and delusion, that is, BhG1 2000, 73–74; BhG3 1936, 39–40; BhG4 2015, 31–32: *atra ca dṛṣṭvā tu pāṇḍavānīkam ity ārabhya yāvat na yotsya iti govindam uktvā tūṣṇīṃ babhūva ha ity etadantaḥ prāṇināṃ śokamohādisaṃsārabījabhūtadoṣodbhavakāraṇapradarśanārthatvena vyākhyeyo granthaḥ | tathā hi—arjunena rājyaguruputramitrasuhṛtsvajanasaṃbandhibāndhaveṣu aham eteṣāṃ mamaite ity evaṃ bhrāntipratyayanimittasnehavicchedādinimittau ātmanaḥ śokamohau pradarśitau | kathaṃ bhīṣmam ahaṃ saṃkhye ity ādinā* |.

5. BhG1 2000, 74; BhG3 1936, 40–41; BhG4 2015, 32–33: *śokamohābhyāṃ hy abhibhūtavivekavijñānaḥ svata eva kṣatradharme yuddhe pravṛtto 'pi tasmād yuddhād upararāma | paradharmaṃ ca bhikṣājīvanādikaṃ kartuṃ pravavṛte | tathā ca sarvaprāṇināṃ śokamohādidoṣāviṣṭacetasāṃ svabhāvata eva svadharmaparityāgaḥ pratiṣiddhasevā ca syāt | svadharme pravṛttānām api teṣāṃ*

vāṅmanaḥkāyādīnāṃ pravṛttiḥ phalābhisaṃdhipūrvikaiva sāhaṃkārā ca bhavati | tatraivaṃ sati dharmādharmopacayād iṣṭāniṣṭajanmasukhaduḥkhādiprāptilakṣaṇaḥ saṃsāro 'nuparato bhavati | ity ataḥ saṃsārabījabhūtau śokamohau | tayoś ca sarvakarmasaṃnyāsapūrvakād ātmajñānān nānyato nivṛttir iti tadupadidikṣuḥ sarvalokānugrahārtham arjunaṃ nimittīkṛtya āha bhagavān vāsudevaḥ — aśocyān ityādi |.

6. BhG1 2000, 79; BhG3 1936, 46; BhG4 2015, 44–45: *yasmāt gatāsūn gataprāṇān mṛtān, agatāsūn agataprāṇān jīvataś ca nānuśocanti paṇḍitāḥ ātmajñāḥ | paṇḍā ātmaviṣayā buddhir yeṣāṃ te hi paṇḍitāḥ, pāṇḍityaṃ nirvidya iti śruteḥ | paramārthatas tu tān nityān aśocyān anuśocasi, ato mūḍho 'si ity abhiprāyaḥ* |. On *paṇḍā* and *paṇḍita*, see Aklujkar (2001, 17–21).

7. BhG1 2000, 79; BhG3 1936, 46; BhG4 2015, 43–44: *na śocyā aśocyāḥ bhīṣmadroṇādayaḥ | sadvṛttatvāt paramārthasvarūpeṇa ca nityatvāt, tān aśocyān anvaśoco 'nu śocitavān asi te mriyante mannimittam, ahaṃ tair vinābhūtaḥ kiṃ kariṣyāmi rājyasukhādinā iti | tvaṃ prajñāvādān prajñāvatāṃ buddhimatāṃ vādāṃś ca vacanāni ca bhāṣase* |.

8. See *Bṛhadāraṇyaka Upaniṣad* 3.5.1: "Thus, having surpassed wisdom, he should rest like a child. Then, having surpassed wisdom and childhood, he becomes a silent sage. And having surpassed [both] non silence and silence, he becomes a [true] Brahmin" (*tasmād pāṇḍityaṃ nirvidya bālyena tiṣṭhaset | bālyaṃ ca pāṇḍityaṃ ca nirvidyātha muniḥ | amaunaṃ ca maunaṃ ca nirvidyātha brāhmaṇaḥ*). See also Olivelle (1998, 83).

9. It is commonly believed that Anubhūtisvarūpācārya wrote the *Prakaṭārthavivaraṇa*, an independent commentary on Śaṅkara's *Brahmasūtrabhāṣya* that follows Vivaraṇa tenets (Chintamani 1989, x-xi). The date of the *Prakaṭārthavivaraṇa* can be established between Prakāśātman (975; Potter 1995, 370) and Rāmādvaya (mid-fourteenth century; Pellegrini 2016, 490). There is a problem concerning the relative chronology of the author of the *Prakaṭārthavivaraṇa* and Ānandagiri, whose *terminus post quem* according to Thangaswami (1980, 387) cannot be placed beyond 1320 (see also Mahadevan 2003, 153–56). Based on this relative chronology (Saha 2017, 263; Potter 1995, 1326), Anubhūtisvarūpācārya seems to be earlier than Ānandagiri (Mahadevan 2003, 320–22). This is relevant for us since we find similar passages in their glosses. Indeed, in his commentary to Śaṅkara's *bhāṣya* Ānandagiri often borrows from Anubhūtisvarūpācārya (see BhG4 2015, 33). Like his predecessors, Anubhūtisvarūpācārya does not comment upon the *BhG*'s first chapter and the opening ten verses of the second (BhG4 2015, 33).

10. BhG1 2000, 71; BhG3 1936, 38–39; BhG4 2015, 31: *tam arjunaṃ senayoḥ vāhinyor ubhayor madhye viṣīdantaṃ viṣādaṃ kurvantam atiduḥkhitaṃ śokamohābhyām abhibhūtaṃ svadharmāt pracyutaprāyaṃ pratītya prahasann iva upāhasaṃ kurvann iva tadāśvāsārthaṃ, he bhārata bharatānvaya ity evaṃ*

sambodhya bhagavān idaṃ praśnottaraṃ niḥśreyasādhigamasādhanaṃ vacanam ūcitavān ity āha—tam uvāceti |.

11. BhG1 2000, 74; BhG3 1936, 40; BhG4 2015, 33: [. . .] *arjunasyānyeṣāṃ ca śokamohayoḥ saṃsārabījatvam upapāditam upasaṃharati—ity ata iti* | *tad evaṃ prathamādhyāyasya dvitīyādhyāyaikadeśasahitasya ātmājñānotthanirvartanīyaśokamohākhyasaṃsārabījapradarśanaparatvaṃ darśayitvā vakṣyamāṇasandarbhasya sahetukasaṃsāranirvartakasamyagjñānopadeśe tātparyaṃ darśayati—tayoś ceti* |.

12. Though "trust in the words of the *guru* and the deity" (*gurudaivatavākyaviśvāsa*) does not figure among the four prerequisites (*sādhanacatuṣṭaya*), yet *viśvāsa* "trust" can be understood as a synonym of *śraddhā* "faith," which is the last among the set of six virtues (*śamadamādiṣaṭkasampatti*) taken from *Bṛhadāraṇyaka Upaniṣad* 4.4.24. For a survey of the four prerequisites, see *Brahmasūtrabhāṣya ad* 1.1.1 (2000, 36–37).

13. While commenting on *BhG* 2.7, Paṇḍita Sūrya quotes from *Chāndogya Upaniṣad* 6.14.2: "The man with a teacher knows!" (*ācāryavān puruṣo veda*; BhG2 2001, 67).

14. *athārjunaṃ viṣādena na yotsya iti niścitya tūṣṇībhūtaṃ bhagavān āha—tam uvāceti* | *hṛṣīkeśa āśayajñaḥ kṛṣṇas tam arjunaṃ prati prahasann iva prahāsagarbham iva vacanam uvāca* | *nanu viṣādāvasare hāsānupakrame 'pi katham uktaṃ prahasann iveti, tatrocyate* | *viṣādotpatter akāraṇatvād yato dīnānāthavadhe eva viṣādotpatter darśanāt* | *prakṛte tu bhīṣmadroṇakarṇaduryodhanādyāḥ śauryeṇa śakram apy agaṇayantaḥ kṣātradharmam anusṛtya pravṛttā na tu mūrkhatvena teṣu kathaṃ kṛpāpātratvam* | [. . .] *ato yadviṣādakāraṇam uktaṃ tat pratāraṇamātraṃ karma naiṣkarmyamārgabahirbhūtam ity āśayena īṣaddhāsyamukho bhūtvā provācety arthaḥ* |.

15. For instance, having quoted from the *Gūḍhārthadīpikā* Śrīveṅkaṭanātha expresses some doubts on its reading of *BhG* 2.8 (*etac cintyam*; BhG1 2000, 69).

16. See also Śrīveṅkaṭanātha *ad* 2.8 (BhG1 2000, 69): *śaraṇāgatir api ananyaśaraṇatvādhyavasayāyapūrvikā tvam eva śaraṇam iti tvadutpattiḥ, na tv anyasmiñ charaṇe sthite 'pi tvam api śaraṇam ity evaṃlakṣaṇatvād upasadanarūpety āha—yad vastu mama śokam apanudet tan na paśyāmīty ananyaśaratvoktiḥ* |.

17. BhG1 2000, 73: *evaṃvidho 'pi śoko yadi svasenāmadhyasthitikāla eva syāt tadā sāvakāśaṃ samādhātuṃ śakyeta, na tv evaṃ, kintu svabalān nirgatya yuyutsuḥ parakīyaśūramukhe sthitvā svayaṃ dhanur udyamya pravṛtte śastrasampāte yadā bandhūn avaikṣata, tadānīm utpannaḥ, tato mahat kaṣṭaṃ jātam ity abhipretyāha—senayor ubhayor madhya iti* |.

18. BhG1 2000, 73: *evaṃ saty api bhagavato 'rjunasaṅkaṭanirāse 'nāyāsaṃ darśayati—prahasann iveti* |.

19. *arjunasya paitṛṣv asevatayā taṃ prati bhagavataḥ sarvadā 'pi parihāsoktaya eva bhavantīti tadā saṅkaṭe 'pi tannirācikīrṣur bhagavān parihāsarītyaiva idaṃ*

vakṣyamāṇam aśocyān ityādikam atigambhīrārtham aśeṣavedāntasārabhūtaṃ vacanam uvāca | tatra ca vinodaphalakatvena loke parihāsaḥ prasiddhaḥ, ayaṃ tv arjunasya tattvajñānotpādanaphalaka iti prasiddhaparihāsavailakṣaṇyadyotanārthaḥ prahasann ivetīvakāraḥ | sarvadhīprerakasya jñānotpādanaṃ hāsamātreṇaiva sukaram iti hṛṣīkeśapadenoktam | [. . .]

20. On this issue, see Śaṅkara's commentaries—*pādabhāṣya* and *vākyabhāṣya*—on *Kena Upaniṣad* 1.1.1–2 (Śāstrī 2004, 17–21).

21. The last passage of *BhG* 2.10 is irrelevant for the issue at stake.

22. *tad evaṃ mohasāgaranimagnasyārjunasya ātmatattvajñānād anyatroddhāraṇopāyam apaśyan prahasann iva iti pūrvaślokam arjunāpahāsaṃ viśadayann eva* [. . .] *ātmatattvajñānam* [. . .] |.

23. *Bṛhadāraṇyaka Upaniṣad* (2.4.10 and 4.5.11): [. . .] *asya mahato bhūtasya niḥśvasitam etad yad ṛgvedo yajurvedaḥ sāmavedo 'tharvāṅgirasa itihāsaḥ purāṇaṃ vidyā upaniṣadaḥ ślokāḥ sūtrāṇy anuvyākhyānāni vyākhyānāni* | *asyaitāni niśvasitāni* | "[. . .] So indeed the *Ṛgveda, Yajurveda, Sāmaveda, Atharvāṅgirasa,* histories, ancient tales, sciences, hidden teachings (*upaniṣad*), verses, aphorisms, explanations and glosses—all these are the exhalation of this Immense Being." See also Olivelle (1998, 69).

24. BhG1 2000, 81: *atra hṛṣīkeśa uvācety uktvā 'pi punar bhagavān uvāceti vadatā saṃjayena deśakālādyanapekṣatvarūpaṃ bhagavanmāhātmyaṃ darśitam* | *atha vyavasthitān dṛṣṭvā dhārtarāṣṭrān kapidhvajaḥ* | *pravṛtte śastrasampāte dhanur udyamya pāṇḍavaḥ ity evaṃvidhāvasthāyāṃ kathaṃ śrīkṛṣṇena jñānam upadeṣṭuṃ pravṛttam? kathaṃ vā 'rjunasya tathāvidhopadeśāj jñānalābhaḥ? deśakālau vinā sarvatra kāryānudayād iti na śaṅkanīyam, acintyādbhūtamahāmahimaśālini bhagavati deśakālayor akiñcitkaratvād iti* |.

25. BhG1 2000, 81: *atrādyapādena prathamādhyāyagatārjunoktānuvādaḥ* | *dvitīyapādena tu kathaṃ bhīṣmam aha ityādidvitīyādhyāyagatataduktānuvādaḥ* | *uttarārdhena ca tatra ko mohaḥ kaḥ śoka ekatvam anupaśyataḥ tarati śokam ātmavit ityādiśrutiprasiddhasarvaśokamohanivartakabhāvasya kṛtsnagītāpratipādyasyādvitīyātmatattvajñānasya nirdeśa iti* |.

26. *Īśa Upaniṣad* 7: "What delusion, what sorrow can there be for the one who sees the oneness?" (*tatra ko mohaḥ kaḥ śoka ekatvam anupaśyataḥ*); *Chāndogya Upaniṣad* 7.1.3: "The knower of the Self goes beyond sorrow" (*tarati śokam ātmavit*).

27. *ato bīje vṛkṣasvarūpasyeva kṛtsnagītārthasya atrāntarbhāvād bījaśloko 'yam iti gītānyāsarahasyam* |.

28. The passage runs as follows: *tathā ca mauḍhyaṃ prājñatvaṃ punaḥ śiṣyatvaṃ svātantryaṃ cety etatparasparaviruddhaṃ tvayi dṛśyata ity apahāsakāraṇoktiḥ* |. According to Śrīveṅkaṭanātha, from 2.11 to 2.31 the *BhG* removes the despondency of those who are not worthy of despondency. From 2.32 to 2.38, it removes the words of false wisdom (BhG1 2000, 81).

29. He defends Śaṅkara's *BhGBh* from all opponents; see vss. 7–8 of the *Bhāṣyotkarṣadīpikā* (BhG2 2001, 10; BhG3 1936, 5–6) and the gloss *ad* 2.1 (BhG2 2001, 56; BhG3 1936, 31).

30. Dhanapati Sūri is the father of Śivadatta Sūri, author of the *Arthadīpikā* which is a gloss on Dharmarāja Adhvarin's *Vedāntaparibhāṣā*.

31. BhG2 2001, 71; BhG3 1936, 38: *etad anantaraṃ bhagavān kiṃ kṛtavān ity ata āha — tam iti | taṃ senayor ubhayor madhye viṣīdantaṃ śokamohāv aṅgīkurvantam arjunaṃ hṛṣīkeśo bhagavān vāsudevaḥ prahasann iva madājñāvaśavartini tvayy ahaṃ prasanno 'smīti prakaṭayann ivedaṃ vakṣyamāṇaṃ vaco vacanam uvāca | anucitācaraṇaprakāśanena lajjāmbudhau majjayann iveti kecit | mūḍho 'py ayam amūḍhavad vadatīti prahasann ivety anye |* [. . .]

32. See the *GAD ad BhG* 2.10.

33. Nīlakāṇṭha *ad BhG* 2.10 (BhG1 2000, 73).

34. Dhanapati *ad* 2.11 criticizes Madhusūdana's position on Arjuna's twofold delusion (BhG2 2001, 74–75; BhG3 1936, 39). His contention is that Śaṅkara has explained everything so clearly that it is useless to suggest any other interpretative option. Dhanapati adds that Madhusūdana's interpretation contradicts *BhG* 3.3 (*loke 'smin dvividhā niṣṭhā purā proktā mayā 'nagha | jñānayogena sāṃkhyānāṃ karmayogena yoginām ||*).

35. *he bhārata dhṛtarāṣṭra! ubhayoḥ senayoḥ madhye viṣīdantaṃ tam arjunaṃ prati hṛṣīkeśaḥ prahasann iva, arjunasyonmādapralāpatulyavacanaśravaṇāt kṛṣṇasya hāsa iti bhāvaḥ, idam aśocyān ity ārabhya mā śucaḥ ity antaṃ gītāśāstrarūpaṃ vacaḥ uvāca ||.*

36. *BhG* 18.66: *sarvadharmān parityajya mām ekaṃ śaraṇaṃ vraja | ahaṃ tvā sarvapāpebhyo mokṣayiṣyāmi mā śucaḥ ||.*

37. BhG2 2001, 74: *śokasyāviṣayībhūtān eva bandhūn tvam anvaśocaḥ anuśocitavān asi dṛṣṭvemān svajanān kṛṣṇa ity ādinā | tatra kutas tvā kaśmalam idaṃ viṣame samupasthitam ity ādinā mayā bodhito 'pi punaś ca prajñāvatāṃ paṇḍitānāṃ vādān śabdān kathaṃ bhīṣmam ahaṃ saṅkhye ity ādīn kevalaṃ bhāṣase, na tu paṇḍito 'si, yataḥ gatāsūn gataprāṇān bandhūn agatāsūṃś ca jīvato 'pi, bandhuhīnā ete kathaṃ jīviṣyantīti nānuśocanti paṇḍitā vivekinaḥ ||.*

38. For more information, see Mahadevan (1968, 178–81).

39. BhG2 2001, 55: *sadasadvivekena tajjanitatīvravairāgyeṇa mumukṣayā ca saṃnyāstasarvakarmaṇo mokṣaikakāmasya brāhmaṇasya sadasadvivekavairāgyādisādhanasaṃpatsiddher brāhmaṇatvasiddheś ca sāphalyāya athāto brahmajijñāsā iti, ātmā vā are draṣṭavyaḥ śrotavyaḥ iti tadvijñānārthaṃ sa gurum evābhigacchet ityādiśrutyuktaprakāreṇa sadguruṃ śrotriyaṃ brahmaniṣṭham upasadya brahmavicāraḥ kartavya itīmam arthaṃ sūcayituṃ sadasadvivekino 'rjunasya paramārthāpekṣiṇaḥ śiṣyas te 'haṃ śādhi māṃ tvāṃ prapannam itīśvarapratipattiṃ tasmai īśvareṇa kṛtam ātmānātmajñānopadeśaprakāraṃ ca pratipādayituṃ dvitīyo 'dhyāya ārabhyate |.*

40. BhG2 2001, 55: *tatrādau so 'haṃ bhagavaḥ śocāmi taṃ mā bhagavāñ chokasya pāraṃ tārayatu iti śravaṇāt saṃsāraduḥkhena śocantaṃ svaśaraṇaṃ gataṃ mumukṣum abhayavacanapūrvakam abhimukhīkṛtya gurus tattvaṃ bodhayed iti sūcayituṃ tathā śocitum arjunaṃ vivekavacanair bhagavān bodhayāmāseti vaktuṃ dhṛtarāṣṭraṃ prati saṃjaya uvāca — tam* |.

41. BhG2 2001, 71: *he bhārata, senayor ubhayor madhye viṣīdantaṃ madīyā ete mriyanta iti śocantaṃ etān hatvā taddoṣeṇāhaṃ nirayaṃ yāsyāmīty ātmani niṣkriye nirvikāre kartṛtvādidharmaśūnya evānādyavidyayā 'nātmataddharmān adhyasyāhaṃ kartā, bhokteti viparītabhāvena muhyantaṃ tam arjunaṃ dṛṣṭvā paramakṛpāluḥ śrībhagavān tatra ko mohaḥ kaḥ śoka ekatvam anupaśyata ityādiśrutiprasiddhabrahmātmaikatvajñānena vinā nāyaṃ dvaitabhramapravartakena bhedaśāstreṇa bodhyamānaḥ śokasāgaraṃ bhramamūlakaṃ tartuṃ śaknotīti matvā padārthadvayaśodhanapūrvakaṃ tajjñānam upadidikṣuḥ sann ādau tvaṃpadārthaśodhanam avatārayituṃ tadīyavṛttaṃ bhavān paṇḍita iti mama buddhir eva vā tava pāṇḍityam iti prahasann iva vacanam idam uvāca* ||.

42. *Chāndogya Upaniṣad* 6.8.7–16.3: *tat tvam asi*.

43. A less known commentary is the *Paiśācabhāṣya* or *Hanumadbhāṣya* by Hanumat, whose date is uncertain (he is mentioned in Veṅkaṭanātha's *Tātparyacandrikā*; Saha 2017, 264). Following Śaṅkara, Hanumat notes that *BhG* 1.2 to 2.9 is meant to prove that worldly life is characterized by anguish and delusion and is rooted in ignorance. He elucidates *BhG* 2.10 almost in the same way as Śrīdhara: "The glorious Nārāyaṇa, with a smiling face—in between the two armies—uttered these words, this discourse which is going to be pronounced to Arjuna who was grieving, who was expressing grief" (BhG1 2000, 72; *śrīnārāyaṇaḥ prasannavadanaḥ sann ubhayoḥ senayor madhye viṣīdantaṃ viṣādaṃ kurvantam arjunaṃ pratīdaṃ vakṣyamāṇaṃ vaco vākyam uvāca*). He interprets *prajñā* in *BhG* 2.11 as meaning "knowledge of the supreme Self" (BhG1 2000, 81; *prajñā paramātmajñānam*) and *paṇḍita*s as meaning "knowers of the supreme aim" (*paṇḍitāḥ paramārthavido nānuśocanti*). This is why Kṛṣṇa says: "O Arjuna, you are a fool, where is your supreme wisdom?" (*ato mūḍhas tvaṃ prajñā paramā kutas te*).

44. For more information, see Mahadevan (1968, 207–11).

45. BhG2 2001, 71: *evam apy arjune yuddham upekṣitavatīśvaraḥ* | *naivopekṣitavān ittham andhaṃ pratyāha sañjayaḥ* || 1 || *āgatya senayor madhye yuddhodyogena cārjunam* | *prāpnuvantaṃ viṣādaṃ ca saṃmohaṃ yuddharodhakam* || 2 || *taccеṣṭāyā hy anaucityaṃ hasanena prakāśayan* | *antaryāmī tam āheśo lajjābdhau majjayann iva* || 3 || *vakṣyamāṇam idaṃ cātigambhīraṃ sāravadvacaḥ* || 4 ||.

46. The three bodies (*śarīratraya*) mentioned in Advaita Vedānta texts are the physical body (*sthūlaśarīra*), the subtle body (*sūkṣmaśarīra*) and the causal body (*kāraṇaśarīra*).

47. *maivaṃ dhīmattvam etad bhoḥ prahāsāyaiva kalpate | ye paṇḍitā guroḥ śrutvā vedāntaviṣayaṃ padam || 15 || brahmaikyaṃ yuktibhir matvā nididhyāsya nirantaram | sākṣātkṛtātmatattvās te naṣṭāvidyāmalā budhāḥ* || 16 ||.

48. *yathā svapne mṛto bandhur jīvan vā śocyatāṃ gataḥ | na tannimittako moho jāgare 'py anuvartate* || 19 || *evam ajñānajabhrāntyā kalpitā bandhavo mṛtāḥ | jīvanto vā na te bodhe śokamohapradāḥ satām* || 20 ||.

49. *na ca śreyo 'nupaśyāmi hatvā svajanam āhave* |.

50. *ananyāś cintayanto māṃ ye janāḥ paryupāsate | teṣāṃ nityābhiyuktānāṃ yogakṣemaṃ vahāmy aham* ||.

51. *na kāṅkṣe vijayaṃ kṛṣṇa na ca rājyaṃ sukhāni ca* |.

52. *etān na hantum icchāmi ghnato 'pi madhusūdana | api trailokyarājyasya hetoḥ kiṃ nu mahīkṛte* ||.

53. *utsannakuladharmāṇāṃ manuṣyāṇāṃ janārdana | narake 'niyataṃ vāso bhavatīty anuśuśruma* ||.

54. *kiṃ no rājyena govinda* [. . .]

55. *kiṃ bhogair jīvitena vā* ||.

56. *yady apy ete na paśyanti lobhopahatacetasaḥ | kulakṣayakṛtaṃ doṣaṃ mitradrohe ca pātakam* ||.

57. *yadi mām apratīkāram aśastraṃ śastrapāṇayaḥ | dhārtarāṣṭrā raṇe hanyus tan me kṣemataraṃ bhavet* ||.

58. *gurūn ahatvā hi mahānubhāvān śreyo bhoktuṃ bhaikṣyam apīha loke | hatvārthakāmāṃs tu gurūn ihaiva bhuñjīya bhogān rudhirapradigdhān* ||.

59. *GAD* 2005, 50–52; BhG2 2001, 65–66; BhG3 1936, 36; *gurūpasadanam idānīṃ pratipādyate samadhigatasaṃsāradoṣajātasyātitarāṃ nirviṇṇasya vidhivad gurum upasannasyaiva vidyāgrahaṇe 'dhikārāt | tad evaṃ bhīṣmādisaṃkaṭavaśāt | vyutthāyātha bhikṣācaryaṃ caranti iti śrutisiddhabhikṣācarye 'rjunasyābhilāṣaṃ pradarśya vidhivad gurūpasattim api tatsaṅkaṭavyājenaiva darśayati kārpaṇyeti | yaḥ svalpām api vittakṣatiṃ na kṣamate sa kṛpaṇa iti loke prasiddhaḥ | tadvidhatvād akhilo 'nātmavid aprāptapuruṣārthatayā kṛpaṇo bhavati | yo vā etad akṣaraṃ gārgy aviditvā asmāl lokāt praiti sa kṛpaṇa iti śruteḥ | tasya bhāvaḥ kārpaṇyam anātmādhyāsavattvaṃ tannimitto 'smin janmany eta eva madīyās teṣu hateṣu kiṃ jīvitenety abhiniveśarūpo mamatālakṣaṇo doṣas tenopahatas tiraskṛtaḥ svabhāvaḥ kṣātro yuddhodyogalakṣaṇo yasya sa tathā* |.

60. It should be noted that Baladeva Vidyābhūṣaṇa utilizes several portions of the GAD in his commentary.

61. The rest of the gloss focusses on Arjuna's inner crisis: "What is justice? To kill one's enemies or to protect them? Is it right to protect the earth or is it right to live in the forest?" Being unable to answer these questions, Arjuna asks Kṛṣṇa to tell him what is best. The text adds other considerations accompanied by Upaniṣadic quotes, such as *Muṇḍaka Upaniṣad* 1.2.12 and *Taittirīya Upaniṣad* 3.1.

62. Along these lines, see Śaṅkarānanda's *Tātparyabodhinī* (BhG2 2001, 66) and Baladeva Vidyābhūṣaṇa's *Gītābhūṣaṇa*.

63. It is noteworthy that although complete self-surrender (*prapatti*) is a major concern of Viśiṣṭādvaita authors, none of them has elaborated upon it when dealing with *BhG* 2.7–8.

64. "So, in the way that here the condition acquired through action is exhausted, likewise the world up there, gained through merits, is exhausted" (*tad yatheha karmajito lokaḥ kṣīyata evam evāmutra puṇyajito lokaḥ kṣīyate iti śruteḥ*).

65. See Pellegrini-Sferra (2018, 289–90).

66. GAD 2005, 56–57; BhG2 2001, 70–71; BhG3 1936, 38–39: [. . .] *senayor ubhayor madhye yuddhodyamenāgatya tadvirodhinaṃ viṣādaṃ mohaṃ prāpnuvantaṃ tam arjunaṃ prahasann ivānucitācāraṇaprakāśanena lajjāmbudhau majjayann iva hṛṣīkeśaḥ sarvāntaryāmī bhagavān idaṃ vakṣyamāṇam aśocyān ityādi vacaḥ paramagambhīrārtham anucitācaraṇaprakāśakam uktavān na tūpekṣitavān ity arthaḥ | anucitācaraṇaprakāśanena lajjotpādanaṃ prahāsaḥ | lajjā ca duḥkhātmiketi dveṣaviṣaya eva sa mukhyaḥ | arjunasya tu bhagavatkṛpāviṣayatvād anucitācaraṇaprakāśanasya ca vivekotpattihetutvād* [. . .] *gauṇa evāyaṃ prahāsa iti kathayitum ivaśabdaḥ | lajjām utapādayitum iva vivekam utpādayitum arjunasyānucitācaraṇaṃ bhagavata prakāśyate* [. . .] | *yadi hi yuddhārambhāt prāg gṛhe eva sthito yuddham upekṣeta tadā nānucitaṃ kuryāt | mahatā saṃrambheṇa tu yuddhabhūmāv āgatya tadupekṣaṇam atīvānucitam iti kathayituṃ senayor ity ādiviśeṣaṇam | etac cāśocyān ityādau spaṣṭaṃ bhaviṣyati ||*.

67. See also Viśvanātha Cakravartī Ṭhākura's *Sārārthavarṣiṇīṭīkā* and Baladeva Vidyābhūṣaṇa's *Gītābhūṣaṇa*.

68. GAD 2005, 57; BhG2 2001, 72; BhG3 1936, 39: *tatrārjunasya yuddhākhye svadharme svato jātāpi pravṛttir dvidhena mohena tannimittena śokena ca pratibaddheti |*.

69. This viewpoint was already developed by Sadānanda *ad BhG* 2.11, vs. 1 (BhG2 2001, 74).

70. Here we paraphrase *GAD* 2005, 57; BhG2 2001, 72–73; BhG3 1936, 39: *tatrātmani svaprakāśaparamānandarūpe sarvasaṃsāradharmā 'saṃsargiṇi sthūlasūkṣmaśarīradvayatatkāraṇāvidyākhyopādhitrayāvivekena mithyābhūtasyāpi saṃsārasya satyatvātmadharmatvādipratibhāsarūpa ekaḥ sarvaprāṇisādhāraṇaḥ |*.

71. Here we paraphrase *GAD* 2005, 57; BhG2 2001, 72; BhG3 1936, 39: *aparas tu yuddhākhye svadharme hiṃsādibāhulyenādharmatvapratibhāsarūpo 'rjunasyaiva karuṇādidoṣanibandhano 'sādhāraṇaḥ | evam upādhitrayavivekena śuddhātmasvarūpabodhaḥ prathamasya nirvartakaḥ | dvitīyasya tu hiṃsādimattve 'pi yuddhasya svadharmatvenādharmatvābhāvabodho 'sādhāraṇaḥ |*.

72. A common rule states that effects cannot arise without their causes; see *Vaiśeṣikasūtra* 1.2.1–2, 4.1.3 and 5.2.18 (Sinha 1986, 37–38, 147, 184) along with *Yogasūtra* 2.25 (Āgāśe 2004, 23, 96).

73. The final sections of *GAD ad* 2.11 (GAD 2005, 58–59; BhG2 2001, 73; BhG3 1936, 41–44) focus on the perception of the *paṇḍitas*, whose knowledge of the reality of the Self is generated by reflection (*vicāra-janyātmatattvajñānavantaḥ*): *paṇḍitas* do not care about the dead or the living, whereas Arjuna's perception is completely different from theirs. For *paṇḍitas* the phenomenal world disappears during *samādhi* and thus there is no trace of masters, friends, relatives, etc. And although once they emerge from *samādhi* (*vyutthāna*; see *Yogasūtra* 3.37 with commentaries: Āgāśe 2004, 41, 156) the world reappears, the *paṇḍitas* have ascertained it as being illusory and false (*vyutthānasamaye tatpratibhāse 'pi mṛṣatvena niścayāt*). In the classic example of the rope mistaken for a snake (*rajju-sarpa*), once the illusion of the snake is dissolved by directly perceiving the rope, fear and trembling are no longer justified. Madhusūdana proposes another example: when the normal sense of taste is subdued by hepatitis A, even molasses taste bitter owing to an excess of bile (*pitta*). But once the person is cured, despite such invalid perception he/she will not search for molasses when wanting to taste something bitter because the ascertainment of sweetness is definitely stronger. Hence, since the illusion consisting in the mourning for those who should not be mourned is due to the ignorance of the nature of the Self, once this ignorance is dispelled through knowledge such an illusion disappears.

74. Saha (2017, 264) refers to Nīlakāṇṭha as Nīlakāṇṭha Sūri, who lived in Maharasthra in the sixteenth century. Nīlakāṇṭha was the son of Govinda Sūri, a Marāṭhī-speaking Brahmin whose family had established itself in the modern district of Ahmednagar (Gode 1942, 146–61).

75. This twofold delusion is also explained by Sadānanda Yogīndra *ad BhG* 2.11, vs. 1 (BhG2 2001, 74) and Madhusūdana Sarasvatī *ad* 2.11 (GAD 2005, 57; BhG2 2001, 72; BhG3 1936, 39).

76. He corroborates his position through a passage of the *śruti*, i.e., *Chāndogya Upaniṣad* 6.11.3: "It is indeed this [body] that perishes deprived of the individual Self; the individual Self does not perish!" (*jīvāpetaṃ vā va kiledaṃ mriyate, na jīvo mriyate*).

77. As stated in *Chāndogya Upaniṣad* 7.15.1: "Breath is indeed the father, the mother, the master!" (*prāṇo ha pitā prāṇo mātā prāṇa ācāryaḥ*).

78. *yadi dehaś cetanaḥ syāt mṛte 'pi tatra caitanyam upalabhyeta, tasmād dehanāśenātmanāśaṃ manvāno mūrkha evāsīty arthaḥ* |. Two inferences are presented here. The first is meant to prove that the Self is sentient and gives a negative (*vyatireka*) instance (*dṛṣṭānta*): the Self is different from a pot because it is sentient, whereas the property of the "negative instance" (*vipakṣa*) is opposite to that of the *probandum* (*sādhya*). The second inference has a positive instance (*sapakṣa*) where in both—*sapakṣa* and *sādhya*—the same *dharma* inheres, namely, the property of being the object of empir-

ical experience (*dṛśyatva*, lit. "visibility") gained through the means of knowledge; see Pellegrini-Sferra (2018, 289–90).

79. BhG7 1990, 33–34: *prahasann iva prahasan prakṛṣṭahāsaṃ kurvan jano yathā prasannamukho bhavati tathā prasannamukhaḥ sann ity arthaḥ | hṛṣīkeśatvena sarvāntaryāmitayā bhaktavatsalatayā ca bhagavataḥ svasakalabhaktasamuddhāraphalakaparamārthatattvaprakāśanasya svacikīrṣitasyaiva arjunasya śokamoharūpaṃ nimittam āśritya ayam iṣṭo 'vasaraḥ saṃprāpta iti bhagavataś cetasi saṃjātā, tasya mukhacandre 'pi prādurabhūd ity āśayaḥ* |.

80. According to Saha (2017, 274), Vasugupta (ninth century) the commentator of the *Śivasūtra*s also wrote the *Vāsavīṭīkā*, a commentary on the *BhG*.

81. We say so because in some parts of his commentary Bhāskara seems to follow the vulgate version or, as pointed out by Kato (2014, 1145–46), perhaps an earlier version of the Kashmirian recension followed by Rāmakaṇṭha (tenth century) and Abhinavagupta.

82. BhG5 1965, 41: *tam arjunaṃ senayor madhye yathoktena prakāreṇa sīdamānaṃ yuddhaṃ prati tyaktotsāhaṃ hṛṣīkeśo hasann idaṃ vakṣyamāṇaṃ vākyam āha* |.

83. *tvaṃ mānuṣyeṇopahatāntarātmā viṣādamohābhibhavād visaṃjñaḥ | kṛpāgṛhītaḥ samavekṣya bandhūn abhiprapannān mukham antakasya* ||.

84. See also Zaehner (1973, 125): "Vanquished by dejection and delusion, devoid of wit, your inmost Self has been upset by what is [all too] human; pity has seized upon you because you see your kinsmen enter into the jaws of death." See also Gnoli (1976, 57).

85. See *BhG* 11.14, where Arjuna is *vismayāviṣṭo*, "pervaded by wonder," on seeing Kṛṣṇa's universal shape; see Peterson (2003, 174–75).

86. BhG5 1965, 42: [. . .] *visaṃjño vyavahitadivyajñānaḥ saṃvṛtta iti | itaś copahāsakāraṇam | saṃjñānaṃ saṃjñā viśiṣṭā buddhiḥ | vigatā vyavahitā vā saṃjñā asyeti visaṃjñaḥ | upahatāntarātmā* | [. . .]

87. *Kaṭha Upaniṣad* 1.2.4: *dūram ete viparīte viṣūcī avidyā yā ca vidyeti | vidyābhīpsitaṃ naciketasaṃ manye na tvā kāmā bahavo 'lolupanta* ||.

88. See also Marjanovic (2002, 25–44) and Gnoli (1976, 56–57).

89. BhG6 1941, 27: *taṃ pārtham ubhayoḥ senayor madhye proktaprakāreṇa sīdamānaṃ śokābhibhūtaṃ yuddhaṃ prati tyaktotsāhaṃ prahasann iva vikṛtaceṣṭādarśanād upahasann iva hṛṣīkāṇām indriyāṇām īśaḥ prerayitā paramātmasvarūpaś caturātmā bhagavān | dehāhaṃbhāvanāvirbhūtamithyājñānanivṛtter saṃbhavaḥ iti tattvopadeśapūrvaṃ svakarmaṇi pravartayiṣur* (*sic* for *pravivartayiṣur*) *dehadehinoḥ saṃyogaviyogasvarūpam uddiśann uvācety arthaḥ* ||.

90. Yāmuna Muni's (tenth century) *Gītārthasaṃgraha* or "Compendium of the Meaning of the *BhG*" is the first *viśiṣṭādvaitin* gloss on the *BhG*. Also known as Āḷavantār, that is, "the victorious," Yāmuna is believed to be the predecessor of Rāmānuja in the line of the Śrī Sampradāya school (Saha

2017, 265–66). In just thirty-two stanzas, he presents the essence of the *BhG* which is Viṣṇu Nārāyaṇa, the supreme *Brahman*, who can be attained only by devotion. In stanzas 2 and 3, he divides the text's eighteen chapters into three hexads (*ṣaṭka*), the first of which is devoted to *karmayoga* and *jñānayoga* and the second to *bhaktiyoga*, "which can be brought about by action and knowledge, and whose purpose is to attain the correct understanding of the truth of the Blessed Lord" (Uskokov 2021, 70). The final hexad merely provides a supplement, expanding upon the contents of the first two. For an analysis of the threefold *BhG* division among the Śrīvaiṣṇavas, see Uskokov 2021, 68–79 and Belvalkar 1975[2], 147–49. It is noteworthy that in stanza 5 Yāmuna refers to Ajuna as "the surrendered one" (*pārthaṃ prapannam*), emphasizing the theme of *prapatti* (BhG1 2000, 24).

91. BhG1 2000, 71: *tam evaṃ dehātmanoḥ yāthātmyājñānanimitta-śokāviṣṭaṃ dehātiriktātmajñānanimittaṃ ca dharmaṃ* (on this emendation, see Ādidevānanda 1993, 59–60) *bhāṣamāṇaṃ parasparaviruddhaguṇānvitam ubhayoḥ senayoḥ yuddhāya udyuktayoḥ madhye akasmān nirudyogaṃ pārtham ālokya paramapuruṣaḥ prahasann iva idam uvāca* | [*pārthaṃ prahasann iva*] *parihāsavākyaṃ vadann iva ātmaparamātmayāthātmyatatprāpty upāyabhūtakarmayogabhaktiyogagocaram na tv evāhaṃ jātu nāsam ity ārabhya ahaṃ tvā sarvapāpebhyo mokṣayiṣyāmi mā śucaḥ ity etadantam uvāca ity arthaḥ* |.

92. *patanti pitaro hy eṣāṃ luptapiṇḍodakakriyāḥ* |.

93. Veṅkaṭanātha's *Gītārthasaṃgraharakṣā* is sometimes indispensable for understanding the synthetic wording of the *Gītārthasaṃgraha*. Veṅkaṭanātha says that in the first four stanzas of the *Gītārthasaṃgraha* Yāmuna Muni refers to the content of the entire *BhG* and to the purport of each of its three hexads (BhG1 2000, 24). Each chapter of the *BhG* is briefly explained by Yāmuna from stanza 5 to stanza 23. In stanza 5, Veṅkaṭanātha summarizes the first chapter and the first verses of the second, up to 2.9. He notes that though Vyāsa—the traditional author of the *BhG*—separated the first chapter from the second, *BhG* 1.1 up to 2.9 is to be understood as the introductory portion of the poem since it explains why Arjuna's despondency has arisen. Rāmānuja's commentary *ad BhG* 2.9 quotes and elucidates this passage from the *Gītārthasaṃgraha* specifically to make this point (BhG1 2000, 71). Though Rāmānuja does not comment on *prahasann iva*, he states that since Arjuna surrendered to his lord as a *prapanna* he should be taken as an example of eligibility (*adhikāratva*) for the *upadeśa*. Verses 2.10 to 2.12 mark the beginning of the instruction (*śāstrāvatararūpa*).

94. *Ad* 2.7, Veṅkaṭanātha writes that some thinkers define *kārpaṇya* as "not abandoning what should be abandoned" (BhG 1 2000, 68). Others define it as a psychological attitude that generates pity (*tyājyasyāparityāgo 'tra kārpaṇyam ity eke, dayājanakadīnavṛttiniratatvam ity apare* |).

95. In order to corroborate his question, Veṅkaṭanātha (BhG1 2000, 72) quotes *Mānavadharmaśāstra* 2.110: "No unasked issue should be revealed to anyone" (*nāpṛṣṭaḥ kasyacid brūyāt*).

96. *tasmād yudhyasva bhārata* ||.

97. *yuddhāya kṛtaniścayaḥ* ||.

98. *parihāsayogyatvāya tam iti parāmṛṣṭam āha—evam ityādinā* | [. . .] *adharmādiḥ parājayādir vā yuddhanivṛtteḥ samyagdhetur atra nāsti, ahetukopakrāntatyāge tu parihāsyatvam iti bhāvaḥ* | [. . .] *yadvā dhīram arjunaṃ hṛṣīkeśatayā svayaṃ prakṣobhya prahasann iva jagadupakārāya śāstram uvāceti* [. . .] *parihāsārthatvaucityāt prahāsasya* [. . .] |.

99. *yadvā prapannasya doṣanirīkṣaṇena parihāsāsaṃbhavaṃ śiṣyaṃ praty adhyātmopadeśe prahāsamātraṃ dṛṣṭāntānupayogaṃ ca abhipretya pārthaśabdaḥ* | *ataḥ prahasann iva ity anena phalitaṃ sarasatvaṃ sugrahatvaṃ nikhilanigamāntagahvaranilīnasya mahato 'rthajātasyānāyāsabhāṣaṇam, idaṃśabdasya vakṣyamāṇasamastabhagavadvākyaviṣayatvam, iṅgitenāpi vivakṣitasūcanaṃ ca darśayati—parihāsetyādinā* |.

100. *aśocyān iti ślokasyāpi upadeśārthāvadhānāpādanārthaparihāsacchāyatayā śāstrāvataraṇamātratvena sākṣācchāstratvābhāvāt na tv evāham ity ārabhya ity uktam* | *yadvā 'tra aśocyān iti ślokaḥ prahasann ivety asya viṣayo na tv evāham ityādikam idaṃśabdārthaḥ* | [. . .].

101. Madhva wrote two commentaries on the *BhG*: the *Gītābhāṣya* or *Dvaitabhāṣya* and the *Bhagavadgītātātparyanirṇaya* that is part of his monumental *Mahābhāratatātparyanirṇaya*. Like Śaṅkara's *Bhagavadgītābhāṣya*, the *Gītābhāṣya* begins at 2.10 whereas the *Bhagavadgītātātparyanirṇaya* begins at 2.11 (BhG1 2000, 80; Prabhanjanacharya 1999, 1–12).

102. Jaya Tīrtha also wrote a subcommentary on the *Bhagavadgītātātparyanirṇaya*, the *Nyāyadīpikā*, which we were not able to see; see Saha (2017, 269–70).

103. BhG1 2000, 80: *nanv idānīm eva kuto 'rjunasya mohasamutpattiḥ? na hy ete bāndhavādaya iti prāṅ nājñāsīt, yena yuddhāya mahāntam udyogam akārṣīd ity āha senayor iti* |.

104. BhG1 2000, 80: *mahāpakārasmaraṇenānuvartamāno 'pi kopo mṛdumanasāṃ bāndhavādiṣv antakāle nivartate, snehaś cotpadyate, tato moho iti prasiddham eveti bhāvaḥ* | *arjunasya jñānitvān mohajālasaṃvṛtatvam īṣad eveti mantavyam* |.

105. BhG2 2001, 3: *tatra tāvad aśocyān anvaśocyas tvam ity ārabhyārjunasya śokamohāpanodānāya bhagavadupadeśaṃ varṇayitum arjunasya sahetukaśokadarśanāya prathamādhyāyārambhaḥ* |.

106. "Indeed the *kṛpaṇa* is he who departs from this world without having known that imperishable!" (*yo vā etad akṣaram aviditvā gārgy asmāl lokāt praiti sa kṛpaṇa*).

107. BhG2 2001, 65: *pūrvapratipāditākṣaraśabdavācyasūryacandravāyuvahnīndrādisarvajaganniyantṛparamātmasvarūpaguṇādijñānahīnaḥ kṛpaṇaḥ ity ucyate śāstre* |.

108. BhG2 2001, 65: *ata eva dharme sammūḍhaṃ ceto yasya so 'haṃ tvāṃ svabhāvato 'pāstasamastadoṣaṃ sarvajñaṃ pṛcchāmi* |.

109. BhG2 2001, 70: *evaṃ yuddhatyāgāya kṛtavyavasāye 'rjune mama putrāṇāṃ sukhaṃ jīvanaṃ siddham iti cetanācetananiyantari durjanavināśāyāvatīrṇe bhagavaty adhiṣṭhātari sati nāśāsanīyam iti dhṛtarāṣṭrāya sūcayituṃ saṃjaya āha—tam iti* | *he bhārata! mahāvīrasya bharatasya vaṃśe jātasya tava yuddhoparatau putrasnehena harṣo nocita iti bhāvaḥ* |.

110. *pāṇḍuputrasya kṣatriyasammatasya naitad yuktam iti lajjānimittaṃ kopam utpādayituṃ prahasann ivety uktam* | *arjunaṃ nimittīkṛtya sarvasenāsaṃhārārthaṃ pravṛttasya gurutvenāṅgīkṛtya hitopadeṣṭur bhagavataḥ svadharme pravarttayitum udyatasya prahāso nocitaḥ, kintu tadvidhābuddhikauśalyagarvāpanayanena tattvajñānādhikāritāsampādanāya tathā vacanam itīvaśabdābhiprāyaḥ* ||.

111. *nimittāni ca paśyāmi viparītāni keśava* | *na ca śreyo 'nupaśyāmi hatvā svajanam āhave* ||.

112. *nihatya dhārtarāṣṭrān naḥ kā prītiḥ syāj janārdana* | *pāpam evāśrayed asmān hatvaitān ātatāyinaḥ* ||.

113. *utsannakuladharmāṇāṃ manuṣyāṇāṃ janārdana* | *narake niyataṃ vāso bhavatīty anuśuśruma* ||.

114. *gurūn ahatvā hi mahānubhāvān śreyo bhoktuṃ bhaikṣyam apīha loke* | *hatvārthakāmāṃs tu gurūn ihaiva bhuñjīya bhogān rudhirapradigdhān* ||.

115. The five *sādhanā*s are divided into two groups. The first group is open to all human beings and includes *prapatti*, "self-surrender to the lord," and *gurūpasatti*, "self-surrender to the master," understood to be constitutive of *prapatti* itself. The second group is made up of three types of *sādhanā* that are reserved to the twice-born (*dvija*). These are *vidyā* "learning," *upāsana* or *dhyāna* "meditation/contemplation," and *jñānayoga* "knowledge" (*karman* or "ritual action" is sometimes found in lieu of *jñānayoga*); see Clémentin-Ojha 2011, 442; Uskokov 2018, 4.

116. BhG1 2000, 73: *tataḥ kiṃ jātam iti tam uvāceti* | *aho asyātmatattvājñānataḥ klaibyaṃ kīdṛk? iti prahasan dharmiṣṭhatvād asyaitad apy ucitam iti bhāvenety uktam* |.

117. While commenting on *BhG* 2.11 (BhG1 2000, 82), Vallabha's focus is on the doctrine of Sāṃkhya-Yoga. The passage highlights that Arjuna's anguish is due to lack of discrimination concerning the Self. Arjuna is concerned with what should not be an object of concern, confusing the imperishable Self with the body that is *prakṛti*, that is, non-Self. In order to remove this epistemic distortion, from 2.11 onward Kṛṣṇa teaches him

"discriminative knowledge" (*sāṃkhyabuddhi*). In Puruṣottama's (1668–1764; Saha 2017, 272) *Amṛtataraṅgiṇī*—a gloss on the *Tattvadīpikā*—nothing is said on *prahasann iva* (BhG1 2000, 73). In addition to Puruṣottama's gloss, G. H. Bhatt (1949, 131–34) mentions a few other Śuddhādvaita commentaries that we were unable to see.

118. *nanu madvācas tvaṃ paṇḍitamānitvena khaṇḍayasi cet, kathaṃ brūyām? tatrāha śiṣyas te 'ham asmi | nātaḥ paraṃ vṛthā khaṇḍayāmīti bhāvaḥ* ||. See also the GRETIL e-text: http://gretil.sub.uni-goettingen.de/gretil/1_sanskr/2_epic/mbh/ext/bhg4c02u.htm.

119. *aho tavāpy etāvān khalv aviveka iti sakhyabhāvena taṃ prahasan anaucityaprakāśena lajjāmbudhau nimajjayan iveti tadānīṃ śiṣyabhāvaṃ prāpte tasmin hāsyam anucitam ity adharoṣṭhanikuñcanena hāsyam āvṛṇvaṃś cety arthaḥ* |.

120. *hṛṣīkeśa iti pūrvaṃ premṇāivārjunavāṅniyamyo 'pi sāmpratam arjunahitakāritvāt premṇaivārjunamanoniyantāpi bhavatīti bhāvaḥ | senayor ubhayor madhye ity arjunasya viṣādo bhagavatā prabodhaś ca ubhābhyāṃ senābhyāṃ sāmānyato dṛṣṭa eveti bhāvaḥ* ||. The meaning is that prior to the intervention of Kṛṣṇa-Hṛṣīkeśa, Arjuna's mind was deluded by his affection for his kinsfolk. Now, however, from the very beginning of the *gītopadeśa* his mind is under Kṛṣṇa's control.

121. See *Bṛhadāraṇyaka Upaniṣad* 3.8.10; *Chāndogya Upaniṣad* 6.14.2; *Muṇḍaka Upaniṣad* 1.2.12.

122. [. . .] *taṃ viṣīdantam arjunaṃ prati hṛṣīkeśo bhagavān aśocyān ityādikam atigambhīrārthaṃ vacanam uvāca | aho tavāpīdṛg viveka iti sakhyabhāvena prahasan | anaucityabhāṣitvena trapāsindhau nimajjayann ity arthaḥ | iveti tadaiva śiṣyatāṃ prāpte tasmin hāsānaucityād īṣadadharollāsaṃ kurvann ity arthaḥ | arjunasya viṣādo bhagavatā tasyopadeśaś ca sarvasākṣika iti bodhayituṃ senayor ubhayor ity etat* ||. See also the GRETIL e-text: http://gretil.sub.uni-goettingen.de/gretil/1_sanskr/2_epic/mbh/ext/bhg4c02u.htm.

Chapter 3

1. For both the *MBh* and Vālmīki's *Rām* we have based ourselves on the critical editions available online. Unless otherwise specified, all translations from the Sanskrit are of Gianni Pellegrini.

2. Each *akṣauhiṇī* was a complete army in itself, a *caturaṅginīsenā*: it comprised 21.870 elephants, 21.870 chariots, 65.610 horses (= 21.870 x 3) and 109.350 infantrymen (= 21.870 x 5).

3. The eighteen *adhyāya*s of the *BhG* (= *MBh* 6.25–42) are part of the larger *Bhagavadgītāparvan* (= *MBh* 6.13–42), which is the third subdivision of the *Bhīṣmaparvan* and the sixty-third of the hundred subdivisions of the *MBh*.

4. As is well known, the reflection on the four aims of human life (*puruṣārtha*) occupies a large part of the *MBh*, as programmatically stated at the beginning (1.62.53, *dharme cārthe ca kāme ca mokṣe ca bharatarṣabha | yad ihāsti tad anyatra yan nehāsti na tat kvacit ||*) and—with some variants—also at the end (18.5.50).

5. Even leaving aside the independent *Gītā*s, there are many other *Gītā*s in the *MBh* most of which are included in the *Śāntiparvan* and in the important *upaparvan* known as *Mokṣadharma*. Stefano Piano (1994, 52–54) lists all these *Gītā*s according to the vulgate edition of the *MBh*: *Utathyagītā* (12.90–91), *Vāmadevagītā* (12.92–93), *Ṛṣabhagītā* (12.125–29), *Ṣaḍjagītā* (12.167), *Śaṃpākagītā* (12.176), *Maṅkigītā* (12.177), *Bodhyagītā* (12.178), *Vicakhnugītā* (12.265), *Hārītagītā* (12.278), *Vṛtragīta* (12.279), *Parāśaragītā* (12.290–98), *Haṃsagītā* (12.299) and the *Anugītā* or *Uttaragītā* (14.16–51). This last *Gītā* is especially relevant since it incorporates the *BhG* main contents (Nilakantan 1989).

6. Before publishing the first English translation of the *BhG*, Charles Wilkins wished to translate the entire *MBh* (and indeed he had started doing it) but at Benares, due to the influence of his Sanskrit teacher Kashinatha, his choice shifted to the *BhG*. This shift "reflects the high value that his Brahmin pundits placed on the work" (Davis 2014, 79).

7. A well-known verse, variously attributed to a *Gītāmāhātmya* (5; BhG1 2000, 4; Brodbeck 2018, 202) or to the *Gītāmṛta* (4), states that the *BhG* is the very essence of the *Upaniṣads*: *sarvopaniṣado gāvo dogdhā gopālanandanaḥ | pārtho vatsaḥ sudhīr bhoktā dugdhaṃ gītāmṛtaṃ mahat ||* that is, "All *Upaniṣads* are cows, the milker is the herdsman's son [= Kṛṣṇa], Pārtha [= Arjuna] is the calf, the consumer/enjoyer is the sage, and the milk is the magnificent nectar of the *Gītā*." In his commentary to the *BhG*, Śaṅkara says (BhG1 2000, 4): *gītāśāstraṃ samastavedārthasārasaṃgrahabhūtam* [. . .], "The teaching of the *Gītā* is a compedium of the essence of the meaning of the entire *Veda* [. . .]."

8. Basing ourselves on D'Sa 1996 and Bandhu 1977, we have focused attention on all possible forms of root √*has* as well as on a few important derivatives such as *apahāsa*, *parihāsa*, and *prahāsa*. D'Sa 1996, 136 reports an apparently erroneous occurrence of root √*has* in *Bṛhadāraṇyaka Upaniṣad* 1.3.28 (*āhasat*). Bandhu detects only six occurrences (Bandhu 1977, 544): *hasati* in *Chāndogya Upaniṣad* 3.17.3 (Olivelle 1998, 212), *hasati* and *hasan* in *Yogaśikhā Upaniṣad* 6.67–68 (Śāstrī 1970, 472), *hasanti* in *Mahā Upaniṣad* 3.35 (Śāstrī 1970, 433), *hasaḥ* in *Jaiminīya Upaniṣad Brāhmaṇa* 3.25.8 (Oertel 1896, 185) and *hāsyam* in *Tejobindu Upaniṣad* 4.27 (Śāstrī 1970, 271).

9. The same participle *jakṣat* is found in *Chāndogya Upaniṣad* 8.12.3: "[. . .] He is the highest person. He roams about there, laughing, playing,

and enjoying himself with women, carriages, or relatives, without remembering the appendage that is this body" ([. . .] *sa uttamapuruṣaḥ | sa tatra paryeti jakṣat krīḍan ramamāṇaḥ strībhir vā yānair vā jñātibhir vā nopajanaṃ smarann idaṃ śarīram* || Olivelle 1998, 284–85). Even here, Śaṅkara glosses *jakṣat* with *hasan* (Śāstrī 1982, 418) but he plays with the double meaning of √*jakṣ* as the reduplicated form of √*ghas* ("to eat/devour"), thus interpreting it to mean also *bhakṣayan*, "eating."

10. In the *Ṛgveda*, we find only seven occurrences of root √*has* but no *prahasann iva* or *hasann iva*; see Bandhu 1963, 607. In the other *Saṃhitā*s there are very few occurrences of the root; see Bandhu 1960, 644; Bandhu 1963, 1097; Nair 1992, 2222 and Bandhu 1963, 3565. The situation is pretty much the same in the *Brāhmaṇa*s; see Bandhu 1973, 1024 and 1675. On the *Upaniṣad*s, see Bandhu 1977, 558, 975, and 1183. On the *Vedāṅga* literature, see Nair 1996, 1747; Nair 1994, 2784.

11. Within the *MBh* there are countless present participles in the nominative case that display a reduplication of final *-n* when followed by *iva*, which is the result of the euphonic rule of *sandhi*. Just to mention a few: *parirujann iva* (5.73.8b); *rudann iva* (5.73.10b); *vilahann iva* (5.73.11b); *prajvalann iva* (6.60.17d); *ārujann iva* (7.47.21a); *śvasann iva* (7.91.38d); *pibann iva* (7.103.2a); *utsmayann iva* (7.111.46a); *kampayann iva* (8.24.93d); *smarayann iva* (9.27.46b); *prakrīḍann iva* (12.125.15c); *harṣayann iva* (13.14.170d). The case of *hasann iva* is exemplified in Goldman—Sutherland Goldman 2002, 42.

12. Present participles are used to express simultaneity with the main action. Though *prahasann iva* and *hasann iva* are no exception, what happens here is that we have a complex action (*kriyā*) such as speaking that is accomplished by subsidiary actions (*ceṣṭā*), that is, the opening of the mouth and the smiling that immediately precedes the locutionary act.

13. We owe this critical remark to our friend and colleague Raffaele Torella.

14. A Hindī expression reveals the meaning of *prahasann iva* and *hasann iva* in these contexts: *bāye hāth kā khel*, that is, "a left-hand game," which refers to a Brahmin's reluctance to use the left hand considered to be impure and less capable of carrying out certain deeds. On the excellence of the right hand, see Gonda 1972, 1–23.

15. See for instance 7.142.16d. Here Rādheya (i.e., Karṇa), after addressing Sahadeva, moves against the armies of the Pāñcālas and Pāṇḍavas with a hint of laughter that indicates his disregard of danger (*evam uktvā tu taṃ karṇo rathena rathināṃ varaḥ | prāyāt pāñcālapāṇḍūnāṃ sainyāni prahasann iva* ||). Even at 7.142.13c, Karṇa addresses Sahadeva laughing (*prahasan*).

16. The list of all these *MBh* occurrences is as follows: 1.141.1b, 1.141.18d, 1.151.7b, 1.151.14d, 4.52.23b, 6.43.21d, 6.49.15d, 6.54.15d, 6.60.13d,

6.60.31b, 6.65.22d, 6.75.39f, 6.79.36b, 6.79.48e, 6.107.2d, 7.37.13b, 7.47.26b, 7.77.29c, 7.82.5b, 7.82.14d, 7.82.20d, 7.90.13d, 7.90.26b, 7.90.28d, 7.91.32b, 7.91.35d, 7.91.43d, 7.92.14d, 7.99.16b, 7.102.98c, 7.103.4b, 7.110.31d, 7.111.3b, 7.114.50f, 7.117.14b, 7.130.29b, 7.134.43b, 7.137.18d, 7.137.26d, 7.141.7b, 7.141.10d, 7.142.6d, 7.142.16d, 7.144.6b, 7.144.16d, 7.146.28d, 7.164.45b, 7.169.20d, 7.173.48b, 8.9.26d, 8.10.21d, 8.17.39d, 8.17.84d, 8.24.94c, 8.33.14d, 8.34.16d, 8.35.23b, 8.44.42d, 8.45.5b, 8.55.52d, 9.11.48d, 9.25.9b, 9.26.42d, 9.26.47d, 9.27.24f, 9.27.35d, 9.27.38d, 9.27.51d, 12.125.18d, 14.83.8b, 16.8.49d.

17. *bhīmasenas tu tac chrutvā prahasann iva bhārata* | *rākṣasaṃ tam anādṛtya bhuṅkta eva parāṅmukhaḥ* ||.

18. *kṣiptaṃ kruddhena taṃ vṛkṣaṃ pratijagrāha vīryavān* | *savyena pāṇinā bhīmaḥ prahasann iva bhārata* ||.

19. *tām āpatantīṃ sahasā śaktiṃ kanakabhūṣaṇām* | *tridhā cikṣepa samare bhāradvājo hasann iva* ||.

20. *sa cchādyamāno bahubhiḥ śaraiḥ saṃnataparvabhiḥ* | *svasrīyābhyāṃ naravyāghro nākampata yathācalaḥ* | *prahasann iva tāṃ cāpi śaravṛṣṭiṃ jaghāna ha* ||.

21. At verse 6.79.45a, we find *prahasya* which is the absolutive of root *pra-√has*.

22. *mādhavas tu susaṃkruddho rākṣasaṃ navabhiḥ śaraiḥ* | *ājaghāna raṇe rājan prahasann iva bhārata* ||.

23. *tāṃ tathā bruvato dṛṣṭvā saubhadraḥ prahasann iva* | *yo yaḥ sma prāharat pūrvaṃ taṃ taṃ vivyādha patribhiḥ* ||.

24. *na no jīvan mokṣyase jīvitām iti* |. On the epic use of *jīvanmukta*, see Hara 1996, 185–88.

25. The Dakṣa myth is popular in Sanskrit literature: see *MBh* 12.283–84; *Bhāgavata Purāṇa* 4.2.4–7; *Kūrma Purāṇa* 1.14–15; *Matsya Purāṇa* 82; *Śiva Purāṇa* 2.2.22–37; *Vāmana Purāṇa* 1–5; *Vāyu Purāṇa* 30. On this myth, see O'Flaherty 1975, 118–25, 324–25; Kramrisch 1981, 301–39; Pellegrini 2012, 290.

26. *vivyādha kupito yajñaṃ nirbhayas tu bhavas tadā* | *dhanuṣā bāṇam utsṛjya sa ghoṣaṃ vinanāda ca* || 42 || *te na śarma kutaḥ śāntiṃ lebhire sma surās tadā* | *vidrute sahasā yajñe kupite ca maheśvare* || 43 || *tena jyātalaghoṣeṇa sarve lokāḥ samākulāḥ* | *babhūvur vaśagāḥ pārtha nipetuś ca surāsurāḥ* || 44 || *āpaś cukṣubhire sarvāś cakampe ca vasuṃdharā* | *parvatāś ca vyaśīryanta diśo nāgāś ca mohitāḥ* || 45 || *andhāś ca tamasā lokā na prakāśanta saṃvṛtāḥ* | *jaghnivān saha sūryeṇa sarveṣāṃ jyotiṣāṃ prabhāḥ* || 46 || *cukruśur bhayabhītāś ca śāntiṃ cakrus tathaiva ca* | *ṛṣayaḥ sarvabhūtānām ātmanaś ca sukhaiṣiṇaḥ* || 47 || *pūṣāṇam abhyadravata śaṅkaraḥ prahasann iva* | *puroḍāśaṃ bhakṣayato daśanān vai vyaśātayat* || 48 || *tato niścakramur devā vepamānā natāḥ sma tam* | *punaś ca saṃdadhe dīptaṃ devānāṃ niśitaṃ śaram* || 49 || *rudrasya yajñabhāgaṃ ca viśiṣṭaṃ te nv akalpayan* | *bhayena tridaśā rājañ śaraṇaṃ ca prapedire* || 50 ||.

27. In this same chapter, at 8.24.43cd, Śiva smiles before allowing the gods to speak (*brūta brūteti bhagavān smayamāno 'bhyabhāṣata*).

28. *sa śobhamāno varadaḥ khaḍgī bāṇī śarāsanī | hasann ivābravīd devo sārathiḥ ko bhaviṣyati* || 94 || *tam abruvan devagaṇā yaṃ bhavan saṃniyokṣyate | sa bhaviṣyati deveśa sārathis te na saṃśayaḥ* || 95 || *tān abravīt punar devo mattaḥ śreṣṭhataro hi yaḥ | taṃ sārathiṃ kurudhvaṃ me svayaṃ saṃcitya māciram* || 96 ||.

29. The charioteer will be Brahmā; see 8.24.97–112.

30. In this passage the formula occurs at the very beginning of the *pada*.

31. *tato gavyūtimātreṇa mṛgayūthapayūthapaḥ | tasya bāṇapathaṃ tyaktvā tasthivān prahasann iva* ||.

32. An example of the multivalence of *prahasann iva,* which signifies ease as well as mockery.

33. *chittvā vajranikāśena rāghavaḥ prahasann iva | trayodaśenendrasamo bibheda samare kharam* ||.

34. A second occurrence that we can refer to this section is 6.95.21c: *vyāyacchamānaṃ taṃ dṛṣṭvā tatparaṃ rāvaṇaṃ raṇe | prahasann iva kākutsthaḥ saṃdadhe sāyakāñ śitān* ||. On seeing Rāvaṇa violently fighting in battle, Rāma (Kākutstha) notches a sharp arrow with a hint of laughter (*prahasann iva*). Here *prahasann iva* is at the beginning of a half-verse, which is unusual.

35. Twenty-one including *BhG* 2.10b (= *MBh* 6.24.10b). The other five occurrences are: 3.290.8b (*madhupiṅgo mahābāhuḥ kambugrīvo hasann iva | aṅgadī baddhamukuṭo diśaḥ prajvālayann iva* ||; "Yellow like honey, with great arms, with a shell-shaped neck, with a hint of laughter, with a bracelet, wearing a crown as if he were inflaming the sky [. . .]"), where *hasann iva* anticipates that the sun god Sūrya is going to bestow a boon on princess Kuntī. Since the god is somehow forced to comply with Kuntī's will, it could also be interpreted as a sarcastic hint of laughter given that he has no alternative but to satisfy her wish; 7.148.39d (*tatas taṃ meghasaṃkāśaṃ dīptāsyaṃ dīptakuṇḍalam | abhyabhāṣata haiḍimbaṃ dāśārhaḥ prahasann iva* ||; "Then Dāśārha [= Kṛṣṇa], with a hint of laughter, addressed the son of Hiḍimbā [= Ghaṭotkaca], similar to a cloud, with a blazing face and shining earrings"), where Kṛṣṇa's *prahasann iva,* akin to a sly grin, introduces a command to the mighty Ghaṭotkaca—son of Bhīma by the *rākṣasī* Hiḍimbā—to attack Karṇa; 10.7.59d (*tam ūrdhvabāhuṃ niśceṣṭaṃ dṛṣṭvā havir upasthitam | abravīd bhagavān sākṣān mahādevo hasann iva* ||; "Seeing him [= Aśvatthāman] with lifted arm, motionless, presented (*upasthitam*) as an oblation, the glorious Mahādeva in person, with a hint of laughter, said [. . .]"), where *hasann iva* shows that Śiva is pleased with the offering of Aśvatthāman and is ready to bestow his favor upon him; 12.310.27b (*uvāca cainaṃ bhavavāṃś tryambakaḥ prahasann iva | evaṃvidhas te tanayo*

dvaipāyana bhaviṣyati ||; "[Śiva Maheśvara], with a hint of laughter, said to him: 'O Dvaipāyana [Vyāsa], you will have a son' "), where through his *prahasann iva* the god bestows his grace upon Vyāsa; 18.1.11b (the last occurrence at the opening of the last *parvan*, the *Svargārohaṇa*, where Yudhiṣṭhira reaches paradise and sees Duryodhana in all his glory: *maivam abravīt taṃ tu nāradaḥ prahasann iva* | *svarge nivāso rājendra viruddhaṃ cāpi naśyati* ||; "[Yudhiṣṭhira said:] 'It can't be like that!' Nārada then replied to him with a hint of laughter: 'O chief among kings, residence in paradise destroys even hostility' "), where *prahasann iva* introduces a moral teaching.

36. *tatra caṅkramyamāṇau tau vasudevasutāṃ śubhām* | *alaṅkṛtāṃ sakhīmadhye bhadrāṃ dadṛśatus tadā* || 14 || *dṛṣṭvaiva tām arjunasya kandarpaḥ samajāyata* | *taṃ tathaikāgramanasaṃ kṛṣṇaḥ pārtham alakṣayat* || 15 || *athābravīt puṣkarākṣaḥ prahasann iva bhārata* | *vanecarasya kim idaṃ kāmenāloḍyate manaḥ* || 16 || *mamaiṣā bhaginī pārtha sāraṇasya sahodarā* | *yadi te vartate buddhir vakṣyāmi pitaraṃ svayam* || 17 ||.

37. *tam uvāca tataḥ prītaḥ sa dvijaḥ prahasann iva* | *varaṃ vṛṇīṣva bhadraṃ te śakro 'ham arisūdana* || 36 || *evam uktaḥ pratyuvāca sahasrākṣaṃ dhanaṃjayaḥ* | *prāñjaliḥ praṇato bhūtvā śūraḥ kurukulodvahaḥ* || 37 || *īpsito hy eṣa me kāmo varaṃ cainaṃ prayaccha me* | *tvatto 'dya bhagavann astraṃ kṛtsnam icchāmi veditum* || 38 || *pratyuvāca mahendras taṃ prītātmā prahasann iva* | *iha prāptasya kiṃ kāryam astrais tava dhanaṃjaya* | *kāmān vṛṇīṣva lokāṃś ca prāpto 'si paramāṃ gatim* || 39 ||.

38. The same story is narrated in *MBh* 3.183–90 and *Matsya Purāṇa* 165.1–22 and 167.13–67. See Zimmer 1972, 35–53.

39. The *śrīvatsa* is a distinctive sign of Viṣṇu-Kṛṣṇa: a wisp of hair in the middle of his chest; see Mani 1996, 139–41, 738.

40. *tato mām abravīd vīra sa bālaḥ prahasann iva* | *śrīvatsadhārī dyutimān pītavāsā mahādyutiḥ* ||.

41. *etac chrutvā mahābāhuḥ keśavaḥ prahasann iva* | *abhūtapūrvaṃ bhīmasya mārdavopagataṃ vacaḥ* || 1 || *girer iva laghutvaṃ tac chītatvam iva pāvake* | *matvā rāmānujaḥ śaurī śārṅgadhanvā vṛkodaram* || 2 || *saṃtejayaṃs tadā vāgbhir mātariśveva pāvakam* | *uvāca bhīmam āsīnaṃ kṛpayābhipariplutam* || 3 || *tvam anyadā bhīmasena yuddham eva praśaṃsasi* | *vadhābhinandinaḥ krūrān dhārtarāṣṭrān mimardiṣuḥ* || 4 || *na ca svapiṣi jāgarṣi nyubjaḥ śeṣe paraṃtapa* | *ghorām aśāntāṃ ruśatīṃ sadā vācaṃ prabhāṣase* || 5 || *niḥśvasan agnivat tena saṃtaptaḥ svena manyunā* | *apraśāntamanā bhīma sadhūma iva pāvakaḥ* || 6 || *ekānte niḥśvasan śeṣe bhārārta iva durbalaḥ* | *api tvāṃ kecid unmattaṃ manyante tadvido janāḥ* || 7 || *ārujya vṛkṣān nirmūlān gajaḥ parirujann iva* | *nighnan padbhiḥ kṣitiṃ bhīma niṣṭanan paridhāvasi* || 8 || *nāsmiñ jane 'bhiramase rahaḥ kṣiyasi pāṇḍava* | *nānyaṃ niśi divā vāpi kadācid abhinandasi* || 9 || *akasmāt smayamānaś ca rahasy āsse rudann iva* | *jānvor mūrdhānam ādhāya ciram āsse pramīlitaḥ* || 10 || *bhrukuṭiṃ ca punaḥ kurvann oṣṭhau ca vilihann*

iva | abhīkṣṇaṃ dṛśyase bhīma sarvaṃ tan manyukāritam || 11 ||. With reference to verse 6ab, we follow the emendation proposed by Garbutt 2008, 622 rather than the reading of the critical edition (*niḥśvasan agnivarṇena saṃtaptaḥ svena manyunā*). With reference to the verb *kṣiyasi* in verse 9b, it should be noted that Garbutt 2008, 622 reads *kṣipasi*.

42. *kasmād annāni pānāni vāsāṃsi śayanāni ca | tvadartham upanītāni nāgrahīs tvaṃ janārdana* || 13 || *ubhayoś cādadaḥ sāhyam ubhayoś ca hite rataḥ | saṃbandhī dayitaś cāsi dhṛtarāṣṭrasya mādhava* || 14 || *tvaṃ hi govinda dharmārthau vettha tattvena sarvaśaḥ | tatra kāraṇam icchāmi śrotuṃ cakragadādhara* || 15 ||.

43. *sa evam ukto govindaḥ pratyuvāca mahāmanāḥ | oghameghasvanaḥ kāle pragṛhya vipulaṃ bhujam* || 16 || *anambhūkṛtam agrastam anirastam asaṃkulam | rājīvanetro rājānaṃ hetumadvākyam uttamam* || 17 ||.

44. *kṛtārthā bhuñjate dūtāḥ pūjāṃ gṛhṇanti caiva hi | kṛtārthaṃ māṃ sāhātyas tvam arciṣyasi bhārata* || 18 || *evam uktaḥ pratyuvāca dhārtarāṣṭro janārdanam | na yuktaṃ bhavatāsmāsu pratipattum asāṃpratam* || 19 || *kṛtārthaṃ ca tvāṃ vayaṃ madhusūdana | yatāmahe pūjayituṃ govinda na ca śaknumaḥ* || 20 || *na ca tatkāraṇaṃ vidmo yasmin no madhusūdana | pūjāṃ kṛtāṃ prīyamāṇair nāmaṃsthāḥ puruṣottama* || 21 || *vairaṃ no nāsti bhavatā govinda na ca vigrahaḥ | sa bhavan prasamīkṣyaitan naidṛśaṃ vaktum arhati* || 22 || *evam uktaḥ pratyuvāca dhārtarāṣṭraṃ janārdanaḥ | abhivīkṣya sahāmātyaṃ dāśārhaḥ prahasann iva* || 23 || *nāhaṃ kāmān na saṃraṃbhān na dveṣān nārthakāraṇāt | na hetuvādāl lobhād vā dharmaṃ jahyāṃ kathaṃcana* || 24 || *saṃprītibhojyāny annāni āpadbhojyāni vā punaḥ | na ca saṃprīyase rājan na cāpy āpadgatā vayam* || 25 || *akasmād dviṣase rājañ janmaprabhṛti pāṇḍavān | priyānuvartino bhrātṝn sarvaiḥ samuditān guṇaiḥ* || 26 || *akasmāc caiva pārthānāṃ dveṣaṇaṃ nopapadyate | dharme sthitāḥ pāṇḍaveyāḥ kas tān kiṃ vaktum arhasi* || 27 || *yas tān dveṣṭi sa māṃ dveṣṭi yas tān anu sa mām anu | aikātmyaṃ māṃ gataṃ viddhi pāṇḍavair dharmacāribhiḥ* || 28 || *kāmakrodhānuvartī hi yo mohād virurutsate | guṇavantaṃ ca yo dveṣṭi tam āhuḥ puruṣādhamam* || 29 || *yaḥ kalyāṇaguṇāñ jñātīn mohāl lobhād didṛkṣate | so 'jitātmājitakrodho na ciraṃ tiṣṭhati śriyam* || 30 || *atha yo guṇasampannān hṛdayasyāpriyān api | priyeṇa kurute vaśyāṃś ciraṃ yaśasi tiṣṭhati* || 31 || *sarvam etad abhoktavyam annaṃ duṣṭābhisaṃhitam | kṣattur ekasya bhoktavyam iti me dhīyate matiḥ* || 32 ||.

45. *evam ābhāṣyamāṇo 'pi bhrātṛbhiḥ kurunandana | novāca vāgyataḥ kiñcid gacchaty eva yudhiṣṭhiraḥ* ||.

46. *tān uvāca mahāprajño vāsudevo mahāmanāḥ | abhiprāyo 'sya vijñāto mayeti prahasann iva* || 16 || *eṣa bhīṣmaṃ tathā droṇaṃ gautamaṃ śalyam eva ca | anumānya gurūn sarvān yotsyate pārthivo 'ribhiḥ* || 17 || *śrūyate hi purākalpe gurūn ananumānya yaḥ | yudhyate sa bhaved vyaktam apadhyāyo mahattaraiḥ* || 18 || *anumānya yathāśāstraṃ yas tu yudhyen mahattaraiḥ | dhruvas tasya jayo yuddhe bhaved iti matir mama* || 19 ||; van Buitenen 1981, 147.

47. On the *pāśupata* weapon, see Bakker and Bisschop 2016, 239 and 247–52; Kramrisch 1981, 257–59.

48. *tatas tāv āgatau śarvaḥ provāca prahasann iva | svāgataṃ vāṃ naraśreṣṭhāv uttiṣṭhetāṃ gataklamau | kiṃ ca vām īpsitaṃ vīrau manasaḥ kṣipram ucyatām* || 46 || *yena kāryeṇa saṃprāptau yuvāṃ tat sādhayāmi vām | vriyatām ātmanaḥ śreyas tat sarvaṃ pradadāni vām* || 47 || *tatas tad vacanaṃ śrutvā pratyutthāya kṛtāñjalī | vāsudevārjunau śarvaṃ tuṣṭuvāte mahāmatī* || 48 ||.

49. On Karṇa's figure, see McGrath 2004.

50. On the story of Karṇa's spear, see Hiltebeitel 2011, 417, 426–27.

51. *etac chrutvā mahārāja govindaḥ prahasann iva | abravīd arjunaṃ tūrṇaṃ kauravāñ jahi pāṇḍava* ||.

52. *iti sma kṛṣṇavacanāt pratyuccārya yudhiṣṭhiram | babhūva vimanāḥ pārthaḥ kiñcit kṛtveva pātakam* || 1 || *tato 'bravīd vāsudevaḥ prahasann iva pāṇḍavam | kathaṃ nāma bhaved etad yadi tvaṃ pārtha dharmajam* || 2 ||.

53. *tam uvāca bhṛguśreṣṭhaḥ saroṣaḥ prahasann iva | bhūmau nipatitaṃ dīnaṃ vepamānaṃ kṛtāñjalim* || 29 || *yasmān mithyopacarito astralobhād iha tvayā | tasmād etad dhi te mūḍha brahmāstraṃ pratibhāsyati* || 30 || *anyatra vadhakālāt te sadṛśena sameyuṣaḥ | abrāhmaṇe na hi brahma dhruvaṃ tiṣṭhet kadācana* || 31 || *gacchedānīṃ na te sthānam anṛtasyeha vidyate | na tvayā sadṛśo yuddhe bhavitā kṣatriyo bhuvi* || 32 ||.

54. Jambavatī is the daughter of Jambavān, king of the Vidyādharas, who will become Kṛṣṇa's wife; see Mani 1996, 342.

55. The story of Upamanyu's father Vyāghrapāda is narrated in this same chapter of the *MBh*.

56. In the *MBh* there are several characters named Dhaumya. One of them is the chief priest (*purohita*) of the Pāṇḍavas, who performed the rites at the royal consecration of Yudhiṣṭhira and, later, walked on ahead of the Pāṇḍavas when they were going to the forest. Here, however, the reference is to another Dhaumya (i.e., an ascetic that is Upamanyu's younger brother); see Mani 1996, 232–33; Rāy 1982, 355.

57. *evam uktas tataḥ śarvaḥ surair brahmādibhis tathā | āha māṃ bhagavān īśaḥ prahasann iva śaṅkaraḥ* || 174 || *vatsopamanyo prīto 'smi paśya māṃ munipuṅgava | dṛḍhabhakto 'si viprarṣe mayā jijñāsito hy asi* || 175 || *anayā caiva bhaktyā te atyarthaṃ prītimān aham | tasmāt sarvān dadāmy adya kāmāṃs tava yathepsitān* || 176 ||. With reference to the last word, the critical edition reads *yathepśitān* (*yathā īpśitān*).

58. *yathā svakoṣṭhe prakṣipya koṣṭhaṃ bhāṇḍamanā bhavet | tathā svakāye prakṣipya mano dvārair aniścalaiḥ | ātmānaṃ tatra mārgeta pramādaṃ parivarjayet* || 42 || *evaṃ satatam udyuktaḥ prītātmā nacircād iva | āsādayati tad brahma yad dṛṣṭvā syāt pradhānavit* || 43 || *na tv asau cakṣuṣā grāhyo na ca sarvair apīndriyaḥ | manasaiva pradīpena mahān ātmani dṛśyate* || 44 || *sarvataḥpāṇipādaṃ taṃ sarvatokṣiśiromukham | jīvo niṣkrāntam ātmānaṃ śarīrāt saṃprapaśyati* ||

45 || *sa tad utsṛjya dehaṃ svaṃ dhārayan brahma kevalam* | *ātmānam ālokayati manasā prahasann iva* || 46 || *idaṃ sarvarahasyaṃ te mayoktaṃ dvijasattama* | *āpṛcche sādhayiṣyāmi gaccha śiṣya yathāsukham* || 47 ||.

59. *evam uktaḥ sa śāntātmā tām uvāca hasann iva* | *subhage nābhyasūyāmi vākyasyāsya tavānaghe* || 5 || *grāhyaṃ dṛśyaṃ ca śrāvyaṃ ca yad idaṃ karma vidyate* | *etad eva vyavasyanti karma karmeti karmiṇaḥ* || 6 || *moham eva niyacchanti karmaṇā jñānavarjitāḥ* | *naiṣkarmyaṃ na ca loke 'smin maurtam ity upalabhyate* || 7 ||. The last verse reminds us of *BhG* 3.5.

60. *tasyādhaḥ srotaso 'paśyad vāri bhūri dvijottamaḥ* || 16cd || *smarann eva ca tam prāha mātaṅgaḥ prahasann iva* | *ehy uttaṅka pratīcchasva matto vāri bhṛgūdvaha* || 17 || *kṛpā hi me sumahatī tvāṃ dṛṣṭvā tṛṭsamāhatam* | *ity uktas tena sa munis tat toyaṃ nābhyanandata* || 18 ||.

61. The other six occurrences are: 1.38.3b (*viśvāmitras tu kākutstham uvāca prahasann iva* | *śrūyatāṃ vistaro rāma sagarasya mahātmanaḥ* || "But Viśvāmitra, with a hint of laughter, said to the heir of [King] Kākutstha: 'Listen, o Rāma, to the story of the great soul Sagara [. . .]' "); 1.51.12d (*tato vasiṣṭho bhagavān kathānte raghunandana* | *viśvāmitram idaṃ vākyam uvāca prahasann iva* || "Then, o joy of the Raghus, at the end of the conversation the glorious Vasiṣṭha, with a hint of laughter, said this to Viśvāmitra [. . .]"); 2.30.22b (*pratīkṣamāṇo 'bhijanaṃ tadārtam anārtarūpaḥ prahasann iva* | *jagāma rāmaḥ pitaraṃ didṛkṣuḥ pitur nideśaṃ vidhivac cikīrṣuḥ* || "Looking at his family that was troubled by his decision, untouched by any turmoil, with a hint of laughter, Rāma left, desirous to see his father and eager to duly respect his father's instruction;" Pollock 2007, 147 translates *prahasann iva* as "he was smiling [instead as he walked on . . .]"); 4.8.19d (*evam uktas tu tejasvī dharmajño dharmavatsalaḥ* | *pratyuvāca sa kākutsthaḥ sugrīvaṃ prahasann iva* || "In this way spoke the mighty knower of the law, devoted to it. Kākutstha [= Rāma], with a hint of laughter, replied to Sugrīva"); 4.10.26d (*evam uktaḥ sa tejasvī dharmajño dharmasaṃhitam* | *vacanaṃ vaktum ārebhe sugrīvaṃ prahasann iva* || "Having thus spoken, the mighty knower of the law, established in the law, almost laughing said to Sugrīva [. . .];" Lefeber 2007, 74 translates *prahasann iva* as "smiled slightly"); 5.1.118d (*ity uktvā pāṇinā śailam ālabhya haripuṅgavaḥ* | *jagāmākāśam āviśya vīryavān prahasann iva* || "Once he said so, having touched the mountain with his hand, the mighty bull among monkeys departed, ascending to the sky with a hint of laughter;" Goldman—Sutherland Goldman 2007, 109 translate *prahasann iva* as "smiling gently").

62. *prajāpatis tu tāny āha sattvāni prahasann iva* | *ābhāṣya vācā yatnena rakṣadhvam iti mānadaḥ* || 11 || *rakṣāma iti tatrānyair yakṣāma iti tathāparaiḥ* | *bhuṅkṣitābhuṅkṣitair uktas tatas tān āha bhūtakṛt* || 12 || *rakṣāma iti yair uktaṃ rākṣasās te bhavantu vaḥ* | *yakṣāma iti yair uktaṃ te vai yakṣā bhavantu vaḥ* || 13 ||.

63. The other thirteen occurrences are: 1.147.21c (*mā rodīs tāta mā mātar mā svasas tvam iti bruvan | prahasann iva sarvāṃs tān ekaikaṃ so 'pasarpati ||*); 1.152.15d (*paripṛcchya sa māṃ pūrvaṃ parikleśaṃ purasya ca | abravīd brāhmaṇaśreṣṭha āśvāsya prahasann iva ||*); 1.181.2b (*tān evaṃ vadato viprān arjunaḥ prahasann iva | uvāca prekṣakā bhūtvā yūyaṃ tiṣṭhata pārśvataḥ ||*); 1.206.16c (*agnikāryaṃ sa kṛtvā tu nāgarājasutāṃ tadā | prahasann iva kaunteya idaṃ vacanam abravīt ||*); 2.54.11b (*tam evaṃvādinaṃ pārthaṃ prahasann iva saubalaḥ | jitam ity eva śakunir yudhiṣṭhiram abhāṣata ||*); 2.60.37d (*duḥśāsanaś cāpi samīkṣya kṛṣṇām avekṣamāṇāṃ kṛpaṇān patīṃs tān | ādhūya vegena visaṃjñākalpām uvāca dāsīti hasann ivograḥ ||*; the present participle of root √*has* in the nominative singular is also used in verse 2.60.38b, where Karṇa laughs (*hasan*) loudly, greatly pleased by Duḥśāsana's words); 3.227.21d (*tathā kathayamānau tau ghoṣayātrāviniścayam | gāndhārarājaḥ śakuniḥ pratyuvāca hasann iva ||*; in 3.227.18b Karṇa addresses Duryodhana laughing, *prahasan*, and in 3.227.24a there is another occurrence of root √*has* + *pra*, i.e., *prahasitāḥ*, "cheerful"); 4.13.5c (*sa tu kāmāgnisaṃtaptaḥ sudeṣṇām abhigamya vai | prahasann iva senānīr idaṃ vacanam abravīt ||*); 5.194.16d (*ācārya kena kālena pāṇḍuputrasya sainikān | nihanyā iti taṃ droṇaḥ pratyuvāca hasann iva ||*); 6.115.34b (*abravīc ca naravyāghraḥ prahasann iva tān nṛpān | naitāni vīraśayyāsu yuktarūpāṇi pārthivāḥ ||*); 7.21.10d (*tān paśyan sainyamadhyastho rājā svajanasaṃvṛtaḥ | duryodhano 'bravīt karṇaṃ prahṛṣṭaḥ prahasann iva ||*); 7.96.13d (*tān abhidravataḥ sarvān samīkṣya śinipuṃgavaḥ | śanair yāhīti yantāram abravīt prahasann iva ||*); 12.151.10b (*evam uktas tataḥ prāha śalmaliḥ prahasann iva | pavana tvaṃ vane kruddho darśayātmānam ātmanā ||*).

64. *taṃ dṛṣṭvā sūtaputro 'yam iti niścitya pāṇḍavaḥ | bhīmasenas tadā vākyam abravīt prahasann iva ||*.

65. *na tvam arhasi pārthena sūtaputra raṇe vadham | kulasya sadṛśas tūrṇaṃ pratodo gṛhyatāṃ tvayā || 6 || aṅgarājyaṃ ca nārhas tvam upabhoktuṃ narādhama | śvā hutāśasamīpasthaṃ puroḍāśam ivādhvare || 7 ||*.

66. The wild boar is the demon Mūka in disguise; see *MBh* 3.40.7–10.

67. Lit. "victorious," "triumphant."

68. *dadarśātha tato jiṣṇuḥ puruṣaṃ kāñcanaprabham | kirātaveṣapracchannaṃ strīsahāyam amitrahā | tam abravīt prītamanāḥ kaunteyaḥ prahasann iva ||*.

69. *ity uktaḥ pāṇḍaveyena kirātaḥ prahasann iva | uvāca ślakṣṇayā vācā pāṇḍavaṃ savyasācinam || 21 || mamaivāyaṃ lakṣyabhūtaḥ pūrvam eva parigrahaḥ | mamaiva ca prahāreṇa jīvitād vyavaropitaḥ || 22 || doṣān svān nārhase 'nyasmai vaktuṃ svabaladarpitaḥ | abhiṣakto 'smi mandātman na me jīvan vimokṣyase || 23 || sthiro bhavasva mokṣyāmi sāyakān aśanīn iva | ghaṭasva parayā śaktyā muñca tvam api sāyakān || 24 ||*; see Hara 1996, 185–88.

70. The story of the two demon brothers Ilvala and Vātāpi is first narrated in the *Vanaparvan* of the *MBh* (3.97) and further developed in several other texts; see Mani 1996, 5, 9, 20, 318, 840; Rāy 1982, 134, 613–14.

71. *dhuryāsanam athāsādya niṣasāda mahāmuniḥ | taṃ paryaveṣad daityendra ilvalaḥ prahasann iva || 5 || agastya eva kṛtsnaṃ tu vātāpiṃ bubhuje tataḥ | bhuktavaty asuro 'hvānam akarot tasya ilvalaḥ || 6 || tato vāyuḥ prādurabhūd agastyasya mahātmanaḥ | ilvalaś ca viṣaṇṇo 'bhūd dṛṣṭvā jīrṇaṃ mahāsuram || 7 || prāñjaliś ca sahāmātyair idaṃ vacanam abravīt | kim artham upayātāḥ stha brūta kiṃ karavāṇi vaḥ* || 8 ||. In the verse that follows there is another occurrence of *prahasann* but without the *iva* particle: *pratyuvāca tato 'gastyaḥ prahasann ilvalaṃ tadā*, i.e., "Then Agastya, laughing, replied to Ilvala."

72. *yadā nānyaṃ pravṛṇute varaṃ vai dvijasattamaḥ | tadainam abravīd bhūyo rādheyaḥ prahasann iva || 9 || sahajaṃ varma me vipra kuṇḍale cāmṛtodbhave | tenāvadhyo 'smi lokeṣu tato naitad dadāmy aham || 10 || viśālaṃ pṛthivīrājyaṃ kṣemaṃ nihatakaṇṭakam | pratigṛhṇīṣva mattas tvaṃ sādhu brāhmaṇapuṃgava || 11 || kuṇḍalābhyāṃ vimukto 'haṃ varmaṇā sahajena ca | gamanīyo bhaviṣyāmi śatrūṇāṃ dvijasattama* || 12 ||. In the verse that follows, Karṇa again addresses the Brahmin laughing (*prahasya*).

73. *bṛhannaḍe kiṃ nu tava sairandhryā kāryam adya vai | yā tvaṃ vasasi kalyāṇi sadā kanyāpure sukham || 21 || na hi duḥkhaṃ samāpnoṣi sairandhrī yad upāśnute | tena māṃ duḥkhitām evaṃ pṛcchase prahasann iva* || 22 ||.

74. *harṣayuktas tathā pārthaḥ prahasann iva vīryavān | rathaṃ rathena droṇasya samāsādya mahārathaḥ || 14 || abhivādya mahābāhuḥ sāntvapūrvam idaṃ vacaḥ | uvāca ślakṣṇayā vācā kaunteyaḥ paravīrahā* || 15 ||.

75. *na ca mām adya saubhadraḥ prahṛṣṭho bhrātṛbhiḥ saha | raṇād āyāntam ucitaṃ pratyudyāti hasann iva* ||.

76. *tasya tad vacanaṃ śrutvā bhāradvājo hasann iva | anvavartata rājānaṃ svasti te 'stv iti cābravīt || 23 || ko hi gāṇḍīvadhanvānaṃ jvalantam iva tejasā | akṣayaṃ kṣapayet kaścit kṣatriyaḥ kṣatriyarṣabham* || 24 ||.

77. *sa kadācit samudrānte vasan drāravatīm anu | eka ekaṃ samāgamya mām uvāca hasann iva || 12 || yat tad ugraṃ tapaḥ kṛṣṇa caran satyaparākramaḥ | agastyād bhāratācāryaḥ pratyapadyata me pitā || 13 || astraṃ brahmaśiro nāma devagandharvapūjitam | tad adya mayi dāśārha yathā pitari me tathā || 14 || asmattas tad upādāya divyam astraṃ yadūttama | mamāpy astraṃ prayaccha tvaṃ cakraṃ ripuharaṃ raṇe* || 15 ||.

78. In the epics there are several characters named Sudyumna. The *Śāntiparvan* refers to a king who, born as a female, subsequently became a male and, at last, became a female again; see Mani 1996, 317; Rāy 1982, 714. The *MBh* narrates a story which took place during the reign of Sudyumna, when the hands of the young ascetic Likhita were cut off. Because of Sudyumna's adherence to his royal duties he attained heaven; see Mani 1996, 755; Rāy 1982, 603.

79. For a detailed analysis of this story, see Granoff 2012, 190–91; Kane 1930, 136–42.

80. *kutaḥ phalāny avāptāni hetunā kena khādasi* || 7cd || *so 'bravīt bhātaraṃ jyeṣṭham upaspṛśyābhivādya ca* | *ita eva gṛhītāni mayeti prahasann iva* || 8 || *tam abravīt tadā śaṅkhas tīvrakopasamanvitaḥ* | *steyaṃ tvayā kṛtam idaṃ phalāny ādadatā svayam* || 9 || *gaccha rājānam āsādya svakarma prathayasva vai* || 10ab ||.

81. *abravīc ca tato jiṣṇuḥ prahasann iva bhārata* | *nivartadhvam adharmajñāḥ śreyo jīvitam eva vaḥ* ||.

82. Toasted chickpea flour.

83. Here the text refers to a well-known paretimology of the word *putra*, "son," which goes back to *Mānavadharmaśāstra* 9.138: *puṃnāmno narakād trāyate pitaraṃ sutaḥ* | *tasmāt putra iti proktaḥ svatam eva svayambhuvā* ||, i.e., "The Self-Existent One himself has called him 'son' (*putra*) because he rescues (*trā*) his father from the hell named Put;" Olivelle 2005, 197, 771.

84. *rūpeṇa sadṛśas tvaṃ me śīlena ca damena ca* | *parīkṣitaś ca bahudhā saktūn ādadmi te tataḥ* || 38 || *ity uktvādāya tān saktūn prītātmā dvijasattamaḥ* | *prahasann iva viprāya sa tasmai pradadau tadā* || 39 ||.

85. Lit. "what sort of man;" a category of semi-divine beings. The males are usually called *kiṃnara*/*kinnara* and the females *kinnarī*. They are often identified with Gandharvas and carry a lute in their hands. The LGBT community of the *hijra*s holds the story of the origin of *kimpuruṣa*s in high regard; see Nanda 1999.

86. *sarvās tā vidrutā dṛṣṭvā kiṃnarīr ṛṣisattamaḥ* | *uvāca rūpasaṃpannāṃ tāṃ striyaṃ prahasann iva* ||.

87. Two more cases can be referred to this section: 2.85.3b (*athovāca bharadvājo bharataṃ prahasann iva* | *jāne tvāṃ prītisaṃyuktaṃ tuṣyes tvaṃ yena kenacit* ||; "Then Bharadvāja, with a hint of laughter, said to Bharata: 'I know that you are full of love, and that you are pleased by whatever [comes]!' ") and 7.60.13b (*tasmiṃs tathā bruvāṇe tu rākṣasaḥ prahasann iva* | *pratyuvāca naraśreṣṭhaṃ diṣṭyā prāpto 'si durmate* ||; "But then, while he [= Śatrughna] was still speaking, the demon, with a hint of laughter, replied to the best among men: 'O fool, thank heavens you have come!' ").

88. For other ambiguous occurrences of *prahasann iva*, see *MBh* 3.77.11b, 5.179.1b, 9.30.15f.

89. *tato duryodhanaḥ kṛṣṇam uvāca prahasann iva* | *vigrahe 'smin bhavān sāhayaṃ mama dātum ihārhati* ||.

90. *tataḥ satyapratijño vai sa pakṣī prahasann iva* | *tam agniṃ triḥ parikramya praviveśa mahīpate* ||.

91. *plavamānaś ca me dṛṣṭaḥ sa tasmin gomayahrade* | *pibann añjalinā tailaṃ hasann iva muhur muhuḥ* ||.

92. On this type of laughter, see Plessner 2020, 32–38. Another occurrence that we can refer to this section is 7.17.3d (*sa dṛṣṭvā rūpasampannāṃ kanyāṃ tāṃ sumahāvratām* | *kāmakrodhaparītātmā papraccha prahasann iva* ||; "Having seen that beautiful girl well-established in her great vow, with

his mind filled with lust and anger, with a hint of laughter, he asked her: [. . .]").

93. These are 1.211.16b, 5.73.1b, 5.89.23d, 6.41.16d, 7.148.39d, 8.40.85b, 8.50.2b.

94. The case in which Kṛṣṇa's hint of laughter is not referred to Arjuna is 7.148.39d, where his *prahasann iva* is directed toward Ghaṭotkaca.

95. See in particular 5.73.1b, 5.89.23d and 6.41.16d.

Chapter 4

1. From Latin *risus*. For its etymology, see A. Ernout and A. Meillet, *Dictionnaire étymologique de la langue latine. Histoire des mots* (Paris: Klincksieck, 2001[5]), 573.

2. For an introduction, see P.-S. Filliozat, "Le sourire dans la littérature sanscrite et la statuaire de l'Inde," *Comptes rendus des séances de l'Académie des Inscriptions et Belles-Lettres*, 153, no. 4 (2009): 1629–54. By the same author, see "Smile in Indian and Khmer Art," http://www.ignca.nic.in/Lectures_PDFs/pl_20121123_Smile_in_Indian_and_Khmer_Art.pdf.

3. An epic text with several occurrences of verbal root √*smi* as well as √*has* is the popular *Nalopakhyāna* or "The story of Nala and Damayantī" (= *MBh* 3.50–78), familiar to many Sanskrit students; see for instance 3.52.18, 3.53.1, 3.53.8, and 3.53.14. On the *Nalopakhyāna*, see C. R. Lanman, *A Sanskrit Reader: Text and Vocabulary and Notes* (Cambridge, MA: Harvard University Press, 1963 [1884]), 1–16, 297–310.

4. See K. Śarmā, *The Dhātupāṭha of Pāṇini. With the Dhātvartha Prakāśikā Notes* (Varanasi: The Chowkhamba Sanskrit Series Office, 1969[2]). Herein, all Sanskrit roots—approximately 2.300—are grouped by the form of their stem in the present tense.

5. For a general introduction to Indian drama and theater, see K. Binder, "Drama and Theatre," in *Brill's Encyclopedia of Hinduism Online*, eds. K. A. Jacobsen, H. Basu, A. Malinar, and V. Narayanan (Leiden: Brill, 2018; https://referenceworks.brillonline.com/browse/brill-s-encyclopedia-of-hinduism). See also G. H. Tarlekar, *Studies in the Nāṭyaśāstra: With Special Reference to the Sanskrit Drama in Performance* (Delhi: Motilal Banarsidass, 1999 [1975]); R. V. M. Baumer and J. R. Brandon, eds., *Sanskrit Drama in Performance* (Delhi: Motilal Banarsidass, 1993 [1981]); and E. W. Marasinghe, *The Sanskrit Theatre and Stagecraft* (Delhi: Sri Satguru Publications, 1989).

6. On the comic, see the seminal article by Har Dutt Sharma, "*Hāsya* as a *rasa* in Sanskrit Rhetoric and Literature," *Annals of the Bhandarkar Oriental Research Institute* 22, no. 1/2 (1941): 103–15. See also S.

Ramaratnam, *Sanskrit Drama: With Special Reference to Prahasana and Vīthī*, foreword by Satyavrat Shastri (New Delhi: D. K. Printworld, 2014), 12–34; D. Meyer-Dinkgräfe, "Comedy, Consciousness and the *Natyasastra*," in *The Natyasastra and the Body in Performance: Essays on Indian Theories of Dance and Drama*, ed. S. Nair, foreword by M. Krzysztof Byrski (Jefferson, NC: McFarland & Company, 2015), 89–98.

7. On the distinction between *hāsya* and *hāsa*, see S. Visuvalingam, "*Hāsa* and *Hāsya* Distinguished in *Rasa*-Theory," http://www.infinityfoundation.com/mandala/i_es/i_es_visuv_cha_7.htm.

8. For an appreciation of *hāsyarasa* in modern and contemporary Bengali theater, see A. De, *The Boundary of Laughter: Popular Performances Across Borders in South Asia* (New Delhi: Oxford University Press, 2021).

9. The whiteness of the teeth calls to mind the whiteness of the jasmine flowers which are widely used in Kṛṣṇa's worship. As already noted, it is remarkable that *prahasantī* is the name of a kind of jasmine.

10. The term *pramatha* literally means "tormentor." Sunthar Visuvalingam notes:

> The deformed (Mahā-)Gaṇapati, "Lord of the Pramathas," who presides over the comic sentiment (*hāsya*) in the Sanskrit drama, is himself born from Omkāra's bi-unity (*mithuna*). Issuing thunderously from the sacrificial stake in the form of the cosmic *liṅga*, Omkāra's mysterious laughter, while affirming the supremacy of Rudra, is indistinguishable from the violent laughter (*aṭṭahāsa*) of the Great God (Mahādeva) himself. (S. Visuvalingam, "The Transgressive Sacrality of the Dīkṣita: Sacrifice, Criminality and *Bhakti* in the Hindu Tradition," in *Criminal Gods and Demon Devotees: Essays on the Guardians of Popular Hinduism*, ed. A. Hiltebeitel [Albany: State University of New York Press, 1989], 430)

11. *Hasita*, which can also mean "blooming," is the name of the bow of Kāma, the god of erotic love, "whose bow is flowers" (*puṣpadhanus*). In the *Purāṇa*s it is said that Kāma, who had been reduced to ashes by the fiery glance of Śiva, was reborn as Pradyumna, the son of Kṛṣṇa and Rukmiṇī. On Kāma, see C. Benton, *God of Desire: Tales of Kāmadeva in Sanskrit Story Literature* (Albany: State University of New York Press, 2006).

12. For instance, when in Kampaṉ's *Irāmāvatāram* (the Tamil retelling of the *Rāmāyaṇa*, c. twelfth century CE) as it is performed in the shadow puppet theater of Kerala Rāma suppresses a laugh at Śūrpaṇakhā's stupidity, this he does because—as the editor points out—"loud laughter would not be appropriate to his excellence;" S. H. Blackburn, "Hanging

in the Balance: Rāma in the Shadow Puppet Theater of Kerala," in *Gender, Genre, and Power in South Asian Expressive Traditions*, ed. A. Appadurai, F. J. Korom, and M. A. Mills (Philadelphia: University of Pennsylvania Press, 1991), 388.

13. Though the date of the *Nāṭyaśāstra*, which was composed through successive incorporations, might be later than that of the *Bhagavadgītā*, it is our contention that its aesthetic canons are not the compiler's creation or a recent innovation but reflect a deep-rooted tradition of the dramatic arts that extends itself to epic literature. Significantly, the *Nāṭyaśāstra* is ascribed to the mythical sage Bharata, who is celebrated as the earliest actor, and the treatise characterizes itself as a fifth *Veda*: that is, as the one primeval authority. On these issues, see K. Gönc Moačanin, "The *Nāṭyaśāstra* as a (Distorting?) Mirror to the Epic/Purāṇic Mythic Image: The Question of Its Dating," in *Stages and Transitions: Temporal and Historical Frameworks in Epic and Purāṇic Literature: Proceedings of the Second Dubrovnik International Conference on the Sanskrit Epics and Purāṇas, August 1999*, ed. M. Brockington (Zagreb: Croatian Academy of Sciences and Arts, 2002), 221–38.

14. In many devotional hymns, the beautiful cheeks (*gaṇḍa, kapola*) are compared to radiant, full-blown lotuses.

15. See C. Packert, *The Art of Loving Krishna: Ornamentation and Devotion* (Bloomington: Indiana University Press, 2010), 49. We are here reminded of the first verse of Vallabhācārya's *Madhurāṣṭaka*: *adharaṃ madhuraṃ vadanaṃ madhuraṃ nayanaṃ madhuraṃ hasitaṃ madhuram | hṛdayaṃ madhuraṃ gamanaṃ madhuraṃ madhurādhipater akhilaṃ madhuram* ||, "Sweet the lower lip, sweet the face, sweet the eye, sweet the slight laughter, sweet the heart, sweet the gait: everything about the Supreme Lord is sweet!"

16. Draupadī's mockery of Duryodhana in the Tamil drama *Cūtutukilurital* ("Dice Match and Disrobing") of Iramaccantira Kavirāyar (early nineteenth century), when she looks at him "shaking in mirth" (*kuluṅka nakaittāḷē*) and destroying his pride, can be regarded as an example of *upahasita* or even *apahasita*; see A. Hiltebeitel, *The Cult of Draupadī. 1 Mythologies: From Gingee to Kurukṣetra* (Chicago and London: University of Chicago Press, 1988), 230–31.

17. As a popular saying (*subhāṣita*) goes: "The wise laughs with the eyes, medium-level people laugh showing the teeth, the vilest people laugh loudly, while the best among the silent ascetics don't laugh" (*cakṣurbhyāṃ hasate vidvān dantodghāṭena madhyamāḥ | adhamā aṭṭahāsena na hasanti munīśvarāḥ* ||); O. Böhtlingk, *Indische Sprüche*, Sanskrit und Deutsch herausgegeben, Vol. 2 (St. Petersburg, 1872–73), 1 (2221). To refer to an eye that is "bright with a smile" the compound *smitojjvala* is used.

18. See M. Ramakrishna Kavi, ed., *Nāṭyaśāstra of Bharata Muni. With the Commentary Abhinavabhāratī by Abhinavaguptācārya* (Baroda: Oriental Institute, 1956²), 1:315.

19. As he writes: "[But] it is in the nature of [most] people that when they see someone else laugh they will at once begin to laugh themselves. A parallel case is the taste of the juice of pomegranate, or of the tamarind [which is sour], which [we can call] 'infectious,' in the sense that just by seeing that juice, other people's mouths begin to water, [the taste, as it were], passing over [from one person to another]. In the same way laughter is infectious by its very nature, and so it is similar to dry wood [that ignites immediately];" J. L. Masson and M. V. Patwardhan, *Aesthetic Rapture: The Rasādhyāya of the Nāṭyaśāstra in Two Volumes*. Vol. 2, *Notes* (Poona: Deccan College Postgraduate Research Institute, 1970), 86 n. 438.

20. On *rasa*, see S. Pollock, ed., *A Rasa Reader: Classical Indian Aesthetics* (New York: Columbia University Press, 2016); S. L. Schwartz, *Rasa: Performing the Divine in India* (New York: Columbia University Press, 2004). For a survey of Indian aesthetics, see A. Pelissero, *Estetica indiana* (Brescia: Morcelliana, 2019). On Abhinavagupta's aesthetics, see Gnoli, *The Aesthetic Experience According to Abhinavagupta*, and E. Ganser, *Theatre and Its Other: Abhinavagupta on Dance and Dramatic Acting* (Leiden: Brill, 2022).

21. Masson and Patwardhan, *Aesthetic Rapture: The Rasādhyāya of the Nāṭyaśāstra in Two Volumes*. Vol. 1, *Text*, 50–51.

22. Along these lines, a popular saying goes: "Four things are ridiculous: the poem composed by a fool, the song of one who has no voice, the dalliance of one who is destitute of wealth, and the desire for sensual enjoyment of an old man" (*mūrkhasya kāvyakaraṇaṃ gītamakaṇṭhasya | lalitamadhanasya vṛddhasya viṣayavāñchā parihāsyakarāṇi catvāri ||*); Böhtlingk, *Indische Sprüche*, 3:58 (4913). On the value of *aucitya* or proportion/harmony, see V. Raghavan, *Studies on Some Concepts of the Alaṃkāra Śāstra* (Adyar: The Adyar Library, 1942), 194–257.

23. See Ramakrishna Kavi, *Nāṭyaśāstra of Bharata Muni. With the Commentary Abhinavabhāratī by Abhinavaguptācārya*, 296.

24. See Masson and Patwardhan, *Aesthetic Rapture: The Rasādhyāya of the Nāṭyaśāstra in Two Volumes*. Vol. 2, *Notes*, 76–78 n. 399. It is noteworthy that even in Kampaṉ's *Irāmāvatāram* the erotic sentiment is mixed with mockery (*hāsyarasa*) and distaste (*jugupsā*); see Hart, *Archetypes in Classical Indian Literature and Beyond*, 173–74.

25. The noun is derived from *sa* + *ratha*, lit. "with a chariot." *Ratha*, lit. "goer," is derived from verbal root √ṛ and refers especially to a two-wheeled war chariot. Two horses were usually used per chariot, though there could also be three or four. With reference to Kṛṣṇa's and Arjuna's

chariot, *BhG* 1.14 speaks of white horses in the plural: they are usually believed to be four or five, five being symbolic of the five senses. The warrior stood on the left of the chariot or sat on a seat (the *upastha, garta* or *vandhura)*; the charioteer stood on the right and remained standing. On *rathas*, see U. P. Thapliyal, *Chariot in Indian History* (New York: Routledge, 2023); A. Lal, "Chariots in Ancient Indian Warfare," in *World History Encyclopedia* (accessed February 26, 2024) https://www.worldhistory.org/article/1269/chariots-in-ancient-indian-warfare/. On the iconography of carriages, see J. Deloche, *Contribution to the History of the Wheeled Vehicle in India* (Pondichéry: Institut Français de Pondichéry—École Française d'Extrême-Orient, 2014), 13–48. On the ethics and philosophy of warfare in Vedic and Epic India, see K. Roy, *Hinduism and the Ethics of Warfare in South Asia: From Antiquity to the Present* (Cambridge: Cambridge University Press, 2012), 13–39.

26. Pārthasārathi is a well-known epithet of Kṛṣṇa. In the *Śrīkṛṣṇasahasranāmastotra,* the hymn of the thousand names of lord Kṛṣṇa, at verse 169 he is praised as "the one who is devoted to the office of charioteer of the son of Pṛthā" (*pārthasārathyaniratah̤*). In the *Mahābhārata,* Kṛṣṇa leads Arjuna's chariot throughout the duration of the battle; see M. Biardeau, "Nala et Damayantī. Héros épiques. Part 2," *Indo-Iranian Journal* 28 (1985): 6. In his role as charioteer, he transforms a weapon into a garland, seems to make the sun set, and cures wounds; see E. W. Hopkins, *Epic Mythology* (Delhi: Motilal Banarsidass, 1986), 215. J. A. B. van Buitenen aptly notes: "This role [of charioteer] assumed by Kṛṣṇa, because of the conventional camaraderie between warrior and driver, provides the intimacy which makes his exhortations possible and appropriate;" van Buitenen, *The Bhagavadgītā in the Mahābhārata,* 5. Kṛṣṇa *bhaktas* revere their lord as the Sanātanasārathi, the eternal charioteer, who directs them toward their ultimate destination. Representing the intellect (*buddhi*) in its pristine purity, he is regarded as the charioteer of everyone's chariot, i.e., of each and every individual *jīva;* on the imagery of the chariot (*rathakalpanā*), see *Kaṭha Upaniṣad* 3.3–6, 9.

27. On this manual containing a wealth of ritual and iconographic prescriptions on Viṣṇu's icons, Gérard Colas observes: "The iconographic and architectural teachings of Vaikhānasa texts like the *Vimānārcanakalpa* (*Marīcisaṃhitā*) remained a major source of reference even for 20th-century temple builders and sculptors;" see G. Colas, "Vaikhānasa," in *Brill's Encyclopedia of Hinduism Online,* eds. K. A. Jacobsen, H. Basu, A. Malinar, and V. Narayanan (Leiden: Brill, 2018; https://referenceworks.brillonline.com/browse/brill-s-encyclopedia-of-hinduism), 9. On this important source, see G. Colas, *Le temple selon Marīci* (Pondichéry: Institut Français d'Indologie, 1986).

28. In *BhG* 1.20 and often in the epic, Arjuna is referred to as "monkey-bannered" (*kapidhvaja*). It is assumed that this monkey is none other than Hanumān, the son of the wind god Vāyu and of the *apsaras* Añjanā. Indeed, Hanumān had promised Bhīma that he would place himself on the banner of Arjuna's chariot, and his presence terrified the Kauravas. From his perch on the hero's flag, the monkey god—extolled as the exemplary *bhakta*—enjoyed the privilege of hearing the *Bhagavadgītā* and witnessing the revelation of Kṛṣṇa's cosmic form. Hanumān is the paradigm of *dāsyabhakti*, in which one considers himself/herself as the slave/servant of god. On these issues, see P. Lutgendorf, *Hanuman's Tale: The Messages of a Divine Monkey* (Oxford and New York: Oxford University Press, 2007), 231–33.

29. Arjuna's bow is the *gāṇḍīva* (*BhG* 1.30), which was made of the backbone of a rhinoceros (*gāṇḍīmaya*). *BhG* 11.33 refers to Arjuna as an ambidextrous archer (*savyasācin*) and *BhG* 18.78 as the bowman (*dhanurdharas*). On the Indian bow, see M. B. Emenau, "The Composite Bow in India," *Proceedings of the American Philosophical Society* 97, no. 1 (1953): 77–87. On the science of archery, see P. Zarrilli, "Martial Arts (*Dhanurveda*)," in *Brill's Encyclopedia of Hinduism Online*, eds. K. A. Jacobsen, H. Basu, A. Malinar, and V. Narayanan (Leiden: Brill, 2018; https://referenceworks.brillonline.com/browse/brill-s-encyclopedia-of-hinduism).

30. T. A. Gopinatha Rao, *Elements of Hindu Iconography, Vol. 1, Part 1* (Madras: Law Printing House, 1914), 211. The *vyākhyānamudrā* is the gesture of teaching. In his *Vishṇu-Kosha*, S. K. Ramachandra Rao adds a few more details:

> Pārtha-sārathi: representing Kṛshṇa as a teacher of Arjuna on the battlefield. Kṛshṇa and Arjuna, both two armed, are shown here alongside a chariot (*ratha*). Kṛshṇa is shown as about to get into the chariot; his right leg planted on the ground (*daksha-pādam sthitam*), and the left leg lifted up and placed on the rampart of the chariot (*vāmam-uddhṛtya ratha-bhittau saṃsthāpya*). He has his right hand in the posture of teaching or exposition (*vyākhyāna-nirṇāyaṅguli-mudrā*). Or he may be shown as holding the whip in one hand and the reins of the horses in the other (*yashṭi-pāśān gṛhītvā*). Arjuna is shown as standing on the ground with his hands in the gesture of supplication; a bow is tucked up in his arms (*pārtham sachāpam prāñjalīkṛtya adhah-sthale sthitam*).
> (S. K. Ramachandra Rao, *Vishṇu-Kosha* [Bangalore: Kalpatharu Research Academy, 1998], 265–67)

The author further specifies:

> *Vimānārchanā-kalpa* (*Paṭala* 79) prescribes that Kṛshṇa as Pārthasārathi must be represented as two-armed, holding the reins of the horses and a whip (*chāpa-yantra-yashṭi-pāśam gṛhītvā*) mounted upon a chariot (*rathārūḍham*); but the right foot is firmly placed on the floor of the chariot, while the left foot is raised and placed on the railings of the chariot (*dakshiṇam pādam sthitam vāmam uddhṛtya ratha-bhittau saṃsthāpya*). His right hand is in the gesture of counseling (*dakshiṇa-hastena vyāsa-nirṇayāṅguli-mudrayā saṃyuktam*). Arjuna must be shown to the god's left, sitting on the floor of the chariot, joining his hands in supplication (*vāme prāñjali-kṛtyādhas-sthale sthitam*). (Ibid., 275)

Here is the drawing that accompanies Ramachandra Rao's description of the Pārthasārathi icon (ibid., 267):

Figure 4.22. Drawing of the Pārthasārathi icon. *Source*: S. K. Ramachandra Rao, *Vishṇu-Kosha*. Bangalore: Kalpatharu Research Academy, 1998.

Apart from other differences, it should be noted that in the iconography Arjuna is not always shown to the god's left.

31. See ibid., 242, 275.

32. For instance, in contemporary India the diplomat G. Pārthasārathi, the theatrical author Indra Pārthasārathi, and the litterateurs N. Pārthasārathi and R. Pārthasārathi, all hailing from Tamil Nadu; see Ch. Jaffrelot, ed., *L'Inde contemporaine de 1950 à nos jours* (Paris: Fayard / CERI, 2006), 353, 796, 855, 857.

33. On Pārthasārathi Miśra, see K. H. Potter, *Philosophy of Pūrva-mīmāṃsā. Encyclopedia of Indian Philosophies*, Vol. 16 (Delhi: Motilal Banarsidass, 2014), 364–90.

34. On this famous temple highly revered by the Āḻvār saints and renovated at the time of the Pallava dynasty, see http://sriparthasarathytemple.tnhrce.in/history-parthasarathy.html. On the politics of worship at this sacred site, see A. Appadurai, *Worship and Conflict under Colonial Rule: A South Indian Case* (Cambridge: Cambridge University Press, 1981). Other South Indian temples worth mentioning are the small sixteenth- or seventeenth-century Venugopāla Pārthasārathi Temple in Chengam, about 34 km west of Tiruvannamalai in Tamil Nadu; the old ninth-century Pārthasārathi Temple in Parthivapuram, c. 50 km north-west of Kanyakumari in Tamil Nadu and 50 km south-east of Trivandrum, Kerala's capital; and the Pārthasārathi Temple in Aranmula near Pattanamthitta in Kerala, also believed to be quite old, on the left bank of the Pampa River, which hosts a famous annual snake-boat race. On the Pārthasārathi Temple in Parthivapuram, see H. Sarkar, *An Architectural Survey of Temples of Kerala* (New Delhi: Archaeological Survey of India, 1978), 135–38.

35. S. K. Ramachandra Rao shows three drawings of Pārthasārathi icons, two located in Kerala (in the Thali temple, Kozhikode District, and in the Ananthapur temple of Kumble, Kasaragod District) and one in Karnataka (in the Viṣṇumūrti temple of Kodipadi, Mangalore); Ramachandra Rao, *Vishṇu-Kosha*, 266, 268. It is noteworthy that Sir Monier Monier-Williams (1819–1899) observed that Pārthasārathi is the title under which Kṛṣṇa is worshipped at Madras, today's Chennai, and viewed it as a merely local epithet; M. Monier-Williams, *Religious Thought and Life in India. An Account of the Religions of the Indian Peoples, Based on a Life's Study of Their Literature and on Personal Investigations in Their Own Country. Part 1: Vedism, Brāhmanism, and Hindūism* (London: John Murray, 1883), 107.

36. See Gopinatha Rao, *Elements of Hindu Iconography*, 211–12; Ramachandra Rao, *Vishṇu-Kosha*, 268. The image of Kṛṣṇa as Pārthasārathi, with conch in the right hand and the left hand in *varadamudrā*, is made of black granite—according to legend it was brought here by *ṛṣi* Atreya—with images of his wife Rukmiṇī and of his devoted friend and powerful warrior Sātyaki standing to his right and left respectively, while his elder brother

Balarāma is to the right of Rukmiṇī. Images of his son Pradyumna and of his grandson Aniruddha are also present in the inner sanctum.

37. In this hand gesture the thumb is held perpendicular to the palm, and the index finger is bent forward to touch the tip of the thumb. The remaining three fingers are held close together vertically above the palm.

38. See H. Krishna Sastri, *South-Indian Images of Gods and Goddesses* (Madras: Madras Government Press, 1916), 49; fig. 31. See also C. Sivaramamurti, *Rishis in Indian Art and Literature* (New Delhi: Kanak, 1981), 234; figs. 8 and 9.

39. See https://www.wisdomlib.org/definition/parthasarathi. On the classical gestures used in Hindu dance and drama, see M. Ghosh, *Nandikeśvara's* Abhinayadarpaṇam*: A Manual of Gesture and Posture Used in Hindu Dance and Drama*. English Translation, Notes and the Text Critically Edited for the First Time from Original Manuscripts with Introduction (Calcutta: Firma K. L. Mukhopadhyay, 1957[2]).

40. See S. R. Balasubrahmanyam, *Early Chola Temples: Parantaka I to Rajaraja I (A. D. 907–985)* (New Delhi: Orient Longman, 1971), 34.

41. See S. Kramrisch, *Indian Sculpture* (London: Oxford University Press, 1933), 197–98, plate XLVII.

42. See B. Preciado-Solis, *The Kṛṣṇa Cycle in the Purāṇas: Themes and Motifs in a Heroic Saga* (Delhi: Motilal Banarsidass, 1984).

43. John Stratton Hawley, who surveyed eight hundred panels of Indian sculpture dating from 500 to 1500 CE in which Kṛṣṇa is the subject, found out that only three refer to the scene of the *Bhagavadgītā* and just a few more depict scenes from the *Mahābhārata*; J. S. Hawley, "Krishna's Cosmic Victories," *Journal of the American Academy of Religion* 47 (1979): 201–21. In the temple complex of Pattadakal (seventh-eighth century CE) in northern Karnataka, the episode of the *Bhagavadgītā* is sculpted on a column of the Virūpākṣa temple, see https://www.alamy.com/bhagavad-gita-narrative-sculpture-on-a-column-in-the-virupaksha-temple-pattadakal-1885-photo-image218375144.html.

44. See A. Truschke, "The Mughal *Book of War*: A Persian Translation of the Sanskrit *Mahabharata*," *Comparative Studies of South Asia, Africa and the Middle East* 31, no. 2 (2011): 500–520. For the Persian translation of the *Bhagavadgītā* sponsored by Prince Dārā Šikōh (1615–1659), that is, the *Āb-i zindagī* or "The Water of Life," see M. R. Jalālī Nā'īnī, ed., *Bhagawad Gītā. Surūd-i ilāhī* (Tehran: Tahūrī, 1980). For an overview of the extant Persian translations, see F. Mujtabai, *Aspects of Hindu-Muslim Cultural Relations* (Delhi: Zakir Husain Educational and Cultural Foundation, 1978), 74–75. See also R. Vassie, *Persian Interpretations of the* Bhagavadgītā *in the Mughal Period: With Special Reference to the Sufi Version of 'Abd al-Raḥmān*

Chishtī (London: School of Oriental and African Studies, 1988); M. L. Roychaudhary, "The *Bhagavad Gītā* in Persian," *Proceedings of the Indian History Congress, 1956*, 19 (1956): 260–63.

45. See A. Bhalla and C. P. Deval, *The Gita: Mewari Miniature Painting (1680–1698) by Allah Baksh* (New Delhi: Niyogi Books, 2019).

46. This school of painting of the Rājasthānī rulers is distinctive and should not be subsumed under the broader classification of Rājput paintings.

47. Bhalla and Deval, *The Gita: Mewari Miniature Painting (1680–1698) by Allah Baksh*, 14.

48. See A. L. Dallapiccola and J. Jain, eds., *Paithan Paintings: The Epic World of the Chitrakathis Picture Showmen: Insights into the Narrative Tradition in Indian Art* (Mumbai: Marg, 1978); *Chitrakathi: Folk Painting of Paithan* (Pune: Raja Dinkar Kelkar Museum, 1996). See also M. Gaonkar, "Contemporary Practices of *Chitrakathi* in the Twenty-first Century Art Market," *The Chitrolekha Journal on Art and Design* 2, no. 2 (2018): 40–46.

49. See U. King, "The Iconography of the *Bhagavad Gītā*," *Journal of Dharma* 7, 2 (1982): 146–63. By the same author, see also "Some Reflections on Sociological Approaches to the Study of Modern Hinduism," *Numen* 36, no. 1 (1989): 72–97 (85).

50. And also through narrative retellings such as the *Arjunopākhyāna* in the sixth book of the *Mokṣopāya* (c. 950 CE); see T. Cohen, "*Arjunopākhyāna*: An Idealist Non-dualistic Translation of the *Bhagavadgītā*," *Journal of South Asian Intellectual History* 2, no. 2 (2019): 122–52.

51. The *Bhagavadgītā* is a secret teaching. Words such as *rahasya* and especially *guhya*, which both mean "secret," are often found in the poem; see *BhG* 4.3, 9.1, 10.38, 11.1, 15.20, 18.63–64, 18.68, 18.75.

52. According to the *Mahābhārata*'s own framing account, Vyāsa's pupil Vaiśaṃpāyana was the first to recite the text—including the *Bhagavadgītā*—to King Janamejaya at the great snake sacrifice performed to avenge Parikṣit's death by snakebite.

53. What Richard H. Davis aptly calls a "meta-*Gītā*"; Davis, *The Bhagavad Gita: A Biography*, 65–71. On this vernacular manifesto, see C. L. Novetzke, *The Quotidian Revolution: Vernacularization, Religion, and the Premodern Public Sphere in India* (New York: Columbia University Press, 2016), 213–84. Through the centuries, the quintessence of Maharashtrian *advaitabhakti* spirituality is represented by Kṛṣṇaism and the tradition of the Vārkarī movement of poet-saints (*santkavī*) centered in Pandharpur; see E. R. Sand, "Pandharpur and Vitthal," *Oxford Bibliographies in Hinduism*. (New York: Oxford University Press, 2019; https://www.oxfordbibliographies.com).

54. A diadem. *BhG* 11.35 presents Arjuna as the diademed one (*kirīṭin*).

55. *Panicum Dactylon*, a kind of grass.

56. See S. Kramrisch, trans., *The Vishnudharmottara (Part III). A Treatise on Indian Painting and Image-Making* (Calcutta: Calcutta University Press, 1928²), 116.

57. See P. Banerjee, *The Life of Krishṇa in Indian Art* (New Delhi: National Museum, 1978), 48.

58. As stated in *BhG* 11.2, one of Kṛṣṇa's epithets is *kamalapatrākṣa*.

59. See J. Leroy Davidson, *Art of the Indian Subcontinent from Los Angeles Collections* (Los Angeles: Ward Ritchie Press, 1968), 87; fig. 131.

60. See King, "The Iconography of the *Bhagavad Gītā*," 157.

61. On the interpretations of the *Bhagavadgītā* within neo-Hinduism, see R. N. Minor, ed., *Modern Indian Interpreters of the Bhagavad Gita* (Albany: State University of New York Press, 1986). See also W. Halbfass, ed., *Philology and Confrontation: Paul Hacker on Traditional and Modern Vedānta* (Albany: State University of New York Press, 1995), 258–70, 273–89, 296–302, 307–9, 337–48. On Charles Wilkins and his translation of the *Bhagavadgītā*, see J. Patterson, *Religion, Enlightenment and Empire: British Interpretations of Hinduism in the Eighteenth Century* (Cambridge: Cambridge University Press, 2021), 239–62; R. H. Davis, "Wilkins, Kasinatha, Hastings, and the First English '*Bhagavad Gītā*,'" *International Journal of Hindu Studies* 19, no. 1–2 (2015): 39–57.

62. The covers and the many illustrations of the *Bhagavadgītā* published by the International Krishna Consciousness Movement are a case in point.

63. See for instance V. G. Vitsaxis, *Hindu Epics, Myths and Legends in Popular Illustrations* (New Delhi: Oxford University Press, 1977), 57. On these issues, see S. Inglis, "*Citrakathā*, Paintings, and Popular Prints," in *Brill's Encyclopedia of Hinduism Online*, eds. K. A. Jacobsen, H. Basu, A. Malinar, and V. Narayanan (Leiden: Brill, 2018; https://referenceworks.brillonline.com/browse/brill-s-encyclopedia-of-hinduism).

64. See F. W. Pritchett, "The World of *Amar Chitra Katha*," in *Media and the Transformation of Religion in South Asia*, ed. L. A. Babb and S. S. Wadley (Philadelphia: University of Pennsylvania Press, 1995), 85, 96–97.

65. The site of Kurukṣetra is located in the northeastern part of the state of Haryana, at a distance of approximately 160 km from Delhi. For an appreciation of the Shri Krishna Museum, see https://www.youtube.com/watch?v=YL7AMPgj9U4&t=1106s.

66. See A. Bharati, "Ritualistic Tolerance and Ideological Rigour: The Paradigm of the Expatriate Hindus in East Africa," *Contributions to Indian Sociology* 10, no. 2 (1976): 341–65.

67. On these issues, see R. H. Davis, "The Greatness of the *Gītā*, as Icon and Mantra," in Theodor, *The Bhagavad-gītā: A Critical Introduction*, 94–103. By the same author, see *Lives of Indian Images* (Princeton, NJ: Princeton University Press, 1997).

68. On Indian classical traditions of dance, see A. Satkunaratnam, "Dance: Classical Tradition," in *Brill's Encyclopedia of Hinduism Online*, eds. K. A. Jacobsen, H. Basu, A. Malinar, and V. Narayanan (Leiden: Brill, 2018; https://referenceworks.brillonline.com/browse/brill-s-encyclopedia-of-hinduism). See also K. Ambrose and R. Gopal, *Classical Dances and Costumes of India* (London: A & C Black, 1983^{2} [1950]).

69. On folk interpretations of the *Mahābhārata*, see A. Hiltebeitel, *Rethinking India's Oral and Classical Epics: Draupadī among Rajputs, Muslims, and Dalits* (Chicago and London: The University of Chicago Press, 1999). On the *Pāṇḍav līlā*, a ritual dramatization of the *Mahābhārata* performed in the Garhwal region of the Himalayas, see W. S. Sax, "Fathers, Sons, and Rhinoceroses: Masculinity and Violence in the *Pāṇḍav līlā*," *Journal of the American Oriental Society* 117, no. 2 (1997): 278–93.

70. N. Hein, *The Miracle Plays of Mathura* (New Haven, CT: Yale University Press, 1972), 259.

71. For examples of the contemporary recitation of the *Bhagavadgītā*, see https://www.youtube.com/watch?v=80D8b3a0Bis; https://www.youtube.com/watch?v=-VHuO7F_q7E. It takes approximately two hours and forty minutes to collectively chant the entire poem. The recitation is typically performed during the festival of *Gītājayantī* or *Gītāmahotsav*, the supposed day on which Kṛṣṇa imparted his teaching to Arjuna: it falls on the eleventh day of the waxing moon (*śukla ekādaśī*) of the lunar month of *mārgaśīrṣa* (December-January). In 2024, the festival will be celebrated on December 11. The *Bhagavadgītā* is worshipped not only as a textual object but as a goddess (*devī*). *Gītā* temples have been built in her honor and their walls are inscribed with the full text of the poem in Sanskrit.

72. Monier-Williams, *Sanskrit-English Dictionary*, 363. The term *gīta* refers to vocal music, as in the case of treatises such as the *Gītaprakāśa* and the *Gītālaṃkāra*; see N. Biondi, *A Descriptive Catalogue of Sanskrit Manuscripts in the Alain Daniélou's Collection at the Giorgio Cini Foundation* (Udine: NOTA, 2017), 69–73.

73. On *BhG* 9.14 and the relevance of *kīrtana*, the collective singing of Kṛṣṇa's glory, see for instance Swami Mukundananda's commentary: https://www.holy-bhagavad-gita.org/chapter/9/verse/14. *Kīrtana* is presented as the second of the nine forms of *bhakti* in *Bhāgavata Purāṇa* 7.5.23, being preceded by *śravaṇa* (hearing the holy word) and followed by *smaraṇa* (recollection of the divine name); on the practice of *kīrtana*, see G. L. Beck,

"*Kīrtan* and *Bhajan*," in *Brill's Encyclopedia of Hinduism Online*, eds. K. A. Jacobsen, H. Basu, A. Malinar, and V. Narayanan (Leiden: Brill, 2018; https://referenceworks.brillonline.com/browse/brill-s-encyclopedia-of-hinduism). On the *Gītā* genre, see J. Gonda, *Medieval Religious Literature in Sanskrit*, vol. 2, fasc. 1 of *A History of Indian Literature* (Wiesbaden: Otto Harrassowitz, 1977), 271–86. On the performativity of a sacred text, see the case study of P. Lutgendorf, *The Life of a Text: Performing the* Rāmcaritmānas *of Tulsidas* (Berkeley: University of California Press, 1991). On the function and creative role of text recitation, see A. Malik, "Bards and Reciters," in *Brill's Encyclopedia of Hinduism Online*, eds. K. A. Jacobsen, H. Basu, A. Malinar, and V. Narayanan (Leiden: Brill, 2018; https://referenceworks.brillonline.com/browse/brill-s-encyclopedia-of-hinduism); F. Orsini and K. B. Schofield, eds., *Tellings and Texts: Music, Literature and Performance in North India* (Cambridge, UK: Open Book, 2015).

74. On the rationale behind Kṛṣṇa's theophany, see G. R. Ashton, "The Soteriology of Role-Play in the *Bhagavad Gītā*," *Asian Philosophy* 23, no. 1 (2013): 1–23. The totalizing metaphysical connotation of *viśvarūpa* as divine "omniform"—Kṛṣṇa being also extolled as *sahasrabāhu*, "he who has a thousand arms" (*BhG* 11.46)—is understood to have been vital to the development of multiform iconography; see D. M. Srinivasan, *Many Heads, Arms and Eyes* (Leiden: Brill, 1997), 137–41.

75. For an ethnographic analysis of danced *Bhagavadgītā*s and the dancers' effort to convey abstract ideas such as *saṃsāra*, the *ātman*, and the performance of one's duty devoid of attachment (*naiṣkarmya*), see K. C. Zubko, "Dancing the *Bhagavadgītā*: Embodiment as Commentary," *Journal of Hindu Studies* 7 (2014): 392–417.

76. On these issues, see Narayan, *Storytellers, Saints, and Scoundrels*. On the performance of *kīrtan*s in contemporary India, with particular reference to the Marāṭhī cultural area, see A. C. Schultz, *Singing a Hindu Nation: Marathi Devotional Performance and Nationalism* (New York: Oxford University Press, 2013); G. N. Dandekar, "The Last Kīrtan of Gadge Baba," in *The Experience of Hinduism: Essays on Religion in Maharashtra*, ed. E. Zelliot and M. Berntsen (Albany: State University of New York Press, 1988), 223–50.

77. See M. Bush Ashton-Sikora, R. P. Sikora, A. Purushothaman, A. Harindranath, *The Royal Temple Theater of Krishnattam* (New Delhi: D. K. Printworld, 2016^2 [1993]), 197–98. Kṛṣṇāṭṭam is subdivided in eight plays: *Avataram* (in fourteen scenes), *Kaliyamardanam* (in eleven scenes), *Rasakrida* (in four scenes), *Kamsavadham* (in twelve scenes), *Svayamvaram* (in thirteen scenes), *Banayuddham* (in eight scenes), *Vividavadham* (in seven scenes), and *Svargarohanam* (in five scenes); see http://www.dvaipayana.net/krishnanattam/krish_summary.html. Kerala has a long and complex

history involving enactments of *Mahābhārata* narratives via the Kūṭiyāṭṭam tradition of Sanskrit drama, which emphasizes the devotional element; see B. M. Sullivan, "Kerala's *Mahābhārata* on Stage: Texts and Performative Practices in Kūṭiyāṭṭam Drama," *Journal of Hindu Studies* 3, no. 1 (2010): 124–42. On these issues, see also N. Shapiro Hawley and S. S. Pillai, eds., *Many Mahābhāratas* (Albany: State University of New York Press, 2021).

78. See M. Stella, *The Significance of the* Mūla Beras *in the Hindu Temples of Tamil Nadu with Special Reference to Bharatanatyam and Hindu Iconography* (PhD diss., Tiruchirapalli: Kalai Kaviri College of Fine Arts, 2009), 203.

79. An Italian-born Odissi and Chhau dancer based in Bhubaneswar, Orissa, in 2006 Ileana Citaristi was the first dancer of foreign origin to be conferred the *Padma Shri* award for her contributions to Odissi dance. Her teacher was the famous Kelucharan Mohapatra (1926–2004), on whom she wrote a biography; I. Citaristi, *The Making of a Guru: Kelucharan Mohapatra, His Life and Times* (Delhi: Manohar, 2005).

80. See https://www.youtube.com/watch?v=oTp7YFEHD3w.

81. Ileana Citaristi's personal communication via email, May 16, 2021. For an appreciation of her interpretation of *hāsyarasa*, see https://www.youtube.com/watch?v=eVbMhsPtiVs. Also noteworthy is the solo dance recital of the *Bhagavadgītā* by the Bharatanāṭyam artist Padma Subrahmanyam; see https://www.youtube.com/watch?v=-nUaywzaDug (in particular her interpretation of *BhG* 2.2–7 and of Kṛṣṇa's smile at minutes 15–18).

82. See C. A. Robinson, *Interpretations of the* Bhagavad-Gītā *and Images of the Hindu Tradition: The Song of the Lord* (Routledge: London and New York, 2006), 145–46.

83. See Rosen, *Vaiṣṇavism: Contemporary Scholars Discuss the Gauḍīya Tradition*, 54.

84. See https://www.youtube.com/watch?v=GODqBiI3pgs; Robinson, *Interpretations of the* Bhagavad-Gītā *and Images of the Hindu Tradition*, 151.

85. On the rendering of the *Bhagavadgītā*, see A. Malinar, "The *Bhagavadgītā* in the *Mahābhārata* TV Serial: Domestic Drama and Dharmic Solutions," in *Representing Hinduism: The Construction of Religious Traditions and National Identity*, ed. V. Dalmia and H. von Stietencron (New Delhi: SAGE, 1995), 442–67. For a survey of actors who have played the part of Kṛṣṇa on Indian television, see https://www.youtube.com/watch?v=vwuEHxSw9aM.

86. See https://www.youtube.com/watch?v=PwFDQWauIJw.

87. We are reminded of Ninian Smart's model of the six dimensions of religion—doctrinal, mythic, ethical, ritual, experiential, and social—as a useful device for trying to get a rounded picture of religion; see N. Smart, *The Religious Experience of Mankind* (New York: Charles Scribner's

Sons, 1976[2]); N. Smart, *Worldviews: Crosscultural Explorations of Human Beliefs* (New York: Charles Scribner's Sons, 1983).

88. See https://youtu.be/NM-CespJ7Do.

89. An instance can be found in *Taittirīya Āraṇyaka* 5.1 which refers to the wry smile of Makha who is none other than Viṣṇu and the personification of sacrifice; see C. Malamoud, *La Danse des pierres: Études sur la scène sacrificielle dans l'Inde ancienne* (Paris: Éditions du Seuil, 2005), 36–37, 53, 170 n. 18.

90. As Oscar Wilde (1854–1900) writes in *The Picture of Dorian Gray*, at the beginning of chapter 14: "But youth smiles without any reason. It is one of its chiefest charms."

91. Yet it is noteworthy that the biographical traits of Kṛṣṇa in the *Viṣṇuparvan* of the *Harivaṃśa* (c. second–third centuries CE) are essentially the same as the ones we find in the *Ghaṭa Jātaka* (454) of the Pāli *Suttapiṭaka*; see https://obo.genaud.net/dhamma-vinaya/pts/kd/jat/jat.4/jat.4.454.rous.pts.htm.

92. For an English translation, see L. Siegel, trans., *Gītagovinda: Love Songs of Rādhā and Kṛṣṇa by Jayadeva* (New York: Clay Sanskrit Library, 2009).

93. For an overview, see A. Malinar, "Kṛṣṇa," in *Brill's Encyclopedia of Hinduism*. Vol. 1: *Regions, Pilgrimages, Deities*, eds. K. A. Jacobsen, H. Basu, A. Malinar, and V. Narayanan (Leiden: Brill, 2009), 605–19. See also G. L. Beck, ed., *Alternative Krishnas: Regional and Vernacular Variations on a Hindu Deity* (Albany: State University of New York Press, 2005). On the textualization of Kṛṣṇa and kṛṣṇaite devotion in a Persian translation of the tenth *skandha* of the *Bhāgavata Purāṇa*, see S. Pellò, "Black Curls in a Mirror: The Eighteenth-Century Persian Kṛṣṇa of Lāla Amānat Rāy's *Jilwa-yi ẕāt* and the Tongue of Bīdil," *International Journal of Hindu Studies* 22, no. 1 (2018): 71–103.

94. Also known as Braj, it is the area surrounding the ancient city of Mathurā on the banks of the Yamunā River. It is here that Kṛṣṇa grew up, played among the *gopīs*, and accomplished many extraordinary feats. It includes his specific home of Vṛndāvana. The Gauḍīyas view the earthly Vraja as coterminous with the heavenly Vraja, where Kṛṣṇa is thought to play eternally with Rādhā and the milkmaids.

95. Dvārakā, the capital of Kṛṣṇa's kingdom, is one of India's seven holy cities and *tīrthas*.

96. See S. S. Pillai, *Krishna's Mahabharatas: Devotional Retellings of an Epic Narrative* (New York: Oxford University Press, 2024). Herein, the author examines over forty retellings in eleven different regional South Asian languages composed over a period of nine hundred years (800–1700 CE).

97. Lit. "increasing cattle." The name of a hill in the Vraja region near Mathurā.

98. For a general examination of Kṛṣṇa's laughter, see Siegel, *Laughing Matters*, 339–72.

99. For instance, we are reminded of the icon of Viṭṭhala/Viṭhobā of Pandharpur, the main form under which Kṛṣṇa is worshipped in the Marāṭhī cultural area. The legend goes that the god decided to remain in this locale because of the extraordinary filial piety (*mātāpitṛbhakti*) of a saintly man called Puṇḍalīka. While he was in search of his spouse Rukmiṇī, the god came to Puṇḍalīka's house, and the latter asked him to wait at his threshold until he finished massaging the feet of his parents. Thus in the iconography Viṭṭhala/Viṭhobā is represented standing on a brick with his hands on his hips and a compassionate smile on his lips, while waiting for Puṇḍalīka to come and receive him. On this famous story, see E. R. Sand, "*Mātāpitṛbhakti*: Some Aspects of the Development of the Puṇḍalīka Legend in Marathi Literature," in *Devotional Literature in South Asia: Current Research, 1985–1988*, ed. R. S. McGregor (Cambridge: Cambridge University Press, 1992), 138–47. On Kṛṣṇa in the Marāṭhī cultural area, see also A. Feldhaus, "Kṛṣṇa and the Kṛṣṇas: Kṛṣṇa in the Mahānubhāva Pantheon," in *Bhakti in Current Research, 1979–1982*, ed. M. Thiel-Horstmann (Berlin: Dietrich Reimer, 1983), 133–42.

100. For an introductory survey of Kṛṣṇa's iconography, see W. M. Spink, *Krishnamandala: A Devotional Theme in Indian Art* (Ann Arbor: University of Michigan, 1971).

101. In a comparative perspective, see K. Johnston Largen, *Baby Krishna, Infant Christ: A Comparative Theology of Salvation* (Maryknoll, NY: Orbis, 2011).

102. On the icon of child Kṛṣṇa stealing butter in literature and in the arts, in Sūr Dās's *Sūr Sāgar* and in the *rāslīlās*, see J. S. Hawley, *Krishna, the Butter Thief* (Princeton, NJ: Princeton University Press, 1983).

103. See A. Okada, *Sculptures indiennes du musée Guimet* (Paris: Trésors du musée Guimet—Réunion des musées nationaux, 2000), 211–12.

104. On this episode, see W. D. O'Flaherty, "Inside and Outside the Mouth of God: The Boundary Between Myth and Reality," *Daedalus* 109, no. 2 (1980): 93–125. For a full English translation, see W. D. O'Flaherty, *Hindu Myths: A Sourcebook Translated from the Sanskrit* (Harmondsworth, UK: Penguin, 1975), 218–21. This story is based on an earlier *Mahābhārata* myth (3.183–90, later taken up by *Matsya Purāṇa* 165.1–22, 166.13–67): the sage Mārkaṇḍeya was floating in the cosmic ocean after the dissolution of the universe, when he came upon a young boy sleeping under a banyan tree. He entered the mouth of the boy—who was Viṣṇu—and saw within him the entire universe, whereupon he came out of Viṣṇu's mouth. On these issues, see A. J. Gail, "Kṛṣṇa on the Banyan Leaf (*vaṭa-patra-śayana*)," *Pandanus* 8, no. 1 (2014): 31–45.

105. Lit. "long-haired one." An epithet of Kṛṣṇa which is also found in *BhG* 1.31, 2.54, 3.1, 10.14, 11.35, 18.76.

106. Lilasuka, *Sri Krishna Karnamrita*, trans. M. K. Acharya (Madras: V. Ramaswamy Sastrulu & Sons, 1948), 92–93. In the book's frontispiece, titled *Vivrta-mukha Visvarupa Darsanam*, is a nice image of child Kṛṣṇa showing the universe in his mouth to his awestruck foster mother. Līlāśuka Bilvamaṅgala also wrote the *Bilvamaṅgalastava*; see D. Wujastyk, "The Love of Kṛṣṇa in Poems and Paintings," in *Pearls of the Orient: Asian Treasures from the Wellcome Library*, ed. N. Allan (London and Chicago: Serindia, 2003), 87–105.

107. On the origins of Kṛṣṇa Veṇugopāla and his link with Arjuna as master of music and dance in the *Mahābhārata*, see the insightful remarks of Biardeau, *Études de mythologie hindoue*, 285–86.

108. On the call of Kṛṣṇa's flute, see D. R. Kinsley, *The Sword and the Flute: Kālī and Kṛṣṇa, Dark Visions of the Terrible and the Sublime in Hindu Mythology* (Berkeley: University of California Press, 1975), 32–41.

109. F. Wilson, ed., *The Love of Krishna*. The *Kṛṣṇakarṇāmṛta* of Līlāśuka Bilvamaṅgala (Philadelphia: University of Pennsylvania Press, 1975), 110.

110. Gopinatha Rao, *Elements of Hindu Iconography*, 207.

111. Sathya Sai Baba, *Sathya Sai Speaks, Vol. 1. Discourses of Bhagawan Sri Sathya Sai Baba (Delivered during 1953–1960)* (Prasanthi Nilayam: Sri Sathya Sai Sadhana Trust, 2015), 22.

112. See D. R. Kinsley, *The Divine Player (A Study of Kṛṣṇa Līlā)* (Delhi: Motilal Banarsidass, 1996).

113. Lit. "the forest of Vṛndā." The forest area on the banks of the Yamunā River in which Kṛṣṇa is said to have grown up, located in the western part of the Mathurā district of Uttar Pradesh. The name is frequently used as a synonym of the surrounding region of Vraja/Braj.

114. For an introduction to Kṛṣṇa's most beloved *gopī*, see H. Pauwels, "Rādhā," in *Brill's Encyclopedia of Hinduism Online*, eds. K. A. Jacobsen, H. Basu, A. Malinar, and V. Narayanan (Leiden: Brill, 2018; https://referenceworks.brillonline.com/browse/brill-s-encyclopedia-of-hinduism). See also D. M. Wulff, "Rādhā: Consort and Conquerer of Krishna," in *Devī: Goddesses of India*, ed. J. S. Hawley and D. M. Wulff (Berkeley: University of California Press, 1996), 109–33; D. R. Kinsley, *Hindu Goddesses: Visions of the Divine Feminine in the Hindu Religious Tradition* (Berkeley: University of California Press, 1988), 81–94.

115. See D. V. Mason, *Theatre and Religion on Krishna's Stage: Performing in Vrindavan* (New York: Palgrave Macmillan, 2009); J. S. Hawley, *At Play with Krishna: Pilgrimage Dramas from Brindavan* (Princeton, NJ: Princeton University Press, 1981). See also M. H. Case, *Seeing Krishna:*

The Religious World of a Brahman Family in Vrindaban (New York: Oxford University Press, 2000).

116. A *nāga* king who lived in the Yamunā River near Vṛndāvana. On *nāgas*, see G. Lange, "Cobra Deities and Divine Cobras: The Ambiguous Animality of Nāgas," *Religions* 10, no. 8 (2019), https://doi.org/10.3390/rel10080454.

117. See C. Dimmitt and J. A. B. van Buitenen, eds., trans., *Classical Hindu Mythology: A Reader in the Sanskrit Purāṇas* (Philadelphia: Temple University Press, 1978), 116–17.

118. Ibid., 115.

119. Kinsley, *The Divine Player*, 217–18. Within the Caitanya tradition, a fine example of *līlāsmaraṇa* or remembering the sport of one's chosen deity is the sixteenth-century text *Govindalīlāmṛta*, the "Ambrosia of the Sport of Govinda," of Kṛṣṇadāsa Kavirāja; see N. Delmonico, "How to Partake in the Love of Kṛṣṇa," in *Religions of India in Practice*, ed. D. S. Lopez Jr. (Princeton, NJ: Princeton University Press, 1995), 244–68.

120. See for instance *Gītagovinda* 1.4.1: "[Kṛṣṇa] is wearing forest garlands, a yellow garment, and has his blue body smeared with the paste of sandalwood. He is always smiling, and his cheeks are adorned with jeweled ear-ornaments, which move during his play" (*candana-carcita-nīla-kalevara-pīta-vasana-vana-mālī | keli-calan-maṇi-kuṇḍala-maṇḍita-gaṇḍa-yuga-smita-śālī ||*); M. M. Deshpande, *Saṃskṛta-Subodhinī. A Sanskrit Primer* (Ann Arbor: Center for South and Southeast Asian Studies, University of Michigan, 2007), 275–76.

121. Wilson, *The Love of Krishna*, 130.

122. A case in point is the smile of the goddess: she is celebrated as *mandasmitamukhāmbujā*, "she who displays a tender smile on her lotus face;" see C. Mackenzie Brown, *The Devī Gītā. The Song of the Goddess: A Translation, Annotation, and Commentary* (Albany: State University of New York Press, 1998), 64, 134, 329.

123. Dabholkar, *Shri Sai Satcharita*, 327 (chap. 20, v. 35). Moreover: "As one gazes into your [= Sai Baba's] smiling countenance, all the sorrows of worldly life are forgotten and hunger and thirst satisfied, there and then! So marvellous is your *darshan*!"; ibid., 722 (chap. 44, v. 3); "His jokes always had a natural ease and novelty about them. Their spirit heightened by the smiling countenance, the play of the eyes, their charm was simply indescribable;" ibid., 319 (chap. 24, v. 14). As Ganesh Shrikrishna Khaparde (1854–1938), lieutenant of the nationalist leader Bal Gangadhar Tilak (1856–1920), wrote in a diary entry dated December 7, 1910: "Sayin Sahib [= Sai Baba] spoke with such a wonderful sweetness and he smiled so often and with such extraordinary grace that the con-

versation will always remain engraved in my memory;" *Shirdi Diary of the Hon'ble Mr. G. S. Khaparde* (Bombay: Shri Sai Baba Sansthan, n.d.), 4. To mention just another case, here is how Viswanatha Swami (1904–1979) describes his first *darśan* of Śrī Ramaṇa Maharṣi in January 1921: "I saw in him something quite arresting which clearly distinguished him from all others I had seen. His look and smile had remarkable spiritual charm. When he spoke, the words seemed to come out of an abyss;" see J. Greenblatt and M. Greenblatt, eds., *Bhagavan Sri Ramana: A Pictorial Biography*. A Birth Centenary Offering (Tiruvannamalai: Sri Ramanasramam, 1985^2), 94.

124. For an introduction to his figure, see R. Lutjeharms, "Rūpa Gosvāmī," in *Brill's Encyclopedia of Hinduism Online*, eds. K. A. Jacobsen, H. Basu, A. Malinar, and V. Narayanan (Leiden: Brill, 2018; https://referenceworks.brillonline.com/browse/brill-s-encyclopedia-of-hinduism).

125. Naturally Rūpa Gosvāmin's focus is on the Kṛṣṇa of the *Bhāgavata Purāṇa* and not on the Kṛṣṇa of the *Bhagavadgītā*, who is beyond his self-delimited purview.

126. A legendary *devarṣi*. In the *Mahābhārata* and *Purāṇas*, Nārada is revered as the son of Brahmā and thus as one of the Prajāpatis. To him are ascribed the eighty-four *sūtras* of the *Bhaktisūtras*, a text perhaps datable to the tenth century CE and dependent upon the *Bhāgavata Purāṇa*.

127. D. L. Haberman, *The Bhaktirasāmṛtasindhu of Rūpa Gosvāmin* (New Delhi: Indira Gandhi National Centre for the Arts—Motilal Banarsidass, 2003), 548–51.

128. The only difference from Bharata's list is that here *avahasita* takes the place of *upahasita*. The two terms, however, are synonymous.

129. Haberman, *The Bhaktirasāmṛtasindhu of Rūpa Gosvāmin*, 550–51.

130. Lit. "very powerful." One of Kṛṣṇa's most dear cowherd friends.

131. In the *Mahābhārata* he is the son of Arjuna and Subhadrā. Killed in a cowardly fashion on the thirteenth day of the war against the Kauravas, he will leave his widow, Uttarā, pregnant with the future Parīkṣit. In Vṛndāvana, Abhimanyu plays the part of the so-called husband of Rādhā.

132. The maternal grandmother of Rādhā.

133. Abhimanyu's sister. Kuṭilā as well as Jaṭilā perform the service of facilitating the *parakīyā rasa* (i.e., the paramour love of Rādhā and Kṛṣṇa).

134. Haberman, *The Bhaktirasāmṛtasindhu of Rūpa Gosvāmin*, 552–57.

135. On the darker characteristics of Hindu dieties, see Hiltebeitel, *Criminal Gods and Demon Devotees*.

136. For more examples of the power of Kṛṣṇa's smile/laughter, see A. Balasubramanya, "A Smile Can Change Your Life," at https://www.youtube.com/watch?v=Yh_q6twJXiw (minutes 0–4); "Traditional Tales: Anger Should Subside," *Prabuddha Bharata or Awakened India. A monthly*

journal of the Ramakrishna Order started by Swami Vivekananda in 1896, 122, no. 2 (2017): 331–32 (translated from the Tamil book *Arulneri Kathaigal*).

137. As the Marāṭhī poet-saint Tukārām (seventeenth century) says, the "holy face" of Viṭṭhala/Viṭhobā, that is, of Kṛṣṇa, is "moulded out of happiness;" J. Nelson Fraser and K. B. Marathe, trans., *The Poems of Tukārāma*. With Notes and Introduction (Delhi: Motilal Banarsidass, 2000 [1909]), 49.

138. For an appreciation of this *bhajan*, see https://www.youtube.com/watch?v=7L3z1k-SdKA

139. See Śastri—Pansīkar, *The Brahmasūtra Śankara Bhāshya with the Commentaries Bhāmatī, Kalpataru and Parimala, Bhāmatī*, 4.

140. The Neoplatonist philosopher Proclus (412–485 CE), in his commentary on Plato's *Timaeus*, analogously states: "For the smile of the gods gave to the things of the cosmos their being and their power to continue;" quoted in Kinsley, *The Divine Player*, ix.

Bibliography

Primary Sources

Āgāśe, Kāśīnātha Śāstrī, ed. *Vācaspatimiśraviracitaṭīkāsaṃvalitavyāsabhāṣyasametāni pātañjalayogasūtrāṇi tathā bhojadevaviracitarājamārtaṇḍābhidhavṛttisametāni pātañjalayogasūtrāṇi*. Pūṇe: Ānandāśrama, 2004.

Belvalkar, Shripad Krishna. *The Bhagavadgītā, Being Reprint of Relevant Parts of Bhīṣmaparvan*. Poona: Bhandarkar Oriental Research Institute, 1945.

Bhagavadgītā with the commentary of Bhāskara, http://gretil.sub.uni-goettingen.de/gretil/1_sanskr/6_sastra/3_phil/vedanta/bhbhg_cu.htm (last accessed December 5, 2022).

Bhagavadgītā with the commentaries of Śrīdhara, Madhusūdana, Viśvanātha and Bāladeva, http://gretil.sub.uni-goettingen.de/gretil/1_sanskr/2_epic/mbh/ext/bhg4c02u.htm (last accessed January 7, 2023).

BhG1 2000 = *Śrīmadbhagavadgītā śāṅkarabhāṣyādyekadaśaṭīkopetā*. Edited by Shastri Gajanana Shambhu Sadhale. Vol. 1. Bombay 1859. Reprint, Delhi: Parimal Publications, 2000.

BhG2 2001 = *Śrīmadbhagavadgītā tattvaprakāśiketyādyaṣṭaṭīkopetā*. Critically Edited by Shastri Jivaram Lallurama. Vol. 1. Bombay 1917. Delhi: Parimal Publications, 2001.

BhG3 1936 = *Śrīmadbhagavadgītā with the Commentaries Śrīmat-Śānkarabhāṣya with Ānandagiri; Nīlakanṭhī; Bhāṣyotkarṣadīpikā of Dhanapati; Śrīdharī; Gītārthasañgraha of Abhinavaguptāchārya; and Gūḍhārthadīpikā of Madhu-sūdana Sarasvatī with Gūḍhārtha-tattvāloka of Śrī-dharma-datta-śarmā (Bachchā-śarmā)*. Edited by Wāsudev Laxmaṇ Shāstrī Paṇśīkar. Bombay: "Nirṇaya Sâgar" Press, 1936.

BhG4 2015 = *Śrīśaṅkarabhagavatpāda's Śrīmadbhagavadgītābhāṣyam, with Commentaries of Śrīmadanubhūtisvarūpācārya, Śrīmadānandagiri and Śrī Bellaṅkoṇḍa Rāmarāya Kavi*. Critically Edited with Notes etc. by Dr. Maṇi Drāviḍa. Vol. 1, chaps. 1–9. Vārāṇasī: Śrīdakṣiṇāmūrti Maṭha Prakāśan, 2015.

BhG5 1965 = Bhāskara. *Śrīmadbhagavadgītābhāṣyam*. Edited by Subhadra Jha. Vārāṇasī: Vārāṇaseya Saṅskṛta Viśvavidyālaya, 1965.

BhG6 1941 = *Śrīmadbhagavadgītā with the "jñānakarmasamuccaya" Commentary of Ānand[vardhana]*. Edited, from a unique Śāradā Manuscript, by Shripad Krishna Belvalkar. Poona: Bilvakunja Publishing House, 1941.

BhG7 1990 = *Śrīmadbhagavadgītā, śrīvaṃśīdharamiśrapraṇītayā vaṃśīvyākhyayā vibhūṣitā*, Vyākhyākāraḥ sampādakaś ca Paṇḍita Vaṃśīdharamiśra. Vārāṇasī: Sampūrṇānanda Saṃskṛta Viśvavidyālaya, 1990.

BhG8 1966 = *Śrīmadbhagavadgītā śrīpādaviśvanāthacakravarttimahodayaviracitasārārthavarṣiṇīṭīkayā evaṃ śrīyutabaladevavidyābhūṣaṇamahodayaviracitagītābhūṣaṇabhāṣyeṇa samalaṃkṛtā*, Prakāśaka Śrīkṛṣṇadāsa Bābā. Mathurā: Gaurahari Press, 1966.

BhGBh = see BhG1 2000, BhG3 1936 and BhG4 2015.

Brahmasūtrabhāṣya 2000 = *Brahmasūtraśāṅkarabhāṣyaṃ śrīgovindānandakṛtayā bhāṣyaratnaprabhayā śrīvācaspatimiśraviracitayā bhāmatyā śrīmadānandagiripraṇītena nyāyanirṇayena samupetam*. Edited by Jagadīśa Lāl Śāstrī. Delhi 1980. Reprint, Delhi: Motilal Banarsidass, 2000.

Dimitrov, Dragomir. *Lehrschrift über die Zwanzig Präverbien im Sanskrit*. Kritische Ausgabe der *Viṃśatyupasargavṛtti* und der tibetischen Übertzung *Ñe bar bsgyur ba ñi śu pa'i 'grel pa*. Editionen von Texten der Cāndra-Schule. Band I. Von Dragomir Dimitrov nach Vorarbeien von Thomas Oberlies. *Indica et Tibetica* 49. Marburg: Indica et Tibetica Verlag, 2007.

GAD 2005 = Sarasvatī, Madhusūdana. *Śrīmadbhagavadgītā Madhusūdanīsaṁskṛtahindīvyākhyopetā*. Hindīvyākhyākāra Svāmī Śrī Sanātanadeva, Ṭippaṇī evaṁ bhūmikā lekhaka. Vārāṇasī 1962. Reprint, Vārāṇasī: Caukhamba Saṁskṛta Saṁsthāna, 2005.

Jhalakikar, Vamanacharya Ramabhatta, ed. *Kāvyaprakāśa of Mammaṭa. With the Sanskrit Commentary Bālabodhinī*. Poona: Bhandarkar Oriental Research Institute, 1983[8].

KSTS 1943 = *The Bhagavadgītā, with the commentary called Sarvatobhadra by Rājānaka Rāmakaṇṭha*. Edited by Paṇḍit Madhusūdan Kaul Shāstrī. *Kashmir Series of Texts and Studies*, n. LXIV. Bombay: Nirnaya Sagar Press, 1943.

Lilasuka. *Sri Krishna Karnamrita*. Translated and introduced by M. K. Acharya. Madras: V. Ramaswamy Sastrulu & Sons, 1948.

Masson, J. L., and M. V. Patwardhan, eds. *Aesthetic Rapture: The Rasādhyāya of the Nāṭyaśāstra in Two Volumes*. Vol. 1, *Text*; Vol. 2, *Notes*. Poona: Deccan College Postgraduate Research Institute, 1970.

MBh = *The Mahābhārata*. For the First Time Critically Edited by Vishnu S. Sukthankar, S. K. Belvalkar, P. L. Vaidya. 19 Vols. Poona: Bhandarkar

Oriental Research Institute, 1933–1966. Electronic version at http://bombay.indology.info/mahabharata/welcome.html (last accessed April 10, 2023).

Oertel, Hanns. "The *Jāiminīya* or *Talavakāra Upaniṣad Brāhmaṇa*," *Journal of the American Oriental Society* 16, no. 1 (1896): 79–260.

Olivelle, Patrick, ed., trans. *Manu's Code of Law: A Critical Edition and Translation of the Mānava-Dharmaśāstra*. New York: Oxford University Press, 2005.

Prabhanjanacharya 1999 = *Śrīmadānandatīrthapraṇīta-sarvamūlagranthāḥ, prathamasaṃpuṭam, (gītāprasthānagranthau) śrīmadbhagavadgītābhāṣyam, śrīmadbhagavadgītātātparyanirṇayaḥ*. Edited critically with an Introduction, explanatory Notes & Appendices by Vyasanakere Prabhanjanacharya. Vol. 1. Bangalore: Śrī Vyāsamadhwa Sevā Pratiṣṭhāna, 1999.

Prakaṭārthavivaraṇa 1989 = Anubhūtisvarūpācārya. *The Prakaṭārthavivaraṇa of Anubhūtisvarūpācārya being a Commentary on the Brahmasūtrabhāṣya of Śaṅkarācārya*, edited by T. R. Chintamani. 2 Vols. Madras 1935. Reprint, New Delhi: Navrang, 1989.

Rām = Bhatt G. H. *The Vālmīki-Rāmāyaṇa*. Critical Edition. 7 Vols. Vadodara 1958. Reprint, Vadodara: Oriental Institute, 2001. Electronic version at https://sanskritdocuments.org/mirrors/ramayana/valmiki.htm (last accessed April 2, 2023).

Ramakrishna Kavi, M., ed. *Nāṭyaśāstra of Bharata Muni. With the Commentary Abhinavabhāratī by Abhinavaguptācārya*. Chapters 1–7 Illustrated, Vol. 1. Baroda: Oriental Institute, 1956[2].

Śarmā, Kanakalāl. *The Dhātupāṭha of Pāṇini. With the Dhātvartha Prakāśikā Notes*. Varanasi: The Chowkhamba Sanskrit Series Office, 1969[2].

Śarmā, Someśvara Appala, ed. *Nipātāvyayopasargavṛttiḥ. Śrīveṅkaṭeśvaraprācyamahāvidyālayavyākaraṇopādhyāyena "vyākaraṇāsāhityavidyāpravīṇā"—dyupādhibhjā kautsena Appala Someśvaraśarmā, ity anena saviśeṣaṃ pariṣkṛta*. Śrīveṅkaṭeśvaraprācyagranthāvalī. Tirupati: Tirupati Devasthānamudrālaya, 1951.

Śāstrī 2004 = *Śrīśaṅkarabhagavatpādācāryaviracitam upaniṣadbhāṣyam. khaṇḍaḥ 1 (āditaḥ 8 upaniṣadām). samagrabhāṣyasya śrīmadānandagiryācāryakṛtaṭīkayā kaṭhamāṇḍūkyataittirīyabhāṣyāṇāṃ prasiddhācāryāntaraṭīkābhiḥ ca samalaṃkṛtam*. Edited by Subrahmaṇya Śāstrī. Mount Abu-Varanasi: Mahesh Research Institute, 2004.

Śāstrī 1986 = *Kāṇvaśākhīyā bṛhadāraṇyakopaniṣat (upaniṣadbhāṣyam—khaṇḍaḥ 3) śrīmadānandagiryācāryaviracitaṭīkopetaśrīśaṅkarabhagavatpādapraṇītabhāṣyavibhūṣitā tathā śrīmādhyandinaśākhīyopaniṣatpāṭhena tadanusāriṇyā śrīvidyāraṇyamuniviracitayā dīpikayā ca saṃvardhitā.*

Edited with Introduction, Notes, etc. by Subrahmaṇya Śāstrī. Mount Abu-Varanasi: Mahesh Research Institute, 1986.

Śāstrī 1982 = *Sāmavedīyā chāndogyopaniṣat (upaniṣadbhāṣyam—khaṇḍaḥ 2) śrīśaṅkarabhagavatpādācāryabhāṣyavibhūṣitā. samagrabhāṣyaṃ śrīmannarendrapurīśrīmadānandagiryācāryadvayakṛtaṭīkābhyāṃ tathā ṣaṣṭasaptamāṣṭamādhyāyabhāṣyaṃ śrīmadabhinavanārāyaṇānandendrasarasvatīviracitaṭīkayā ca samalaṅkṛtam*. Edited with Introduction, Notes etc. by Subrahmaṇya Śāstrī. Mount Abu-Varanasi: Mahesh Research Institute, 1982.

Śāstrī 1970 = *Upaniṣatsaṃgrahaḥ*. Edited by Jagadīśa Śāstrī. Delhi: Motilal Banarsidass, 1970.

Śastri, Ananta Krishna, and V. L. S. Pansīkar, eds. *The Brahmasūtra Śankara Bhāshya with the Commentaries Bhāmatī, Kalpataru and Parimala*. Bombay: Nirnaya Sagar Press, 1917.

Sinha 1986 = *The Vaiśeṣikasūtras of Kaṇāda with the Commentary of Śaṅkara Miśra and Extracts from the Gloss of Jayanārāyaṇa, Together with Notes from the Commentary of Candrakānta and an Introduction by the Translator*. Translated by Nandlal Sinha. Calcutta 1911. Reprint, Delhi: S. N. Publications, 1996.

Śrīmadbhagavadgītā, padaccheda-anvaya aur sadharaṇa-bhāṣāṭīkāsahita. Gorakhpur: Gītā Press, 1974[27] (1922).

Secondary Sources

Achtemeier, Paul J., ed. *Harper's Bible Dictionary*. San Francisco: Harper & Row, 1985.

Ādidevānanda, Svāmī, trans. *Śrī Rāmānuja Gītā Bhāṣya*. Madras: Sri Ramakrishna Math, 1983.

Aklujkar, Ashok. "Paṇḍita and Pandits in History." In *The Pandit. Traditional Scholarship in India*, edited by A. Michaels, 17–38. Delhi: Manohar, 2001.

Alighieri, Dante. *Convivio*. A cura di P. Cudini. Milan: Garzanti, 1980.

———. *La Divina Commedia, Paradiso*. Commento di A. M. Chiavacci Leonardi. Milan: Mondadori, 2009.

Ambrose, Kay, and Ram Gopal. *Classical Dances and Costumes of India*. London: A & C Black, 1983[2] (1950).

Appadurai, Arjun. *Worship and Conflict under Colonial Rule: A South Indian Case*. Cambridge: Cambridge University Press, 1981.

Apte, Mahadev L. *Humor and Laughter: An Anthropological Approach*. Ithaca and London: Cornell University Press, 1985.

Apte, Vaman Shivaram. *The Practical Sanskrit-English Dictionary*. Revised & Enlarged Edition. Kyoto: Rinsen Book Company, 1986.

Arnold, Edwin, trans. *The Song Celestial or* Bhagavad-Gita *(From the* Mahabharata*)*. Being a Discourse Between Arjuna, Prince of India, and the Supreme Being Under the Form of Krishna. New York: Truslove, Hanson & Comba, 1900.

Ashton, Geoffrey R. "The Soteriology of Role-Play in the *Bhagavad Gītā*," *Asian Philosophy* 23, 1 (2013): 1–23.

Ashton-Sikora, Martha Bush, Robert P. Sikora, A. Purushothaman, and A. Harindranath. *The Royal Temple Theater of Krishnattam*. New Delhi: D. K. Printworld, 2016[2] (1993).

Babb, Lawrence A. "Glancing: Visual Interaction in Hinduism," *Journal of Anthropological Research* 37, no. 4 (1981): 387–401.

Bakker, Hans. "Dakṣiṇāmūrti." In *Vidyārṇavavandanam. Essays in Honour of Asko Parpola*, edited by K. Karttunen & P. Koskikallio, 41–53. Helsinki: Finnish Oriental Society, 2001.

Bakker, Hans T., and Peter Bisschop. "The Quest for the Pāśupata Weapon. The Gateway of the Mahādeva Temple at Madhyamikā (Nagarī)," *Indo-Iranian Journal* 59 (2016): 217–58.

Balasubrahmanyam, S. R. *Early Chola Temples: Parantaka I to Rajaraja I (A. D. 907–985)*. New Delhi: Orient Longman, 1971.

Balasubramanya, Aravind. "A Smile Can Change Your Life;" https://www.youtube.com/watch?v=Yh_q6twJXiw.

Balkaran, Raj. "Arjuna and Acyuta: The Import of Epithets in the *Bhagavad-gītā*." In *The Bhagavad-gītā: A Critical Introduction*, edited by I. Theodor, 137–44. London and New York: Routledge, 2021.

Bandhu, Vishva, ed. *A Grammatical Word-Index to the Four Vedas*. I Part (*a-pha*). Hoshiarpur: Vishveshvaranand Vedic Research Institute, 1960.

———. *A Grammatical Word-Index to the Four Vedas*. II Part (*ba-ha*). Hoshiarpur: Vishveshvaranand Vedic Research Institute, 1963.

———. *Vaidika-pādānukrama-koṣaḥ (A Vedic Word-Concordance). Brāhmaṇa-bhāgaḥ (Brāhmaṇa section)*. Part II (*pa-ha*). Hoshiarpur: Vishveshvaranand Vedic Research Institute, 1973.

———. *Vaidika-pādānukrama-koṣaḥ (A Vedic Word-Concordance). Upaniṣad-bhāgaḥ (Upaniṣad section)*. Part II (*pa-ha*). Hoshiarpur: Vishveshvaranand Vedic Research Institute, 1977 (1966).

Banerjee, Priyatosh. *The Life of Krishṇa in Indian Art*. New Delhi: National Museum, 1978.

Barnett, Lionel D., trans. *Bhagavad-Gītā or The Lord's Song*. London: J. M. Dent & Sons, 1928 (1905).

Baumer, Rachel Van M., and James R. Brandon, eds., *Sanskrit Drama in Performance*. Delhi: Motilal Banarsidass, 1993 (1981).

Beard, Mary. *Laughter in Ancient Rome: On Joking, Tickling, and Cracking Up*. Berkeley: University of California Press, 2014.

Beck, Guy L. "*Kīrtan* and *Bhajan*." In *Brill's Encyclopedia of Hinduism Online*, edited by K. A. Jacobsen, H. Basu, A. Malinar, and V. Narayanan. Leiden: Brill, 2018. https://referenceworks.brillonline.com/browse/brill-s-encyclopedia-of-hinduism.

———, ed. *Alternative Krishnas: Regional and Vernacular Variations on a Hindu Deity*. Albany: State University of New York Press, 2005.

Beekes, Robert. *Etymological Dictionary of Greek*. With the Assistance of L. van Beek. Vol. 1, 264–65. Leiden: Brill, 2010.

Belvalkar 1941 = See BhG6 1941.

Belvalkar, Shripad Krishna. "The Bhagavad Gītā: A General Review of Its History and Character." In *Cultural Heritage of India*, 2: 135–57. Calcutta: The Ramakrishna Mission Institute of Culture, 1975.

Benedetti, Marina. "«Ma qual è la vera letizia?» Realtà e metamorfosi di Francesco." In *Francesco da Assisi. Storia, arte, mito*, edited by M. Benedetti and T. Subini, 29–40. Rome: Carocci, 2019.

Benton, Catherine. *God of Desire: Tales of Kāmadeva in Sanskrit Story Literature*. Albany: State University of New York Press, 2006.

Berger, Peter L. *Redeeming Laughter: The Comic Dimension of Human Experience*. New York and Berlin: Walter De Gruyter, 1997.

Bergson, Henri. *Laughter. An Essay on the Meaning of the Comic*. New York: Macmillan, 2018 (1900).

Besant, Annie, and Bhagavân Dâs, trans. *The Bhagavad-Gîtâ*. With Saṃskrit Text, free translation into English, a word-for-word translation, and an Introduction on Saṃskrit Grammar. London and Benares: Theosophical Publishing Society, 1905.

Bhalla, Alok, and Chandra Prakash Deval. *The Gita: Mewari Miniature Painting (1680–1698) by Allah Baksh*. New Delhi: Niyogi Books, 2019.

Bharati, Agehananda. "Ritualistic Tolerance and Ideological Rigour: The Paradigm of the Expatriate Hindus in East Africa," *Contributions to Indian Sociology* 10, no. 2 (1976): 341–65.

Bhargava, P. L. "Names and Epithets of Kṛṣṇa in the *Bhagavadgītā*," *Indologica Taurinensia* 7 (1979): 93–96.

Bhatt, G. H. "The Literature on the *Gītā* in the Śuddhādvaita School," *Annals of the Bhandarkar Oriental Research Institute* 30, no. 1/2 (1949): 131–34.

Biagetti, Erica, Oliver Hellwig, and Sven Sellmer. "Hedging in Diachrony: The Case of Vedic Sanskrit *iva*," *Proceedings of the 21st International Workshop on Treebanks and Linguistic Theories, March 9–12, 2023, Association for Computational Linguistics* 2023, 21–31; https://www.academia.edu/98485196/Hedging_in_diachrony_the_case_of_Vedic_Sanskrit_iva.

Biardeau, Madeleine. *Études de mythologie hindoue. 2. Bhakti et avatāra*. Pondichéry: Publications de l'École Française d'Extrême-Orient, 1994.

———. "Nala et Damayantī. Héros épiques. Part 2," *Indo-Iranian Journal* 28 (1985): 1–34.

———. "Nara et Nārāyaṇa," *Wiener Zeitschrift für die Kunde Südasiens* 35 (1991): 75–108.

Binder, Katrin. "Drama and Theatre." In *Brill's Encyclopedia of Hinduism Online*, edited by K. A. Jacobsen, H. Basu, A. Malinar, and V. Narayanan. Leiden: Brill, 2018. https://referenceworks.brillonline.com/browse/brill-s-encyclopedia-of-hinduism.

Biondi, Nicola. *A Descriptive Catalogue of Sanskrit Manuscripts in the Alain Daniélou's Collection at the Giorgio Cini Foundation*. Udine: NOTA, 2017.

Blackburn, Stuart H. "Hanging in the Balance: Rāma in the Shadow Puppet Theater of Kerala." In *Gender, Genre, and Power in South Asian Expressive Traditions*, edited by A. Appadurai, F. J. Korom, and M. A. Mills, 379–94. Philadelphia: University of Pennsylvania Press, 1991.

Bloomfield, Maurice. "On Recurring Psychic Motifs in Hindu Fiction, and the Laugh and Cry Motif," *Journal of the American Oriental Society* 36 (1916): 54–89.

Bobde, P. V., trans. *Garland of Divine Flowers: Selected Devotional Lyrics of Saint Jñāneśvara*. Delhi: Motilal Banarsidass, 1999.

Böhtlingk, Otto. *Indische Sprüche*, Sanskrit und Deutsch herausgegeben, Vols. 2–3. St. Petersburg, 1872–73.

Bolle, Keyes W., trans. *The Bhagavadgītā: A New Translation*. Berkeley: University of California Press, 1979.

Bowles, Adam. *Dharma, Disorder and the Political in Ancient India: The* Āpaddharmaparvan *of the* Mahābhārata. Leiden: Brill, 2007.

Brereton, Joel P. "The Particle *iva* in Vedic Prose," *Journal of the American Oriental Society* 102, no. 3 (1982): 443–50.

Brodbeck, Simon. "The *Upaniṣads* and the *Bhagavadgītā*." In *The Upaniṣads. A Complete Guide*, edited by S. Cohen, 200–18. London and New York: Routledge, 2018.

Brooks, Douglas Renfrew. *Poised for Grace: Annotations on the Bhagavad Gita from a Tantric View*. The Woodlands, TX: Anusara Press, 2008.

Brown, C. Mackenzie. *The Devī Gītā. The Song of the Goddess: A Translation, Annotation, and Commentary*. Albany: State University of New York Press, 1998.

Burnouf, Eugène. "Sur les trente-deux signes caractéristiques d'un grand homme." In *Le lotus de la bonne loi: Traduit su sanscrit, accompagné d'un commentaire et de vingt et un mémoires relatifs au buddhisme*. Nouvelle édition avec une Préface de Sylvain Lévi, 553–647. Paris: Maisonneuve, 1925.

Burton, Adrian P. *Temples, Texts, and Taxes: The Bhagavad-gītā and the Politico-Religious Identity of the Caitanya Sect*. PhD diss., Canberra: The Australian National University, 2000.

Bynum, Caroline W. *Dissimilar Similitudes: Devotional Objects in Late Medieval Europe*. Princeton, NJ: Princeton University Press, 2020.

Callewaert, Winand M., and Shilanand Hemraj. *Bhagavadgītānuvāda: A Study in Transcultural Translation*. Ranchi: Satya Bharati Publication, 1982.
Case, Margaret H. *Seeing Krishna: The Religious World of a Brahman Family in Vrindaban*. New York: Oxford University Press, 2000.
Cecil, Elizabeth A. "Mapping the Pāśupata Landscape: Narrative, Tradition, and the Geographic Imaginary," *The Journal of Hindu Studies* 11, no. 3 (2018): 285–303.
Chapman, Antony J., Hugh C. Foot, and Peter Derks, eds. *Humor and Laughter: Theory, Research, and Applications*. New York: Routledge, 1996.
Chapple, Christopher K. "Arjuna's Argument: Family Secrets Unveiled," *Journal of Vaiṣṇava Studies* 9, no. 2 (2001): 23–31.
Cherniak, Alex, trans. *Mahābhārata. Book Six. Bhīṣma, Volume 1. Including the 'Bhagavad Gītā' in Context*. New York: The Clay Sanskrit Library—New York University Press and the JJC Foundation, 2008.
Chidbhavananda, Swami, trans. *The Bhagavad Gita*. Tirupparaitturai: Sri Ramakrishna Tapovanam, 1972[6] (1965).
Chinmayananda, Swami, trans. *The Bhagavad Geeta*. Langhorne, PA: Chinmaya, 2000.
Chintamani 1989 = See *Prakaṭārthavivaraṇa* 1989.
Chitluri, Vinny. *Baba's Divine Symphony*. New Delhi: Sterling, 2014.
Chitrakathi: Folk Painting of Paithan. Pune: Raja Dinkar Kelkar Museum, 1996.
Citaristi, Ileana. *The Making of a Guru: Kelucharan Mohapatra, His Life and Times*. Delhi: Manohar, 2005.
Classen, Albrecht, ed. *Laughter in the Middle Ages and Early Modern Times: Epistemology of a Fundamental Human Behavior, Its Meaning, and Consequences*. Berlin: De Gruyter, 2010.
Clémentin-Ojha, Catherine. "Nimbārka sampradāya." In *Brill's Encyclopedia of Hinduism*. Vol. 3: *Society, Religious Specialists, Religious Traditions, Philosophy*, edited by K. A. Jacobsen, H. Basu, A. Malinar, and V. Narayanan, 429–44. Leiden: Brill, 2011.
Coburn, Thomas B. *Devī-Māhātmya: The Crystallization of the Goddess Tradition*. Delhi: Motilal Banarsidass, 1988.
Cohen, Tamara. "*Arjunopākhyāna*: An Idealist Non-dualistic Translation of the *Bhagavadgītā*," *Journal of South Asian Intellectual History* 2, no. 2 (2019): 122–52.
Colas, Gérard. *Le temple selon Marīci*. Pondichéry: Institut Français d'Indologie, 1986.
———. "Vaikhānasa." In *Brill's Encyclopedia of Hinduism Online*, edited by K. A. Jacobsen, H. Basu, A. Malinar, and V. Narayanan. Leiden: Brill, 2018. https://referenceworks.brillonline.com/browse/brill-s-encyclopedia-of-hinduism.

Couture, André. "*Avatāra*." In *Brill's Encyclopedia of Hinduism Online*, edited by K. A. Jacobsen, H. Basu, A. Malinar, and V. Narayanan. Leiden: Brill, 2018. https://referenceworks.brillonline.com/browse/brill-s-encyclopedia-of-hinduism.

Dabholkar, Govind R. (Hemad Pant), *Shri Sai Satcharita: The Life and Teachings of Shirdi Sai Baba*. Translated from the Original Marathi by Indira Kher. New Delhi: Sterling, 1999.

Dallapiccola, Anna Libera, and Jyotindra Jain, eds. *Paithan Paintings: The Epic World of the Chitrakathis Picture Showmen: Insights into the Narrative Tradition in Indian Art*. Mumbai: Marg, 1978.

Dandekar, G. N. "The Last Kīrtan of Gadge Baba." In *The Experience of Hinduism: Essays on Religion in Maharashtra*, edited by E. Zelliot and M. Berntsen, 223–50. Albany: State University of New York Press, 1988.

Davidson, Joseph Leroy. *Art of the Indian Subcontinent from Los Angeles Collections*. Los Angeles: The Ward Ritchie Press, 1968.

Davis, Richard H. *Lives of Indian Images*. Princeton, NJ: Princeton University Press, 1997.

———. *The Bhagavad Gita: A Biography*. Princeton and Oxford: Princeton University Press, 2015.

———. "The Greatness of the *Gītā*, as Icon and Mantra." In *The Bhagavad-gītā: A Critical Introduction*, edited by I. Theodor, 94–103. London and New York: Routledge, 2021.

———. "Wilkins, Kasinatha, Hastings, and the First English '*Bhagavad Gītā*,'" *International Journal of Hindu Studies* 19, no. 1–2 (2015): 39–57.

De, Aniket. *The Boundary of Laughter: Popular Performances Across Borders in South Asia*. New Delhi: Oxford University Press, 2021.

Delmonico, Neal. "How to Partake in the Love of Kṛṣṇa." In *Religions of India in Practice*, edited by D. S. Lopez Jr., 244–68. Princeton, NJ: Princeton University Press, 1995.

Deloche, Jean. *Contribution to the History of the Wheeled Vehicle in India*. Pondichéry: Institut Français de Pondichéry—École Française d'Extrême-Orient, 2014.

Deshpande, Madhav M. *Saṃskṛta-Subodhinī. A Sanskrit Primer*. Ann Arbor: Center for South and Southeast Asian Studies, University of Michigan, 2007.

Deutsch, Eliot, trans. *The Bhagavad Gītā*. New York-Chicago-San Francisco: Holt, Rinehart and Winston, 1968.

Di Bernardi, Vito. *Mahābhārata. L'epica indiana e lo spettacolo di Peter Brook*. Rome: Bulzoni, 1990[2].

Dimmitt, Cornelia, and Johannes Adrianus Bernardus van Buitenen, eds., trans. *Classical Hindu Mythology: A Reader in the Sanskrit Purāṇas*. Philadelphia: Temple University Press, 1978.

D'Sa, Francis Xavier, ed. *Word-Index to Bṛhadāraṇyaka Upaniṣad*. Pune: Institute for the Study of Religion, 1996.

Easwaran, Eknath, trans. *The Bhagavad Gita*. Tomales, CA: Nilgiri Press, 2007[2] (1985).

Eck, Diana L. *Darśan: Seeing the Divine Image in India*. New York: Columbia University Press, 1998[3].

Eco, Umberto. *Il nome della rosa*. Milan: Bompiani, 1980.

———. *The Name of the Rose*. Translated from the Italian by W. Weaver. New York: Warner Books, 1983.

Edelman, Jonathan. "*Bhāgavatapurāṇa*." In *Brill's Encyclopedia of Hinduism Online*, edited by K. A. Jacobsen, H. Basu, A. Malinar, and V. Narayanan. Leiden: Brill, 2018. https://referenceworks.brillonline.com/browse/brill-s-encyclopedia-of-hinduism.

Edgerton, Franklin. "The Hour of Death: Its Importance for Man's Future Fate in Hindu and Western Religions," *Annals of the Bhandarkar Oriental Research Institute* 8, no. 3 (1926–27): 219–49.

———, trans. *The Bhagavad Gītā*. New York: Harper Torchbooks—The Cloister Library, 1964 (1944).

Emeneau, Murray Barnson. "*Bhagavadgītā* Notes." In *Mélanges d'indianisme à la mémoire de Louis Renou*. Paris: Éditions de Boccard, 1968.

———. "The Composite Bow in India," *Proceedings of the American Philosophical Society* 97, 1 (1953): 77–87.

Ernout, Alfred, and Antoine Meillet. *Dictionnaire étymologique de la langue latine. Histoire des mots*. Paris: Klincksieck, 2001[5].

Feldhaus, Anne. "Kṛṣṇa and the Kṛṣṇas: Kṛṣṇa in the Mahānubhāva Pantheon." In *Bhakti in Current Research, 1979–1982*, edited by M. Thiel-Horstmann, 133–42. Berlin: Dietrich Reimer, 1983.

Feuerstein, Georg, and Brenda Feuerstein, trans. *The Bhagavad-Gītā: A New Translation*. With the Sanskrit Text, a Romanized Transliteration, a Word-for-Word Translation, and Extensive Notes and Supporting Essays. Boulder: Shambhala Publications, 2014 (2011).

Figueroa-Dorrego, Jorge, and Cristina Larkin-Galiñanes, eds. *A Source Book of Literary and Philosophical Writings about Humour and Laughter: The Seventy-Five Essential Texts from Antiquity to Modern Times*. Lewiston, NY: Edwin Mellen Press, 2009.

Filliozat, Pierre-Sylvain, "Le sourire dans la littérature sanscrite et la statuaire de l'Inde," *Comptes rendus des séances de l'Académie des Inscriptions et Belles-Lettres* 153, no. 4 (2009): 1629–54.

———. "Smile in Indian and Khmer Art," http://www.ignca.nic.in/Lectures_PDFs/pl_20121123_Smile_in_Indian_and_Khmer_Art.pdf.

Filliozat, Pierre-Sylvain, and Michel Zink. *Sourires d'Orient et d'Occident*. Paris: Académie des Inscriptions et Belles-Lettres, 2013.

Fitzgerald, James L. "*Mahābhārata*." In *Brill's Encyclopedia of Hinduism Online*, edited by K. A. Jacobsen, H. Basu, A. Malinar, and V. Narayanan. Leiden: Brill, 2018. https://referenceworks.brillonline.com/browse/brill-s-encyclopedia-of-hinduism.

Flood, Gavin, and Charles Martin, trans. *The Bhagavad Gita: A New Translation*. New York and London: W. W. Norton, 2013.

Fosse, Lars Martin, trans. *The Bhagavad Gita*. Woodstock, NY: YogaVidya, 2007.

Frame, Douglas. "Echoes of the Indo-European Twin Gods in Sanskrit and Greek Epic: Arjuna and Achilles;" https://chs.harvard.edu/CHS/article/display/5901.

Fraser, James Nelson, and K. B. Marathe, trans. *The Poems of Tukārāma*. With Notes and Introduction. Delhi: Motilal Banarsidass, 2000 (1909).

Freiberger, Oliver. *Considering Comparison: A Method for Religious Studies*. New York: Oxford University Press, 2019.

Gail, Adalbert J. *Bhakti im Bhāgavatapurāṇa. Religionsgeschichtliche Studie zur Idee der Gottesliebe in Kult und Mystik des Viṣṇuismus*. Wiesbaden: Otto Harrassowitz, 1969.

———. "Kṛṣṇa on the Banyan Leaf (*vaṭa-patra-śayana*)," *Pandanus* 8, no. 1 (2014): 31–45.

———. "The Enlightened Buddha and the Preaching Śiva: More Light on the Dakṣiṇāmūrti Icon." In *South Asian Archaeology 1999*. Proceedings of the Fifteenth International Conference of the European Association of South Asian Archaeologists, held at the Universiteit Leiden, 5–9 July 1999, edited by E. M. Raven, 457–62. Leiden: Brill, 2008.

Gallaher Branch, Robin. "Laughter in the Bible? Absolutely!" https://www.biblicalarchaeology.org/daily/biblical-topics/bible-interpretation/laughter-in-the-bible-absolutely/.

Gambhirananda, Swami, trans. *Bhagavad Gita. With the Annotation Gūḍārtha Dīpikā of Madhusudana Sarasvati*. Mayavati-Pithoragarh: Advaita Ashrama, 1998.

———. *Bhagavad Gītā with the Commentary of Śaṅkarācārya*. Kolkata: Advaita Ashram, 1995 (1984).

Ganser, Elisa. *Theatre and Its Other: Abhinavagupta on Dance and Dramatic Acting*. Leiden: Brill, 2022.

Gaonkar, Manik. "Contemporary Practices of *Chitrakathi* in the Twenty-first Century Art Market," *The Chitrolekha Journal on Art and Design* 2, no. 2 (2018): 40–46.

Garbutt, Kathleen, trans. *Mahābhārata. Book Five. Preparations for War*, Vol. 1. New York: New York University Press and the JJC Foundation, 2008.

Geetha, M. "Image of Siva Dakshinamurti in the Early Chola Temples: A Glance," *The Quarterly Journal of the Mythic Society* 103, no. 2 (2012): 74–85.

Ghosh, Manomohan. *Nandikeśvara's* Abhinayadarpaṇam*: A Manual of Gesture and Posture Used in Hindu Dance and Drama*. English Translation, Notes and the Text Critically Edited for the First Time from Original Manuscripts with Introduction. Calcutta: Firma K. L. Mukhopadhyay, 1957[2].

Gift, Kristine. "Sarah's Laughter as Her Lasting Legacy: An Interpretation of *Genesis* 18:9–15," Coe College, 2012; http://research.monm.edu/mjur/files/2019/02/MJUR-i02-2012-7-Gift.pdf.

Ginzburg, Jonathan, Ellen Breitholtz, Robin Cooper, Julian Hough, and Ye Tian. "Understanding Laughter." Proceedings of the 20th Amsterdam Colloquium, 2015. https://hal-univ-diderot.archives-ouvertes.fr/hal-01371396.

Gnoli, Raniero. *The Aesthetic Experience According to Abhinavagupta*. Varanasi: The Chowkhamba Sanskrit Series Office, 1985[3].

———, trans. *Il canto del beato (Bhagavadgītā)*. Turin: Unione Tipografico-Editrice Torinese, 1976.

Gode, Parshuram Krishna. "Nīlakaṇṭha Caturdhara, the Commentator of the *Mahābhārata*: His Genealogy and Descendants," *Annals of the Bhandarkar Oriental Research Institute* 23 (1942): 146–61.

Goldman, Robert E. "'*The Great War and Ancient Memory*:' Modern *Mahābhāratas* and the Limits of Cultural Translation," *Visual Anthropology* 5, no. 1 (1992): 87–96.

Goldman, Robert, and Sally J. Sutherland Goldman. *Devavāṇīpraveśikā. An Introduction to the Sanskrit Language*. Berkeley: Center for South Asia Studies, University of California, 2002.

———, trans. *The Rāmāyaṇa of Vālmīki. An Epic of Ancient India. Volume V: Sundarakāṇḍa*. Princeton, NJ: Princeton University Press, 1984. Reprint, Delhi: Motilal Banarsidass, 2007.

Gönc Moačanin, Klara. "The *Nāṭyaśāstra* as a (Distorting?) Mirror to the Epic/Purāṇic Mythic Image: The Question of Its Dating." In *Stages and Transitions: Temporal and Historical Frameworks in Epic and Purāṇic Literature*. Proceedings of the Second Dubrovnik International Conference on the Sanskrit Epics and Purāṇas, August 1999, edited by M. Brockington, 221–38. Zagreb: Croatian Academy of Sciences and Arts, 2002.

Gonda, Jan. *Medieval Religious Literature in Sanskrit*. Vol. 2, fasc. 1 of *A History of Indian Literature*. Wiesbaden: Otto Harrassowitz, 1977.

———. "The Significance of the Right Hand and the Right Side in Vedic Ritual," *Religion* 2 (1972): 1–23.

Goodman, Hananya, ed. *Between Jerusalem and Benares: Comparative Studies in Judaism and Hinduism*. Albany: State University of New York Press, 1994.

Gopinatha Rao, T. A. *Elements of Hindu Iconography, Vol. 1, Part 1*. Madras: Law Printing House, 1914.

Govindanātha. *Il Poema di Śaṅkara:* Śrīśaṅkarācāryacarita. Edited by M. Piantelli. Turin: Promolibri, 1994.

Granoff, Phyllis. "After Sinning: Some Thoughts on Remorse, Responsibility and the Remedies for Sin in Indian Religious Traditions." In *Sins and Sinners: Perspectives from Asian Religions*, edited by Ph. Granoff and K. Shinohara, 175–215. Leiden: Brill, 2012.

Greenblatt, Joan, and Matthew Greenblatt, eds. *Bhagavan Sri Ramana: A Pictorial Biography*. A Birth Centenary Offering. Tiruvannamalai: Sri Ramanasramam, 1985[2].

Grinshpon, Yohanan. *Silence Unheard: Deathly Otherness in Pātañjala-Yoga*. Albany: State University of New York Press, 2001.

Gupta, Mahendranath. *The Gospel of Sri Ramakrishna (Sri Sri Ramakrishna Kathamrita)*. Translated from the Bengali by Swami Nikhilananda. New York: Ramakrishna-Vivekananda Center, 1942.

Haas, George C. O. "Recurrent and Parallel Passages in the Principal *Upanishads* and the *Bhagavad-gītā* with References to Other Sanskrit Text." In *The Thirteen Principal Upanishads Translated from the Sanskrit. With an Outline of the Philosophy of the Upanishads and an Annotated Bibliography*, edited by R. E. Hume, 560–62. Madras: Geoffrey Cumberlege, Oxford University Press, 1949[2].

Haberman, David L. *The Bhaktirasāmṛtasindhu of Rūpa Gosvāmin*. Translated with Introduction and Notes. New Delhi: Indira Gandhi National Centre for the Arts—Motilal Banarsidass, 2003.

Halbfass, Wilhelm, ed. *Philology and Confrontation: Paul Hacker on Traditional and Modern Vedānta*. Albany: State University of New York Press, 1995.

Hale, Mark. "Some Notes on the Syntax of *iva* clauses in Vedic." https://www.researchgate.net/profile/Mark_Hale/publication/286626021_Some_Notes_on_the_Syntax_of_iva_Clauses_in_Vedic_Handout/links/566c9c0408ae1a797e3d9d85/Some-Notes-on-the-Syntax-of-iva-Clauses-in-Vedic-Handout.pdf.

Halliwell, Stephen. *Greek Laughter: A Study of Cultural Psychology from Homer to Early Christianity*. Cambridge: Cambridge University Press, 2008.

Hara, Minoru. "A Note on the Epic Phrase *jīvan-mukta*," *Adyar Library Bullettin* 60 (1996): 181–97.

———. "Note on Two Sanskrit Religious Terms: *bhakti* and *śraddhā*," *Indo-Iranian Journal* 7, no. 2/3 (1964): 132–45.

———. *Pāśupata Studies*. Edited by J. Takashima. Vienna: Sammlung De Nobili, 2002.

———. "Words for Love in Sanskrit," *Rivista degli Studi Orientali* 80, no. 1–4 (2007): 81–106.

Hart, George L. "Archetypes in Classical Indian Literature and Beyond." In *Syllables of Sky: Studies in South Asian Civilization in Honour of Velcheru Narayana Rao*, edited by D. Shulman, 165–82. Delhi: Oxford University Press, 1995.

Hawley, John Stratton. *At Play with Krishna: Pilgrimage Dramas from Brindavan*. In Association with Shrivatsa Goswami. Princeton, NJ: Princeton University Press, 1981.

———. *Krishna, the Butter Thief*. Princeton, NJ: Princeton University Press, 1983.

———. "Krishna's Cosmic Victories," *Journal of the American Academy of Religion* 47 (1979): 201–21.

Hawley, John Stratton, and Kimberley C. Patton, eds. *Holy Tears: Weeping in the Religious Imagination*. Princeton, NJ: Princeton University Press, 2005.

Hein, Norvin. *The Miracle Plays of Mathura*. New Haven, CT: Yale University Press, 1972.

Hejib, Alaka, and Katherine K. Young. "*Klība* on the Battlefield: Towards a Reinterpretation of Arjuna's Despondency," *Annals of the Bhandarkar Oriental Research Institute* 61 (1980): 235–44.

Hill, W. Douglas P., trans. *The Bhagavad-gītā: An English Translation and Commentary*. Madras: Oxford University Press, 1953[2] (1928).

Hiltebeitel, Alf. "Kṛṣṇa and the *Mahābhārata* (A Bibliographical Essay)," *Annals of the Bhandarkar Oriental Research Institute* 60, no. 1/4 (1979): 65–107.

———. "Kṛṣṇa in the *Mahābhārata*: The Death of Karṇa." In *Reading the Fifth Veda. Studies on the Mahābhārata. Essays by Alf Hiltebeitel*, edited by V. Adluri and J. Bagchee, 411–59. Leiden: Brill, 2011.

———. *Rethinking India's Oral and Classical Epics: Draupadī among Rajputs, Muslims, and Dalits*. Chicago and London: University of Chicago Press, 1999.

———. *Rethinking the Mahābhārata: A Reader's Guide to the Education of the Dharma King*. Chicago and London: University of Chicago Press, 2001.

———. *The Cult of Draupadī. 1 Mythologies: From Gingee to Kurukṣetra*. Chicago and London: University of Chicago Press, 1988.

———. *The Ritual of Battle: Krishna in the Mahābhārata*. Albany: State University of New York Press, 1990.

———. "The Two Kṛṣṇas on One Chariot: Upaniṣadic Imagery and Epic Mythology," *History of Religions* 24, no. 1 (1984): 1–26.

———, ed. *Criminal Gods and Demon Devotees: Essays on the Guardians of Popular Hinduism*. Albany: State University of New York Press, 1989.

Holdrege, Barbara. *Bhakti and Embodiment: Fashioning Divine Bodies and Devotional Bodies in Kṛṣṇa Bhakti*. New York: Routledge, 2015.

Hopkins, Edward Washburn. *Epic Mythology*. Delhi: Motilal Banarsidass, 1986 (1915).

Hospital, Clifford. "*Līlā* in Early Vaiṣṇava Thought." In *The Gods at Play: Līlā in South Asia*, edited by W. Sax, 21–34. New York: Oxford University Press, 1995.

Hudson, Dennis. "Arjuna's Sin: Thoughts on the *Bhagavad-gītā* in Its Epic Context," *Journal of Vaiṣṇava Studies* 4 (1996): 65–84.

Ingalls, Daniel H. H. "Cynics and Pāśupatas: The Seeking of Dishonor," *Harvard Theological Review* 55 (1962): 281–98.

Inglis, Stephen. "*Citrakathā*, Paintings, and Popular Prints." In *Brill's Encyclopedia of Hinduism Online*, edited by K. A. Jacobsen, H. Basu, A. Malinar, and V. Narayanan. Leiden: Brill, 2018. https://referenceworks.brillonline.com/browse/brill-s-encyclopedia-of-hinduism.

Jacobi, Hermann. "Über die Einfugüng der *Bhagavadgītā* im *Mahābhārata*," *Zeitschrift der Deutschen Morgenländischen Gesellschaft* 72 (1918): 323–27.

Jaffrelot, Christophe, ed. *L'Inde contemporaine de 1950 à nos jours*. Paris: Fayard / CERI, 2006.

Jain-Neubauer, Jutta. *Feet & Footwear in Indian Culture*. Toronto: The Bata Shoe Museum Foundation, 2000.

Jalālī Nā'īnī, M. R., ed. *Bhagawad Gītā. Surūd-i ilāhī*. Tehran: Tahūrī, 1980.

Ježić, Mislav. "Textual Layers of the *Bhagavadgītā* as Traces of Indian Cultural History." In *Sanskrit and World Culture*. Proceedings of the Fourth World Sanskrit Conference, Weimar, May, 23–30, 1979, edited by W. Morgenroth, 628–38. Berlin: Akademie Verlag, 1986.

———. "The Relationship Between the *Bhagavadgītā* and the Vedic *Upaniṣads*: Parallels and Relative Chronology." In *Epic Undertakings*, edited by R. P. Goldman and M. Tokunaga, 215–82. Delhi: Motilal Banarsidass, 2009.

Johnston Largen, Kristin. *Baby Krishna, Infant Christ: A Comparative Theology of Salvation*. Maryknoll, NY: Orbis Books, 2011.

Kalyana-Kalpataru. Gita-Tattva Number 1. Gorakhpur: Gita Press, 1946.

Kane, Pandurang Vaman. *History of Dharmaśāstra. Ancient and Medieval Religious and Civil Law in India*. Vol. 1, Part 1. Poona: Bhandarkar Oriental Research Institute, 1930.

Kato, Takahiro. "A Note on the Kashmirian Recension of the *Bhagavadgītā*: *Gītā* Passages in Bhāskara's *Gītābhāṣya* and *Brahmasūtrabhāṣya*," *Journal of Indian and Buddhist Studies* 62, no. 3 (2014): 1144–50.

———. "Interpretation of the *Bhagavadgītā* II.11," *Journal of Indian and Buddhist Studies* 64, no. 3 (2016): 1106–12.

Katz, Ruth Cecily. *Arjuna in the Mahabharata: Where Krishna Is, There Is Victory*. Columbia, SC: University of South Carolina Press, 1989.

King, Ursula. "Some Reflections on Sociological Approaches to the Study of Modern Hinduism," *Numen* 36, 1 (1989): 72–97.

———. "The Iconography of the *Bhagavad Gītā*," *Journal of Dharma* 7, no. 2 (1982): 146–63.

Kinsley, David R. *Hindu Goddesses: Visions of the Divine Feminine in the Hindu Religious Tradition*. Berkeley: University of California Press, 1988.

———. *The Divine Player (A Study of Kṛṣṇa Līlā)*. Delhi: Motilal Banarsidass, 1996.

———. *The Sword and the Flute. Kālī and Kṛṣṇa, Dark Visions of the Terrible and the Sublime in Hindu Mythology*. Berkeley: University of California Press, 1975.

Kramrisch, Stella. *Indian Sculpture*. London: Oxford University Press, 1933.

———. *The Presence of Śiva*. Princeton, NJ: Princeton University Press, 1981.

———, trans. *The Vishnudharmottara (Part III). A Treatise on Indian Painting and Image-Making*. Calcutta: Calcutta University Press, 1928[2].

Kripananda, Swami, trans. *Jnaneshwar's Gita*. Albany: State University of New York Press, 1989.

Krishna Sastri, H. *South-Indian Images of Gods and Goddesses*. Madras: Madras Government Press, 1916.

Laine, James W. *Visions of God: Narratives of Theophany in the Mahābhārata*. Vienna: Publications of the De Nobili Research Library, 1989.

Lal, Avantika. "Chariots in Ancient Indian Warfare." In *World History Encyclopedia* at https://www.worldhistory.org/article/1269/chariots-in-ancient-indian-warfare/ (published on October 2, 2018).

Lange, Gerrit. "Cobra Deities and Divine Cobras: The Ambiguous Animality of Nāgas," *Religions* 10, no. 8 (2019). https://doi.org/10.3390/rel10080454.

Lanman, Charles Rockwell. *A Sanskrit Reader: Text and Vocabulary and Notes*. Cambridge, MA: Harvard University Press, 1963 (1884).

Larson, Gerald James. "The Song Celestial: Two Centuries of the *Bhagavad Gītā* in English," *Philosophy East and West* 31, no. 4 (1981): 513–41.

Larson, Gerald James, and Eliot Deutsch, eds. *Interpreting Across Boundaries: New Essays in Comparative Philosophy*. Princeton, NJ: Princeton University Press, 1988.

Lefeber, Rosalind, trans. *The Rāmāyaṇa of Vālmīki. An Epic of Ancient India. Volume IV: Kiṣkindhākāṇḍa*. Princeton, NJ: Princeton University Press, 1984. Reprint, Delhi: Motilal Banarsidass, 2007.

Lester, Robert C. "Rāmānuja and Śrī-vaiṣṇavism: The Concept of *prapatti* or *śaraṇāgati*," *History of Religions* 5, no. 2 (1966): 266–82.

Lightfoot, Jessica. *Wonder and the Marvellous from Homer to the Hellenistic World*. Cambridge: Cambridge University Press, 2021.

Lipner, Julius J. "A God at Play? Reexamining the Concept of *Līlā* in Hindu Philosophy and Theology," *International Journal of Hindu Studies* 26 (2022): 283–326.

Lorenz, Konrad. *On Aggression*. Translated by M. K. Wilson. London and New York: Routledge, 1966.

Lorenzen, David N. *Praises to a Formless God: Nirguṇī Texts from North India*. Albany: State University of New York Press, 1996.

———. *The Kāpālikas and Kālāmukhas: Two Lost Śaivite Sects*. Berkeley and Los Angeles: University of California Press, 1972.

Lutgendorf, Philip. *Hanuman's Tale: The Messages of a Divine Monkey*. Oxford and New York: Oxford University Press, 2007.

———. *The Life of a Text: Performing the* Rāmcaritmānas *of Tulsidas*. Berkeley: University of California Press, 1991.

Lutjeharms, Rembert. "Rūpa Gosvāmī." In *Brill's Encyclopedia of Hinduism Online*, edited by K. A. Jacobsen, H. Basu, A. Malinar, and V. Narayanan. Leiden: Brill, 2018. https://referenceworks.brillonline.com/browse/brill-s-encyclopedia-of-hinduism.

Madhurananda, Swami, ed. *Bhagavad Gita. As Viewed by Swami Vivekananda*. Kolkata: Advaita Ashrama, 2022[10].

Magnone, Paolo. "*Tejas* Transactions in the Itihāsa-Purāṇa." In *The Churning of the Epics and Purāṇas*, edited by S. Brodbeck, A. Bowles, and A. Hiltebeitel, 341–65. New Delhi: Dev Publishers, 2018.

———. "The Development of *tejas* from the Vedas to the Purāṇas," *Wiener Zeitschrift für die Kunde Südasiens* 36 (1992): 137–47.

Mahadeva Sastry, Alladi, trans. *The Bhagavad Gita with the Commentary of Sri Sankaracharya*. Madras: Samata Books, 1977[7] (1897).

Mahadevan, Telliyavaram Mahadevan Ponnambalam. *The Hymns of Śaṅkara*. Madras: Ganesh & Co., 1970.

Mahadevan, Telliyavaram Mahadevan Ponnambalam, ed. *Preceptors of Advaita*. Secunderabad: Sri Kanchi Kamakoti Sankara Mandir, 1968. Reprint, Madras: Samata Books, 2003.

Maharishi Mahesh Yogi. *On the Bhagavad-Gita: A New Translation and Commentary. Chapters 1 to 6*. New York: Penguin, 1969.

Malamoud, Charles. *La Danse des pierres. Études sur la scène sacrificielle dans l'Inde ancienne*. Paris: Éditions du Seuil, 2005.

Malik, Aditya. "Bards and Reciters." In *Brill's Encyclopedia of Hinduism Online*, edited by K. A. Jacobsen, H. Basu, A. Malinar, and V. Narayanan. Leiden: Brill, 2018. https://referenceworks.brillonline.com/browse/brill-s-encyclopedia-of-hinduism.

Malinar, Angelika. "*Bhagavadgītā*." In *Brill's Encyclopedia of Hinduism Online*, edited by K. A. Jacobsen, H. Basu, A. Malinar, and V. Narayanan. Leiden: Brill, 2018. https://referenceworks.brillonline.com/browse/brill-s-encyclopedia-of-hinduism.

———. "Kṛṣṇa." In *Brill's Encyclopedia of Hinduism*. Vol. 1: *Regions, Pilgrimages, Deities*, edited by K. A. Jacobsen, H. Basu, A. Malinar, and V. Narayanan, 605–19. Leiden: Brill, 2009.

———. *The Bhagavadgītā: Doctrines and Contexts*. Cambridge: Cambridge University Press, 2007.

———. "The *Bhagavadgītā* in the *Mahābhārata* TV Serial: Domestic Drama and Dharmic Solutions." In *Representing Hinduism: The Construction of Religious Traditions and National Identity*, edited by V. Dalmia and H. von Stietencron, 442–67. New Delhi: SAGE, 1995.

———. "Yoga Powers in the *Mahābhārata*." In *Yoga Powers: Extraordinary Capacities Attained Through Meditation and Concentration*, edited by K. A. Jacobsen, 33–60. Leiden: Brill, 2012.

Mani, Vettam. *Purāṇic Encyclopaedia: A Comprehensive Dictionary with Special Reference to the Epic and Purāṇic Literature*. Delhi: Motilal Banarsidass, 1996 (1975).

Marasinghe, E. W. *The Sanskrit Theatre and Stagecraft*. Delhi: Sri Satguru, 1989.

Marchignoli, Saverio. "*Bhagavadgītābhāṣya* di Śaṅkara *ad* 18.66." In *Filosofie dell'India. Un'antologia di testi*, edited by F. Sferra, 233–35. Rome: Carocci, 2018.

Marjanovic, Boris, trans. *Abhinavagupta's Commentary on the Bhagavad Gita. Gītārtha Saṁgraha*. Varanasi: Indica, 2002.

Markschies, Christoph. *God's Body: Jewish, Christian, and Pagan Images of God*. Waco, TX: Baylor University Press, 2019.

Martin, Nancy M. "Grace and Compassion." In *Brill's Encyclopedia of Hinduism Online*, edited by K. A. Jacobsen, H. Basu, A. Malinar, and V. Narayanan. Leiden: Brill, 2013. https://referenceworks.brillonline.com/browse/brill-s-encyclopedia-of-hinduism.

Mascaró, Juan, trans. *The Bhagavad Gita*. New York: Penguin, 1978 (1962).

Mason, David V. *Theatre and Religion on Krishna's Stage: Performing in Vrindavan*. New York: Palgrave Macmillan, 2009.

Mason, Peggy, Sandra Lévy, and M. Veeravahu, eds. *Sai Humour*. Prasanthi Nilayam: Sri Sathya Sai Towers Hotels, 1999.

Matilal, Bimal Krishna. "Kṛṣṇa: In Defence of a Devious Divinity." In *The Collected Essays of Bimal Krishna Matilal. Philosophy, Culture and Religion. Ethics and Epics*, edited by J. Ganeri, 91–108. Oxford and New York: Oxford University Press, 2002.

Maurer, Walter Harding. *The Sanskrit Language: An Introductory Grammar and Reader*. Rev. ed. London and New York: Routledge, 2009.

McDaniel, June E. "Kālī." In *Brill's Encyclopedia of Hinduism*. Vol. 1: *Regions, Pilgrimages, Deities*, edited by K. A. Jacobsen, H. Basu, A. Malinar, and V. Narayanan, 587–604. Leiden: Brill, 2009.

McGrath, Kevin. *The Sanskrit Hero. Karṇa in Epic Mahābhārata*. Leiden: Brill, 2004.

Meyer-Dinkgräfe, Daniel. "Comedy, Consciousness and the *Natyasastra*." In *The Natyasastra and the Body in Performance: Essays on Indian Theories of Dance and Drama*, edited by S. Nair, 89–98. Jefferson, NC: McFarland & Company, 2015.

Minnema, Lourens. *Tragic Views of the Human Condition: Cross-Cultural Comparisons Between Views of Human Nature in Greek and Shakespearean Tragedy and the Mahābhārata and Bhagavadgītā*. New York: Bloomsbury, 2013.

Minor, Robert N. "Krishna in the *Bhagavad Gita*." In *Krishna: A Sourcebook*, edited by E. F. Bryant, 77–94. New York: Oxford University Press, 2007.

———, ed. *Modern Indian Interpreters of the Bhagavad Gita*. Albany: State University of New York Press, 1986.

———, trans. *Bhagavad-Gita: An Exegetical Commentary*. Columbia, MO: South Asia Books, 1982.

Mitchell, Stephen, trans. *Bhagavad Gita: A New Translation*. New York: Harmony, 2000.

Monier-Williams, Monier. *Religious Thought and Life in India. An Account of the Religions of the Indian Peoples, Based on a Life's Study of Their Literature and on Personal Investigations in Their Own Country. Part 1: Vedism, Brāhmanism, and Hindūism*. London: John Murray, 1883.

———. *Sanskrit-English Dictionary*. New Delhi: Munshiram Manoharlal, 1988^3 (1899).

Morreall, John, ed. *The Philosophy of Laughter and Humor*. Albany: State University of New York Press, 1986.

Mucciarelli, Elena. "The Steadiness of a Non-steady Place: Re-adaptations of the Imagery of the Chariot." In *Adaptive Reuse: Aspects of Creativity in South Asian Cultural History*, edited by E. Freschi and P. A. Maas, 169–94. Wiesbaden: Harrassowitz, 2017.

Mujtabai, Fathollah. *Aspects of Hindu-Muslim Cultural Relations*. Delhi: Zakir Husain Educational and Cultural Foundation, 1978.

Mukundananda, Swami, trans. *Bhagavad Gita: The Song of God*, 2014. https://www.holy-bhagavad-gita.org.

Nair, Bhaskaran S., ed. *Vaidika-pādānukrama-koṣaḥ (A Vedic Word-Concordance). Saṃhitā-bhāgaḥ (Saṃhitās section)*. Part IV (*pa-la*). Hoshiarpur: Vishveshvaranand Vedic Research Institute, 1992.

———. *Vaidika-pādānukrama-koṣaḥ (A Vedic Word-Concordance). Vedāṅga-bhāgaḥ (Vedāṅga section)*. Part III (*pa-la*). Hoshiarpur: Vishveshvaranand Vedic Research Institute, 1996.

———. *Vaidika-pādānukrama-koṣaḥ (A Vedic Word-Concordance). Vedāṅga-bhāgaḥ (Vedāṅga section).* Part IV (*va-ha*). Hoshiarpur: Vishveshvaranand Vedic Research Institute, 1994.

Nanda, Serena. *Neither Man nor Woman: The Hijras of India.* Toronto: Wadsworth, 1999.

Narayan, Kirin. *Storytellers, Saints, and Scoundrels: Folk Narrative in Hindu Religious Teaching.* Philadelphia: University of Pennsylvania Press, 1989.

Narayan, Rasipuram Krishnaswami. *The Mahabharata: A Shortened Modern Prose Version of the Indian Epic.* London: Mandarin, 1978.

Nataraja Guru, trans. *The Bhagavad Gita.* Bombay: Asia Publishing House, 1961.

Nikhilananda, Swami, trans. *Self-Knowledge: An English Translation of Śaṅkarācārya's Ātmabodha with Notes, Comments, and Introduction.* Madras: Sri Ramakrishna Math, 1947[10].

———. *The Bhagavad Gita.* New York: Ramakrishna-Vivekananda Center, 1944.

Nikolaev, Alexander. "Deep Waters: The Etymology of Vedic *gabhīrá-*," *Historische Sprachforschung* 132 (2019 [2021]): 191–207.

Nilakantan, Ratnam. *Gītās in the Mahābhārata and Purāṇas.* Delhi: Nag, 1989.

Novetzke, Christian Lee. *The Quotidian Revolution: Vernacularization, Religion, and the Premodern Public Sphere in India.* New York: Columbia University Press, 2016.

O'Flaherty, Wendy Doniger. *Hindu Myths: A Sourcebook Translated from the Sanskrit.* Harmondsworth, UK: Penguin, 1975.

———. "Inside and Outside the Mouth of God: The Boundary Between Myth and Reality," *Daedalus* 109, no. 2 (1980): 93–125.

Okada, Amina. *Sculptures indiennes du musée Guimet.* Paris: Trésors du musée Guimet—Réunion des musées nationaux, 2000.

Olivelle, Patrick. "Contributions to the Semantic History of *saṃnyāsa*." In *Collected Essays II. Ascetics and Brahmins: Studies in Ideologies and Institutions*, 127–43. Florence: Firenze University Press, 2008.

———, trans. *Upaniṣads.* New York: Oxford University Press, 1998.

Olson, Carl. "*Līlā*." In *Hinduism and Tribal Religions. Encyclopedia of Indian Religions*, edited by J. D. Long, R. D. Sherma, P. Jain, and M. Khanna. Dordrecht: Springer, 2022. https://doi.org/10.1007/978-94-024-1188-1_87K.

Orsini, Francesca, and Katherine Butler Schofield, eds. *Tellings and Texts: Music, Literature and Performance in North India.* Cambridge, UK: Open Book, 2015.

Osho. *Inner War and Peace: Timeless Solutions to Conflict from the Bhagavad Gita.* London: Watkins, 2005 (1970).

Otto, Rudolf. *The Idea of the Holy. An Inquiry into the Non-Rational Factor in the Idea of the Divine and Its Relation to the Rational.* Translated by J. W. Harvey. London: Oxford University Press, 1950[2] (1923).

Packert, Cynthia. *The Art of Loving Krishna: Ornamentation and Devotion.* Bloomington and Indianapolis: Indiana University Press, 2010.

Panikkar, Raimon. *Lo spirito della parola.* Turin: Bollati Boringhieri, 2021.

———. *Myth, Faith and Hermeneutics: Cross-cultural Studies.* Toronto: Paulist, 1979.

Parodi, Massimo. "Disarmonia. Una causa del riso da Umberto Eco al Medioevo," *I castelli di Yale online* 5, no. 2 (2017): 267–77. https://cyonline.unife.it/article/view/1540.

Patterson, Jessica. *Religion, Enlightenment and Empire: British Interpretations of Hinduism in the Eighteenth Century.* Cambridge: Cambridge University Press, 2021.

Pauwels, Heidi. "Rādhā." In *Brill's Encyclopedia of Hinduism Online,* edited by K. A. Jacobsen, H. Basu, A. Malinar, and V. Narayanan. Leiden: Brill, 2018. https://referenceworks.brillonline.com/browse/brill-s-encyclopedia-of-hinduism.

Pelissero, Alberto. *Estetica indiana.* Brescia: Morcelliana, 2019.

———. *Il riso e la pula. Vie di salvezza nello śivaismo del Kaśmīr.* Alessandria: Edizioni dell'Orso, 1998.

Pellegrini, Gianni. "Old is Gold! Madhusūdana Sarasvatī's Way of Referring to Earlier Textual Tradition," *Journal of Indian Philosophy* 43, no. 23 (2015): 277–334.

———. "On the Alleged Indebtedness of the *Vedānta Paribhāṣā* Towards the *Vedānta Kaumudī*: Some Considerations on an Almost Forgotten Vivaraṇa text (Studies in *Vedānta Kaumudī* I)," *Journal of Indian Philosophy* 44, no. 3 (2016): 485–505.

———. "Śiva, l'icona del tempo." In *Miti stellari e cosmogonici. Dall'India al Nuovo Mondo,* edited by M. Marchetto, 289–316. Rimini: Il Cerchio, 2012.

Pellegrini, Gianni, and Francesco Sferra. "*Tarkabhāṣā.*" In *Filosofie dell'India. Un'antologia di testi,* edited by F. Sferra, 83–92, 279–319. Rome: Carocci Editore, 2018.

Pellò, Stefano. "Black Curls in a Mirror: The Eighteenth-Century Persian Kṛṣṇa of Lāla Amānat Rāy's *Jilwa-yi ẓāt* and the Tongue of Bīdil," *International Journal of Hindu Studies* 22, no. 1 (2018): 71–103.

Peterson-Viswanathan, Indira. *Design and Rhetoric in a Sanskrit Court Epic: The Kīrātārjunīya of Bhāravi.* Albany: State University of New York Press, 2003.

Philpot, Joshua M. "*Exodus* 34:29–35 and Moses' Shining Face," *Bulletin for Biblical Research* 23, no. 1 (2013): 1–11.

Piano, Stefano, trans. *Bhagavadgītā (Il Canto del Glorioso Signore)*. Cinisello Balsamo: Edizioni San Paolo, 1994. Reprint, Turin: Magnanelli, 2017.

Piantelli, Mario. "Aspetti della preghiera dell'India." In *L'uomo davanti a Dio. La preghiera nelle religioni e nella tradizione cristiana*, edited by E. Guerriero, 34–89. Cinisello Balsamo: Edizioni San Paolo, 1998.

———. "La concezione del tempo nell'esperienza dell'Induismo. Spunti di riflessione." In *Tempo e Apocalisse.* Atti dell'incontro del 19–20 settembre 1981 al monastero di Montebello, edited by S. Quinzio, 117–56. Milazzo: SPES, 1985.

———. "Lo Hinduismo. I. Testi e dottrine." In *Storia delle religioni. 4. Religioni dell'India e dell'Estremo Oriente*, edited by G. Filoramo, 49–131. Bari: Laterza, 1996.

———. "Nota sulla '*Bhagavadgītā*.'" In *Bhagavadgītā*, edited by A.-M. Esnoul, 179–96. Milan: Adelphi, 1996[4] (1976).

———. *Śaṅkara e la rinascita del brāhmanesimo*. Fossano: Editrice Esperienze, 1974.

Pierdominici Leão, David Paolo. *The* Somavallīyogānandaprahasana *of Aruṇagirinātha Ḍiṇḍimakavi (critical text, translation and study)*. PhD diss., Rome: Università "La Sapienza," 2018.

Pillai, Sohini Sarah. *Krishna's Mahabharatas: Devotional Retellings of an Epic Narrative*. New York: Oxford University Press, 2024.

Pinault, Georges-Jean. "On the Usages of the Particle *iva* in the Ṛgvedic Hymns." In *The Vedas: Texts, Language and Ritual.* Proceedings of the Third International Vedic Workshop, Leiden 2002, edited by A. Griffiths and J. E. M. Houben, 285–306. Groningen: Egbert Forsten, 2004.

Plessner, Helmuth. *Laughing and Crying: A Study of the Limits of Human Behavior*. Translated by J. Spencer Churchill and M. Grene. Evanston, IL: Northwestern University Press, 2020.

Pollock, Sheldon, trans. *The Rāmāyaṇa of Vālmīki. An Epic of Ancient India. Volume II: Ayodhyākāṇḍa*. Princeton, NJ: Princeton University Press, 1984. Reprint, Delhi: Motilal Banarsidass, 2007.

———, ed., trans. *A Rasa Reader: Classical Indian Aesthetics*. New York: Columbia University Press, 2016.

Potter, Karl H. *Bibliography. Encyclopedia of Indian Philosophies*. Vol. 1. Delhi: Motilal Banarsidass, 1995 (1970).

———. *Philosophy of Pūrva-mīmāṃsā. Encyclopedia of Indian Philosophies*. Vol. 16. Delhi: Motilal Banarsidass, 2014.

———. *Presuppositions of India's Philosophies*. Delhi: Motilal Banarsidass, 1991.

Prabhavananda, Swami, and Christopher Isherwood, trans. *The Song of God: Bhagavad-Gita*. With an Introduction by Aldous Huxley. New York: The New American Library, 1958[5] (1944).

Prabhupāda, Abhay Caranaravinda Bhaktivedanta Swami, trans. *Bhagavad-gītā As It Is*. New York: The Bhaktivedanta Book Trust, 1976 (1968).

Preciado-Solis, Benjamin. *The Kṛṣṇa Cycle in the Purāṇas: Themes and Motifs in a Heroic Saga*. Delhi: Motilal Banarsidass, 1984.

Prentiss, Karen Pechilis. *The Embodiment of Bhakti*. New York and Oxford: Oxford University Press, 2000.

Pritchett, Frances W. "The World of *Amar Chitra Katha*." In *Media and the Transformation of Religion in South Asia*, edited by L. A. Babb and S. S. Wadley, 76–106. Philadelphia: University of Pennsylvania Press, 1995.

Radhakrishnan, Sarvepalli, trans. *Bhagavadgītā*. London: George Allen & Unwin, 1963[7] (1948).

Raghavachar, Singra Srinivasa. *Śrī Rāmānuja on the Gītā*. Mayavati: Advaita Ashram, 1990 (1969).

Raghavan, Venkataraman. *Readings from the Bhagavadgītā*. Adyar, Chennai: Dr. V. Raghavan Centre for Performing Arts, 2010.

———. *Studies on Some Concepts of the Alaṃkāra Śāstra*. Adyar, Madras: The Adyar Library, 1942.

———. *The Concept of the Beautiful in Sanskrit Literature*. Chennai: The Kuppuswami Sastri Research Institute, 2008 (1988).

Raj, Selva J., and Corinne G. Dempsey, eds. *Sacred Play: Ritual Levity and Humor in South Asian Religions*. Albany: State University of New York Press, 2010.

Ramachandra Rao, S. K. *Vishṇu-Kosha*. Bangalore: Kalpatharu Research Academy, 1998.

Raman, Srilata. *Self-Surrender (*prapatti*) to God in Śrīvaiṣṇavism: Tamil Cats and Sanskrit Monkeys*. London and New York: Routledge, 2007.

Ramana Maharshi, Shri. *Opere*. Rome: Ubaldini, 2012.

Ramaratnam, S. *Sanskrit Drama: With Special Reference to Prahasana and Vīthī*. New Delhi: D. K. Printworld, 2014.

Ravasi, Gianfranco. *I salmi. Introduzione, testo e commento*. Cinisello Balsamo: Edizioni San Paolo, 2006[3].

Rāy, Rāmkumār. *Mahābhāratakośaḥ*. Vārāṇasī: Caukhamba Sanskrit Series Office, 1982.

Rhys Davids, Thomas William, and William Stede, eds. *The Pali Text Society's Pali-English Dictionary*. London, Henley and Boston: Routledge & Kegan Paul, 1986 (1921–25).

Rigopoulos, Antonio. "Declinazioni della compassione nella *Bhagavad-gītā*: da vile debolezza del cuore a virtù suprema." In *Religioni e compassione*, edited by M. Dal Corso, 71–97. Villa Verucchio: Pazzini, 2023.

———. *Guru. Il fondamento della civiltà dell'India*. Con la prima traduzione italiana del "Canto sul Maestro." Rome: Carocci, 2009.

———. *Hindūismo*. Brescia: Queriniana, 2005.

———. "La *Bhagavadgītā*." In *Hinduismo antico. Volume primo. Dalle origini vediche ai Purāṇa*, edited by F. Sferra, CLXXIII-CXCII, 1500–1504. Milan: Mondadori, 2010.

———. "Negazioni e silenzi sotto i cieli dell'India. Orizzonti upaniṣadici e buddhisti a confronto." In *Forme della negazione. Un percorso interculturale tra Oriente ed Occidente*, edited by L. Marcato, 101–17. Milan: Mimesis, 2015.

———. *Oral Testimonies on Sai Baba. As Gathered During a Field Research in Shirdi and Other Locales in October-November 1985*. Venice: Edizioni Ca' Foscari, 2020.

———. "Sorrisi e silenzi nell'Induismo e nel Buddhismo. Dimensioni apofatiche a confronto nella riflessione di Raimon Panikkar." In *Le pratiche del dialogo dialogale. Scritti su Raimon Panikkar*, edited by M. Ghilardi and S. La Mendola, 287–304. Milan: Mimesis, 2020.

———. *The Hagiographer and the Avatar: The Life and Works of Narayan Kasturi*. Albany: State University of New York Press, 2021.

———. *The Life and Teachings of Sai Baba of Shirdi*. Albany: State University of New York Press, 1993.

Robinson, Catherine A. *Interpretations of the* Bhagavad-Gītā *and Images of the Hindu Tradition: The Song of the Lord*. London and New York: Routledge, 2006.

Rocher, Ludo. "*Bhagavadgītā* 2.20 and *Kaṭhopaniṣad* 2.18: A New Interpretation," *The Adyar Library Bulletin* 27 (1963): 45–58.

Rosen, Steven J., ed. *Vaiṣṇavism: Contemporary Scholars Discuss the Gauḍīya Tradition*. New York: FOLK Books, 1992.

Rossella, Daniela. "Satire, Wit and Humour on Kings and Ascetics in *kāvya* Literature: «He who laughs last, laughs best»." In *Kings and Ascetics in Indian Classical Literature*. International Seminar Proceedings, 21–22 September 2007, edited by P. M. Rossi and C. Pieruccini, 117–33. Milan: Cisalpino, 2009.

Roy, Kaushik. *Hinduism and the Ethics of Warfare in South Asia: From Antiquity to the Present*. Cambridge: Cambridge University Press, 2012.

Roychaudhary, M. L. "The *Bhagavad Gītā* in Persian," *Proceedings of the Indian History Congress, 1956*, 19 (1956): 260–63.

Saha, Niranjan. "Vedāntic Commentaries on the *Bhagavadgītā* as a Component of Three Canonical Texts (*prasthāna-trayī*)," *Journal of Indian Philosophy* 45, no. 2 (2017): 257–80.

Sand, Erik Reenberg. "*Mātāpitṛbhakti*: Some Aspects of the Development of the Puṇḍalīka Legend in Marathi Literature." In *Devotional Literature in South Asia: Current Research, 1985–1988*, edited by R. S. McGregor, 138–47. Cambridge: Cambridge University Press, 1992.

———. "Pandharpur and Vitthal." In *Oxford Bibliographies in Hinduism*. New York: Oxford University Press, 2019. https://www.oxfordbibliographies.com.

Sargeant, Winthrop, trans. *The Bhagavad Gītā*. Edited by Christopher Key Chapple. Albany: State University of New York Press, 2009 (1984).

Sarkar, H. *An Architectural Survey of Temples of Kerala*. New Delhi: Archaeological Survey of India, 1978.

Sarkar, Mahendra Nath. "The *Bhagavad Gītā*: Its Early Commentaries." In *Cultural Heritage of India*, 2:190–203. Calcutta: Ramakrishna Mission Institute of Culture, 1975.

Sathya Sai Baba. *Sathya Sai Speaks, Vol. 1. Discourses of Bhagawan Sri Sathya Sai Baba (Delivered during 1953–1960)*. Prasanthi Nilayam: Sri Sathya Sai Sadhana Trust, 2015.

Satkunaratnam, Ahalya. "Dance: Classical Tradition." In *Brill's Encyclopedia of Hinduism Online*, edited by K. A. Jacobsen, H. Basu, A. Malinar, and V. Narayanan. Leiden: Brill, 2018. https://referenceworks.brillonline.com/browse/brill-s-encyclopedia-of-hinduism.

Sax, William S. "Fathers, Sons, and Rhinoceroses: Masculinity and Violence in the *Pāṇḍav līlā*," *Journal of the American Oriental Society* 117, no. 2 (1997): 278–93.

Schultz, Anna C. *Singing a Hindu Nation: Marathi Devotional Performance and Nationalism*. New York: Oxford University Press, 2013.

Schwartz, Susan L. *Rasa: Performing the Divine in India*. New York: Columbia University Press, 2004.

Schweig, Graham. "*Līlā*." In *Brill's Encyclopedia of Hinduism Online*, edited by K. A. Jacobsen, H. Basu, A. Malinar, and V. Narayanan. Leiden: Brill, 2018. https://referenceworks.brillonline.com/browse/brill-s-encyclopedia-of-hinduism.

———, trans. *Bhagavad Gita: The Beloved Lord's Secret Love Song*. San Francisco: Harper, 2007.

Sellmer, Sven. *Formulaic Diction and Versification in the Mahābhārata*. Poznań: Adam Mickiewicz University Press, 2015.

Seybold, Klaus, Martin Jacobs, and Don E. Saliers. "Aaronic Blessing." In *Religion Past and Present. Encyclopedia of Theology and Religion*. Leiden: Brill Online 2011. http://dx.doi.org/10.1163/1877-5888_rpp_COM_00010.

Sferra, Francesco. "Introduzione." In *Filosofie dell'India. Un'antologia di testi*, edited by F. Sferra, 68–70. Rome: Carocci, 2018.

Shapiro Hawley, Nell, and Sohini Sarah Pillai, eds. *Many Mahābhāratas*. Albany: State University of New York Press, 2021.

Sharma, B. N. Krishnamurti. *History of the Dvaita School of Vedānta and Its Literature*. Bombay 1961. Reprint, Delhi: Motilal Banarsidass, 1981.

Sharma, Har Dutt. "*Hāsya* as a *rasa* in Sanskrit Rhetoric and Literature," *Annals of the Bhandarkar Oriental Research Institute* 22, no. 1/2 (1941): 103–15.

Sheridan, Daniel P. *The Advaitic Theism of the Bhāgavata Purāṇa*. Delhi: Motilal Banarsidass, 1986.

Shirdi Diary of the Hon'ble Mr. G. S. Khaparde. Bombay: Shri Sai Baba Sansthan, n.d.

Shulman, David Dean. *More than Real: A History of the Imagination in South India*. Cambridge, MA: Harvard University Press, 2012.

———. *The King and the Clown in South Indian Myth and Poetry*. Princeton, NJ: Princeton University Press, 1985.

Siegel, Lee. *Laughing Matters: Comic Tradition in India*. Delhi: Motilal Banarsidass, 1989.

———, trans. *Gītagovinda: Love Songs of Rādhā and Kṛṣṇa by Jayadeva*. New York: Clay Sanskrit Library, 2009.

Sivananda, Swami, trans. *The Bhagavad Gita*. Shivanandanagar: The Divine Life Society, 1996^3 (1979).

Sivaramamurti, Calambur. *Rishis in Indian Art and Literature*. New Delhi: Kanak, 1981.

Sloterdijk, Peter. *You Must Change Your Life: On Anthropotechnics*. Translated by W. Hoban. Cambridge: Polity, 2013.

Smart, Ninian. *The Religious Experience of Mankind*. New York: Charles Scribner's Sons, 1976^2.

———. *Worldviews: Crosscultural Explorations of Human Beliefs*. New York: Charles Scribner's Sons, 1983.

Smoak, Jeremy D. "The Priestly Blessing in Inscription and Scripture: The Early History of *Numbers* 6:24–26," *Oxford Scholarship Online*, October 2015. https://academic.oup.com/book/10129.

Spink, Walter M. *Krishnamandala: A Devotional Theme in Indian Art*. Ann Arbor: University of Michigan, 1971.

Srinivasan, Doris Meth. *Many Heads, Arms and Eyes*. Leiden: Brill, 1997.

Stavrakopoulou, Francesca. *God: An Anatomy*. New York: Alfred A. Knopf, 2021.

Steinmann, Ralph Marc. *Guru-śiṣya-sambandha. Das Meister-Schüler-Verhältnis im Traditionellen und Modernen Hinduismus*. Stuttgart: Steiner Verlag Wiesbaden GMBH, 1986.

Stella, Marie. *The Significance of the* Mūla Beras *in the Hindu Temples of Tamil Nadu with Special Reference to Bharatanatyam and Hindu Iconography*. PhD diss., Tiruchirapalli: Kalai Kaviri College of Fine Arts, 2009.

Stoler Miller, Barbara, trans. *The Bhagavad-Gita: Krishna's Counsel in Time of War*. New York: Bantam, 1986.

Stroumsa, Guy. *Le rire du Christ. Essais sur le christianisme antique*. Paris: Bayard, 2006.

Sullivan, Bruce M. "Kerala's *Mahābhārata* on Stage: Texts and Performative Practices in Kūṭiyāṭṭam Drama," *The Journal of Hindu Studies* 3, no. 1 (2010): 124–42.

Swarupananda, Swami, trans. *Srimat-Bhagavad-Gita*. Calcutta: Advaita Ashrama, 1967[10] (1909).

Tarlekar, Ganesh Hari. *Studies in the Nāṭyaśāstra: With Special Reference to the Sanskrit Drama in Performance*. Delhi: Motilal Banarsidass, 1999 (1975).

Telang, Kāshināth Trimbak, trans. *The Bhagavadgītā with the Sanatsujātīya and the Anugītā*. Oxford: Clarendon, 1908[2] (1882).

Thangaswami, R. *Advaita Vedānta Literature. A Bibliographical Survey*. Madras: University of Madras, 1980.

Thapliyal, U. P. *Chariot in Indian History*. New York: Routledge, 2023.

Theodor, Ithamar, ed. *The Bhagavad-gītā: A Critical Introduction*. London and New York: Routledge, 2021.

Torella, Raffaele. "Beauty." In *Burlesque of the Philosophers: Indian and Buddhist Studies in Memory of Helmut Krasser*, edited by V. Eltschinger, J. Kramer, P. Patil, Ch. Yoshimizu, 2:755–80. Hamburg: Numata Center for Buddhist Studies, 2023.

"Traditional Tales: Anger Should Subside," *Prabuddha Bharata or Awakened India. A monthly journal of the Ramakrishna Order started by Swami Vivekananda in 1896*, 122, no. 2 (2017): 331–32.

Tripurari, B. V. Swami, trans. *Bhagavad Gita: Its Feeling and Philosophy*. San Rafael, CA: Mandala Publishing, 2010.

Tritle, Lawrence. "Laughter in Battle." In *The Many Faces of War in the Ancient World*, edited by W. Heckel, S. Müller and G. Wrightson, 117–34. Cambridge: Cambridge Scholars Publishing, 2015.

Trueblood, Elton. *The Humor of Christ*. New York: Harper & Row, 1964.

Truschke, Audrey. "The Mughal *Book of War*: A Persian Translation of the Sanskrit *Mahabharata*," *Comparative Studies of South Asia, Africa and the Middle East* 31, 2 (2011): 500–20.

Tschannerl, Volker M. *Das Lachen in der altindischen Literatur*. Frankfurt: Peter Lang, 1992.

Tubb, Gary A., and Emery R. Boose. *Scholastic Sanskrit: A Handbook for Students*. New York: American Institute of Buddhist Studies, Columbia University Press, 2007.

Uskokov, Aleksandar. "Nimbārka." In *Hinduism and Tribal Religions. Encyclopedia of Indian Religions*, edited by J. D. Long, R. D. Sherma, P. Jain, and M. Khanna. Dordrecht: Springer, 2018. https://doi.org/10.1007/978-94-024-1036-5_282-1.

———. "The Soteriology of Devotion, Divine Grace, and Teaching: *Bhagavadgītā* and the Śrīvaiṣṇavas." In *The Bhagavad-gītā: A Critical Introduction*, edited by I. Theodor, 68–79. London and New York: Routledge, 2021.

Valpey, Kenneth. "*Pūja* and *darśana*." In *Brill's Encyclopedia of Hinduism*. Vol. 2: *Sacred Texts and Languages, Ritual Traditions, Arts, Concepts*, edited by K. A. Jacobsen, H. Basu, A. Malinar, and V. Narayanan, 380–94. Leiden: Brill, 2010.

van Buitenen, Johannes Adrianus Bernardus, ed., trans. *The Bhagavadgītā in the Mahābhārata: Text and Translation*. Chicago and London: University of Chicago Press, 1981.

Vassie, Roderic. *Persian Interpretations of the* Bhagavadgītā *in the Mughal Period: With Special Reference to the Sufi Version of 'Abd al-Raḥmān Chishtī*. London: School of Oriental and African Studies, 1988.

Vasugupta. *Gli aforismi di Śiva con il commento di Kṣemarāja (Śivasūtravimarśinī)*, edited by R. Torella. Milan: Adelphi, 2013.

Venkatesananda, Swami, trans. *The Song of God (Bhagavad Gita)*. Daily Readings. Elgin, South Africa: The Chiltern Yoga Trust, 1984[4] (1972).

Vireswarananda, Swami, trans. *Srimad-Bhagavad-Gita*. Text, Translation of the Text and of the Gloss of Sridhara Swami. Mylapore: Sri Ramakrishna Math, 1991 (1948).

Visuvalingam, Sunthar. "*Hāsa* and *Hāsya* Distinguished in *Rasa*-Theory." http://www.infinityfoundation.com/mandala/i_es/i_es_visuv_cha_7.htm.

———. "The Transgressive Sacrality of the Dīkṣita: Sacrifice, Criminality and *Bhakti* in the Hindu Tradition." In *Criminal Gods and Demon Devotees: Essays on the Guardians of Popular Hinduism*, edited by A. Hiltebeitel, 427–62. Albany: State University of New York Press, 1989.

Vitsaxis, Vassilis G. *Hindu Epics, Myths and Legends in Popular Illustrations*. New Delhi: Oxford University Press, 1977.

Vivekananda, Swami. *Thoughts on the Gita*. Calcutta: Advaita Ashrama, 1995[14].

Vollkommer, Rainer. "Gelos." In *Lexicon Iconographicum Mythologiae Classicae*. Vol. 4.1, 179. Zürich-München: Artemis, 1988.

Wacławczyk, Aleksandra, and Adam Mickiewicz. "What is Aphrodite Laughing at? An Attempt at Interpretation of the Epithet φιλομμειδής in the Archaic Greek Poetry." In *Święto—Zabawa—Uroczystość w świecie starożytnym (Feast—Play—Celebration in the Ancient World)*, edited by L. Ożarowska, K. Sekita and J. Simo, 133–41. Warsaw: Wydawniktwo Naukowe Sub Lupa, 2011.

Watson, Walter. *The Lost Second Book of Aristotle's "Poetics."* Chicago and London: University of Chicago Press, 2012.

Wilkins, Charles, trans. *The Bhagvat-Geeta or Dialogues of Kreeshna and Arjoon*. London: C. Nourse, 1785.

Wilson, Frances, ed. *The Love of Krishna*. The *Kṛṣṇakarṇāmṛta* of Līlāśuka Bilvamaṅgala. Philadelphia: University of Pennsylvania Press, 1975.

Wujastyk, Dominik. "The Love of Kṛṣṇa in Poems and Paintings." In *Pearls of the Orient: Asian Treasures from the Wellcome Library*, edited by N. Allan, 87–105. London and Chicago: Serindia, 2003.

Wulff, Donna Marie. "Rādhā: Consort and Conquerer of Krishna." In *Devī: Goddesses of India*, edited by J. S. Hawley and D. M. Wulff, 109–33. Berkeley: University of California Press, 1996.

Zaehner, Robert Charles, trans. *The Bhagavad-Gītā*. London: Oxford University Press, 1973.

Zarrilli, Phillip. "Martial Arts (*Dhanurveda*)." In *Brill's Encyclopedia of Hinduism Online*, edited by K. A. Jacobsen, H. Basu, A. Malinar, and V. Narayanan. Leiden: Brill, 2018. https://referenceworks.brillonline.com/browse/brill-s-encyclopedia-of-hinduism.

Zimmer, Heinrich. *Myths and Symbols of Indian Art and Civilization*, edited by J. Campbell. New York: Pantheon, 1946.

Zubko, Katherine C. "Dancing the *Bhagavadgītā*: Embodiment as Commentary," *The Journal of Hindu Studies* 7 (2014): 392–417.

Zucker, David J. "Isaac: A Life of Bitter Laughter," *Jewish Bible Quarterly*; https://jbqnew.jewishbible.org/assets/Uploads/402/jbq_402_isaaclaughter.pdf.

Internet Sites

http://bombay.indology.info/mahabharata/welcome.html

http://nrs.harvard.edu/urn-3:hul.ebook:CHS_TravisR.The_Descent_of_the_Goddess.1990

http://sriparthasarathytemple.tnhrce.in/history-parthasarathy.html

http://www.bbc.com/future/story/20170407-why-all-smiles-are-not-the-same

http://www.dvaipayana.net/krishnanattam/krish_summary.html

http://www.vedanta-nl.org/GOSPEL.pdf

https://blog.cancellieri.org/umberto-eco-sul-riso-e-la-comicita

https://dante.princeton.edu/dante/pdp/commedia.html

https://dante.princeton.edu/pdp/convivio.html

https://factmuseum.com/pdf/upaveda/Holy-Geeta-by-Swami-Chinmayananda.pdf

https://letterepaoline.files.wordpress.com/2013/12/ev-th-comm.pdf

https://obo.genaud.net/dhamma-vinaya/pts/kd/jat/jat.4/jat.4.454.rous.pts.htm

https://www.alamy.com/bhagavad-gita-narrative-sculpture-on-a-column-in-the-virupaksha-temple-pattadakal-1885-photo-image218375144.html
https://www.auro-ebooks.com/bhagavad-gita
https://www.biblestudytools.com/nrs/
https://www.holy-bhagavad-gita.org
https://www.holy-bhagavad-gita.org/chapter/9/verse/14
https://www.unodc.org/pdf/india/Bhagavad.pdf
https://www.wisdomlib.org/definition/parthasarathi
https://www.youtube.com/watch?v=eVbMhsPtiVs
https://www.youtube.com/watch?v=tONcYzfW8hQ
https://www.youtube.com/watch?v=vwuEHxSw9aM
https://www.youtube.com/watch?v=xSqM7Qw3HlM
https://www.youtube.com/watch?v=YL7AMPgj9U4&t=1106s
https://www.youtube.com/watch?v=7L3z1k-SdKA
https://www.youtube.com/watch?v=80D8b3a0Bis
https://www.youtube.com/watch?v=-nUaywzaDug
https://www.youtube.com/watch?v=-VHuO7F_q7E

Index

Locators in *italic* refer to figures and tables

Abhinavagupta—*Gītārthasaṃgraha*: *anaucitya* (inappropriateness) thematized by, 2; on Arjuna's eligibility (*adhikāra*) to receive Kṛṣṇa's *upadeśa* (gloss on *BhG* 2.5–6), 83

Alighieri, Dante, 1

Allah Baksh: paintings of the *Bhagavadgītā*, 146–48

Ānanda Giri—*Gītābhāṣyavivecana*: *BhG* 2.10 identified as a transition in the text, 64, 98; on the opening verses of *BhGBh*, 63; *prahasann iva* elucidated, 63–64

ānanda (pure joy): communication by Kṛṣṇa's smile of, 37, 177–78, 255n137; the perfect joy exalted by Saint Francis of Assisi compared with, 206n146

anaucitya (inappropriateness): of Arjuna's stubbornness and mental confusion that triggers Kṛṣṇa's *prahasann iva*, 3, 28, 65, 74, 82, 96, 97, 99, 141; Western philosophical advocates of, 2

Anubhūtisvarūpācārya: *Ānanda Giri*'s indebtedness to, 63; *Prakaṭārthavivaraṇa* commentary on Śaṅkara's *Brahmasūtrabhāṣya*, 212n9

Apte, Vaman Shivaram: on *pra* + √*has*, 14; on *prahāsa*, 5; on *prasannamukha* (with a pleased countenance), 198n94

Aristotle: laughter triggered by inappropriateness advocated by, 2; on θαῦμα ("wonder," "awe"), 207n154

Arjuna (Pārtha). *See also* Pārthasārathi and the Pārthasārathi icon: *anaucitya* (inappropriateness) of his stubbornness and mental confusion that triggers Kṛṣṇa's *prahasann iva (BhG* 2.10), 3, 28, 65, 74, 82, 96, 97, 99, 141; "becoming silent" (*tūṣṇīṃ babhūva*) by (*BhG* 2.9), 22, 46; as a eunuch at the court of Virāṭa: 20, 94, 127, 195n69; his expression of words of wisdom, viewed as *prajñāvādān ca bhāṣase* by Kṛṣṇa, 22, 60, 69–70, 81, 82, 94, 196n77; Kṛṣṇa's death as a premonition of his impending

Arjuna (Pārtha) *(continued)*
death, 200n100; last words by that he shall not fight (*na yotsya iti*; *BhG* 2.9), 3, 22, 31, 57, 68, 85, 88, 221n93; as the main warrior-hero among the Pāṇḍavas, 22; as "monkey-bannered" (*kapidhvaja*), 241n28; as the son of Indra, 22, 209n168; as the son of Pṛthā, 142, 199n100, 208–209n168; surrender to Kṛṣṇa (*īśvarapratipatti*) (*BhG* 2.7), 9, 10–11, 21, 24, 30, 36, 38, 48, 52, 57, 60, 66, 71, 76, 99, 146; as "the thick-haired one" (*guḍā-keśa*), 192n33

Arnold, Edwin: *prahasann iva* translated as "with a tender smile," 14

Aurobindo, Sri: *prahasann iva* translated as "smiling as it were," 188n18

Banerjee, Priyatosh, 149

Barnett, Lionel D.: *prahasann iva* translated as "with seeming smile," 187n18

Bellarmino, Roberto, 199n98

Bergson, Henri: on imitation as the essence of the ludicrous, 3; theory of inconsistency, 2

Besant, Annie, and Bhagavân Dâs: *prahasann iva* translated as "smiling," 187n18

Bhagavadgītā (*BhG*). *See also* Kṛṣṇa—names and epithets in the *BhG* and *MBh*; Pārthasārathi and the Pārthasārathi icon; *prahasann iva* and *hasann iva* in the *Bhagavadgītā*: authorship attributed to Vyāsa, 221n93; chapters 1 to 6 identified as the *karmayoga* section extolling "the discipline of action," 39; chapters 7 to 12 identified as the *bhaktiyoga* section extolling the "the discipline of devotion," 43; chapters 13 to 18 identified as the *jñānayoga* section extolling the "discipline of knowledge," 49; first English translation published by Charles Wilkins, 151, 225n6; *Gītācārya* representation of Kṛṣṇa teaching the *Bhagavadgītā* to Arjuna, 151, *152*; identification as a secret teaching, 245; Kṛṣṇa's identification with Viṣṇu as one of his embodiments (*avatāra*) in, 161; location in the *Bhīṣmaparvan* of the *MBh*, 101; reading it as an independent work, 102–103; the term *vairāgya* (detachment) found in, 49, 54, 147, 161, 193n46; transition of from elite status to popular work, 148; Vaiśaṃpāyana identified as the first to recite it, 245n52

Bhagavadgītā (*BhG*)—chapter 1: *acyuta* (changeless) used by Arjuna acknowledging Kṛṣṇa's divinity (1.21), 36; Nīlakāṇṭha on the words of Arjuna in *BhG* 1.37, 79; Śaṅkara's argument that *BhG* 1.2 to 2.9 is meant to identify the root of the defects that are intrinsic to worldly life, 61; starting from verse 1.28, Śrīdhara Svāmin highlights the object of Arjuna's anguish as his kinsfolk, 71

Bhagavadgītā (*BhG*)—chapter 2: Abhinavagupta's gloss on Arjuna's eligibility (*adhikāra*) to receive Kṛṣṇa's *upadeśa* (*BhG* 2.5–6), 83; Allah Baksh's color rendering of *BhG* 2.15, 147; Arjuna's "becoming silent" (*tūṣṇīṃ babhūva*) (2.9), 22, 46; Arjuna's last words that he shall not fight (*na yotsya iti*; *BhG* 2.9), 3, 22, 31, 57, 68, 85, 88, 221n93; Arjuna's surrender to Kṛṣṇa (*īśvarapratipatti*) (2.7), 9, 10–11, 21, 24, 30, 36, 38, 48, 52, 57, 60, 66, 71, 76, 99, 146; the *BhG* viewed as part of the *prasthānatraya* or the "triad of the points of departure" by the schools of Vedānta, 103; connection between *BhG* verses 2.1–10 and the Upaniṣadic requirements for approaching a master for instruction suggested by Śaṅkarānanda Sarasvatī, 71; instruction of the *Bhagavadgītā*, beginning with *aśocyān* (2.11) and ending with *mā śucaḥ* (18.66), 22, 57, 60, 61–62, 67–68, 70, 78, 81, 87, 90; Kṛṣṇa on "holding pleasure and pain alike" (*sama*; 2.37), 196n80; Kṛṣṇa's definition of the *muni* (2.56), 46; Kṛṣṇa's definition of *yoga* as equanimity (2.48), 8, 23, 193n45; Kṛṣṇa's laugh prompted by Arjuna's mixture of foolishness (*mauḍhya*) and wisdom (*prājñatva*), discipleship (*śiṣyatva*) and independence (*svātantrya*), 68; Kṛṣṇa's removal of Arjuna's delusion, 77, 89, 96; the meter changes from *śloka* to *triṣṭubh* to highlight importance (2.5–8, 2.20, 2.29, 2.70), 21, 195n70; on *prasāda* (2.64–66), 45; *prasāda* found at 2.64, 2.65, 198n94; Śaṅkara's argument that *BhG* 1.2 to 2.9 is meant to identify the root of the defects that are intrinsic to worldly life, 61; Śrīdhara Svāmin notes that Arjuna's anguish comes from the lack of discrimination between the body and Self (2.11), 71; Śrīveṅkaṭanātha on *BhG* 2.11–2.38, 214n28

Bhagavadgītā (*BhG*)—chapter 2.10: *anaucitya* (inappropriateness) of Arjuna's stubbornness and mental confusion that triggers Kṛṣṇa's *prahasann iva*, 3, 28, 65, 74, 82, 96, 97, 99, 141; English renderings of *prahasann iva* in, 14; Kṛṣṇa eloquent silence contrasted with Arjuna's "becoming silent" (*tūṣṇīṃ babhūva*) (2.9), 46; Nīlakāṇṭha Caturdhara on Arjuna as the victim of two types of delusion in, 79–80; *prahasann iva* identified by Śrīdhara as "having a happy face," 70; *prahasann iva* interpreted by Dhanapati Sūri as "I am happy for you, who are under the control of my authority!," 69; resonance of Kṛṣṇa's *prahasann iva* with Arjuna's *vismaya* (amazement) in *BhG* 11.14, 8–9; Viśvanātha's gloss on Kṛṣṇa's *prahasann iva*, 96–97

Bhagavadgītā (*BhG*)—chapter 3: Kṛṣṇa instructs Arjuna on how to act in the world without karmic repercussions (3.27), 39–40; Kṛṣṇa provides an example that all should follow

Bhagavadgītā (*BhG*)—chapter 3 *(continued)*
to participate in his divine play (3.22–23), 41

Bhagavadgītā (*BhG*)—chapter 4: Arjuna advised to abandon all egotistic attachments and to be "always satisfied/content": (*nityatṛpto*; 4.20), 41, 195n75; Kṛṣṇa reveals to Arjuna that he has been teaching *karmayoga* from time immemorial, 40; on piercing the veil of *māyā* (4.6), 41

Bhagavadgītā (*BhG*)—chapter 5: Kṛṣṇa reveals to Arjuna that path of *karmayoga* is ultimately subsumed in *bhakti*, 40; Kṛṣṇa's definition of the *muni* (5.6, 5.28), 47

Bhagavadgītā (*BhG*)—chapter 6: Kṛṣṇa reiterates to Arjuna that true renunciation culminates in attaining *nirvāṇa*, 40; Kṛṣṇa's definition of the *muni* (6.3), 46; Kṛṣṇa teaches the essential characteristic of perfect serenity (6.8), 45

Bhagavadgītā (*BhG*)—chapter 7: on piercing the veil of *māyā* (7.14), 41

Bhagavadgītā (*BhG*)—chapter 8: Kṛṣṇa proclaims to Arjuna the supreme reality of *Brahman*, 44

Bhagavadgītā (*BhG*)—chapter 9: Kṛṣṇa teaches Arjuna that all existence originates from him, 44

Bhagavadgītā (*BhG*)—chapter 10: Kṛṣṇa states that nobody knows the origin (*prabhava*) of the Bhagavat, 44–45; Kṛṣṇa tells Arjuna what "wise men" (*budhā*) do (*BhG* 10.9), 154, 160

Bhagavadgītā (*BhG*)—chapter 11: *acyuta* (changeless) used by Arjuna in acknowledging Kṛṣṇa's divinity (11.42), 36; Arjuna's *vismaya* upon seeing a doomsday fire in Kṛṣṇa's mouths (11.26–30), 167; Kṛṣṇa as able to swallow all beings with his flaming mouths "like moths entering a burning flame" (*BhG* 11.29), 42; Kṛṣṇa's face/mouths as flaming fire (11.19), 47; wrathful vision of Kṛṣṇa's mouths and terrible tusks (*daṃṣṭrākarāla*) in the theophany of (*BhG* 11.23, 11.25, and 11.27), 37, 42

Bhagavadgītā (*BhG*)—chapter 12: Kṛṣṇa explains to Arjuna that the best ones among the adepts of *yoga* are those who have *bhakti* toward him (12.6–7), 48; *prahasann iva* shows itself in the meaning of *prasāda* as both clarity of mind and pure grace (12.11, 12.20), 49

Bhagavadgītā (*BhG*)—chapter 13: Kṛṣṇa defines the human body as the field (*kṣetra*) and he himself as the knower of the field (*kṣetrajña*), 49; revelation of Kṛṣṇa as light (13.17, 13.33), 47–48, 49

Bhagavadgītā (*BhG*)—chapter 14: Kṛṣṇa's *prahasann iva* discloses the equanimity that substantiates his teaching (14.22–25), 50; Kṛṣṇa teaches Arjuna that the great *Brahman* is the womb (*yoni*), 49–50

Bhagavadgītā (*BhG*)—chapter 15: *asaṅga* (nonattachment) used in (15.3), 50, 193n46; devotees encouraged to contemplate Kṛṣṇa's radiant beauty in their hearts (15.15), 37; Kṛṣṇa's *prahasann iva* identified with liberation (15.4, 15.19), 51; Kṛṣṇa's *prahasann iva* identified with light (15.6, 15.12), 51; parable of the mythic *aśvattha* tree that must be cut down with the stout axe of nonattachment (*asaṅga*) (15.3), 50, 193n46

Bhagavadgītā (*BhG*)—chapter 16: abandonment (*tyāga*) discussed (16.2), 52, 193n46; Kṛṣṇa's illustrates to Arjuna the virtues of those men who are endowed with a divine nature (16.21, 16.24), 51–52; *prasāda* of Kṛṣṇa's *prahasann iva* described as both tranquility of mind and compassionate grace (16.1–3), 52

Bhagavadgītā (*BhG*)—chapter 17: *prasāda* found at 17.16, 45, 198n94; silence presented as a characteristic of austerity of the mind (*tapo mānasam*) (17.16), 45, 46, 52, 198n94

Bhagavadgītā (*BhG*)—chapter 18: abandonment (*tyāga*) discussed (18.1–11), 53, 193n46; *acyuta* (changeless) used by Arjuna acknowledging Kṛṣṇa's divinity (18.73), 36; Arjuna's loyalty to Kṛṣṇa as the highest godhead (18.61, 18.66), 39; on detachment (*vairāgya*) (18.52), 54, 193n46; difference between renunciation (*saṃnyāsa*) and abandonment (*tyāga*) explained to Arjuna by Kṛṣṇa, 53–54; instruction of the *Bhagavadgītā,* beginning with *aśocyān* (2.11) and ending with *mā śucaḥ* (18.66), 57, 70, 81, 87, 215n36; *prasāda* found at 18.37, 18.56, 18.58, 18.62, 18.73, 18.75, 9, 54, 85, 198n94, 211n200; on the pure joy that originates from the serenity of the soul and intellect (*ātmabuddhiprasādajam;* 18.37), 45, 85; Saṃjaya's statement that Vyāsa's grace enabled him to hear the secret *yoga* taught by Kṛṣṇa to Arjuna (18.75), 211n200; Śaṅkara on *līlā* in *BhG* 18.61, 42, 209n172; that everything is but god's unfathomable *līlā* is revealed to Arjuna (11.32–33), 42–43; the theology of *prapatti* understood in Śrī Vaiṣṇava circles as a development of *BhG* 18.66, 208n161

bhakti: Arjuna's loyalty to Kṛṣṇa as the highest godhead (*BhG* 18.61, 18.66), 39, 209n162; chapters 7 to 12 of the *BhG* identified as the *bhaktiyoga* section extolling "the discipline of devotion," 43; the emotional *bhakti* of the *Purāṇas* distinguished from the intellectual *bhakti* of the *Bhagavadgītā,* 161; the nine forms of *bhakti* presented in the *Bhāgavata Purāṇa* (7.5.23), 36, 247n73; *rasa* theory of Sanskrit poetics applied to the practice of Kṛṣṇa *bhakti* by Rūpa Gosvāmin, 174; as a term, 198n92

Bhalla, Alok, and Chandra Prakash Deval, 146
Bharata: his telling about a nightmare he had and of Daśaratha's *hasann iva* (*Rām* 2.63.9d), 132
Bharata—*Nāṭyaśāstra*: dating of, 238n13; six states of ecstatic love (*hāsyabhaktirasa*) listed in, 136–37, 254n128
Bhāskara—commentary on BhG 2.10: on Great souls on smiling before they speak, 60, v
Bhīma: dialogue between Yudhiṣṭhira, Bhīma, and Draupadī (*MBh* 3.27–35), 102; Ghaṭotkaca identified as the son of Bhīma by the *rākṣasī* Hiḍimbā, 228n35; his heroic ease expressed in (*MBh* 1.151.7b) and (*MBh* 1.51.14d), 108; identified as the son of Pṛthā/Kuntī and Pāṇḍu, 208–209n168; Karṇa's humble origins ridiculed by his *prahasann iva* (*MBh* 1.127.5d), 125; Kṛṣṇa's reply to Bhīma's despondency (*MBh* 5.73), 113–14, 194n66; vision of the ancient form of Hanumān (*MBh* 3.146–50), 102
Bhīṣma: as Arjuna's teacher, 18, 21, 66, 94; Kṛṣṇa's cosmic form as Viśvarūpa revealed to him, 102
Bible. *See* Christianity and the Bible
Brahmasūtras. *See also* Śaṅkara—*Brahmasūtrabhāṣya*: on *līlā* as lighthearted attitude through which god carries out every action for pure amusement (2.1.33), 7, 68, 184n23; on requirements for approaching a master for instruction (1.1.1), 71; viewed as part of the *prasthānatraya* or the "triad of the points of departure" by the schools of Vedānta, 103
Brereton, Joel P., 15
Brook, Peter—staging of the *Mahābhārata*: actors' ideas about Kṛṣṇa and Arjuna, 192n39; Kṛṣṇa's hint of a smile not conveyed in, 16–17, 157, xii
Buddhist influence: use of the term *nirvāṇa* as an indication of, 197n87

Caitanya: Baladeva Vidyābhūṣaṇa as a later follower of, 97; Gauḍīya Vaiṣṇavism established by, 172, 174
charioteers: Kṛṣṇa worshipped as the charioteer in the Pārthasārathi icon, 142, 145, 146, 149, *150*, 151, 240n26, 241–42n30, *242n30*, 243n35
Cherniak, Alex: *prahasann iva* translated as "almost laughing," 14
Christianity and the Bible: chariots and horses in, 199n98; laughter in the Bible and early Christianity, 2, 182n7, 184n28; Moses's encounter with Yahweh in *Exodus*, 10; "priestly blessing" (*birkat kohanim*) in the book of *Numbers*, 9–10; on the rebirth of the soul, 196–97n81; saying attributed to Jesus in the *Gospel of Thomas* compared with *vismaya*, 207n156; the splendor of Moses' face related to Jesus' transfiguration in the Bible, 185n33
Ciotti, Giovanni, 205n135

Citaristi, Ileana: background of, 249n79; on the depiction of Kṛṣṇa's *prahasann iva* in Odissi dance, 156–57; Parthasarathi performed with Saswat Joshi, 156, *156*, 157
Clémentin-Ojha, Catherine: on the importance of *prapatti* in the Nimbārka *sampradāya*, 94

Dabholkar, Govind R. (Hemad Pant), 184–85n20, 253n123
darśan and *darśana* (vision): coexistence of the benevolent *darśana* of Kṛṣṇa with the wrathful vision of the god's mouths and terrible tusks (*daṃṣṭrākarāla*), 37; *darśana* (vision) as a meaning of *pra*, 190n27; explanation of, 33–34; jasmine flowers associated with the *darśana* of the god's laughter/smile in the kṛṣṇaite traditions, 37, 206n145; of Kṛṣṇa offering his teaching to Arjuna, 142; longing for Kṛṣṇa's radiant, smiling face and his flute, 169; the pivotal *darśana* of Kṛṣṇa's serene hint of laughter, 50, 178; Viswanatha Swami's description of his first *darśan* of Ramaṇa Maharṣi, 254n123
Davidson, Joseph Leroy, 149
Davis, Richard H.: on the coexistence of "supremacy" (*paratva*) and "easy accessibility" (*saulabhya*) in Kṛṣṇa, 183n14; on "meta-*Gītā*," 245n53; on Wilkins' translation of the *MBh*, 225n6
death. *See also* liberation (*mokṣa*); *saṃsāra*: as an occasion for "changing old clothes" (*vāsāṃsi jīrṇāni*), 22; the idea that the Self dies with the death of the body identified as one of Arjuna's delusions in *BhG* 2.10, 79–80; two paths for the soul after death explained in *BhG* chapter 8, 44
Deutsch, Eliot: *prahasann iva* translated as "faintly smiling," 14
Dhanapati Sūri: background of, 68–69, 215n30; his *Arthadīpikā* identified as a gloss on Dharmarāja Adhvarin's *Vedāntaparibhāṣā*, 215n30; Madhusūdana's position on Arjuna's twofold delusion criticized by, 215n34; *prahasann iva* in *BhG* 2.10 interpreted as "I am happy for you, who are under the control of my authority!," 69
Dharmarāja Adhvarin: Dhanapati Sūri's *Arthadīpikā* identified as a gloss on his *Vedāntaparibhāṣā*, 215n30; Śrīveṅkaṭanātha identified as his teacher, 66
Dhaumya: characters named Dhaumya in the *MBh*, 231n56; as Upamanyu's brother, 121, 231n56
Dhṛtarāṣṭra: blindness of, 192n34; Saṃjaya identified as his charioteer, 191n32; Vyāsa's appeal to stop the battle considered futile by (*MBh* 6.4.44–46), 193n51
doubts (*saṃśaya, saṃdeha*): dissolution of, 204n126
Draupadī: dialogue between Yudhiṣṭhira, Bhīma, and Draupadī (*MBh* 3.27–35), 102; *prahasann iva* expressed by Arjuna/Bṛhannaḍā contrasted

Draupadī *(continued)*
with Draupadī/Sairandhrī's distress (*MBh* 4.23.22d), 127; *upahasita* exemplified by her mockery of Duryodhana in the Tamil drama *Cūtutukilurital,* 238n16
Droṇa: Arjuna's resistance to the idea of having to fight Bhīṣma and Droṇa, 18, 21, 65; as Arjuna's teacher, 18, 21, 66, 94, 192n48, 193n48; Bhīṣma and Droṇa identified as "those who are not to be mourned" (*aśocya*) by Śaṅkara, 62–63; death of, 109, 118; exhibition of heroic ease (6.49.15d), 108; *hasann iva* in response to Duryodhana's assessment of Arjuna (7.160.23b), 128; secret of an extraordinary weapon called *brahmaśiras* revealed to his son Aśvatthāman (10.12.12d), 128–29

Eco, Umberto, 3–4
Edgerton, Franklin: *avahāsārtham* translated as "to make sport," 35; *prahasann iva* rendered as "with a semblance of a smile," 14; *prajñāvādikaḥ* translated as "talking as (pretending to be) wise," 196n77
eunuchs *(klība)*: Arjuna disguised as a eunuch at the court of Virāṭa, 20, 94, 127, 195n69; Kṛṣṇa's admonishing of Arjuna to stop acting like one, 20–21, 27, 94, 95, 99, 140, 159; as a symbol of impotence and cowardice, 20, 194n67

feet of the *guru*: Arjuna's prostration at Kṛṣṇa's feet at *BhG* 2.7, 6, 10–11, 21, 24, 30–31, 33–34, 36, 70, 99, 141, 159, xi; in devotional hymns, 204n128; the hero as a man who takes refuge at his lord's feet as his *śiṣya*, 27, 36; illustration of Arjuna kneeling at Kṛṣṇa's feet on the Kurukṣetra battlefield in the *Amar Chitra Katha* collection of children's comics and storybooks, 151; infinite grace and compassion represented by Kṛṣṇa's feet, 25, 48–49, 199n95
Feuerstein, Georg, and Brenda Feuerstein: *prahasann iva* translated as "laughingly, as it were," 14, 187n18
Fitzgerald, James L.: on the divine freedom of Kṛṣṇa-Vāsudeva, 29–30

Garbutt, Kathleen, 230n41
Gauḍīya Vaiṣṇavism: earthly Vraja viewed as coterminous with heavenly Vraja, 250n94; establishment by Caitanya, 172, 174
Goldman, Robert, and Sally J. Sutherland Goldman: *prahasann iva* translated as "smiling gently," 232n61
Gopinatha Rao, T. A.: on the depiction of the rapture of music on the face, 169; on Kṛṣṇa Pārthasārathi, 142
grace (*kṛpā, prasāda*). See also *prahasann iva* and *hasann iva*—2. as expressions of divine grace: in the *BhG*, 9, 54, 85, 198n94,

211n200; infinite grace and compassion represented by Kṛṣṇa's feet, 25, 199n95; its revelation by Kṛṣṇa's *prahasann iva* described in *BhG* chapters 8 through 10, 45; *pra* with √*sad* (to be clear/bright/tranquil): 9, 25; revelation of his divine grace (*prasāda*) as crucial to Kṛṣṇa's *prahasann iva*, 99; sacredness of, expressed in devotional hymns, 204n128; smiles of deities and saints regarded as tokens of, 174, 253n123

grace (*kṛpā, prasāda*) expressed by Kṛṣṇa toward Arjuna: described as both tranquility of mind and compassionate grace (*BhG* 16.1–3), 52; Jñāneśvar on how the sweetness of Kṛṣṇa's grace is hidden by the bitter taste of medicine (mocking expression), 141; Kṛṣṇa as the *prasanna*, 9, 33–34, 210n180; signaling by Kṛṣṇa's hint of laughter (*prahasann iva*), 48, 141, xi

Gupta, Mahendranath, 208n162

Hanumān: Arjuna as "monkey-bannered" (*kapidhvaja*), 241n28; Bhīma's vision of the ancient form of (*MBh* 3.146–50), 102

Hanumat, *Paiśācabhāṣya*, 216n43

Hart, George L., 210n180

hasann iva. See *prahasann iva* and *hasann iva* in the *Bhagavadgītā*

Hawley, John Stratton: on depictions of the Pārthasārathi icon in Indian sculpture, 244n43; *navanītacora* Kṛṣṇa image for *Krishna, the Butter Thief*, 163

hearing (*śravaṇa*): as one of the nine forms of *bhakti* in *Bhāgavata Purāṇa* 7.5.23, 247n73; as one of three fundamental steps to achieve self-realization in nondual Vedānta, 11, 185n31

Hill, W. Douglas P.: *prahasann iva* translated as "as one smiling," 188n18

Hiltebeitel, Alf: on Arjuna's supplicant words to Kṛṣṇa, 35; criticism of Kṛṣṇa's lack of a smile in Brook's staging of the *Mahābhārata*, 16–17, 157

humor: as double meaning of *prasāda*, 25

iconography. *See* Kṛṣṇa—iconography of; Pārthasārathi and the Pārthasārathi icon

imitation: of divine *līlā*, 8; as the essence of the ludicrous, 3, 182n4; *hāsyarasa* as the imitation of *śṛṅgārarasa*, 136, 140; in the sphere of *anaucitya* (inappropriateness), 3; transgressive laughter that imitates the "loud laughter" (*aṭṭahāsa*) of Rudra, 201n106, 237n10

iva (as if). See also *prahasann iva* ("hint of laughter") in the *Bhagavadgītā*: action affirmed as true by (but that its realization or its extent is uncertain), 15; applied to Kṛṣṇa's smile and traced to the *lingua mystica* of the *Upaniṣads*, 191n30; liminal character of Kṛṣṇa's hint of laughter reinforced by, 29; present participles in the

iva (as if) *(continued)*
nominative case that display a reduplication of final *-n* when followed by *iva* in the *MBh*, 226n11; softening of the effect of expressions by, 15
Iyer, G.V.: Kṛṣṇa's smile/hint of laughter featured in *Bhagvad Gita: Song of the Lord* directed by, 157, *158*

Jacobi, Hermann, 104n66
Jayadeva's *Gītagovinda*, 161
Jaya Tīrtha: standardization of Dvaita thought, 90–91; works by, 90, 222n102
Jñāneśvar: background of, 84–85; on Kṛṣṇa's dazzling splendor, 210n187
Jñāneśvar—*Jñāneśvarī*: Advaita-oriented Marāṭhī gloss on Kṛṣṇa's *prahasann iva*, 6, 59, 85, 141; on how the sweetness of Kṛṣṇa's grace is hidden by the bitter taste of medicine, 141; on Kṛṣṇa's mouth as the receptacle of an otherworldly effulgence through which he reveals his divinity, 31

kārpaṇya ("poorness of spirit"): identified by Rāmānuja as the sixth stage of *prapatti*, 24–25; Veṅkaṭanātha on definitions of *kārpaṇya*, 221nn93–94; weakness of pity (*kārpaṇyadoṣa*), 21, 31
Kasturi, Narayan: excerpt from a poem by, 13; as a humorist, 182n5
Kaṭha Upaniṣad. See *Upaniṣads—Kaṭha Upaniṣad*
Kato, Takahiro: on the *BhGk* and its interpretation, 81, 196n77, 220n81; study of the *Bhagavadāśayānusaraṇa*, 82
Keśava Kaśmīrī Bhaṭṭācārya—*Tattvaprakāśikā*: on the importance of first chapter of the *BhG* in understanding Arjuna's despondency, 92, 94; on *kārpaṇya*, 93; on Kṛṣṇa's *prahasann iva* as like a bitter medicine to cure Arjuna's despondency, 6, 60, 94
King, Ursula: on the iconography of the *Bhagavadgītā*, 147–48; on the terrace scene featuring Kṛṣṇa and Arjuna, 151
Kinsley, David R., 172–73
Kṛṣṇa: care for the world that he both transcends and encompasses, 199n99; death of, 199n96, 199n100; genealogy of, 199n96, 199n100; how the intellect (*buddhi*) of the tranquil-minded (*prasannacetaso*) becomes steady pointed out by, 204n127
Kṛṣṇa—Bālakṛṣṇa as butter thief (*navanītacora*): Kṛṣṇa's granting vision of the universe to his foster-mother Yaśodā, 165–68, *167*, 203n118, 252n106; mischievous form as starting point, 163; as *navanītanṛttamūrti*, 164–65, *166*, 251n104; smile featured in, 163–64, *165*; Tanjore painting, 163, *164*
Kṛṣṇa—cosmic form as Viśvarūpa: Arjuna's *vismaya* in response to Kṛṣṇa's revelation of his supernal form, 8–9, 37–38, 167, 220n85; revelation to Bhīṣma,

102; revelation to Duryodhana, 205n132; revelation to Uttaṅka, 102, 123–24

Kṛṣṇa—iconography of. *See also* Pārthasārathi and the Pārthasārathi icon: icon of child Kṛṣṇa stealing butter in literature and in the arts, 251n102; icon of Viṭṭhala/Viṭhobā, 251n99, 255n137; of Kṛṣṇa lifting the Govardhana mountain, 162, 170–71, *172*; of Kṛṣṇa vanquishing the five-headed serpent-demon Kāliya, 170, 171–72, *173*; *līlā* expressed in, 170–71; longing for Kṛṣṇa's radiant, smiling face and his flute, 169; *śrīvatsa* is a distinctive sign of Viṣṇu-Kṛṣṇa, 113, 229n39; as Veṇugopāla, *168*, 168–69, 208n166, 252n107; *Viṣṇudharmottara* on depictions of Kṛṣṇa and Arjuna, 149

Kṛṣṇa—mouth/mouths (*mukha*) of: Arjuna's vision of doomsday fire in them (*BhG* 11.26–30), 167; faces/mouths as flaming fire (*BhG* 11.19)., 47; Kṛṣṇa as able to swallow all beings with his flaming mouths "like moths entering a burning flame" (*BhG* 11.29):, 42; Kṛṣṇa's granting vision of the universe to his foster-mother Yaśodā, 165–68, *167*, 203n118, 252n106; the partial opening of his mouth that makes his glittering teeth slightly visible (*BhG* 2.10), 137; as the receptacle of an otherworldly effulgence through which he reveals his divinity, 31; wrathful vision of Kṛṣṇa's mouths and terrible tusks (*daṃṣṭrākarāla*) in the theophany of chapter 11 (*BhG* 11.23, 11.25, and 11.27), 37, 42

Kṛṣṇa—names and epithets in the *BhG* and *MBh*, 191–92n33; as Keśava (the "long-haired one") (*BhG*: 1.31, 2.54, 3.1, 10.14, 11.35, 18.76), 113, 166, 176, 252n105; as the lord of the gods (*deveśa*; *BhG* 11.25, 11.37, 11.45), 42; Pārthasārathi as an epithet of, 240n26, 243n35; Vāsudeva as a patronymic of Kṛṣṇa, 16, 29–30, 192n35

Kṛṣṇa's love toward Arjuna expressed by *prahasann iva*, 5, 11, 25, 133, 236n93. See also *prapatti* (surrender)—Arjuna's surrender to Kṛṣṇa; *prasāda* expressed by Kṛṣṇa toward Arjuna; Arjuna as pretext (*nimitta*) for, explained by Śaṅkara, 61–63, xi; Arjuna as pretext (*nimitta*) for, explained by Vaṃśīdhara, 80–81; Arjuna's *vismaya* in response to Kṛṣṇa's revelation of his supernal form, 8–9, 37–38, 167, 220n85; as a bridging point between silence and the word, 27, 200n104; English renderings of, 14, 187–89n18, 232n61; impact on the poem's central teachings, xiii; as inspiration to Arjuna and all beings to tread the triune paths of *karmayoga, bhaktiyoga,* and *jñānayoga*, 54–55; Jñāneśvar's Advaita-oriented Marāṭhī gloss on, 6, 59, 85, 141; *līlā* associated

Kṛṣṇa's love toward Arjuna expressed by *prahasann iva* (continued)
with, 7–8, 41–43; list of authors and works that comment on it, 58–59; *loci* of *hasann iva*, 186n4; *loci* of *prahasann iva*, 186n3; the meaning of *prahasann iva* and *hasann iva* revealed in the Hindī expression: *bāye hāth kā khel* ("a left-hand game"), 226n14; mocking and mirth combined in, 7, 27–30; as the most powerful *darśana* he bestows upon Arjuna, 178; as a natural reaction to Arjuna's betrayal of his *kṣatriyadharma*, 3; pedagogical function of, 6, 28–29, 63–64; "priestly blessing" (*birkat kohanim*) in the book of *Numbers* compared with, 9–10; pure joy (*ānanda*) and blissful equanimity exhibited by Kṛṣṇa, 37, 206n146; revelation of his divine grace (*prasāda*) as crucial to, 99; summary of the moment of, xi; in theater and dance, 154–57; theories of superiority and inconsistency used to explain it, 2–5; verse 2.11 associated with, 16, 22, 57–58, 60, 61, 70, 82, 87; the view that it is mere mockery not favored by authors examined in this book, 60

Kṛṣṇāṭṭam: eight plays of, 248–49n77; *Vividavadham* ("Slaying of Vivida"), 155, *155*

kṣatriya and *kṣatriyadharma*: Kṛṣṇa's hint of laughter is but a natural reaction to Arjuna's betrayal of, 3

laughter. *See also* Kṛṣṇa's love toward Arjuna expressed by *prahasann iva*; *prahasann iva* ("hint of laughter"): ambivalence of, 29; in the Bible and early Christianity, 2, 182n7, 184n28; of Democritus of Abdera, 200n103; Umberto Eco on the danger of, 3–4; *hāsa*, derived from verbal root √*has*, 104, 135, 183n15; of Homeric heroes, 201n106; popular saying (*subhāṣita*) on, 238n17; six states of laughter in ecstatic love (*hāsyabhaktirasa*) identified by Bharata, 136–37, 254n128; six states of laughter in ecstatic love (*hāsyabhaktirasa*) identified by Rūpa Gosvāmin, 175–77, 254n128

laughter—"slight laughter" (*hasita*): common characteristics identified by Rūpa Gosvāmin, 175; as the name of the bow of Kāma, 237n11; as one of six varieties of *hāsyarasa*, 136, 175; pairing with *smita* in the six varieties of *hāsyarasa* identified by Bharata, 135, 138–39; *prahasann iva* as a hearty laugh contrasted with, 81; smiles (*smita*) and *hasita* associated with noble persons, 136; as a sure sign of Kṛṣṇa's grace toward Arjuna, 70

laughter—"open laughter" (*vihasita*): common characteristics identified by Bharata, 138; common characteristics identified by Rūpa Gosvāmin, 175; as one of six varieties of *hāsyarasa*, 136, 175

laughter—"mocking laughter" (*upahasita* or *avahasita*): common characteristics identified by Bharata, 137; common characteristics identified by Rūpa Gosvāmin, 175; as one of six varieties of *hāsyarasa*, 136, 175; "shaking in mirth" (*kuluṅka nakaittāḷē*) by Draupadī as an example of, 238n16; of Yaśodā upon seeing Kṛṣṇa, 176
laughter—"loud laughter" (*apahasita*): common characteristics identified by Bharata, 137; common characteristics identified by Rūpa Gosvāmin, 175; the loud laugh (*aṭṭahāsa*) of Rudra-Śiva, 161, 201n106, 237n10; of Nārada at the sight of Kṛṣṇa dancing for the cowherd women, 176; as one of six varieties of *hāsyarasa*, 136, 175; "shaking in mirth" (*kuluṅka nakaittāḷē*) by Draupadī as an example of, 238n16
laughter—"excessive laughter" (*atihasita*): common characteristics identified by Bharata, 137; common characteristics identified by Rūpa Gosvāmin, 175; of girls upon hearing an exchange between Kṛṣṇa and Mukharā, 176; as one of six varieties of *hāsyarasa*, 136, 175
Lefeber, Rosalind: *prahasann iva* translated as "smiled slightly," 232n61
liberation (*mokṣa*): *brahmanirvāṇa* as, 24, 197n87; every person's fight for the attainment of, 8; Śaṅkara's refutation of the view that ritual activities and knowledge *karmajñānasamuccaya* are equally involved in its attainment, 62
līlā (play): association with Kṛṣṇa's love toward Arjuna expressed by *prahasann iva*, 7–8, 41; celebration in painting of, 147; development as a theological concept, 206n147; Kṛṣṇa's *līlā*s extolled in the *Bhāgavata Purāṇa*, 161; as the lighthearted attitude through which god carries out every action for pure amusement (*Brahmasūtra* 2.1.33), 7, 68, 184n23; *māyā* associated with, 42, 209n172; *rāslīlā* (dance pastime) of Kṛṣṇa dancing with all the *gopī*s, 169–70, *171*; that everything is but god's unfathomable *līlā* is revealed to Arjuna (*BhG* 11.32–33), 42–43
Līlāśuka Bilvamaṅgala—*Kṛṣṇakarṇāmṛta*: Kṛṣṇa's graceful smile described in, 174; Kṛṣṇa's granting vision of the universe to Yaśodā, 166, 252n106; song of love for his chosen deity, 13, 169
Lorenz, Konrad, 29
luminosity: golden color of the skin of *yogins*, 43–44, 210n178; Kṛṣṇa's dazzling splendor, 47–48, 210n187

Madhusūdana Sarasvatī—*Gūḍhārthadīpikā* (*GAD*): on the perception of the *paṇḍitas*, 219n73; Śrīveṅkaṭanātha criticism of, 65–66, 213n15

Mahābhārata (*MBh*): *Gītās* in, 225n5; present participles in, 106, 189n19, 226nn11–12; reflection on the four aims of human life (*puruṣārtha*), 101, 225n4
Mahābhārata (*MBh*)—1. *Ādiparvan*: Arjuna's desire for Kṛṣṇa's sister Subhadrā acknowledged with divine grace (1.211.16b), 111–12; Bhīma's heroic ease expressed in (1.151.7b), 108; Bhīma's heroic ease expressed in (1.151.14d), 108; Karṇa's humble origins ridiculed by Bhīma's *prahasann iva* (1.127.5d), 125; *prahasann iva* + *hasann iva* used in, 105, *105*, 108
Mahābhārata (*MBh*)—2. *Sabhāparvan*: *prahasann iva* + *hasann iva* used in, *105*
Mahābhārata (*MBh*)—3. *Āraṇyakaparvan* (or *Vanaparvan)*: Arjuna's *prahasann iva* harshly addresses a hunter (*kirāta*) (3.40.17 and 3.40.21b), 125–26; Arjuna's search for divine weapons from Indra (3.38.36b, 3.38.39b), 112–13; Bhīma's vision of the ancient form of Hanumān (3.146–50), 102; dialogue between Yudhiṣṭhira, Bhīma, and Draupadī (3.27–35), 102; Mārkaṇḍeya tells Yudhiṣṭhira how Viṣṇu appeared to him in disguise as a divine boy (3.186.116b), 113; *Nalopakhyāna* or "The story of Nala and Damayantī" (*MBh* 3.50–78), 236n3; *prahasann iva* expressed by Karṇa in response to a Brahmin's request for his armor (3.294.9d), 127; *prahasann iva* + *hasann iva* used in, *105*, 112–13, 125–26, 127, 235n88; story of Ilvala and Vātāpi (3.97), 126, 233n70
Mahābhārata (*MBh*)—4. *Virāṭaparvan*: *prahasann iva* expressed by Arjuna/Bṛhannaḍā contrasted with Draupadī/Sairandhrī's distress (4.23.22d), 128; *prahasann iva* + *hasann iva* used in, *105*; *prahasann iva* signaling Arjuna's delight in fighting a loyal combat with Droṇa (4.53.14b), 128; story of Arjuna as a eunuch, 195n69
Mahābhārata (*MBh*)—5. *Udyogaparvan*: Duryodhana's *prahasann iva* toward Kṛṣṇa before asking him to side with the Kauravas (5.7.9b), 131; Kṛṣṇa's *prahasann iva* in response to Bhīma's despondency (5.73.1–11), 113–14, 194n66; Kṛṣṇa's revelation of his cosmic form as Viśvarūpa to Duryodhana, 205n132; Kṛṣṇa's revelation of his cosmic form to the Kauravas (5.129.1–16), 102; Kṛṣṇa visits the Kauravas before the war (5.89.23d), 114–16; *prahasann iva* + *hasann iva* used in, *105*, 235n88; present participles in the nominative case that display a reduplication of final *-n* when followed by iva (5.73.8b, 5.73.10b, 5.73.11b), 226n11; Saṃjaya's advice to Yudhiṣṭhira (5.27.2), 194n72; *Sanatsujātīya* of (5.42–45), 102; Vidurā's son questions the value

(*artha*) of a warrior's *svadharma* (5.1.31.36, 5.133.3), 194n53

Mahābhārata (*MBh*)—6. *Bhīṣmaparvan*: Droṇa's exhibition of heroic ease (6.49.15d), 108; Kṛṣṇa's heroic ease in piercing a demon (*rākṣasa*) with nine arrows (6.107.2d), 108–109; location of the *BhG* in, 101, 224n3; Madrarāja's brushing aside of shower of arrows shot at him by Sahadeva (6.79.48e), 108; as the narrative pivot of the *MBh*, 101; *prahasann iva* + *hasann iva* used in, 13–14, 104–105, *105*, 108, 109; present participles in the nominative case that display a reduplication of final *-n* when followed by *iva* (6.60.17d), 226n11; Vyāsa's appeal to stop the battle considered futile by Dhṛtarāṣṭra (6.4.44–46), 193n51; Yudhiṣṭhira's unarmed approaching of the Kauravas before the battle (6.41.16d), 116–17

Mahābhārata (*MBh*)—7. *Droṇaparvan*: *hasann iva* associated with Subhadra [=Abhimanyu] (7.50.16d), 128; *hasann iva* by Droṇa in response to Duryodhana's assessment of Arjuna (7.160.23b), 128; Kṛṣṇa's *prahasann iva* directed toward Ghaṭotkaca (7.148.39d), 228n35, 236n94; *prahasann iva* as a sign of Arjuna's delight in fighting a loyal combat with Droṇa (4.53.14b), 128; *prahasann iva* + *hasann iva* used in, 13–14, 104–105, *105*, 109; present participles in the nominative case that display a reduplication of final *-n* when followed by *iva* (7.47.21a, 7.91.38d, 7.103.21, 7.11.46a), 226n11; Sahadeva addressed by Karṇa with a hint of laughing (*prahasan*) (7.142.16d), 226n15; Śiva's expression of his *kṛpā* when Kṛṣṇa and Arjuna visit him before Arjuna's fight against Jayadratha (7.57.46b), 117–18; Subhadra's indication of his fearlessness (7.37.13b), 109; three-eyed Śaṅkara explained to Arjuna (7.173.48b), 109–10

Mahābhārata (*MBh*)—8. *Karṇaparvan*: Kṛṣṇa's *prahasann iva* revealing his grace and foreseeing wisdom in restoring harmony between Yudhiṣṭhira and Arjuna (8.50.2b), 118–20; Kṛṣṇa's *prahasann iva* signaling his grace to Arjuna before his fight against Karṇa (8.40.85b), 118; Mahādeva's ease in defeating the *asuras* (8.24), 110; *prahasann iva* + *hasann iva* used in, *105*, 110; present participles in the nominative case that display a reduplication of final *-n* when followed by *iva* (8.24.93d), 226n11

Mahābhārata (*MBh*)—9. *Śalyaparvan*: *prahasann iva* + *hasann iva* used in, 14, *105*; present participles in the nominative case that display a reduplication of final *-n* when followed by *iva* (9.27.46b), 226n11

Mahābhārata (*MBh*)—10. *Sauptikaparvan*: Bhīma's

Mahābhārata (*MBh*)—10 *(continued)*
experiencing of the terrifying appearances of Kṛṣṇa and Śiva (10.6–7), 102; Droṇa's revelation of the secret of an extraordinary weapon called *brahmaśiras* to his son Aśvatthāman (10.12.12d), 128–29; Kṛṣṇa's identification with Kapila (10.26) and Vyāsa (10.37), 46; *prahasann iva* + *hasann iva* used in, *105*

Mahābhārata (*MBh*)—11. *Strīparvan*: *prahasann iva* + *hasann iva* used in, *105*

Mahābhārata (*MBh*)—12. *Śāntiparvan*: Kṛṣṇa's revelation of his eternal form to Bhīṣma (12.51.310), 102; *Mokṣadharma* of (12.174–365), 102; Paraśurāma's hint of laughter when admonishing Karṇa (12.3.29b), 120; *prahasann iva* expressed by Likhita in a tale told by Vyāsa to Yudhiṣṭhira about King Sudyumna (12.24.8d), 129; *prahasann iva* transferred to a bird in a story that Bhīṣma narrates to a king about a pigeon (12.142.41b), 131; *prahasann iva* transferred to a deer that fearlessly challenges Sumitra (12.125.13d), 111; present participles in the nominative case that display a reduplication of final *-n* when followed by *iva* (12.125.15c), 226n11

Mahābhārata (*MBh*)—13. *Anuśāsanaparvan*: *prahasann iva* + *hasann iva* used in, *105*; present participles in the nominative case that display a reduplication of final *-n* when followed by *iva* (13.14.170d), 226n11; Śiva's hint of laughter when showering his grace on Upamanyu (13.14.174d), 120–22

Mahābhārata (*MBh*)—14. *Āśvamedhikaparvan*: *hasann iva* expressed by a Brahmin in story narrated by Vāsudeva about a learned Brahmin and his wife (14.20.5b), 111–12; Kṛṣṇa's manifestation of his glory to Uttaṅka (14.54.1–3), 102, 123–24; the main contents of the *BhG* incorporated in the *Anugītā* or *Uttaragītā* (14.16–51), 102, 225n5; *prahasann iva* expressed by a Brahmin in his dialogue with Kṛṣṇa in the *Anugītā* or *Uttaragītā* (14.19.46d), 122–23; *prahasann iva* expressed by Arjuna in a story told by Vaiśaṃpāyana (14.73.6b), 130; *prahasann iva* expressed in a story told by a mongoose (14.93.39c), 128; *prahasann iva* + *hasann iva* used in, 102, *105*, 111–12, 122–23, 130

Mahābhārata (*MBh*)—15. *Āśramavāsikaparvan*: *prahasann iva* + *hasann iva* used in, *105*

Mahābhārata (*MBh*)—16. *Mausalaparvan*: *prahasann iva* + *hasann iva* used in, *105*

Mahābhārata (*MBh*)—17. *Mahāprasthānikaparvan*: *prahasann iva* + *hasann iva* used in, *105*

Mahābhārata (*MBh*)—18. *Svargārohaṇaparvan*: *prahasann iva* + *hasann iva* used in, *105*

Mahadeva Sastry, Alladi: *prahasann iva* translated as "as if smiling," 187n18

Maharishi Mahesh Yogi, 200n104

Malinar, Angelika: on Kṛṣṇa's unique position, 26; *prahasann iva* translated as "almost bursting out in laughter," 14, 15; on social relationships placed in the framework of *bhakti*, 35
Mānavadharmaśāstra: on the fruitlessness and bad reputation of the *klība*, 194n67; on the right of the attacked to defend himself/herself, 197n83
Maurer, Walter Harding: *prahasann iva* translated as "almost bursting into laughter," 15
Miśra, Vācaspati—*Bhāmatī* subcommentary on Śaṅkara's *Brahmasūtrabhāṣya*: on the Absolute *Brahman*, 179; Śaṅkara addressed as *prasanna* and *gambhīra* (serene and profound) in, 9; three reasons for the Bhagavat's manifestation of the universe distinguished by, 184n23
Miśra, Vaṃśīdhara: background information on, 80; *BhG* divided into two main sections, 81; on *prahasann iva*, 80–81, 220n79
Monier-Williams, Monier: on *pra* + √*has*, 15; on *prahāsa* translated as "loud laughter," "derision"/"irony," 5; on *prasannamukha*, 198n94; thirteen different meanings of *pra* listed by, 190n27

Nara and Nārāyaṇa: about, 200n101; Arjuna and Kṛṣṇa as incarnations of, 27, 200n101
Nārada: eighty-four *sūtras* of the *Bhaktisūtras* ascribed to, 254n126; *prahasann iva* as a subject in a dialogue between Sanatkumāra and Nārada, 60, 77; "raucous laughter" (*apahasita*) at the sight of Kṛṣṇa dancing for the cowherd women, 176
Nataraja Guru: *iva* applied to Kṛṣṇa's smile traced to the *lingua mystica* of the *Upaniṣads*, 191n30; *prahasann iva* translated as "with a semblance of smiling," 188n18
Nikhilananda, Swami: *prahasann iva* translated as "smiling," 188n18
Nīlakāṇṭha Caturdhara—*Bhāvadīpa* (or *Bhāratabhāvadīpa*): on Arjuna as the victim of two types of delusion in *BhG* 2.10, 79–80; *navya* style and a meta-idiom as characteristic of, 79

Osho, 203n119

Pāṇḍavas. *See also* Arjuna; Bhīma: demand that the Kauravas return their half of the kingdom, 194n54; Dhṛṣṭadyumna's attack thwarted by Droṇa's strength and ease, 108; Madrarāja f orced to fight against them, 108
Pāṇḍavas—Nakula: Yudhiṣṭhira's unarmed approaching of the Kauravas observed by, 108
Pāṇḍavas—Sahadeva: Karṇa addresses him laughing (*prahasan*), 226n15; Madrarāja's brushing aside of a shower of arrows he shot at him, 108; Yudhiṣṭhira's unarmed approaching of the Kauravas observed by, 108

Pāṇḍavas—Yudhiṣṭhira: dialogue with Bhīma and Draupadī in the *Vanaparvan* (*MBh* 3.27–35), 102; Kṛṣṇa's *prahasann iva* revealing his grace and foreseeing wisdom in restoring harmony between Yudhiṣṭhira and Arjuna (*MBh* 8.50.2b), 118–20; Mārkaṇḍeya tells Yudhiṣṭhira how Viṣṇu appeared to him in disguise as a divine boy (*MBh* 3.186.116b), 113; Saṃjaya's advice to Yudhiṣṭhira (*MBh* 5.27.2), 195n72; unarmed approaching of the Kauravas before the battle, 116–17

Paṇḍita Sūrya—*Paramārthaprapā*: *prahasann iva* linked to Arjuna's inappropriate reaction when faced with his martial duty, 65; Sadānanda Yogīndra's *Bhāvaprakāśa* compared with, 64–65

Panikkar, Raimon: on pronouns, 190n26

Pārthasārathi and the Pārthasārathi icon: Bharatanāṭyam dance portrayal of, 155–56; contemporary images of, 152, *153*; described, 142, 241–43n30, 243–44n36; drawings of, *242*n30, 243n35; as an epithet of Rāmānuja, 142–43; etymology of *sārathi*, 239–40n25; at the holy site of Kurukṣetra and its attached Shri Krishna Museum, 152, *153*; Kṛṣṇa worshipped as the charioteer in, 142, 145, 146, 149, *150*, 151, 240n26, 241–42n30, *242n30*, 243n35; *prahasann iva* of Kṛṣṇa Pārthasārathi's smile, 160, *160*; scant presence of depictions of, 145, 244n43; temples in South India devoted to, 143–45, *144*; *vyākhyāna* or teaching *mudrā* featured in, 143, 244n37

Piano, Stefano: *Gītās* in the *MBh* listed by, 225n5

Plato: Proclus on the smile of the gods in his commentary on Plato's *Timaeus*, 255n140; on the rebirth of the soul, 197n81; on θαῦμα ("wonder," "awe"), 207n155

Pollock, Sheldon: *prahasann iva* translated by, 232n61

Potter, Karl H.: commentaries on the *BhG* reviewed by, 58

prahasann iva: derivation from verbal root *pra* + √*has*, 5–6, 14–15, 30 34, 35; doubling of *n* in *prahasann iva*, 189n19

prahasann iva and *hasann iva* in the *BhG*. *See also* Kṛṣṇa's love toward Arjuna expressed by *prahasann iva*; *prapatti* (surrender)—Arjuna's surrender to Kṛṣṇa: English renderings of, 14, 187–89n18, 232n61; hint of laughter at *BhG* 2.10 as a bridging point, 15–16, 57; influence on the poem as a whole, 102, xiv; overview of its impact on the *BhG*'s central teachings, 39–55passim

prahasann iva and *hasann iva* in the *MBh*: location at the end of *pāda*s, 106; summary of occurrences of, 104–105, *105*

prahasann iva and *hasann iva*—1. as markers of heroic ease, 184n23;

Bhīma's heroic ease expressed in (*MBh* 1.151.7b) and (*MBh* 1.51.14d), 108; the capacity of various *kṣatriyas* to accomplish difficult tasks with no effort, 107–108; a deer with a hint of laughter fearlessly challenges Sumitra (*MBh* 12.125.13d), 111; Droṇa's easy thwarting of Dhṛṣṭadyumna's attacks (*MBh* 6.49.15d), 108; explanation of and identification of seventy-one instances, 107–108, 226–27n16; Madrarāja's brushing aside of Sahadeva's shower of arrows (*MBh* 6.79.48e), 108; Mahādeva's ease in defeating the *asuras* (*MBh* 8.24), 110; in the *Rām*, 111, 228n34; Subhadra's indication of his fearlessness (*MBh* 7.37.13b), 109; of three-eyed Śaṅkara explained to Arjuna by Vyāsa (*MBh* 7.173.48b), 109–10

prahasann iva and *hasann iva*—2. as expressions of divine grace. *See also* Kṛṣṇa's love toward Arjuna expressed by *prahasann iva*: Arjuna's desire for Kṛṣṇa's sister Subhadrā acknowledged with (*MBh* 1.211.16b), 111–12; the Bhagavat's *prahasann iva* shows itself in the meaning of *prasāda* as both clarity of mind and pure grace in (*BhG* 12.11, 12.20), 49; *BhG* 2.10 associated with, 111; explanation of and identification of twenty instances in the *MBh*, 111, 228–29n35; Indra's bestowing of weapons on Arjuna (*MBh* 3.38.36b, 3.3.8.39b), 112–13; Kṛṣṇa's *prahasann iva* as an expression of grace meant to trigger Arjuna's discrimination (*viveka*) in the *Tattvaprakāśikā*, 93–94; Kṛṣṇa's *prahasann iva* directed toward Ghaṭotkaca (*MBh* 7.148.39d), 228n35, 236n94; Kṛṣṇa's *prahasann iva* in revealing his glory to Uttaṅka (*MBh* 14.54.1–3), 123–24; Kṛṣṇa's *prahasann iva* revealing his grace and foreseeing wisdom in restoring harmony between Yudhiṣṭhira and Arjuna (*MBh* 8.50.2b), 118–20; Kṛṣṇa's response to Bhīma's despondency (*MBh* 5.73.1b), 113–14; Kṛṣṇa's signaling to Arjuna before his fight against Karṇa (*MBh* 8.40.85b), 118; Kṛṣṇa's visiting with the Kauravas before the beginning of the war (*MBh* 5.89.23d), 114–16; Paraśurāma's hint of laughter when admonishing Karṇa (*MBh* 12.3.29b), 120; *prahasann iva* expressed by a Brahmin in his dialogue with Kṛṣṇa in the *Anugītā* or *Uttaragītā* (*MBh* 14.19.46d), 122–23; *prasāda* of Kṛṣṇa's *prahasann iva* described as both tranquility of mind and compassionate grace (*BhG* 16.1–3), 52; in the *Rām*, 124, 232n61; in the *Rām* in Prajāpati's story, 124–25; Śiva's expression of his *kṛpā* when Kṛṣṇa and Arjuna visit him before Arjuna's fight against Jayadratha (*MBh* 7.57.46b), 117–18; Śiva's hint of laughter when showering

prahasann iva and *hasann iva*—2 *(continued)*
his grace on Upamanyu (*MBh* 13.14.174d), 120–22; in a story narrated by Vāsudeva about a learned Brahmin and his wife (*MBh* 14.20.5b), 123; Viṣṇu's appearance in disguise to Mārkaṇḍeya, 112, 251n104; Yudhiṣṭhira's unarmed approaching of the Kauravas before the battle (*MBh* 6.41.16d), 116–17
prahasann iva and *hasann iva*—3. as expressions of mockery, delight and surprise: *anaucitya* (inappropriateness) of Arjuna's stubbornness and mental confusion that triggers Kṛṣṇa's *prahasann iva*, 3, 28, 65, 74, 82, 96, 97, 99, 141; Arjuna's *prahasann iva* harshly addresses a hunter (*kirāta*) (*MBh* 3.40.17, 3.40.21b), 125–26; explanation of and identification of twenty-six instances in the *MBh*, 125, 233n63; *hasann iva* associated with Subhadra [=Abhimanyu] (*MBh* 7.50.16d), 128; *hasann iva* by Aśvatthāman when Droṇa reveals the *brahmaśiras* to him (*MBh* 10.12.12d), 128–29; *hasann iva* by Droṇa in response to Duryodhana's assessment of Arjuna (*MBh* 7.160.23b), 128; Karṇa's humble origins ridiculed by Bhīma's *prahasann iva* (*MBh* 1.127.5d), 125; *prahasann iva* expressed by Arjuna/Bṛhannaḍā contrasted with Draupadī/Sairandhrī's distress (*MBh* 4.23.22d), 127; *prahasann iva* expressed by Arjuna in a story told by Vaiśaṃpāyana (*MBh* 14.73.6b), 128; *prahasann iva* expressed by Droṇa as a sign of Arjuna's delight in fighting a loyal combat with him (*MBh* 4.53.14b), 128; *prahasann iva* expressed by Karṇa in response to a Brahmin's request for his armor (*MBh* 3.294.9d), 127; *prahasann iva* expressed by Likhita in a tale told by Vyāsa to Yudhiṣṭhira about King Sudyumna (*MBh* 12.24.8d), 129; *prahasann iva* expressed in a story told by a mongoose (14.93.39c), 128; *prahasann iva* interpreted as mockery in Sadānanda's commentary on *BhG* 2.11, 74–75; *prahasann iva* that displays Ilvala's ill intentions (*MBh* 3.97.5d), 126; in the *Rām*, 130–31, 235n87
prahasann iva and *hasann iva*—4. as ambiguous or seemingly incongruous expressions: Duryodhana's *prahasann iva* toward Kṛṣṇa before before asking him to side with the Kauravas (*MBh* 5.7.9b), 131; explanation of and identification of cases in the *MBh*, 131, 235n88; *hasann iva* by Daśaratha in the *Rām* (2.63.9.d), 132; *prahasann iva* transferred to a bird in a story that Bhīṣma narrates to a king about a pigeon (*MBh* 12.142.41b), 131
Prajāpati: story in the *Rāmāyaṇa*, 124–25, 232n62
prajñāvādikaḥ (words of wisdom): Arjuna's expression of, viewed as *prajñāvādān ca bhāṣase* by

Kṛṣṇa, 22, 60, 69–70, 81, 82, 94, 196n77
prapatti (surrender): identification with *gurūpasatti* in the *BhG*, 94–95; the importance of *prapatti* in the Nimbārka *sampradāya*, 94; *kārpaṇya* ("poorness of spirit") identified by Rāmānuja as the sixth stage of *prapatti*, 24–25; *pra* + √*pad* (to go forward, throw oneself down), 30–31, 33, 198n89; the theology of *prapatti* understood in Śrī Vaiṣṇava circles as a development of *BhG* 18.66, 208n161
prapatti (surrender)—Arjuna's surrender to Kṛṣṇa: Arjuna's posture as a *prapanna*, 9, 10–11, 21, 30, 33–34, 66, 99, 221n90, 221n93; summary of the moment of, xi
prasāda. *See* grace (*kṛpā*, *prasāda*)
prefixes—*ava* ("down" or "off"): *avahasann iva*, 205n134; *avahāsārtham*, 34–35, 205n135; as a prefix to verbs, 35
prefixes—*pra*. See also *prapatti* (surrender): Greek προ compared with, 15; with √*has* (laughing), 5–6, 14–15, 25, 30, 34, 35; lack of mention in Bhāskara's commentary on *BhG* 2.10 of, 32; *pramāṇa* ("a means to acquire true knowledge"), 15; as a prefix to adjectives *vs.* nouns, 15; with √*sad* (to be clear/bright/tranquil), 9, 25; thirteen meanings given in the *Viṃśatyupasargavṛtti* traditionally ascribed to Candragomin, 190n27
prefixes—*pra* with √*has* (laughing) and the particle *iva*. See also *prahasann iva* and *hasann iva* in the *Bhagavadgītā*: seven occurrences in the *MBh* that see Kṛṣṇa as protagonist, 133
Purāṇas: the emotional *bhakti* of the *Purāṇas* distinguished from the intellectual *bhakti* of the *Bhagavadgītā*, 161; Kāma in, 237n11; teaching in a compassionate way like a friend (*mitrasammita*) in the *Itihāsas* and *Purāṇas*, 6
Purāṇas—Bhāgavata Purāṇa: account of Kṛṣṇa's *līlā*s in Vraja and Dvārakā, 161; episode of the child Kṛṣṇa stealing the butter (10.8.21–45), 163, 165–66, 251n104; iconography of the Pārthasārathi icon drawn from, 145; knowledge (*jñāna*) and devotion (*bhakti*) harmonized in Śrīdhara Svāmin's commentary to, 70–71; Kṛṣṇa identified with Viṣṇu, 161; Kṛṣṇa's granting vision of the universe to Yaśodā, 203n118; Kṛṣṇa's vanquishing of Kāliya (10.1.16), 170; *Mahābhārata* linked with, 161; the meaning of *sakhya* in the story of King Puraṃjana in book 4, 205n140; the nine forms of *bhakti* presented in (7.5.23), 36, 247n73
Purāṇas—Matsya Purāṇa: Dakṣa myth in, 227n25; Mārkaṇḍeya's encounter with Viṣṇu, 229n39, 251n104
Purāṇas—Viṣṇu Purāṇa: Indra's anger over the cowherds shifting their devotion to Kṛṣṇa 1 (5.11.1–25), 171; Kṛṣṇa's portrait in, 161; Kṛṣṇa's vanquishing of Kāliya (5.7.1–83), 171–72

Radhakrishnan, Sarvepalli: Kṛṣṇa's smile interpreted by, 203n120; *prahasann iva* rendered as "smiling as it were," 14
Ramachandra Rao, S. K.: drawings of Pārthasārathi icons, *242*n30, 243n35; on the Pārthasārathi icon, 241n30, 243–44n36
Ramaṇa Maharṣi: on silence, 203n123; Viswanatha Swami's description of his first *darśan* of, 254n123
Rāmānuja: background of, 86; *kārpaṇya* ("poorness of spirit") identified as the sixth stage of *prapatti*, 24–25; Pārthasārathi as an epithet of, 142–43
Rāmānuja—*Gītābhāṣya* commentary on the *BhG*: on Arjuna's surrender to his lord as *prapanna*, 221n93; main themes of, 86; on *prahasann iva*, 87–88; Rāmarāya Kavi's opposition to its interpretation, 69–70; three hexads (*ṣaṭka*) of, 86–87
Rāmarāya Kavi, Śrībellaṅkoṇḍa: about, 69
Rāmarāya Kavi, Śrībellaṅkoṇḍa—*Bhāṣyārkaprakāśa*: *prahasann iva* presented as an expression of Kṛṣṇa's grace, 70; the supremacy of Śaṅkara's interpretation of the *BhG* asserted by, 69–70
Rāmāyaṇa (*Rām*): folk pictures utilized by itinerant bards in their recitation of, 147; *hasann iva* by Daśaratha at a moment when he might be expected to cry (2.63.9.d), 132; *prahasann iva* and *hasann iva* as expressions of divine grace in Prajāpati's story in (7.4.11b), 124–25; *prahasann iva* and *hasann iva* as expressions of mockery, delight and surprise in, 130–31, 235n87; *prahasann iva* as an expression of heroic ease as Rāma breaks the bow and arrow of the demon Khara, 111; *prahasann iva* as an expression of heroic ease as Rāma notches a sharp arrow (6.95.21c), 228n34; *prahasann iva* as an expression of heroic ease in six additional occurrences, 232n61; summary of instances of *prahasann iva* and *hasann iva* in, 14, 186n5
Razmnamah (Book of wars), 145–46
rebirth and transmigration. See *saṃsāra*
Rūpa Gosvāmin: Gauḍīya Vaiṣṇavism established at the behest of Caitanya, 174; *rasa* theory of Sanskrit poetics applied to the practice of Kṛṣṇa *bhakti*, 174; six states of laughter in ecstatic love (*hāsyabhaktirasa*) identified by, 175–77, 254n128

Sadānanda Yogīndra—*Bhāvaprakāśa*: *BhG* divided into three sections (*kāṇḍa*), 73; commentary on *BhG* 2.7, 73–74; the main purpose of the *BhG* identified at 2.11, 75; Paṇḍita Sūrya's *Paramārthaprapā* compared with, 64–65; *prahasann iva* interpreted as mockery in his commentary on *BhG* 2.11, 74–75
Sai Baba of Shirdi: his torrent of abuses understood as a shower

of mercy, 7, 183–84n20; smile of, 253–54n123
saṃsāra: conveyed in danced *Bhagavadgītās*, 248n75; death viewed as an occasion for "changing old clothes" (*vāsāṃsi jīrṇāni*), 22; Śaṅkara's commentary that anguish and delusion are the seeds of, 61–62; underlined as an ocean of defects in Sadānanda's commentary on *BhG* 2.7, 73
Śaṅkara: defined as *prasanna* by his students, 9; foundational *Bhagavadgītābhāṣya* or "Commentary on the *Bhagavadgītā*" (*BhGBh*), 61–63; on the incorruptibility of Supreme Reality, xvii
Śaṅkara—*Brahmasūtrabhāṣya*. *See also* Miśra, Vācaspati—*Bhāmatī* subcommentary on Śaṅkara's *Brahmasūtrabhāṣya*: Anubhūtisvarūpacārya's *Prakaṭārthavivaraṇa* commentary on, 212n9; on Īśvara's manifestation of the universe, 7–8, 184n23; on *līlā* in *BhG* 18.61, 42, 209n172; on the omniscience of *Brahman*, 184n22; survey of the four prerequisites (*sādhanacatuṣṭaya*) (1.1.1), 213n12
Śaṅkara—*Gītābhāṣya*. *See also* Ānanda Giri—*Gītābhāṣyavivecana*: Arjuna as pretext (*nimitta*) for Kṛṣṇa's *prahasann iva*, explained by, 61–63, xi
Śaṅkarānanda Sarasvatī: background of, 71
Śaṅkarānanda Sarasvatī—*Tātparyabodhinī*: connection between *BhG* verses 2.1–10 and the Upaniṣadic requirements for approaching a master for instruction suggested by, 71
Sargeant, Winthrop: *prahasann iva* translated as "beginning to laugh so to speak," 14
seeing and sight. See also *darśan* and *darśana* (vision); luminosity: knowing equated with, 18; Kṛṣṇa's grace conveyed through the sight of him, 37
Sellmer, Sven: on present participles in the *MBh*, 106
Shulman, David Dean: on Kṛṣṇa's laugh in the *MBh*, 17; on *śraddhā*, 198n90
Śiva: hint of laughter when showering his grace on Upamanyu (*MBh* 13.14.174d), 120–22; laugh before he attacks Pūṣan, 161; loud laugh (*aṭṭahāsa*) of, 161
Śiva Dakṣiṇāmūrti: the iconography of the enlightened Buddha compared with, 32, 203n123
Sloterdijk, Peter, 107–108
Smart, Ninian: model of the six dimensions of religion, 249–50n87
smile (*smita*) and smiling. *See also* Kṛṣṇa's love toward Arjuna expressed by *prahasann iva*; *prahasann iva* ("hint of laughter"): Aphrodite's smile, 201–202n110; beings identified as the smiling of the supreme godhead by Vācaspati Miśra, 179; derivation from the word for "laugh" in many languages, 135; as double meaning of

smile (*smita*) and smiling (*continued*)
prasāda, 25, 198–99n94; enigmatic smile of many statues of Greek deities, 201–202n110; in the iconography of Viṭṭhala/Viṭhobā, 251n99; as one of six states of laughter in ecstatic love (*hāsyabhaktirasa*), 136, 175; Proclus on the smile of the gods in his commentary on Plato's *Timaeus*, 255n140; pure joy (*ānanda*) communicated by Kṛṣṇa's smile, 37, 177–78, 255n137; of Sai Baba of Shirdi, 253–54n123; smile featured in Bālakṛṣṇa as butter thief (*navanītacora*), 163–64, *165*; *smitojjvala* (an eye that is "bright with a smile"), 238; verbal roots for "smiling" and "laughing" in the vernacular languages of India, 183n15
śraddhā (faith): as a term, 198n90
Śrīdhara Svāmin: Hanumat's elucidation of *BhG* 2.10 compared with, 216n43; knowledge (*jñāna*) and devotion (*bhakti*) harmonized in his commentary to the *Bhāgavata Purāṇa*, 70–71; *prahasann iva* interpreted as "having a happy face," 70; starting from verse 1.28, he identifies the object of Arjuna's anguish as his kinsfolk, 71
Śrīveṅkaṭanātha: background of, 66
Śrīveṅkaṭanātha—*Brahmānandagiri*: on *BhG* chapter 2 (2.11–2.38), 67–68, 214n28; the *Gūḍhārthadīpikā*'s reading of *BhG* 2.8 criticized, 65–66, 213n15; *prahasann iva* interpreted as an expression of cheerful derision, 67
Stoler Miller, Barbara: *prahasann iva* translated as "mocking him gently," 14
Subhadrā: Arjuna's abduction (*haraṇa*) and marriage of, 199–200n100; the killing of her son Abhimanyu, 128, 254n131; Kṛṣṇa's approval of Arjuna's desire for Subhadrā exemplified by his *prahasann iva*, 111–12
Śuddhādvaita (pure nondualism), 59, 95
Swarupananda, Swami: on Kṛṣṇa's smile at Arjuna's sorrow, 29; *prahasann iva* translated as "as if smiling," 187–88n18

Telang, Kāshināth Trimbak: *prahasann iva* translated as "with a slight smile," 187n18
theater and dramaturgy. *See also* Bharata-*Nāṭyaśāstra*; Brook, Peter—staging of the *Mahābhārata*; Kṛṣṇāṭṭam: Bharatanāṭyam dance: 152, 155–56, 249n81; classical dance forms inspired by the *rāslīlā* of Kṛṣṇa dancing with all the *gopīs*, 170; Kṛṣṇa's love toward Arjuna expressed by *prahasann iva* in, 154–57; Kṛṣṇa's smile/hint of laughter featured in *Bhagvad Gita: Song of the Lord* directed by G.V. Iyer: 157, *158*; Odissi dance, 152, *156*, 156–57, 249n79; *prahasana* as one of ten types of play (*nāṭya*) in which the comic sentiment predominates, 14–15;

serialization of the *Mahābhārata* on Doordarshan, 158–59, *159*
Tukārām: on the "holy face" of Viṭṭhala / Viṭhobā, 255n137

Upamanyu: Dhaumya identified as his brother, 121, 231n56; story of his devotion to Śiva narrated to Kṛṣṇa, 120–22; story of his father Vyāghrapāda, 231n55
Upaniṣads: *Bhagavadgītā* extolled as an *Upaniṣad*, 103, 148, 225n7; connection between *BhG* verses 2.1–10 and the Upaniṣadic requirements for approaching a master for instruction suggested by Śaṅkarānanda Sarasvatī, 71; the term *iva* applied to Kṛṣṇa's smile traced to the *lingua mystica* of the *Upaniṣads*, 191n30; viewed as part of the *prasthānatraya* or the "triad of the points of departure" by the schools of Vedānta, 103
Upaniṣads—Bṛhadāraṇyaka Upaniṣad: connection between *BhG* verses 2.1–10 and the Upaniṣadic requirements for approaching a master for instruction (2.4.5, 4.5.6) suggested by Śaṅkarānanda Sarasvatī, 71; on death (4.4.5), 196n81; on the ease of supreme beings (2.4.10), 67–68, 214n23; erroneous occurrence of root √*has* in (1.3.28), 225n8; on *kṛpaṇa* in (1.4.15, 3.8.10), 77, 93; on the six virtues (*śamadamādiṣaṭkasampatti*), 213n12; *śruti* passage on conducting a wandering life (3.5.1), 63, 76, 218n8; Yājñavalkya instructs King Janaka on the nature of dream (4.3.13), 75, 103–104
Upaniṣads—Chāndogya Upaniṣad: on breath (7.15.1), 219n77; explanation for *tat tvam asi*, 73; *hasati* in (3.17.3), 103, 225n8; on life, death, and the individual Self (6.11.3), 219n76; *prahasann iva* as a subject in a dialogue between Sanatkumāra and Nārada, 60, 77; *śruti* passage from (7.1.3), 71–72
Upaniṣads—Īśa Upaniṣad: *śruti* passage from, 72
Upaniṣads—Jaiminīya Upaniṣad Brāhmaṇa: *hasaḥ* "laughter" in (3.25.8), 103, 225n8
Upaniṣads—Kaṭha Upaniṣad: dialogue between Yama-Mṛtyu and Naciketas, 60, 83, 195n74; imagery of the *ātman* as the traveler in the chariot (3.3–6, 9), 193n44, 240n26; parable of the mythic *aśvattha* tree, with roots above and branches below (6.1), 211n193; passage 2.18 compared with *BhG* 2.20, 196n79; *śruti* passage in (1.2.1), 76, 88
Upaniṣads—Mahā Upaniṣad: *hasanti hasan* in (3.25.8), 104, 225n8
Upaniṣads—Muṇḍaka Upaniṣad: connection between *BhG* verses 2.1–10 and the Upaniṣadic requirements for approaching a master for instruction (1.2.12) suggested by Śaṅkarānanda Sarasvatī, 71; the lord compared to the manner of a bird (3.1.1–2), 205n140

Upaniṣads—Śvetāśvatara Upaniṣad: closing verse on love for God (6.23), 24; the lord compared to the manner of a bird (4.6–7), 205n140
Upaniṣads—Taittirīya Upaniṣad, 217n61
Upaniṣads—Tejobindu Upaniṣad: *hāsyam* in, 225n8
Upaniṣads—Yogaśikhā Upaniṣad: *hasati* and *hasan* in (6.67–68), 104, 225n8

Vaiśaṃpāyana: as the first to recite the *Bhagavadgītā*, 245n52; Kṛṣṇa's *prahasann iva* in revealing his glory to Uttaṅka narrated by (*MBh* 14.54.1–3), 123–24; *prahasann iva* expressed by Arjuna in a story told by (*MBh* 14.73.6b), 130; *prahasann iva* expressed by Karṇa in response to a Brahmin's request for his armor in a story told by (*MBh* 3.294.9d), 127
Vallabha: on Kṛṣṇa's *prahasann iva* in his gloss on *BhG* 2.10 in his *Tattvadīpikā*, 95; lineage of, 95
van Buitenen, Johannes Adrianus Bernardus: on Arjuna's dilemma as real despite Kṛṣṇa's sarcasm, 187n13; *Bhagavadāśayānusaraṇa* studied by, 82; on Kṛṣṇa's assumption of the role of charioteer, 240n26; *prahasann iva* translated as "with a hint of laughter," 14, 15
Vāsudeva: as a patronymic of Kṛṣṇa, 16, 29–30, 192n35; story narrated by about a learned Brahmin and his wife (*MBh* 14.20.5b), 111–12
Vasugupta: *Vāsavīṭīkā*, a commentary on the *BhG* by, 220n80; on *vismayo yogabhūmikāḥ*, ("The stages of Yoga are amazement"), 207n156
Veṅkaṭanātha / Vedānta Deśika: on definitions of *kārpaṇya*, 221nn93–94; *Gītārthasaṃgraharakṣā* on Yāmuna Muni's *Gītārthasaṃgraha*, 88, 221n93
Veṅkaṭanātha / Vedānta Deśika—*Tātparyacāndrikā* subcommentary on Rāmānuja's commentary on the *BhG*, 86; Hanumat mentioned in, 216n43; Rāmarāya Kavi's opposition to, 69–70
vismaya (amazement, bewilderment and terror): Arjuna's *vismaya* upon seeing a doomsday fire in Kṛṣṇa's mouths (*BhG* 11.26–30), 167; Arjuna's *vismaya* / *vismayāviṣṭo* upon seeing Kṛṣṇa's universal shape (*BhG* 11.14), 8–9, 37–38, 48, 167, 220n85; derivation from *vi* + verbal root √*smi* ("to smile"), 38, 135; as a motif in the *Dakṣiṇāmūrtistotra*, 32–33; as the primary emotion prompting Kṛṣṇa's hint of laughter (*BhG* 2.9), 85, 141; saying attributed to Jesus in the *Gospel of Thomas* compared with, 207n156; θαῦμα ("wonder," "awe") compared with, 207n154; Uttaṅka's *vismaya* upon seeing Kṛṣṇa's universal shape (*MBh* 14.54.1–3), 123–24; Vasugupta on *vismayo yogabhūmikāḥ* ("The stages of Yoga are amazement"),

207n156; of Yaśodā's vision of the universe granted by Kṛṣṇa, 165–68, *167*, 203n118, 252n106
Viśvanātha Cakravartī Ṭhākura—*Sārārthavarṣiṇīṭīkā*: gloss on Kṛṣṇa's *prahasann iva* (*BhG* 2.10), 96–97
Viswanatha Swami, 254n123
Vivekānanda, Swami: Kṛṣṇa's *prahasann iva* translated by, 208n165
Vraja/Braj region: Kṛṣṇa (as the divine child of) dancing for cowherd women of, 176; Kṛṣṇa's *līlā*s in, 161; "the forest of Vṛndā" as a name for, 252n113
Vyāsa: authorship of the *Bhagavadgītā* attributed to, 221n93; composition of the *Mahābhārata* associated with, 161; his appeal to stop the battle considered futile by Dhṛtarāṣṭra (*MBh* 6.4.44–46): 193n51; his instructions to Arjuna to search for divine weapons from Indra (*MBh* 3.38.36b, 3.38.39b), 112–13; Kṛṣṇa's identification with (10.37), 46; Saṃjaya's statement that Vyāsa's grace enabled him to hear the secret *yoga* taught by Kṛṣṇa to Arjuna (*BhG* 18.75), 211n200; tale of Likhita and Śaṅkha told to Yudhiṣṭhira about King Sudyumna (*MBh* 12.24.8d), 129; three-eyed Śaṅkara explained to Arjuna (7.173.48b), 109

Wilkins, Charles: first English translation of the *Bhagavadgītā* published by, 151, 225n6; *prahasann iva* translated as "smiling," 14
words of wisdom. See *prajñāvādikaḥ*

Yāmuna Muni (or Yāmunācārya): biographical details, 86; Rāmānuja as likely his disciple, 86, 220–21n90
Yāmuna Muni (or Yāmunācārya)—*Gītārthasaṃgraha* ("Compendium on the Meaning of the *Gītā*"): on Arjuna as "the surrendered one" (*pārthaṃ prapannam*), 221n90; as the first *viśiṣṭādvaitin* gloss on the *BhG*, 86, 220n90; three hexads (*ṣaṭka*) of, 208n163, 221n90, 221n93; Veṅkaṭanātha's *Gītārthasaṃgraharakṣā* on, 221n93
Yaśodā: Kṛṣṇa granting vision of the universe to, 165–68, *167*, 203n118, 252n106

Zaehner, Robert Charles: *prahasann iva* translated as "faintly smiling," 14; translation of a passage that some manuscripts add to *BhG* 2.11, 220n84